INDIAN OCEAN HISTORIES

This book offers a global history of the Indian Ocean and focuses on a holistic perspective of the worlds of water. It builds on maritime historian Michael Naylor Pearson's works, his unorthodox approach and strong influence on the study of the Indian Ocean in viewing the oceanic space as replete with human experiences and not as an artefact of empire or as the theatre of European commercial and imperial transits focused only on trade.

This interdisciplinary volume presents several ways of writing the history of the Indian Ocean. The chapters explore the changing nature of Indian Ocean history through diverse themes, including state and capital, regional identities, maritime networking, South Asian immigrants, Bay of Bengal linkages, the East India Company, Indian seamen, formal and informal collaboration in imperial networking, scientific transfers, pearling, the issues of colonial copyright, customs, excise and port cities.

The volume will be useful to scholars and researchers of global history, modern history, maritime history, medieval history, Indian history, colonial history and world history.

Rila Mukherjee is a professor, Department of History, University of Hyderabad, India. She works on spatial categories in the eastern Indian Ocean, especially in the northern Bay of Bengal, comprising the coasts of northern Odisha and West Bengal in India, littoral Bangladesh and Arakan. Her most recent publications are the co-edited *Subversive Sovereigns Across the Sea: Indian Ocean Ports-of-Trade from Early Historic Times to Late Colonialism* (2017); the book chapter 'Silver-Links! Bagan-Bengal and Shadowy Metal Corridors: 9th to 13th Centuries' in Yian, Miksic and Aung-Thwin (eds), *Bagan and the World: Early Myanmar and Its Global Connections* (2018); and articles in *Topoi*, the *International Journal of Maritime History* and *Asian Review of World Histories*.

Radhika Seshan is a professor and the head of the Department of History, Savitribai Phule Pune University, India, where she has worked since 1996. She is the author of *Trade and Politics on the Coromandel Coast* (2012) and *Ideas and Institutions in Medieval India* (2013). Her most recent publications are the edited volumes *Narratives, Routes and Intersections in the Pre-Modern Asian World* (2016) and *Re-searching Transition in Indian History* (co-edited with Shraddha Kumbhojkar, 2018).

INDIAN OCEAN HISTORIES

The Many Worlds of
Michael Naylor Pearson

*Edited by Rila Mukherjee
and Radhika Seshan*

LONDON AND NEW YORK

First published 2020 by Routledge

2 Park Square, Milton Park, Abingdon, Oxon, OX14 4RN
605 Third Avenue, New York, NY 10017

Routledge is an imprint of the Taylor & Francis Group, an informa business

First issued in paperback 2020

Copyright © 2020 selection and editorial matter, Rila Mukherjee and Radhika
Seshan; individual chapters, the contributors

The right of Rila Mukherjee and Radhika Seshan to be identified
as the authors of the editorial material, and of the authors for their
individual chapters, has been asserted in accordance with sections 77
and 78 of the Copyright, Designs and Patents Act 1988.

All rights reserved. No part of this book may be reprinted or
reproduced or utilised in any form or by any electronic, mechanical,
or other means, now known or hereafter invented, including
photocopying and recording, or in any information storage or
retrieval system, without permission in writing from the publishers.

Notice:
Product or corporate names may be trademarks
or registered trademarks, and are used only for identification and
explanation without intent to infringe.

British Library Cataloguing-in-Publication Data
A catalogue record for this book is available from the British Library

Library of Congress Cataloging-in-Publication Data
Names: Mukherjee, Rila, editor. | Seshan, Radhika, editor.
Title: Indian Ocean histories : the many worlds of Michael Naylor
Pearson / edited by Rila Mukherjee and Radhika Seshan.
Description: Abingdon, Oxon ; New York, NY : Routledge, 2020. |
Includes bibliographical references and index. |
Identifiers: LCCN 2019020444 (print) | LCCN 2019981060 (ebook) |
ISBN 9781138611818 (hardback) | ISBN 9780367334864 (ebook)
Subjects: LCSH: Pearson, M. N. (Michael Naylor), 1941– | Indian
Ocean Region—Historiography. | Indian Ocean Region—History.
Classification: LCC DS340 .I523 2020 (print) | LCC DS340 (ebook) |
DDC 909/.09824—dc23
LC record available at https://lccn.loc.gov/2019020444
LC ebook record available at https://lccn.loc.gov/2019981060

ISBN: 978-1-138-61181-8 (hbk)
ISBN: 978-0-367-78459-1 (pbk)

Typeset in Sabon
by Apex CoVantage, LLC

CONTENTS

List of figures	viii
List of tables	ix
List of contributors	x
Preface	xiii

Introduction: Indian Ocean histories	**1**
RILA MUKHERJEE	

PART I
Historiographies, methodologies and scale
in the Indian Ocean — **17**

1 The Indian Ocean: global nexus (1500–1800)	19
PATRICK MANNING	

2 The sodden archive: Africa, the Atlantic and the Indian Ocean	32
ISABEL HOFMEYR	

PART II
Case studies — **49**

3 The Kakatiyas, Motupalli and the Southern Bay of Bengal linkages	51
RADHIKA SESHAN	

CONTENTS

4 Regional identities, maritime networking and Islamic conversions in fifteenth-century Java 62
KENNETH R. HALL

5 Brokers and go-betweens within the Portuguese State of India (1500–1700) 97
AMÉLIA POLÓNIA

6 South Asian settlers at Batavia in the seventeenth and eighteenth centuries 124
RYUTO SHIMADA

7 Physicians, surgeons, merchants and healers: production, circulation and reconfiguration of knowledge in eighteenth-century Portuguese India 137
FABIANO BRACHT

8 Indian seamen (lascars), shipboard labor regime and the East India Company in the first half of the nineteenth century 156
GHULAM A. NADRI

PART III
New histories 173

9 Hazards and history on the Western Australian coast: the 'Pearling Fleet Disaster' of 1887 175
JOSEPH CHRISTENSEN

10 Landscape, Rajah and wax prints: contemporary archaeologies of India in Mozambique 196
PEDRO POMBO

11 Littoral shell tracks: tracing Burma's transregional pearl histories 214
PEDRO MACHADO

CONTENTS

PART IV
Reminiscences   247

12 Michael Naylor Pearson: the discipline of history,
    the sea and the man   249
    RILA MUKHERJEE

13 Afterword   264
    RADHIKA SESHAN

    Index   269

FIGURES

4.1	Two contemporary Java literary conceptions of the Majapahit Java Mandala State	66
4.2	Fifteenth/sixteenth-century Majapahit Emblem of State, Jakarta National Museum	70
4.3	Java knowledge agencies, c. 1500	89
9.1	Map of Northwest Australia, showing locations mentioned in the chapter	176
11.1	Map of Burma	216
11.2	House on stilts	217
12.1	Michael Pearson advancing on the Bay of Bengal in a dinghy from Masulipatnam, India, 2011	248
12.2	Michael Pearson at Bijapur, 2011	255
12.3	Michael Pearson at the pier in Masulipatnam, 2011	256
12.4	Michael Pearson at a temple at Saptagrama [Satgaon], 2015	258
12.5	Michael Pearson in a toy shop, Kondapalli, Andhra Pradesh, 2011	259
12.6	Michael Pearson at the old Masulipatnam shipyard, 2011	260

TABLES

6.1	Population of Batavia in 1699	129
6.2	Population of Batavia in 1769	130
6.3	Population of Batavia in 1835	131
8.1	Wages of native seafaring persons	160

CONTRIBUTORS

Fabiano Bracht is a post-doctoral researcher at the University of São Paulo, USP, Brazil, and researcher at CITCEM (Transdisciplinary Research Centre Culture, Space of Memory), University of Porto. He has a PhD in history from the University of Porto, Portugal. His current research field is the history of medicine and natural sciences in eighteenth-century South and East Asia and the production and circulation of knowledge within colonial empires.

Joseph Christensen is a postdoctoral fellow at the Asia Research Centre, Murdoch University, Australia, where he works in the fields of maritime and environmental history. He is a graduate (PhD, BA hons) of the University of Western Australia. He is co-editor of the collections *Historical Perspectives of Fisheries Exploitation in the Indo-Pacific* (2014), *Natural Hazards and Peoples in the Indian Ocean World* (2016) and (with Pedro Machado and Steve Mullins) of a forthcoming volume on pearling in the history of the Indian Ocean worlds.

Kenneth R. Hall is a professor of history at Ball State University, USA, and a specialist on the Eastern Indian Ocean, with a focus on Chola-era South India and pre-1500 Southeast Asia. His most recent books are *Networks of Trade, Polity, and Societal Integration in Chola-Era South India 875–1200* (2014) and *A History of Early Southeast Asia, 100–1500* (2011). He attributes his research specialisation to early mentorship at the University of Michigan by Michael Pearson, who recruited him to an Indian Ocean doctoral program.

Isabel Hofmeyr is a professor of African literature at the University of the Witwatersrand in Johannesburg, South Africa, and Global Distinguished Professor in the English Department of New York University, USA. Her most recent book is *Gandhi's Printing Press: Experiments in Slow Reading* (2013). Along with Antoinette Burton, she edited *Ten Books That Shaped the British Empire: Creating an Imperial Commons* (2014). She currently heads up a project on Oceanic Humanities for the Global South in Johannesburg.

CONTRIBUTORS

Pedro Machado is an associate professor at the Department of History, Indiana University, Bloomington, USA. He is the author of several works, most recently *Ocean of Trade: South Asian Merchants, Africa and the Indian Ocean, c. 1750–1850* (2014); "Views from Other Boats: On Amitav Ghosh's Indian Ocean 'Worlds," *American Historical Review*, Vol. 121, No. 5 (December 2016); and *Textile Trades, Consumer Cultures and the Material Worlds of the Indian Ocean* (2018). He also has a new volume on the Indian Ocean's pearling histories forthcoming and is currently at work on a global history of pearl shell collection and exchange while also developing research on eucalyptus and colonial forestry in the Portuguese empire in the nineteenth and twentieth centuries.

Patrick Manning was the Andrew W. Mellon Professor of World History at the University of Pittsburgh and served as president of the American Historical Association in 2016–2017. He is an emeritus professor, Department of History, University of Pittsburgh, USA. He is president of the World History Network, Inc., a nonprofit corporation fostering research in world history. A specialist in world history and African history, his current research addresses global historiography, early human history, migration in world history, the African diaspora and the demography of African slavery.

Rila Mukherjee is a professor, Department of History, University of Hyderabad, India. She works on spatial categories in the eastern Indian Ocean, especially in the northern Bay of Bengal, comprising the coasts of northern Odisha and West Bengal in India, littoral Bangladesh and Arakan. Her most recent publications are the co-edited *Subversive Sovereigns Across the Sea: Indian Ocean Ports-of-Trade from Early Historic Times to Late Colonialism* (2017); the book chapter 'Silver-Links! Bagan-Bengal and Shadowy Metal Corridors: 9th to 13th Centuries' in Yian, Miksic and Aung-Thwin (eds), *Bagan and the World: Early Myanmar and its Global Connections* (2018); and articles in *Topoi*, the *International Journal of Maritime History*, and *Asian Review of World Histories*.

Ghulam A. Nadri is a professor of history at Georgia State University, USA. He has published two monographs, *The Political Economy of Indigo in India, 1580–1930: A Global Perspective* and *Eighteenth-Century Gujarat: The Dynamics of Its Political Economy, 1750–1800* and numerous journal articles and book chapters on commodities, merchants, labour markets and Indian Ocean trade. His current research explores the role of political, socio-cultural and institutional factors in the entrepreneurial accomplishments of the Parsis (Zoroastrians) in India in the eighteenth and nineteenth centuries.

Amélia Polónia is an associate professor at the University of Porto, Portugal; vice president of IMHA (International Maritime History Association); and director of CITCEM (Transdisciplinary Research Centre Culture,

Space of Memory). Her research interests focus on seaport history, maritime history and colonial history in the Early Modern Age (1500–1800). She co-edited *Beyond Empires: Global, Self-Organizing, Cross-Imperial Networks, 1500–1800* (2016) and *Seaports in the First Global Age: Portuguese agents, networks and interactions (1500–1800)* (2016) and authored *Brokers and Go-betweens within the Portuguese State of India (1500–1700)* (2016) and *Connecting Worlds: Women as Intermediaries in the Portuguese Overseas Empire* (2017).

Pedro Pombo is an assistant professor (visiting faculty) at Goa University, India. He received a PhD in anthropology from ISCTE-IUL, Lisbon (Portugal), on ethnographic exploration on space, belonging, local history and personal narratives in Southern Mozambique. He investigates traces of maritime circulations though dialogues between cartography and archives, heritage and material culture. He presently researches topographies between Africa and India through textile aesthetics, stories of migration and contemporary art, inquiring into possible archaeologies of the contemporary in the Indian Ocean world.

Radhika Seshan is a professor and the head of the Department of History, Savitribai Phule Pune University, India, where she has worked since 1996. She is the author of *Trade and Politics on the Coromandel Coast* (2012) and *Ideas and Institutions in Medieval India* (2013). Her most recent publications are the edited volumes *Narratives, Routes and Intersections in the Pre-Modern Asian World* (2016) and *Re-searching Transition in Indian History* (co-edited with Shraddha Kumbhojkar, 2018).

Ryuto Shimada has been an associate professor in Asian History, Faculty of Letters, the University of Tokyo, Japan, since 2012. He obtained his PhD from Leiden University in 2005 and taught economic history at Seinan Gakuin University, Fukuoka, Japan, between 2006 and 2012. He works on Asian maritime history since the sixteenth century and has published several books and articles including *The Intra-Asian Trade in Japanese Copper by the Dutch East India Company During the Eighteenth Century* (2006).

PREFACE

This collective brings together some of the people and many of the themes that reflect maritime historian Michael Pearson's wide-ranging interests. Pearson engaged with diverse disciplines and scholars from different fields to write a refreshingly different kind of Indian Ocean history. Seeing himself as a magpie, he used concepts from social anthropology, cultural geography, literature, culture studies and history, picking and choosing whatever he felt was relevant to argue for the ocean as a living space of social interactions. Always open to new ideas, he wrote of late on the Anthropocene and the territorialisation of ocean space, concerns addressed by some of the chapters in this collective.

Pearson's work has had tremendous influence on many disciplines and scholars; generous to a fault, his encouragement to a whole new generation of maritime scholars is well known. The contributors to this volume are those who have engaged with him in different ways – socially, intellectually and academically.

Rila Mukherjee
Radhika Seshan

INTRODUCTION
Indian Ocean histories

Rila Mukherjee

Trade and cultural flows have been central to the maritime imaginary of Indian Ocean historians for the early modern period, but Michael Pearson's perspective is unorthodox and refreshingly different. He regards the Indian Ocean as a human space rather than as an artefact of the age of empire or a theatre of European commercial transits between 1500–1800, the overwhelming perspective that still dominates history-writing of the early modern Indian Ocean.

Michael also does not see its space as composed only of fluid passageways dominated by multi-ethnic traders, a perspective marking studies of the pre-1500 Indian Ocean world (Lockard 2010; Hall 2014) or as a theatre of human and biological circulations, which has been the conventional approach to the proto-historical Indian Ocean (Manning 2015; Fuller et al. 2011; Boivin et al. 2012; Fuller and Boivin 2009). He sees it instead as a human ocean, within which far-flung maritime communities were linked by a common material culture across its littorals in the period from 1500 to 1800.

For Michael, therefore, maritime studies are not something to be conducted apart. Along with Karen Wigen, he sees the future of maritime studies as possibly seceding from the land and proceeding alone but preferably modifying and enriching the traditional social sciences (Wigen 2007: 17). Michael is nevertheless critical of some trends emerging in maritime history-writing, such as the question of whether maritime history can be regarded as global or world history (Fusaro and Polónia 2011). He once cautioned scholars that all oceanic history is not always world history:

> If we look at the three greatest oceans, we must at once admit that they are by no means homogeneous bodies of water . . . some are . . . more susceptible to world history analysis than are others . . . the variations are so profound that we may decide the Pacific, or maybe any other ocean, is simply not a category or template which we can use to write world history.
>
> (Pearson 2015: 145, 148, 151)

A human space

Michael's Indian Ocean spans the period from 1500 to 1800. Received history suggests that to control the ocean at that time was to control its trade and riches and was a guarantee, historically, to global ascendancy (Moorthy and Jamal 2010: 2). The Portuguese diarist and apothecary Tomé Pires had noted, 'whoever is lord of Malacca has his hands on the throat of Venice' – this being an instance of supply chain economics operating in the early sixteenth-century Indian Ocean world (Cortesao 1944: I, lxxv).

Michael, however, prioritised individual endeavours and human experience over global ascendance. He often expressed disappointment with the undue emphasis on commerce and commodities in writing Indian Ocean histories for this period, and his dissatisfaction with the present state of Indian Ocean studies can be seen from the interview of 2004 cited in Ghulam Nadri's chapter in this collective.

There is one exception, however. The collective on Indian Ocean trade (Das Gupta and Pearson 1987) made India focal and concentrated on the activities of European merchants and local traders in the ocean in the period from 1500 to 1800. It argued that even though Europeans had crossed the Indian Ocean to trade, their presence was not crucial to India's economic stability at that time, and they did not fundamentally change the Indian Ocean economy. Making that point was important at the time, for it was a fitting response to the imperial sea-borne histories of the Indian Ocean that then dominated the field (Boxer, 1965; Boxer 1969; Parry 1961, Parry 1966, Parry 1971, Parry, 1974; Scammell 1981; Russell Wood 1998).

Apart from this one departure, Michael has always advocated scholarship with what has been called wet ontologies: 'the perspective of a world of flows, connections, liquidities, and becomings, (and) also to propose a means by which the sea's material and phenomenological distinctiveness can facilitate the reimagining and re-enlivening of a world ever on the move' (Steinberg and Peters 2015: 248). He asked scholars writing on the Indian Ocean to get their feet wet to enter the human experience of the time, feeling that a more nautical angle and a whiff of ozone was needed in Indian Ocean studies: 'I want [my book, *The Indian Ocean*] to have a whiff of ozone, not just be a collection of statistics about trade' (Pearson 2003: 8).

Michael Pearson's aquatic vision

Influenced by J. C. Heesterman's foregrounding of the littoral as a free space as opposed to the interior, which was politically and economically regulated (Heesterman 1980), Michael investigated as to whether deep oceanic structures did influence human life and if there was something uniquely maritime about the people who lived on the shores of the ocean. This search led him to the coast, not necessarily by privileging the activities of merchants, rulers and admirals as Heesterman had done but seeing coastlines through the lens of a more fundamental social history.

For scholars, and most particularly for historians, ocean region studies have their origins in an explicit questioning of the assumption that the land-based region is the appropriate scope for conducting social analysis. The coast has a special place in ocean-region-based studies, as it marks both the limit of the region and the points where its regionalisation is achieved. But coastlines also mark the point where the divide between land-covered-by-water and land-not-covered-by-water occurs. This not only divides space but also directs disciplinary enquiries into landward state territories (inside and inward) and external seas (outside and outward) (Steinberg 2013: 161, 163). The present perceptual disarticulation between coast and the interior may arise from early European writings; when Europeans entered the ocean and established port cities on the Indian Ocean littoral, they privileged the coast. Some of the port cities became capitals of colonial empires – Calcutta, for instance, which stayed as the capital of British India until 1911 when the capital was reoriented once again to the interior, to Delhi.

To unpack this binary between coast and interior, Michael adopted an amphibious approach. He studied seafaring and maritime communities, such as fishermen, pearlers, sailors, sail and rope makers and others who were based at sea or on land but who were essentially amphibian in nature and were connected with maritime enterprises for their livelihood. This resulted in the *Great Circle* publication (Pearson 1985), and he returned to the coast again, arguing that 'studies of the littoral can contribute importantly as we try to write not only maritime, but also world, history' (Pearson 2006: 373).

But foregrounding the coast was not easy, and the jury is still out on the methodologies to be adopted in studying oceanic spaces. Steinberg, whom Michael quotes extensively, suggests alternate perspectives that directly engage the ocean's fluid mobility and its tactile materiality. Steinberg does not deny the importance of either the human history of the ocean or the suggestive power of the maritime metaphor, but he asserts that to fully appreciate the ocean as a uniquely fluid and dynamic space, we need to develop an epistemology that views the ocean as continually being reconstituted by a variety of elements: the non-human and the human, the biological and the geophysical, the historic and the contemporary (Steinberg 2013: 157). Michael saw the play of these elements as ressac, borrowing the term from Jean-Claude Penrad. This was the movement of waves breaking on the shore and then receding into the sea again (Penrad 1994).

In 2016, Michael, still in search of deep oceanic structures, wrote,

> One way forward is to be clear about the difference between the pelagic or demersal ocean and coastal waters. It is a fault of most of the people who want to stress the sea and maritime influences

that they fail to make this crucial distinction. Steinberg writes that the sea consists of two regions. 'One region, the coastal zone, is like land in that it is susceptible to being claimed, controlled, regulated, and managed by individual state-actors. In the other region, the deep sea, the only necessary (or even permissible) regulation is that which ensures that all ships will be able to travel freely across its vast surface.'

(Pearson 2016: 41)[1]

Sea mountains, the experience of islands in the middle of oceans and stories of storms at sea challenge Steinberg's notion of the deep sea as a space only to be crossed, and many more such tales are gradually being revealed (Samuelson 2016). But Michael concluded that there was no such thing as a uniquely maritime culture; on the contrary, maritime culture seemed an extension of land-based cultures and institutions even on deep sea: 'If we look at the deep sea ship as a social space, we can clearly see that it is a variant of any social collectivity on land' and 'maritime hierarchies appear similar to landed ones' (Pearson 2016: 41–2). Michael therefore asked historians to adopt 'flexibility and the ability to move, and to accept new ideas. . . . Only on the coast do we find a unique combination of fixed and yet fluid. . . . I am convinced that is the marge, the coast, where we can write the most distinctive maritime, water-based, history' (Pearson 2016: 49–50).

Indian Ocean imaginaries

The history of the Indian Ocean, the world's oldest human ocean, is relatively seamless. Without the newness of the Atlantic, the Indian Ocean holds no comparable sway on contemporary Western or local political imaginary (Moorthy and Jamal 2010: 2). Nevertheless it has generated its own iconography throughout history. In the medieval West, the Indian Ocean was imagined as the original cradle of civilisation, containing perhaps the lost Garden of Eden (Le Goff 1980). In the age of European empires, the Indian Ocean was re-imagined as a route to fabulous riches, eternal youth and possible Shangri-La. Asian and Arabic seafarers, scholars, pilgrims and merchants, in contrast, saw the ocean as a cultural pathway linked through its port cities in a myriad of exchange relationships (Lockard 2010: 221). These relationships spanned diverse seas, each with its own colour, winds and fauna (al-Ya'qubi [d. 897] cited in Lunde 2005), but voyagers travelled seamlessly across this vast oceanic space. Historians have often reduced the Indian Ocean to a place of mobilities, connections and transits, but in doing so, they fail to incorporate the sea as a real, experienced social arena. The ocean region then becomes a series of terrestrial points linked by connections, not the actual oceanic space of connections (Blum 2010; Steinberg 2013: 156–8).

INTRODUCTION

In writing his maritime history, Michael, as we already know, avoided assigning commercial links centre stage, but he also refrained from reducing the sea merely to a place of physical connections. He interrogated instead various aspects of social life at sea to discern specific maritime attributes: religion, violence, gender, class and authority; cosmopolitanism; life on ship board; communication; medical connections; and the roles of brokers, metals and spices in the Indian Ocean world. He wanted to feel how his Indian Ocean of the 1500–1800 period had changed from its earlier avatars.

A non-partisan approach

His interest in these themes and his commitment to the diverse methods they entail ensures that Michael is open to new ideas and disciplinary approaches; his receptive attitude has influenced a new generation of scholars. His openness to new perspectives can be seen from two seminal volumes: *Eyes Across the Water: Navigating the Indian Ocean* (Gupta, Hofmeyr, Pearson 2010) and *Indian Ocean Studies: Cultural, Social, and Political Perspectives* (Moorthy and Jamal 2010). The Gupta, Hofmeyr and Pearson collective firmly placed Africa within the Indian Ocean map from the perspectives of cultural and literary studies. His preface to the Moorthy and Jamal volume noted,

> all the chapters in this important volume demonstrate unequivocally that cultural studies can move forward, even reorient, studies of the Indian Ocean, and indeed maritime studies in general.
> (Pearson 2010: xvii)

His eclectic approach reveals his interest in many of the new trends appearing in maritime studies, such as the work of Mark Ravinder Frost, which outlines a distinctive Indian Ocean public sphere that flourished in Indian Ocean port cities from the 1880s to the 1920s. Based on and sustained by the intelligentsias of intersecting diasporas, this public sphere was rooted in pan-religious movements, be these Buddhist, Muslim or Hindu. The diasporic intelligentsias of the port cities shared 'similar concerns for reform and oversaw parallel campaigns for religious revival, educational improvement and constitutional change' (Frost 2002: 937, 2010: 251–2).

Geographies of the Ocean

Michael is interested in the discipline of geography of ocean spaces (this is seen in his recent engagement with the works of Philip E. Steinberg and Kimberley Peters, for example), but sadly, it has not been possible to include a geographic perspective in this collective. Nor has it been possible to include alternate perspectives from islands – those naturally bounded in history, such as Mauritius with its concept of 'Indienoceanisme' (Hofmeyr 2007: 9) and those that were deliberately repositioned in the ocean through a process of 'islanding' by the colonial state as was the case of colonial Lanka (Sivasundaram 2013: 14). The importance of the three British Crown colonies – Lanka, Mauritius and the Cape, the last as the setting of ambivalent identification and disavowal, and the point of conjuncture between three worlds: African, Atlantic Ocean and Indian Ocean (Samuelson 2016: 526) – ebb and flow in Michael's ocean, revealing the new imperial geographies emerging, much like Sir Thomas Livingstone Mitchell's vision that saw his expedition across the interior of the continent as a way of drawing Australia into what he called 'the Indian Archipelago' in 1848, by linking old and new movements, connections, memories, and histories (Rangan and Kull 2010: 67–8).[2]

There were counter-imaginaries at play as well on both sides of the ocean; these became apparent in the later age of empire, and Michael would have welcomed these new geographies. The Omani Surdhow case of 1893 that was ultimately referred to the Permanent Court of Arbitration in The Hague revealed how native mariners interpreted their rights of sailing and trading in the western Indian Ocean in the age of empire. They flouted British oceanic jurisdiction by re-inventing previous maritime practices and re-invigorating old routes through an innovative application of French legitimacy instead. The French Consul claimed that the Suri mariners belonged not to the Sultan of Muscat, who was at that time under Ottoman overlordship or to any territorial sovereign but were rather members of a maritime community that transcended any of these (Bishara 2018: 339). Another case, also of 1893 but occurring on the other side of the Indian Ocean, is cited in Pedro Machado's chapter in this volume. This case too illustrated the contours of maritime territorial limits and claims. It involved a legal challenge to the (British) Government of Burma from an Australian pearler active in the Mergui Archipelago after it had granted 'a concession of the exclusive right of fishing on these banks.' This unnamed Australian claimed through his legal representatives that he had a right to operate in these waters because he considered 'them to be in the high seas outside the territorial waters [controlled by the Government of Burma]' and that the Government of Burma was therefore acting unlawfully in granting monopoly rights. In raising questions of territoriality and maritime jurisdiction, the two cases exposed not only the anxieties of an incipient colonial state struggling to solidify the 'porous' maritime boundaries of the region but also the ways others interpreted this incipient solidification, informing us to the very diverse aspects of the human experience along the shores of the ocean in the late colonial period. Coastlines are amorphous boundaries, as Pedro Machado reminds us in his chapter in this volume.

The oceanic turn

The contributions in this collective reflect more modestly some of Michael's interests and concerns. While it contains chapters on some of the themes permeating Michael Pearson's work over the last forty years, it is different on certain counts. Contributions have been solicited from diverse fields: literary and cultural studies, environmental studies, the discipline of history and anthropology, all of them concerned with different ways of studying the ocean.

Although the historians' perspective informs the largest portion of contributors to this volume, the editors have consciously refrained from soliciting chapters from only maritime historians because we recognise the limits of historical studies on the Indian Ocean. This collective invited world historian Patrick Manning, literary and cultural studies scholar Isabel Hofmeyr, environmental historian Joseph Christensen and anthropologist Pedro Pombo to contribute alternate views, for Michael, as already noted, has an enduring relationship with diverse approaches. The close disciplinary relationship is particularly visible in Isabel Hofmeyr's chapter on how to make a 'sodden archive' work for scholars, enabling them to navigate between sea and land to write a different, a 'post-humanist', history of the ocean. Her chapter weaves together two of Michael's disciplinary interests: geography and natural science.

Patrick Manning's chapter gives a global overview of the Indian Ocean world in the periods prior to 1500 and post-1800. It is a combined look at the physical extent of the region and its long-term historical experience. The objective of his chapter study is to provide a context reaffirming the particular historical significance of the period from 1500 to 1800 in the long and deep historical experience of the Indian Ocean. To achieve this, Manning looks at human migration, the spread of disease, climate patterns, politics, technology, labour movements and trade over the long-term to confirm the wisdom of Michael's choice of the period 1500 to 1800. By comparing the commercial fortunes of the Indian Ocean with the preceding and following periods, Manning shows that the intermediate 'early modern' era was the time in which the great tropical semicircle played the most central role in the global economy. Finally, Manning argues that to underscore the distinctiveness of the Indian Ocean's global networks, it is not enough to investigate the Indian Ocean alone or the Atlantic Ocean alone. It may well be that resources are becoming available that can enable investigation of the Indian Ocean, East Asia, the North Atlantic and other regions in the context of the world economy as a whole, for the period from the fourteenth century onward, to learn the causes of what we observe.

Unlike what Michael Pearson and Ashin Das Gupta attempted in their collective on *India and the Indian Ocean*, after the academic fashion of the time (Das Gupta and Pearson 1987), this collective hopes to showcase that Indian Ocean studies have moved a long way from privileging India's central place in the Indian Ocean. Instead, it sees the Indian Ocean space as one embracing the Indo-Pacific (Western Australia) and East and South Africa – the last a space where scholars such as Isabel Hofmeyr, Nigel Worden, Meg

Samuelson, Kerry Ward and Preben Karsholm have succeeded in breaking down oceanic boundaries between the Indian and Atlantic oceans. By linking the Indian Ocean with the southern Atlantic at the Cape (as opposed to Manning's chapter in this volume privileging the North Atlantic), their works bring to the surface new textual circuits and suggest the possibility of new ways of seeing, new ways of recounting old stories and hence new ways of writing histories (Hofmeyr et al. 2016).

Case studies

The historical case studies presented in this volume validate the continuing utility of the conventional archive. Radhika Seshan, in her interrogation of peninsular commercial history in the pre-1500 period, plays with the concepts of place, scale, territoriality and networks. She argues that when talking of networks, one cannot stop at the coast because coastal and oceanic networks were part of hinterland networks, and the prosperity of one was reflected in the trade of the other. Thus 'continuities' need to be seen in not just oceanic or coastal trade, but also in the sourcing of the products for that trade and their dissemination in the interior. What she argues is that networks need to focus on hinterlands as well as on inter-port dynamics to highlight the maritime experience.

Kenneth R. Hall's chapter study furthers Seshan's argument through an investigation of coast-hinterland dynamics in fifteenth-century Java. It highlights a network change in studying the island's external 'knowledge networking' contacts over its international marketplace exchanges, including the intellectual dialogue facilitated by 'monks and priests' who travelled on merchant ships and established residency in Java. Consistent with the scholarship of Michael Pearson that contrasts the variety of historical Indian Ocean networked relationships, especially those between coastlines and hinterlands, Hall's study addresses this assertive self-image of Java's cultural accomplishments with a focus on the Majapahit era's legacy to its successors. His chapter examines the tensions of network and hierarchy intersections in Java, as Java evolved from an agricultural economy to one substantively engaged in international trade. It considers networked literary flows consequent to religious transition as also the consequent transitions in political authority, as these linked with Java's religious evolutions from local spirit worship to Hindu-Buddhism and then Islam. Herein religious change was a factor in the de-stabilisation and challenge to Java's existing societal hierarchy that was based in Hindu-Buddhist theology. One can argue that Java's transition from a generally wet-rice agricultural society to one of mixed economic pursuits, due to Java's evolving role as a major marketing centre in the vibrant international maritime trade network, was a factor in the Javanese acceptance of Islam.

INTRODUCTION

While the first two chapters deal with the pre-1500 Indian Ocean world, the next three chapters enter the period from 1500 to 1800. Amélia Polónia furthers Michael's interrogation of the Jesuits in India where he noted that

> in Bassein and Daman . . . the Jesuits had large estates, to a total value of over 180,000 cruzados. It was claimed these should return 10 per cent on their value. Adding in rents from orchards, we find the Jesuits with annual receipts, from the land of about 22,500 cruzados. A traveller in this area in the 1670s claimed that the Jesuits 'govern all [Portuguese] India, in matters both temporal and spiritual, with a superiority and address that render them redoubtable to any who dare to work against this holy Society'. The same sort of stereotype is revealed in another seventeenth-century jingle: 'Guard your wife from the Franciscans and your money from the Jesuits.'
>
> (Pearson 1987: 127)

Polónia argues in her chapter study that the presence of Jesuits in sixteenth-century Japan can also be seen as a historical case study of agents of institutionalised networks getting involved in overseas empire building by way of self-organised individual networks. Ruled by the Roman church and one of the most powerful and well-structured religious orders of the time, the Jesuits were introduced in the East by the Portuguese crown itself, as imperial Portuguese history informs us. Nonetheless, what the Eurocentric approach does not reveal is the fact that Jesuit presence in Japan depended also on active cooperation with local landlords, resulting in a wide process of cultural assimilation, but there were also widespread behaviours of cheating and defection – to the Portuguese crown, to the Portuguese merchants and to the Japanese landlords. Polónia holds that in the case of the Jesuits, missionary activities, as well as political and economic performances, have to be understood within the framework of various networks – Portuguese, Japanese and Chinese, both lay and ecclesiastical – and intermingled in a disentangled way. For her, processes of imposition, negotiation, and adaptation weaved a web of global interactions between European, Japanese and other Asian peoples, and research on these interactions is essential to fully understand the dynamic, open, complex, non-linear system which characterised the First Global Age from 1400 to 1800.

Ryuto Shimada delves into the Dutch records to highlight Batavia's cross-cultural dimensions as centre of VOC trade in the seventeenth century. Batavia was not solely a European or Indonesian township. Investigating the nature of the 'Moorish' population there, Shimada concludes that the existence of the Moor people in Batavia during this time was unique because they were one of the key sources of manual labour. Also, the *Moors* displayed the competitiveness of the Chinese. From the establishment of the city of

Batavia, the VOC had heavily relied on overseas Chinese in terms of sources of manual labour, entrepreneurs for inland industry, and traders for coastal trade and for domestic trade within the city. To avoid undue dependence on overseas Chinese, the VOC was willing to promote immigrants from South Asia and gave privileges to the *Moors* at Batavia. This gave Batavia its distinctive pan-Asian character.

Fabiano Bracht takes up a theme close to Michael's heart: the circulation of medical knowledge in the Indian Ocean realm. Bracht analyses historical sources on the processes of the production of knowledge in Portuguese India during the eighteenth century, interrogating the dynamics of construction, extension and reconfiguration of scientific (chiefly medical) knowledge in the extended Indian Ocean world centred on eighteenth-century Goa. He sees these processes as inseparable from their local contexts and, at the same time, connected with global developments in knowledge production.

Michael has for long advocated the need to explore seamen's lived experiences aboard ships to underscore the oceanic experience. Ghulam A. Nadri does so in his chapter study, arguing that while literature on Indian maritime history recognises the significant role of sailors (lascars) in facilitating navigation and trade in the early modern and colonial periods, the scholarship has been primarily focused on issues related to sailors on shore and in ports at both ends of the journey. Beyond a general assumption and acknowledgement among scholars that lascars were ill-treated on board European ships, there is hardly any discussion and analysis of what the actual journey entailed, how lascars were treated during the journey on European ships, and why the journey was so fraught with violence, death, and desertion. Ghulam Nadri claims that very often the analysis turns into a discussion of the domination of European colonial merchant capital and subordination or submission of Indian labour and the ensuing hardships the latter were forced to endure. But the reality, according to him, was more complex. More than race and racial discrimination, market forces of supply and demand, competition among shipowners and the social/ethnic composition of the crew, as well as the monsoon-driven sailing seasons played an important role in shaping the shipboard labour regime and the relationship between its various constituents. Analysis of lascars' nautical experiences in the early nineteenth century has to go beyond the binary of colonial domination – Indian subordination and take into account the role of market forces and the complex hierarchy through which power and authority were exercised aboard ships. Using the evidence related to lascar recruitment for the vessel *David Scott*, Nadri's chapter illuminates the dynamics of the nineteenth-century Indian Ocean labour market, showing that the flawed system of lascar recruitment was largely responsible for disaffected labour relations on board ships, arguing that labour relations on board a ship depended on how the ship was staffed, who the lascars were and how were they recruited.

INTRODUCTION

Fungible histories

This collective has devoted space to what we have called 'new histories' in the third section; three chapters expound on some of the themes Michael was working on as late as 2015: the history of pearling, the territoriality of ocean spaces and the impact of the Anthropocene, with concern for writing history through non-conventional sources running as the unifying strand between these themes.

The themes come alive in Joseph Christensen's, Pedro Pombo's and Pedro Machado's chapter studies. Joseph Christensen uses Greg Bankoff's recent formulation of the notion of the 'hazardousness of place' to study the 'Pearling Fleet Disaster' of April 1887 on the Western Australian coast (Bankoff 2016). Christensen's chapter captures the subalternity of those who provided the pearling fleets with its essential labour: 'Malays' from Singapore, Timor, the Sulu Archipelago, and many other places in between; Filipinos or 'Manilamen'; Japanese; Chinese; and Pacific or 'South Sea' Islanders. By exploring the Pearling Fleet Disaster, his chapter also poses questions about approaches to, and the possibilities of, Indian Ocean history. To bring these questions together, Christensen's closing section considers a further aspect of Michael's work. This is the distinction he makes, following Peregrine Horden and Nicholas Purcell in *The Corrupting Sea*, between a history of the ocean and a history in it – that is, between an internal one using ocean-wide comparisons, or history of the ocean, and a history shaped by forces emanating from beyond the ocean, which comprises history in the ocean (Horden and Purcell 2000: 8; Pearson 2003: 11–12; Vink 2007: 57). The disaster, Joseph Christensen suggests, cuts across these distinctions, offering an example of how natural hazards might be considered as part of the 'deep structure' shaping the history of the ocean across the longue durée.

In Pedro Pombo's chapter, everydayness, material culture, smells and flavours become sites where memories are constructed, re-built or contested. They are also testimonies of cultural contacts across time and space. Pombo sees an interactive Indian Ocean arena where new histories are forged between Gujarat, Mozambique and South Africa through cashew nuts, curries, Rajah masala and wax prints. His chapter shows that the presence of India in Mozambique can be seen not only through historical documents or statistics of the Indian-origin population in the country but also in the processes whereby the presence of India became part of the everyday at various levels.

Pedro Machado shows us how marine product extraction, involving a sustained search for pearls but, more significantly in terms of quantities fished and their consumption, shell, was a critical dimension in shaping the complex waterways around which the varied littorals of the Indian Ocean took shape. The pearling economies of coastal Burma, including importantly those of the Mergui Archipelago that were located in its southern

11

reaches, were primary sites of marine extraction and trade that represented vital nodes in the many flows of commodities linking the Bay of Bengal and parts of South India to Southeast Asia and the South China Sea and ultimately also to pearling's globalizing markets of the nineteenth and early twentieth centuries. The territorialisation of ocean space became an increasingly dominant feature of British and other European imperial claims from around the middle of the eighteenth century, particularly throughout the many islands and coastal areas of insular Southeast Asia. European and Australian involvement in Mergui pearling has been privileged in scholarship, while the participation of Chinese and South Asian capital and labour has been marginalised or largely occluded in the scholarship. That much of the shell extracted from the Mergui Archipelago was shipped to Chinese markets is undeniable but Machado's chapter asserts that it is important to recognise the multiple circuits through which shipments reached the latter and also the wider importance of South Asian consumer markets for Burmese shell in the nineteenth and early twentieth centuries.

The last section of the volume ends with two chapters of reminiscences of Michael Pearson as a scholar and human being by editors Rila Mukherjee and Radhika Seshan.

End words

The chapter studies in this collective address some of the changes in thinking and seeing that have taken place in Indian Ocean studies in this century: how to integrate Indian Ocean studies at a world-historical scale, how to make an archive work, how to write fungible stories and the new ways of studying histories. In so doing, the collective moves away from many of the enduring themes in studies of the Indian Ocean world, such as its characterisation as the cradle of globalisation or the notion of the ocean and its constituent seas as a cultural and civilisational continuum (Chaudhuri 1991, Chaudhuri 1985; Prakash and Lombard 1999), dominated by what some scholars have seen as a distinctive Asian trade (Meilink-Roelofsz 1962; Das Gupta 1967) and others as a 'peddling trade' (Van Leur 1955). Other themes that have predominated thus far have been the Indian Ocean's similarity (or not) to the Mediterranean (Braudel 1995; Guillot et al. 1998) with over-emphasis on port cities, commodities, merchants and trade (Ptak and Rothermund 1991; Lombard and Aubin 1988; Lombard and Aubin 2000; Polónia and Antunes 2016; Mukherjee 2014).

Such Orientalist, Eurocentric and nationalist approaches are abandoned here. The present collective has concentrated on lived experiences instead from a multitude of disciplinary perspectives, revealing that this generation of Indian Ocean scholars have moved very consciously away from a maritime history written within the confines of the nation-state – imperial or not, as the case may be. At the end of the twentieth century, post-imperial historical studies of seafarers and maritime communities were still being conducted within, as Frank Broeze had put it, the archival, linguistic, conceptual and statistical boundaries of the nation-state (Broeze 1995: xiii–xiv). For example, despite making the coast focal, Heesterman had still seen his littoral operating within national and imperial frames – that of the Mughal state and subsequently of European merchant empires. But it was not marked by the cash-nexus of merchant-monarch relations; he saw instead in the porous littoral a fundamental opposition to the closed-ness of the interior, which ultimately translated to a clash between what Heesterman called a littoral regime versus a territorial one (Heesterman 1980: 89). But the littoral underwent a fundamental change from the end of the seventeenth century. Under the impact of European capital, it became integrated with the interior – in his famous words: 'L'lnde bascule vers la mer' (Heesterman 1980: 90). Despite accepting many of Heesterman's arguments, Michael had consciously eschewed political events and European hegemony when writing his Indian Ocean history. *Merchants and Rulers in Gujarat* (Pearson 1976) was an exception. By continuing to break down such walls, we hope that this collective will demonstrate that Indian Ocean studies have indeed come a long way.

Notes

1 Michael N. Pearson, citing Philip E. Steinberg, *The Social Construction of the Ocean*, 115 (New York: Cambridge University Press, 2001).
2 See figure 3.21.

References

al-Ya'qubi, in Paul Lunde. 2005. "The Seas of Sindbad," *Saudi Aramco World*, 56(4): 20–9, July–August.

Bankoff, Greg. 2016. "Hazardousness of Place: A New Comparative approach to the Study of the Filipino Past," *Philippine Studies*, Special Issue *Disasters in History*, 64(3–4), Manila: Ateneo de Manila University: 335–57.

Bishara, Fahad Ahmad. 2018. " 'No Country but the Ocean': Reading International Law from the Deck of an Indian Ocean Dhow, ca. 1900," *Comparative Studies in Society and History*, 60(2): 338–66.

Blum, Hester. 2010. "The Prospect of Oceanic Studies," *Proceedings of the Modern Language Association of America*: 670–7.

Boivin, Nicole, Dorian Q. Fuller and Alison Crowther. 2012. "Old World Globalization and the Columbian Exchange: Comparison and Contrast," *World Archaeology*, 44: 452–69.

Boxer, C.R. 1965. *The Dutch Seaborne Empire 1600–1800*, New York: Alfred A. Knopf.

Boxer, C.R. 1969. *The Portuguese Seaborne Empire 1415–1825*, New York: Alfred A. Knopf.

Braudel, Fernand. 1995. *A History of Civilizations*, New York: Penguin.

Broeze, Frank. 1995. "Introduction: Maritime History at the Crossroads: A Critical Review of Recent Historiography," in Frank Broeze (ed.), *Maritime History at the Crossroads: A Critical Review of Recent Historiography*, St. John's, Newfoundland: IMEHA: ix–xxi.

Chaudhuri, K.N. 1985. *Trade and Civilisation in the Indian Ocean: An Economic History from the Rise of Islam to 1750*, Cambridge: Cambridge University Press.

Chaudhuri, K.N. 1991. *Asia Before Europe: Economy and Civilisation of the Indian Ocean from the Rise of Islam to 1750*, Cambridge: Cambridge University Press.

Cortesao, Armando. 1944. *Introduction to the Suma Oriental of Tome Pires etc*, 2 vols, London: Hakluyt Society, Reprint, New Delhi: Asian Educational Services, 2005.

Das Gupta, Ashin and M.N. Pearson (eds.). 1987. *India and the Indian Ocean, 1500–1800*, Calcutta and New York: Oxford University Press.

Das Gupta, Ashin. 1967. *Malabar in Asian Trade: 1740–1800*, Cambridge: Cambridge University Press.

Frost, Mark Ravinder. 2002. " 'Wider Opportunities': Religious Revival, Nationalist Awakening and the Global Dimension in Colombo, 1870–1920," *Modern Asian Studies*, 36(4): 937–67.

Frost, Mark Ravinder. 2010. " 'That Great Ocean of Idealism': Calcutta, the Tagore Circle, and the Idea of Asia, 1900–1920," in Shanti Moorthy and Ashraf Jamal (eds.), *Indian Ocean Studies: Cultural, Social, and Political Perspectives*, New York and Abingdon: Routledge: 251–79.

Fuller, Dorian Q. and Nicole Boivin. 2009. "Crops, Cattle and Commensals Across the Indian Ocean: Current and Potential Archaeobiological Evidence," *Études Océan Indien*, 42–43: 13–46.

Fuller, Dorian Q., Nicole Boivin, T. Hoogervorst and R. Allaby. 2011. "Across the Indian Ocean: The Prehistoric Movement of Plants and Animals," *Antiquity*, 85: 544–58.

Fusaro, M. and A. Polónia (eds.). 2011. *Maritime History as Global History*, St. John's, Newfoundland: IMEHA.

Guillot, Claude, Denys Lombard and Roderich Ptak (eds.). 1998. *From the Mediterranean to the China Sea: Miscellaneous Notes*, Wiesbaden: Otto Harrassowitz Verlag.

Hall, Kenneth R. 2014. "Revisionist Study of Cross-Cultural Commercial Competition on the Indian Ocean Coastlines c. 1000–1500 and the Wider Implications," in Rila Mukherjee (ed.), *Vanguards of Globalization, Port Cities from the Classical to the Modern*, New Delhi: Primus Books: 195–21.

Heesterman, J.C. 1980. "Littoral et intérieur de l'Inde," *Itinerario*, 4: 87–92.

Hofmeyr, Isabel. 2007. "The Black Atlantic Meets the Indian Ocean: Forging New Paradigms of Transnationalism for the Global South – Literary and Cultural Perspectives," *Social Dynamics*, 33(2): 3–32.

Hofmeyr, Isabel, Uma Dhupelia-Mesthrie and Preben Kaarsholm. 2016. "Durban and Cape Town as Port Cities: Reconsidering Southern African Studies from the Indian Ocean," *Journal of Southern African Studies*, 42(3): 375–87.

Horden, Peregrine and Nicholas Purcell. 2000. *The Corrupting Sea: A Study of Mediterranean History*, Malden, MA: Blackwell.

Le Goff, Jacques. 1980. "The Medieval West and the Indian Ocean: An Oneiric Horizon," in Jacques le Goff, (Arthur Goldhammer trans.), *Time, Work and Culture in the Middle Ages*, Chicago: University of Chicago Press.

INTRODUCTION

Lockard, Craig A. 2010. "'The Sea Common to All': Maritime Frontiers, Port Cities, and Chinese Traders in the Southeast Asian Age of Commerce, ca. 1400–1750," *Journal of World History*, 21: 219–247, 2 June.

Lombard, Denys and Jean Aubin (eds.). 1988. *Marchands et hommes d'affaires asiatiques dans l'océan Indien et la mer de Chine (13e -20e siècles)*, Paris: Editions EHESS.

Lombard, Denys and Jean Aubin (eds.). 2000. *Asian Merchants and Businessmen in the Indian Ocean and the China Sea*, New Delhi: Oxford University Press.

Manning, Patrick. 2015. "Settlement and Resettlement in Asia: Migration vs. Empire in History," *Asian Review of World Histories*, 3(2): 171–200.

Meilink-Roelofsz, M.A.P. 1962. *Asian Trade and European Influence in the Indonesian Archipelago Between 1500 and About 1630*, The Hague: Martinus Nijhoff.

Moorthy, Shanti and Ashraf Jamal. 2010. "Introduction: New Conjunctures in Maritime Imaginaries," in Shanti Moorthy and Ashraf Jamal (eds.), *Indian Ocean Studies: Cultural, Social, and Political Perspectives*, New York and Abingdon: Routledge: 1–31.

Mukherjee, Rila (ed.). 2014. *Vanguards of Globalization: Port-Cities from the Classical to the Modern*, New Delhi: Primus Books.

Parry, J.H. 1961. *The Establishment of the European Hegemony, 1415–1715: Trade and Exploration in the Age of the Renaissance*, New York: Harper & Row.

Parry, J.H. 1966. *The Spanish Seaborne Empire*, New York: Alfred A. Knopf, Reprint, 1973, 1977, 1990.

Parry, J.H. 1971. *Trade and Dominion: The European Overseas Empires in the Eighteenth Century*, New York: Praeger Publishers, Reprint, 1974, 2000.

Parry, J.H. 1974. *The Discovery of the Sea*, New York: Dial Press, Reprint, 1975, 1981.

Pearson, M.N. 1976. *Merchants and Rulers in Gujarat: The Response to the Portuguese in the Sixteenth Century*, New Delhi: Munshiram Manoharlal.

Pearson, M.N. 1985. "Littoral Society: The Case for the Coast," *The Great Circle*, 7(1): 1–8, April.

Pearson, M.N. 1987. *The Portuguese in India, The New Cambridge History of India, 1.1*, Cambridge: Cambridge University Press.

Pearson, M.N. 2003. *The Indian Ocean*, New York and Abingdon: Routledge.

Pearson, M.N. 2006. "Littoral Society: The Concept and the Problems," *Journal of World History*, 17(4): 353–73.

Pearson, M.N. 2010. "Preface," in Shanti Moorthy and Ashraf Jamal (eds.), *Indian Ocean Studies: Cultural, Social, and Political Perspectives*, New York and Abingdon: Routledge: xv–xvii.

Pearson, M.N. 2015. "Notes on World History and Maritime History," *Asian Review of World Histories*, special issue *Problematizing World History*, 3(1): 137–51, January.

Pearson, M.N. 2016. "Water and History: Some Sceptical Notes," in Rila Mukherjee (ed.), *Living with Water: Peoples, Lives, and Livelihoods in Asia and Beyond*, New Delhi: Primus Books: 39–52.

Penrad, Jean-Claude. 1994. "Societies of the Ressac: The Mainland Meets the Ocean," in David Parkin (ed.), *Continuity and Autonomy in Swahili Communities: Influences and Strategies of Self-Determination*, Wien: Afrika Pub; London: S.O.A.S.: 41–48.

Polónia, Amélia and Catia Antunes (eds.). 2016. *Seaports in the First Global Age Portuguese Agents, Networks and Interactions (1500–1800)*, Porto: UPorto Press.

Prakash, Om and Denys Lombard (eds.). 1999. *Commerce and Culture in the Bay of Bengal, 1500–1800*, New Delhi: Manohar.

Ptak, Roderich and Dietmar Rothermund (eds.). 1991. *Emporia, Commodities and Entrepreneurs in Asian Maritime Trade, c. 1400–1750*, Stuttgart: Franz Steiner Verlag.

Rangan, Haripriya and Christian Kull. 2010. "The Indian Ocean and the Making of Outback Australia: An Ecocultural Odyssey," in Shanti Moorthy and Ashraf Jamal (eds,), *Indian Ocean Studies: Cultural, Social, and Political Perspectives*, New York and Abingdon: Routledge: 45–72.

Russell Wood, A.J.R. 1998. *The Portuguese Empire, 1415–1808: A World on the Move*, Baltimore: JHU Press.

Samuelson, Meg. 2016. "Rendering the Cape-as-Port: Sea-Mountain, Cape of Storms/Good Hope, Adamastor and Local-World Literary Formations," *Journal of Southern African Studies*, 42(3): 523–37.

Scammell, Geoffrey Vaughn. 1981. *The World Encompassed: The First European Maritime Empires, C. 800–1650*, Berkeley and Los Angeles: University of California Press.

Sivasundaram, Sujit. 2013. *Islanded: Britain, Sri Lanka, and the Bounds of an Indian Ocean Colony*, Chicago: University of Chicago Press.

Steinberg, Philip E. 2013. "Of Other Seas: Metaphors and Materialities in Maritime Regions," *Atlantic Studies*, 10(2): 156–69.

Steinberg, Philip E. and K. Peters. 2015. "Wet Ontologies, Fluid Spaces: Giving Depth to Volume Through Oceanic Thinking," *Environment and Planning D: Society and Space*, 33(2): 247–64.

Van Leur, Jacob Cornelius. 1955. *Indonesian Trade and Society: Essays in Asian Social and Economic History*, The Hague and Bandung: W. van Hoeve.

Vink, Markus. 2007. "Indian Ocean Studies and the 'New Thalassology'," *Journal of Global History*, 2: 41–62.

Wigen, Karen. 2007. "Introduction," in Jerry H. Bentley, Renate Bridenthal and Karen Wigen (eds.), *Seascapes: Maritime History, Littoral Cultures and Transoceanic Exchanges*, Honolulu, HI: University of Hawai'i Press.

Part I

HISTORIOGRAPHIES, METHODOLOGIES AND SCALE IN THE INDIAN OCEAN

1

THE INDIAN OCEAN
Global nexus (1500–1800)

Patrick Manning

Space-age technology enables us to gain views of the Earth at night – luminous images of what humankind has done to remake the surface of our planet. Of these views, one of the most arresting is that of the great semicircular littoral of the Indian Ocean, centred on the South Asian peninsula. It shows bright spots in Southern Africa and Western Australia, brighter spots along the coasts of Arabia and Indonesia, glimmers all along the ocean shore and a dense glow throughout South Asia. This tropical semicircle conveys at once the notion of communication along the littoral and of traversing the open ocean to link ports so as to satisfy complementary needs.

This concise overview of the Indian Ocean is an effort to honour the wide-ranging analyses of Michael Pearson, combining a look at the physical extent of the region and its long-term historical experience with citations of his works on these issues. The objective is to provide a context reaffirming the particular historical significance of the period from 1500 to 1800 in the long and deep historical experience of the Indian Ocean (Pearson 2003, 2010a).[1]

Today's Indian Ocean littoral sustains the legacy of human habitation during many thousands of years. The commonality of this landscape and seascape – with shared flora and fauna, terrestrial and maritime, along its lengthy littoral – provided a welcoming habitat for the humans who began expanding ever outward from their Northeast African homeland, once they developed language. Speaking humans moved southward along the African coast and, at much the same time, moved eastward along the Asian coast, in each case moving inland along river valleys when the opportunity arose. The travel was both maritime and terrestrial from the first – across the Bab el Mendeb from Africa to Arabia, along the coast on both continents and eventually across the ocean from Sunda to Sahul. Early human settlers thus formed a great semicircle from South Africa to Australia, on and near the shores of the Indian Ocean. From this base, later generations moved inland, especially via rivers such as the Rovuma, Zambezi, Euphrates, Indus,

Godavari, Ganges, Brahmaputra, Irrawaddy, Mekong and Red River. With the passage of more time, other settlers moved west to Africa's Atlantic, north throughout Eurasia and eventually into the Americas. Nevertheless, as widely as humans were to become dispersed, the initial semicircle of settlement around the Indian Ocean remained an important base of human population, where humanity developed many of its innovations. The descendants of these early settlers gradually developed both diversification and interconnection, as the diversifying languages, cultures and social and economic patterns were linked by recurring migrations and exchanges of heritage.

Continents and subcontinents frame the waters of the Indian Ocean: this terrestrial frame generates the monsoon-centred climate that stands as the outstanding regional characteristic. The great landmasses gain heat in the summer, forcing winds across lands and waters. Asia and Northeast Africa force winds to the south during the northern summer; continental cooling during the winter draws winds to the north. These patterns are reinforced by the heating of southern Africa and Australia in the southern summer – these landmasses, when heated, force winds to the north. The seasonal shifts cause the winds to blow dependably north and south every year; the rains come from the humidity gathered over the oceans. But the monsoons vary over time according to the strength of the sun's impact on each latitude. The strength of monsoons in each part of the ocean basin changed from weak to strong, from south to north, according to the three types of change in insolation resulting from variations in the earth's orbit, from annual changes to cycles of many thousands of years. In addition, an east-west variation in climate imposed itself occasionally on the north-south alternation of the monsoons – the El Niño Southern Oscillation, created by varying insolation of the Pacific Ocean, brought alternations of heat and cold, humid and dry, that cut across the Indian Ocean in cycles ranging from two to seven years.

During the first millennium CE, mariners had learned the monsoons, how to sail them and how to link up the markets for commodities: the littoral linked each region to the next and to the islands, all across the great semicircle. In addition, a few major routes tied the Indian Ocean to other world regions facilitating long-distance commerce and migration. The Red Sea formed a path to the Mediterranean; the Persian Gulf opened the way to the West Asian interior; Khyber Pass was the route to Central Asia; and the Ganges and the Brahmaputra led to the interior of North India and to the mountainous route to Yunnan and south China. Finally, through the straits of Malacca and Sunda, maritime routes led to China and to the Spice Islands.

Michael Pearson's scholarly focus on the Indian Ocean reached back into early times but settled most seriously on the period beginning with 1500, as Portuguese and Spanish navigators entered the region from opposite directions so that global communication and commerce took form, and ending in 1800 as Britain gained hegemony throughout the region and began shipping cotton textiles to India rather than the reverse. This chapter confirms the wisdom of Pearson's choice, by comparing the commercial fortunes of the Indian Ocean, 1500–1800, with the preceding and following periods, to show that the intermediate "early modern" era was the time in which the great tropical semicircle played the most central role in the global economy.

Commerce in an era of Islamic expansion (1200–1500)

The era of the Medieval Warm Period (as it was labelled in northwest Europe) is known to have brought a warm and humid climate to most regions of the world from 900 to 1250 CE. It therefore brought ample harvests and growing population to the Indian Ocean region. From 1250, temperatures stabilised and then declined from 1350 for some four hundred years before beginning to rise. During the period to 1500, the Indian Ocean region experienced relative peace and prosperity.

Within the confines of the Indian Ocean, the ancient commercial system continued to mature. Ships from three traditions crossed the seas, transshipped goods in harbours and underwent repair in home ports and distant workshops. The dhows of the Western and Eastern Indian Ocean, the proas of the Malay mariners and the junks from China, each type built at varying scales, maintained their original designs yet adopted innovations from each other. The principal ports changed, over the centuries, though the regions served by shifting ports changed little. An overlapping set of languages was employed in commerce, varying across the regions and over time.

Regions, ethnicities and religions served as markers of culture and identity: the ancient settlement of the region meant that there was deep cultural diversity in the Indian Ocean region, but it also meant that devices had been developed for exchange and communication across the persistent cultural divides (Pearson 1994).[2] In the era from 1200 to 1500, migrations were relatively small scale and took the form of trade diasporas or missionary diasporas. Trade diasporas included those of Armenian and Gujarati merchants; religious diasporas included those of Islamic missionaries to East Africa and the Malay lands and Buddhist missionaries from Ceylon to Thailand and Burma.

Commerce of the Indian Ocean extended in various directions beyond the limits of the tropical semicircle. From the Western Indian Ocean, exchange had long taken place along the East African coast; with the Mediterranean, through the Red Sea; with West Asia, through the Persian Gulf and the Tigris-Euphrates Valley; and with Central Asia, through the Khyber Pass. From the Eastern Indian Ocean, the valleys of the Ganges, the Brahmaputra and the Irrawaddy led to southwest China, while the Strait of Malacca and the Strait of Sunda led to the Spice Islands and the South China Sea (Pearson 2010b).[3]

In this expanded network, built around an Indian Ocean core, commerce flourished as never before in the era from 1250 to 1350. During that century, a world economy linked markets from Europe to Japan through the Indian Ocean, with overland connections as well. Commodities in this trade included silks from China, cottons from India, pepper from India, spices from the Spice Islands, diamonds from India, pearls from South Asia and the Gulf, ceramics from China and Persia, coffee from Ethiopia, tea from China, horses from Arabia, furs from Siberia and wheat and rice from many farmlands. While the Mongol regime controlled the Silk Road, no one state controlled the commercial links through the Indian Ocean. Mongol-era warfare had spread advanced military techniques back and forth across the Old World, but many other sorts of exchanges took place in peacetime (Pearson 1997).[4] These included exchanges of spoken and literary languages, religious knowledge and belief, maps, astronomy, medical and other knowledge and technical knowledge in agriculture and printing. Cowrie shells from the Maldives spread as far as the Yellow River Valley, the western Mediterranean and the Niger Valley. Cinnamon and nutmeg reached Japan and Iberia.

States rose and fell throughout this commercial network, causing disruption as they fought wars of conquest and sought to repress rebellions but protecting and facilitating commerce in intervening eras of peace. The commercial hub of Srivijaya lost its long hegemony over the straits of Sunda and Malacca as did its competitor Chola on the Coromandel Coast at the end of the thirteenth century, but Majapahit rose to replace Srivijaya and Vijayanagar rose to replace Chola. Ghaznavid rule in India and Persia came to an end in the twelfth century, but the Delhi Sultanate expanded Islam in North India from 1206. Buddhist priests from Ceylon successfully spread Theravada Buddhism to the lands that are now Myanmar, Thailand and Cambodia, while Hinduism rebounded in India with the fourteenth-century rise of Vijayanagar. Muslim communities, commonly maritime, spread to East Africa to North India and along the coast, carrying goods as far as China, where they established diaspora communities. Islam had won over Arabia and Persia in its early days and entered North India from Ghaznavid times. Established mosques were expanded along the Swahili coast; new mosques were constructed in Malay lands.

At a global level, the era from 1200 to 1600 was a time of collisions and crises, which made the Indian Ocean appear peaceful and orderly by comparison with other regions. The Mongol conquests (1206–1280) and the Black Death (beginning in the 1340s) were the two greatest collisions, one in human affairs, the other with the natural world. Genghis Khan had conquered all of the Eurasian steppes before his death in 1227, and his successors had seized all of Persia and China by 1280. (But Mongol expeditions against the Delhi Sultanate were unsuccessful, and their occupation of Java was brief.) The Black Death, an epidemic of plague resulting from the bacterium *Yersina pestis*, killed great numbers in many parts of the eastern hemisphere in the mid-fourteenth century and then returned at less severe levels for centuries. The plague is now thought to have broken out in North China and to have killed millions there. The immense plague mortality in Europe, 1347–1351, has been well documented; a heavy but less well-documented mortality is known for West Asia, Egypt and North Africa. New research is indicating that plague mortality may also have been significant in South Asia and South Arabia and from Ethiopia west to the African Atlantic.

The Indian Ocean region was the largest region of commercial interchange and had the most fully developed practices in exchange within the region, facilitating commerce with other regions. A widely recognised emblem of the region's achievement in commerce and navigation is the work of the maritime scholar Ibn Majid (1421–c.1500), born on the gulf shore, who sailed and documented the western Indian Ocean: his numerous treatises on navigation, along with his poetry on maritime life, brought the art of seamanship to a high level in the fifteenth century (Pearson 2007a).[5]

The nexus of global commerce (1500–1800)

In the sixteenth century, two new commercial routes opened for the Indian Ocean. The cape route to the Atlantic opened with the voyage of Vasco da Gama in 1498; the trans-Pacific route opened in 1571 as the Spanish established regular galleon voyages from Mexico to Manila. This was of course also the era in which maritime travel linked all the populated regions of the world, bringing discovery and disaster at first but eventually bringing growth and transformation. These additional openings to and from the Indian Ocean created the era, from 1500 to 1800, in which the Indian Ocean played a transformed yet distinctive role as a nexus of global commerce and communication. Such expansion of global commercial contacts was to facilitate expanded and transformed trade in every region. Iberia and Northwest Europe developed as a new global commercial centre, relying on shipping routes in all directions. The East Asian commercial hub, linking China, Japan and Korea, maintained its centrality and developed new ties, especially with trans-Pacific trade linking Manila to Acapulco. Smaller commercial centres developed in the Caribbean and West Africa, but they did not thrive. The Indian Ocean arguably benefited the most, especially early in this three-century period, because of its clear links to all other regions.

The conditions of climate and disease in this era were not initially favourable to economic growth. Global temperatures declined slowly but steadily on to 1650, an unusually cool and trying time worldwide, and only then began to rise. Epidemics of plague, while declining in frequency and intensity, continued into this period. The steady expansion in interregional contact during this era meant that diseases, both old and new, struck and occasionally reduced populations. So the expansion in the volume of Indian Ocean trade after 1500 (assuming that it can be firmly documented) is all the more impressive in that it moved ahead despite declining temperatures and the continuation of serious disease.

Changes in the Americas brought effects in the Indian Ocean. From the early sixteenth century, waves of epidemic disease led to dramatic population decline throughout the Americas, as a result of pathogens brought especially from Europe and Africa. Disease spread around the world through human communication – as an instance, syphilis, originating in the Americas, had reached Melaka in 1511 and by 1512 had reached Japan. In the "Columbian Exchange," biota from the eastern hemisphere and the western hemisphere were exchanged, especially beginning in 1492. The results brought new crops to the Indian Ocean, notably chili peppers, peanuts, pineapples, maize, potatoes and squashes, that ultimately changed diet and cuisine.

Yet the trade of the Indian Ocean, while it expanded, did so under complex conditions. From the moment of Portuguese entry into the Indian Ocean, they emphasised the militarisation of trade, an approach later reaffirmed by their Dutch, English and French successors. For the period from 1500 to 1580, Portugal was the one European state with significant trade in the Indian Ocean, monopolizing the trade around the Cape of Good Hope, facilitating trade to China and seeking to dominate trade within the Indian Ocean. While the Portuguese established great military influence, they did not succeed in monopolizing trade within the region (Pearson 1969, 1976a, 1984, 1987, 1998b, 2002, 2007b).[6]

The Ottomans challenged the Portuguese in the mid-sixteenth century with naval campaigns to drive them from the western Indian Ocean but fell short. From 1580, competing European states offered a challenge, seeking to beat the Portuguese at their own Indian Ocean strategy: Spain (under the dual monarchy), Netherlands, England and France each attempted their own version. They neither expelled the Portuguese nor dominated regional commerce, yet they profited because they shared in the expanding total volume of Indian Ocean commerce. Exports of cowries and cotton textiles went to West Africa via Europe to nourish the Atlantic slave trade, which grew at 2 per cent per year. Silver entered the region in unprecedented quantity from the Americas, crossing the Pacific to Manila and crossing the Atlantic to Seville and then dispersing through multiple processes (Pearson 1993, 2001b).[7]

Throughout the early modern era, the Indian Ocean littoral hosted numerous encounters of various types, among peoples of the great oceanic basin, including expatriates. Although the East African encounters have been neglected by some authors, Michael Pearson provided several valuable explorations of the commercial, cultural, and military links along the East African coast (Pearson 1998a, 1998c, 2000, 2007c).[8] Other connections included the exchange of knowledge on medical practice, notably between Portuguese and Hindu practitioners (Pearson 1996, 2001a, 2006).[9] Further exchanges of knowledge in the early modern era included reform movements within Islam, for which ideas developed in Indian Ocean regions could be debated in Mecca during and after the annual hajj (Pearson 1986–87, 2007d).[10]

If one characteristic of European commercial incursions was the militarisation of trade, another characteristic of trade in the post-1500 era was the expanded focus on slavery. While slavery had characterised the previous period in the Indian Ocean (as with the purchase of Turkish slaves from Central Asia and slaves from Northeastern Africa, many of them males for military service), the level of enslavement grew after 1500. Europeans in the Atlantic world expanded the emphasis on enslavement to the greatest degree, and Europeans in the Indian Ocean relied more heavily on slavery than most other merchant and imperial groups, but the demand for cheap labour in a search for rapid profit characterised the socio-economic patterns of every region, with the number of enslaved persons rising each century from the fifteenth century to a peak in the nineteenth century. Dutch merchants in particular gathered captives in Southeast Asia to be sold in Java and the Cape of Good Hope.

The largest states of this era were, in significant measure, successor states of the Mongols: the Safavids and Mughals (and, at greater distance, Ottomans, Romanovs and Ming). Majapahit collapsed in the early sixteenth century, defeated by Muslims. The Persianate Qutb Shahi Dynasty took power in Hyderabad; Vijayanagar survived while Majapahit came to the end of its three centuries of leadership as Muslim forces overwhelmed it. With powerful naval forces but small numbers, the Portuguese were able to join in regional diplomatic affairs without being able to dominate; the same was true for the Dutch and other Europeans after them. The Portuguese seized key ports and made them into colonial outposts: Mozambique, Hormuz, Malacca, Goa and others. The Dutch seized some of these, such as Malacca, and established others. Up to the late eighteenth century, European states in the Indian Ocean were colonial outposts and their immediate hinterland. These had replaced the independent city-states that had existed before, such as Mombasa and Hormuz. One independent city-state that preserved itself well into the eighteenth century was that of the Siddis of Janjira, an island off the Konkan Coast. Founded in the fifteenth century as an independent maritime city-state with a population descended from enslaved Africans, it specialised in naval warfare, at times in alliance with the Mughals. The Mughals declined in the face of the Marathas (Pearson 1976: 221–36).[11]

Although the Portuguese lost military hegemony on the Indian Ocean in the seventeenth century, Portuguese language remained significant as a lingua franca, and people of Portuguese identity remained a significant influence throughout the region. People who spoke the Portuguese language and professed Catholicism, regardless of their ancestry, adopted Portuguese identity and played intermediate roles as headmen of work groups, commercial employees and domestics.

The multi-directional, multi-lingual nature of commerce in the Indian Ocean led to a complex but lively system of work and exchange of knowledge. In ship-building and repair, work on the pre-existing dhows, proas and junks was now supplemented by work on European caravels, fluyts and, briefly, Ottoman galleys. Once the Ming Dynasty reopened the doors to Chinese overseas trade in 1568, merchant vessels went especially to Manila, to exchange silks for silver, and to Batavia, where Dutch vessels assumed the task of distributing their wares throughout the Indian Ocean. In addition, however, Chinese vessels voyaged throughout the eastern Indian Ocean, as is confirmed in the Selden Map, a detailed map of ports and sea routes prepared between 1607 and 1619, identified in Chinese characters. A division of labour developed in which the larger ships were European owned and operated while the smaller vessels were owned and operated by people of the Indian Ocean. Nevertheless, as indicated in Dutch records of ships and crews, the polyglot crews became mixed to a considerable degree.

Commodities flowed within the region and beyond it. Textiles and cowries went to West Africa, to nurture the European-led slave trade that built plantations in the Americas. Textiles went to Europe as well; cottons went to China in return for silks. The spice trade became more worldwide. An expanded commerce in silver chased rising demand – silver from the Americas reached the Indian Ocean by crossing the Pacific, by crossing the Atlantic and then to the east. Demand for gunpowder brought expanded mining of saltpeter.

Late in the eighteenth century, the Indian Ocean revealed hints of big changes to come. As the English East India Company gained military and civil control of much of Bengal with its 1757 victory at Plassey, the company gradually developed a plan for seizing the subcontinent as a whole. The Mughal state had declined significantly in power, especially because of the rise of Maratha influence in the west. The English failed in their first effort to displace the Maratha (1775–1782). Yet during and after the Napoleonic Wars, the English achieved hegemony in India through battles from 1803 to 1818.

Colonisation and decolonisation, since 1800

With the nineteenth century, European-led capitalism expanded outward from the Atlantic basin. Within the Atlantic, North America arose as a supplementary and competing nexus of commercial and industrial activity. The growth of this pair of hubs enabled them to exceed the other great commercial hubs, the Indian Ocean and East Asia, in the volume of commerce and commodity production. Two great canals, across Suez and Panama, facilitated oceanic commerce significantly. Yet in a time when markets in manufactured goods were expanding, the workers of the Indian Ocean found themselves producing primary goods and raw materials. India came to export opium to China, along with cotton yarn and wheat to England, while sugar plantations expanded in India and the Dutch East Indies.

The lands of the Indian Ocean benefited from rapid technological change that brought them telegraphs, steamships, railroads, printing presses and photography, yet at rates in arrears of the advances in Europe and the North Atlantic. Meanwhile, a second slavery had been expanding throughout the tropics from the late eighteenth century, despite the concurrent movement for slave emancipation. In the Atlantic, this second slavery centred in Cuba and Brazil. In addition, it grew in eastern Africa, the Middle East, the western Indian Ocean, Southeast Asia and India – to a peak in about 1860 and an overall decline only thereafter. In other regions, migration of free people rose from the 1840s to an unprecedented level, as Indian workers moved independently or as contract labourers to Fiji, the West Indies, Southeast Asia and western Indian Ocean destinations. At the same time, migrants from South China moved in great numbers, especially to Southeast Asia. Out of these migratory movements, voluntary or involuntary, there arose diaspora communities that later became powerful in the cultural and political affairs of their lands of residence and in their ancestral homes.

Britain had already taken hold of Rangoon and Singapore (and would soon annex Hong Kong) when, in the 1840s, British Indian Ocean patrols began efforts to suppress the oceanic slave trade. This soon led to annexation of ports along the African and Arabian littoral. These ports expanded into protectorates, and, by the 1890s, Great Britain had achieved imperial hegemony over the Indian Ocean. Britain's Indian Ocean empire was complemented by the smaller-scale colonial regimes of France, Netherlands, Germany, Portugal and Italy, thus putting virtually the entirety of the Indian Ocean under direct European rule. For another fifty years, none were in a position to contest British hegemony. During the nineteenth and twentieth centuries, British officials sought with some success to place themselves as leaders in the Islamic community of the Indian Ocean, for instance in conveying pilgrims by sea to Arabia for the hajj (Pearson 1977: 87–103).[12]

Nevertheless, by 1970, virtually all of the Indian Ocean was politically independent, and by 2000, the whole region was economically growing (Pearson and Tonsich 1972: 132–73).[13] Empire had declined, and independent city-states arose where colonial outposts had earlier been: Singapore, Brunei, Qatar, Abu Dhabi and Djibouti. The Indian Ocean, which had been the principal nexus of the world economy from 1500 to 1800 (though in a situation of contested political leadership), lost its economic leadership and lost all political independence in the nineteenth century. By the twenty-first century, however, the region had regained a position as a major nexus in the global economy, although now ranked fourth after North America, Europe and China.

This narrative has recounted the rise of the Indian Ocean region to global centrality (though not global control) in the sixteenth century, as the world economic system completed its intercontinental connections. What followed was the eclipse of the Indian Ocean as the North Atlantic gained the central role in the world economic system during the nineteenth century. This tale is not proposed as an explanation of why Indian Ocean commercial leadership did not reproduce itself from period to period. It does, however, suggest that further study of this question could take place on a scale somewhat larger than that of the previous analysis. That is, rather than investigate the Indian Ocean alone or the Atlantic alone, it may be that resources are becoming available that can enable investigation of the Indian Ocean, East Asia, the North Atlantic and other regions in the context of the world economy as a whole, for the period from the fourteenth century forth. Perhaps then we will learn the causes of what we observe.

Notes

1 Michael N. Pearson, "Introduction: The Idea of the Ocean," in *Eyes Across the Water: Navigating the Indian Ocean*, edited by Pamila Gupta, Isabel Hofmeyr and Michael Pearson, 7–14 (Pretoria: UNISA Press and Penguin India, 2010); Michael N. Pearson, *The Indian Ocean* (London and New York: Routledge, 2003).
2 Michael N. Pearson, *Pious Passengers: The Hajj in Earlier Times* (Delhi: Sterling Publishers; London: C. Hurst and Co., 1994).
3 Michael N. Pearson, "Islamic Trade, Shipping, Port-States and Merchant Communities in the Indian Ocean, 7th–16th Centuries," in *New Cambridge History of Islam*, vol. III, edited by M. A. Cook, 317–65 (Cambridge: Cambridge University Press, 2010).
4 Michael N. Pearson, "World-Systems before Capitalism," in *History, Literature and Society: Essays in Honour of Soumyen Mukherjee*, edited by Mabel Lee and Michael Wilding, 163–78 (Sydney and New Delhi: Manuhar, 1997).
5 Michael N. Pearson, "Ibn Madjid," in *Oxford Encyclopedia of Maritime History*, edited by John B. Hattendorf (Oxford: Oxford University Press, 2007).
6 Michael N. Pearson, *The Portuguese in India* (Cambridge: Cambridge University Press, 1987); Michael N. Pearson, "Markets and Merchant Communities in the Indian Ocean: Locating the Portuguese," in *Portuguese Oceanic Expansion, 1400–1800: A Collection of Essays*, edited by Francisco Bethencourt and Diogo Ramada Curto, 88–108 (New York: Cambridge University Press, 2007); Michael N. Pearson, "Early Relations Between the Portuguese and Gujarat: A New Overview," *Indica* XXXV.2 (1998): 81–95; Michael N. Pearson, "Goa During the First Century of Portuguese Rule," *Itinerario* VIII.1 (1984): 36–57; Michael N. Pearson, "The Spanish 'Impact' on the Philippines," *Journal of the Economic and Social History of the Orient* XII.2 (1969): 165–86; Michael N. Pearson, "Portuguese India Twenty Five Years After Gama: An Important Document from 1523," in *Studies In the History of the Deccan: Medieval and Modern: Professor A.R. Kulkarni Felicitation Volume*, edited by M. A. Nayeem, Anirudha Ray and K. S. Mathew, 179–87 (New Delhi: Pragati Publishers, 2002); Michael N. Pearson, *Merchants and Rulers in Gujarat: The Response to the Portuguese in the Sixteenth Century* (Berkeley: University of California Press, 1976).
7 Michael N. Pearson, "The Flows and Effects of Precious Metals in India and China: 1500–1750," *Annales* II.2 (1993): 51–69; Michael N. Pearson, "Asia and World Precious Metal Flows in the Early Modern Period," in *Evolution of the*

World Economy, Precious Metals and India, edited by John McGuire, Patrick Bertola and Peter Reeves, 21–57 (New Delhi: Oxford University Press, 2001).

8 Michael N. Pearson, *Port Cities and Intruders: The Swahili Coast, India, and Portugal in the Early Modern Era* (Baltimore: The Johns Hopkins University Press, 1998); Michael N. Pearson, "East Africa and the Indian Ocean World," in *Metahistory: History Questioning History*, edited by C.J. Borges and M.N. Pearson, 485–95 (Lisbon: Nova Vega, 2007); Michael N. Pearson, "Gateways to Africa: the Indian Ocean and the Red Sea," in *History of Islam in Africa*, edited by Randall Pouwels and Nehemia Levtzion, 37–59 (Athens, OH: Ohio University Press, 2000); Michael N. Pearson, "Indians in East Africa: The Early Modern Period," in *Politics and Trade in the Indian Ocean World: Essays in Honour of Ashin Das Gupta*, edited by Rudrangshu Mukherjee and Lakshmi Subramanian, 227–49 (New Delhi: Oxford University Press, 1998).

9 Michael N. Pearson, "Hindu Medical Practice in Sixteenth-Century Western India: Evidence from the Portuguese Records," *Portuguese Studies* XVII (2001): 100–13; Michael N. Pearson, "Portuguese and Indian Medical Systems: Commonality and Superiority in the Early Modern Period," *Revista de Cultura* 20 (2006): 116–41; Michael N. Pearson, "First Contacts Between Indian and European Medical Systems: Goa in the Sixteenth Century," in *Warm Climates and Western Medicine: The Emergence of Tropical Medicine, 1500–1900*, edited by David Arnold, 20–41 (Amsterdam: Editions Rodopi [The Wellcome Institute Series in the History of Medicine], 1996).

10 Michael N. Pearson, "Creating a Littoral Community: Muslim Reformers in the Early Modern Indian Ocean World," in *Between the Middle Ages and Modernity: Individual and Community in the Early Modern World*, edited by Charles Parker and Jerry Bentley, 155–65 (Lanham: Rowman and Littlefield, 2007); Michael N. Pearson, "The Mughals and the Hajj," *Journal of the Oriental Society of Australia* XVII–XIX (1986–87): 164–79.

11 Michael N. Pearson, "Shivaji and the Decline of the Mughal Empire," *Journal of Asian Studies* XXXV.2 (1976): 221–36.

12 Michael N. Pearson, "European Relations with South Asian Muslims, 1500–1947," in *The Changeless and the Changing in Islamic-Arabic-Hispanic Cultures, Cultural Studies Conference*, 87–103 (Goulburn, NSW: Goulburn College of Advanced Education, 1977).

13 Michael N. Pearson and Diana Tonsich, "The Partition of India and Pakistan: The Emergence of Bangladesh," in *The Problem of Partition: Peril to World Peace*, edited by T.E. Hachey, 132–73 (Chicago: Rand McNally, 1972).

References

Books

Pearson, M.N. 1976. *Merchants and Rulers in Gujarat: The Response to the Portuguese in the Sixteenth Century*, Berkeley: University of California Press.

Pearson, M.N. 1987. *The Portuguese in India*, Cambridge: Cambridge University Press.

Pearson, M.N. 1994. *Pious Passengers: The Hajj in Earlier Times*, New Delhi: Sterling Publishers; London: C. Hurst & Co.

Pearson, M.N. 1998a. *Port Cities and Intruders: The Swahili Coast, India, and Portugal in the Early Modern Era*, Baltimore: Johns Hopkins University Press.

Pearson, M.N. 2003. *The Indian Ocean*, London and New York: Routledge.

Articles

Pearson, M.N. 1969. "The Spanish 'Impact' on the Philippines," *Journal of the Economic and Social History of the Orient*, XII(2): 165–86.

Pearson, M.N. 1976. "Shivaji and the Decline of the Mughal Empire," *Journal of Asian Studies* XXXV(2): 221–36.

Pearson, M.N. 1977. "European Relations with South Asian Muslims, 1500–1947," in *The Changeless and the Changing in Islamic-Arabic-Hispanic Cultures, Cultural Studies Conference*, Goulburn, NSW: Goulburn College of Advanced Education: 87–103.

Pearson, M.N. 1984. "Goa During the First Century of Portuguese Rule," *Itinerario*, VIII(l): 36–57.

Pearson, M.N. 1986–87. "The Mughals and the Hajj," *Journal of the Oriental Society of Australia*, XVII–XIX: 164–79.

Pearson, M.N. 1993. "The Flows and Effects of Precious Metals in India and China: 1500–1750," *Annales*, II(2): 51–69.

Pearson, M.N. 1996. "First Contacts Between Indian and European Medical Systems: Goa in the Sixteenth Century," in D. Arnold (ed.), *Warm Climates and Western Medicine: The Emergence of Tropical Medicine, 1500–1900*, Amsterdam: Editions Rodopi [The Wellcome Institute Series in the History of Medicine]: 20–41.

Pearson, M.N. 1997. "World-Systems Before Capitalism," in Mabel Lee and Michael Wilding (eds.), *History, Literature and Society: Essays in Honour of Soumyen Mukherjee*, Sydney and New Delhi: Manohar: 163–78.

Pearson, M.N. 1998b. "Early Relations Between the Portuguese and Gujarat: A New Overview," *Indica*, XXXV(2): 81–95.

Pearson, M.N. 1998c. "Indians in East Africa: The Early Modern Period," in Mukherjee Rudrangshu and Subramanian Lakshmi (eds.), *Politics and Trade in the Indian Ocean World: Essays in Honour of Ashin Das Gupta*, New Delhi: Oxford University Press: 227–49.

Pearson, M.N. 2000. "Gateways to Africa: The Indian Ocean and the Red Sea," in Randall Pouwels and N. Levtzion (eds.), *History of Islam in Africa*, Athens, OH: Ohio University Press: 37–59.

Pearson, M.N. 2001a. "Hindu Medical Practice in Sixteenth-Century Western India: Evidence from the Portuguese Records," *Portuguese Studies*, XVII: 100–13.

Pearson, M.N. 2001b. "Asia and World Precious Metal Flows in the Early Modern Period," in J. McGuire, P. Bertola and P. Reeves (eds.), *Evolution of the World Economy, Precious Metals and India*, New Delhi: Oxford University Press: 21–57.

Pearson, M.N. 2002. "Portuguese India Twenty Five Years After Gama: An Important Document from 1523," in M.A. Nayeem, Aniruddha Ray and K.S. Mathew (eds.), *Studies in the History of the Deccan: Medieval and Modern: Professor A.R. Kulkarni Felicitation Volume*, New Delhi: Pragati Publishers: 179–87.

Pearson, M.N. 2006. "Portuguese and Indian Medical Systems: Commonality and Superiority in the Early Modern Period," *Revista de Cultura*, 20: 116–41.

Pearson, M.N. 2007a. "Ibn Madjid," in J. Hattendorf (ed.), *Oxford Encyclopedia of Maritime History*, Oxford: Oxford University Press.

Pearson, M.N. 2007b. "Markets and Merchant Communities in the Indian Ocean: Locating the Portuguese," in F. Berthencourt and Diogo Ramada Curto (eds.),

Portuguese Oceanic Expansion, 1400–1800: A Collection of Essays, New York: Cambridge University Press: 88–108.

Pearson, M.N. 2007c. "East Africa and the Indian Ocean World," in C.J. Borges and M.N. Pearson (eds.), *Metahistory: History Questioning History*, Lisbon: Nova Vega: 485–95.

Pearson, M.N. 2007d. "Creating a Littoral Community: Muslim Reformers in the Early Modern Indian Ocean World," in C. Parker and J. Bentley (eds.), *Between the Middle Ages and Modernity: Individual and Community in the Early Modern World*, Lanham: Rowman and Littlefield: 155–65.

Pearson, M.N. 2010a. "Introduction: The Idea of the Ocean," in Pamila Gupta, Isabel Hofmeyr and M.N. Pearson (eds.), *Eyes Across the Water: Navigating the Indian Ocean*, Pretoria: UNISA Press and Penguin: 7–14.

Pearson, M.N. 2010b. "Islamic Trade, Shipping, Port-States and Merchant Communities in the Indian Ocean, 7th–16th Centuries," in M.A. Cook (ed.), *New Cambridge History of Islam*, Cambridge: Cambridge University Press: 317–65, vol. III.

Pearson, M.N. and Diana Tonsich. 1972. "The Partition of India and Pakistan: The Emergence of Bangladesh," in T.N. Hachey (ed.), *The Problem of Partition: Peril to World Peace*, Chicago: Rand McNally: 132–73.

2

THE SODDEN ARCHIVE

Africa, the Atlantic and the Indian Ocean

Isabel Hofmeyr

The rise of ocean levels has become a tangible sign of climate change and the Anthropocene. These rising waters have precipitated an urgent awareness of the ocean, inaugurating new styles of oceanic studies. There have been long traditions of maritime scholarship on human history at sea, tracing movements of people, ideas and objects across oceans. This work has however been human-centred and concerned only with the ocean as a backdrop. New versions of ocean studies ask us to engage with both human and non-human aspects of the ocean, with both the depth and the surface, with the materiality and seaness of the sea.

Michael Pearson's work has long been pushing us in this direction. One way in which he phrased this was through a call for 'more ozone'. It was an idea he often raised at conferences and also noted in his magisterial monograph on the Indian Ocean, where he observed, 'I want [this book] to have a whiff of ozone, not just be a collection of statistics about trade' (Pearson 2003: 8). In a related observation, he quotes a critic who observes that most histories of the Indian Ocean are unsatisfactory because 'there is too much hot air and not enough wind' (Pearson 2003: 20). Ozone is of course fresh, invigorating air, especially that blowing from the ocean shorewards, and in calling for more such breezes, Pearson was pushing us towards a material engagement with the ocean. Pearson's work, as ever, was ahead of the curve, highlighting environmental, oceanographic and marine science themes alongside the usual human cast of sailors, slaves, pirates, merchants and pilgrims, while also incorporating coral reefs, pearl divers and southern bluefin tuna as 'characters' in, and of, the Indian Ocean world.

The paper that follows was given as a keynote address at a conference entitled 'Place and Mobility: Cultural Practices in Cosmopolitan Networks in Africa, the Atlantic and the Indian Ocean,' held at the Stellenbosch Institute for Advanced Studies in South Africa in September 2015. The conference proposed an ambitious agenda – namely to re-configure three realms: Africa, the Atlantic, the Indian Ocean – a trend which resonated with the concerns of global history, as it becomes ever more global. As scholarship on global systems expands, so too does the recognition that such processes exceed hemispheric, oceanic, continental or indeed any other intellectual boundaries, undoing the myths of continents, oceans and empires. These shifts in turn shake up previously 'settled' areas, be these 'Africa' or indeed the Atlantic or Indian oceans, both a kind of area studies at sea.

This turn seawards holds out a number of radical implications. One is to push us in post-human directions, to investigate more-than-human hydro-material histories of the ocean – examples include tracing imperial or post-imperial assemblages of ship-labour-machines crossing water, current and tide, joining up extractive and energy enclaves. Such histories challenge the epistemological humanist bases of older areas studies models as much as their geographical boundaries.

To think across these three domains is to embark on an adventure in the maritime humanities or, shall I say, maritime post-humanities. It is to think laterally along new global latitudes and axes, many of a southern orientation. Such experiments point back to older ideals of 'southern' universalisms (tricontinentalism for example) while bringing us up against the epistemological limits and contradictions of such projects even as we excavate their meanings in the brave new world of the 'global south.'

The difficulties inherent in engaging with the materiality of the ocean are well set out in Lindsay Bremner's article on the disappearance of the Malaysian airline, 'Fluid Ontologies in the Search for MH370' (2015). The article uses the international search operation for the airline as an occasion to speculate on remote and deep ocean space, 'a privileged, if tragic, moment to see beyond a world constructed by humans and to get a little closer to understanding the properties of the ocean itself' (9). Quoting Gaston Gordillo, she characterises these properties as:

> a vast liquid space whose ambient thickness and intensity is in a permanent state of becoming: folding, shifting, arching, twisting; always in motion, always displacing its volume across vast distances, always indifferent to the life forms enveloped by its mobile flows.
>
> (quoted in Bremner 2015: 9)

The Indian Ocean is the world's deepest ocean, and Bremner examines various attempts to try to make these fathoms legible to media audiences, via infographics that marked depth using known buildings and landmarks (e.g., the Empire State building, 1250 ft.). As Bremner indicates, these patchworks of data 'get us no further in imaging the ocean than the medieval [maps] which depicted the ocean as a two-dimensional surface crossed by rhumb lines and illustrated with astronomical, astrological and religious references and images from travel literature' (Bremner 2015: 19).

Bremner's piece highlights the limits of humanist knowledge when faced with the deep ocean, making one feel adrift at sea on a raft of books, trying to navigate new and epic elements via the miniature, water-logged and rapidly sinking humanist instrument of the book. The early modern world of shipwreck narrative outlined by Josiah Blackmore (2002) comes to mind – shipwreck stories enact a radical sense of catastrophe that splinters the known world and its commonsense epistemologies. Or as Leslie Eckel notes in her discussion of Atlantic literature and the 'global chaosmos,' sea narratives can position us 'on the edge of knowledge, facing the incomprehensible and the theoretically impossible' (Eckel 2014: 131).

Which way to turn? Try to head back for the humanist shore or plough on in a spirit of suicidally ludic experimentation?

This chapter attempts both options, although more of the first than the second. The first part plays it safe and heads for land and the sheltered harbour of social and cultural history and outlines the ways in which the Atlantic and Indian Oceans have variously been conjoined and separated and the modes of work which toggle across both. The second part heads for the open sea and provides some speculations on what a post-humanist oceanic enterprise might look like. A third concluding section returns to Africa and asks what these various historiographical developments might mean for African studies.

Heading for shore

Genealogies of Atlantic and Indian Ocean
studies – together and apart

Hydrographically and historiographically, the Atlantic and Indian oceans assumed their current discrete identities comparatively recently, a process of naming set in motion by the age of European empires and its instrumentalisation of the seas (Lewis 1999). These two oceans have led both separate and conjoined lives, at times defined as integrated (especially during the early modern period and the age of the chartered company) and at times as self-servingly discrete (the first versus the second British empire; the plantation economy versus trade and commerce; the realm of 'race' versus that of 'caste'; Christian versus Muslim; West versus East).

The definition and study of oceans has hence long been entangled with imperialism: Fernand Braudel's influential history of the Mediterranean (Braudel 1949), for example, was conceptualised during his spell as a teacher in Algeria (1923–32) and took shape under imperial mythologies of Graeco-Roman classical civilisation (Horden and Purcell 2006; Borutta and Gekas 2012).

If Braudel's notion of the Mediterranean carried an imperial imprimatur, then other oceanic models acquired an anti-imperial charge. The idea of the black Atlantic, for example, emerged initially from late nineteenth- and early-twentieth-century ideas of diasporic black intellectual traditions and pan-Africanism (with a small 'p'). Boosted by decolonisation, the Cold War and the rise of area studies (which helped to re-centre the Atlantic slave trade), the scholarship on black transnationalism continues powerfully into the present, informing what some call the new Atlantic studies (Boelhoewer 2008).

This new Atlantic studies has been defined in relation to the old, a Cold War–shaped tradition of studying the Atlantic, which emerged in the 1950s as something of an intellectual proxy of NATO, a case of 'victorious states incorporating their respective historical narratives into a shared hyper-narrative' (O'Reilly 2004: 78). In some cases, this version of Atlantic studies became little more than 'a "free world" response to the Cold War' (O'Reilly 2004: 78) and was propagated largely in those countries supporting NATO (Boelhoewer 2008).

With regard to Indian Ocean studies and its formation, the picture is somewhat different, and it is only post-1989 with the rise of Asia that the field starts to gain significant visibility. For the duration of the Cold War itself, Indian Ocean studies was something of a ragtag enterprise taking shape loosely around work on the Swahili coast, studies of the Mascarenes, Portuguese imperial history, scholarship on Indian maritime history and Western Australian–driven analyses of its ocean 'hinterland' (Toussaint 1966; McPherson 1998; Pearson 2003).

If some versions of Atlantic studies then presented themselves as the locus of the first world, Indian Ocean studies fashioned itself as a calling card for the third world. As the earliest long-distance transoceanic arena, the Indian Ocean world had long offered archives of non-Western cosmopolitanism and its dense lattice of interactions. These horizontal and subsequently colony-to-colony exchanges have in turn been seen as an ideal vantage point from which to analyse themes of the third world and its associated projects of non-alignment and Afro-Asian solidarity. Not surprisingly, the Indian Ocean has been labelled the 'ocean of the third world,' the 'ocean of the south' and the 'subaltern sea.'

The fortunes of this field have, however, been considerably boosted by the end of the Cold War, which presaged the advent of the Asian century and the rise of the global south. Within this changed context, the Indian Ocean's status as a third-world proxy has become an especially useful calling card which can both make historical sense of the global south while implying a veneer of supposed solidarity that papers over the growing fault-lines within this bloc (Soske 2009; Burton 2012). Also important in this post-Cold War configuration has been the end of apartheid and the new directions in the South African academy, which have become an important driver of Indian Ocean studies (Hofmeyr 2013). These shifts in turn form part of the broader reorientation of nation and area studies towards oceanic and global approaches.

For much of the twentieth century, then, Atlantic studies and Indian Ocean studies have operated in somewhat parallel universes. Both have been dominated by canonical traditions that focus on the northern portions of each respective ocean. In the case of the Indian Ocean, this has been the monsoon region and the long trajectories of religious and commercial exchange it has enabled. In the case of the Atlantic, the focus (at least in Anglophone scholarship) has likewise been northward, especially in the white-Atlantic-NATO models but also in wider analyses, which seldom go beyond the equator other than to touch on the Gulf of Guinea. From an Anglophone (but not Lusophone) perspective, the southern reaches are less understood – indeed the South Atlantic is increasingly being identified as a 'blank' region that requires analytical definition.

Yet, as global history becomes more global, these myths of discrete oceans are evaporating. Historians now consider the first and second British empires as related theatres across which systems of oppression like race and caste were brought into comparative and reinforcing relationships. Plantations and their associated forms of slavery were not solely an Atlantic phenomenon but characterised parts of the Indian Ocean world, notably Mauritius and Zanzibar (Allen 2014). Maritime, slave and indentured labour moved between the two oceans. The early Portuguese empire and the European chartered companies likewise saw the two oceans as one domain. Rio de Janeiro and St Helena formed key nodes in the maritime system of the East India Company, and during the period of the company's control of St Helena (1673–1704), directors in London routinely described the island as being 'in India,' a geographical liberty which was intended to extend the India-base of the company's authority into the Atlantic (Stern 2007; Bowen 2012).

Ashley Cohen's work on the Global Indies makes a similar point. She argues that the so-called East and West Indies were not discrete domains but were vitally linked. As she notes, 'Although transnational paradigms such as the Atlantic and Indian Ocean worlds have revealed transnational relations within these regions, they have tended to occlude connections between them' (Cohen 2017: 8). She reunites these domains through the term, the *Global Indies*, arguing that these regions form a single unit of analysis.

Ocean arcs

In his discussion of the naming of the oceans, Martin Lewis (1999) tells us that enlightenment cartography at times displaced oceanic definition from the basin to 'skirt or wraparound landmasses.' In a map from 1719, the 'Ethiopian Sea' (a common term for the South Atlantic) arcs around the Cape from the southern Atlantic to the southwest Indian Ocean. The 'Mer Magellanique' curves around both littorals of the southern 'tail' of South America while the 'Eastern Indian Ocean' stretches from the Arabian to the South China sea (Lewis 1999: 203–4). As Lewis indicates, ocean arcs 'can elucidate patterns obscured in the basin schema'. As Atlantic-based slave and plantation economies spread into the Indian Ocean world, they did indeed create an 'Ethiopian Ocean' that stretched from the southern Atlantic to the Mascarenes (Lewis 1999: 204).

In the section that follows, I use this idea of 'ocean arcs' to trace historiographical developments that explore global developments that unfold in and across the two oceans.

Arc 1: transoceanic carceral assemblages

European resource imperialisms were driven by extractive and epistemological imperatives. These global systems depended on the stockpiling of enclaves whether for energy, settlement, trade or the sourcing and transportation of forced and bonded labour. This section sketches out some of the rich scholarship that configures bonded labour, maritime transport, infrastructure and the carceral assemblages that knitted these together across both oceans.

With regard to bonded labour, this field was for some time dominated by discrete historiographies: slavery in the Atlantic; slavery in the Indian Ocean; indenture in the Indian Ocean, the Caribbean or the Pacific; and penal transportation within and across the Indian Ocean, penal transportation to Australia. Increasingly, however, these systems are being understood as cogs of larger imperial carceral assemblages, which in turn leeched off earlier systems of slavery and bondage.

Through the French and Portuguese slave trades, significant numbers of Africans were transported from South East Africa littoral and its insular 'hinterland' to destinations in the Americas (Harms et al. 2013; Harries 2013; Allen 2014). Indentured labour sites across the three oceans were linked in imperial thinking (Tinker 1974). Slaves 'freed' by the British post-1834 in the Indian Ocean were transported to destinations like Cape Town and St Helena (Harries 2013). Penal transportation was a global system that delivered labour for constructing colonial infrastructure, linking the bulkheads of Bermuda to the prisons of the Indian Ocean islands to the Australasian penal colonies (Anderson 2000, 2012; Stanziani 2014).

This work of linking up different institutions of unfree labour has also started to undo the racialised categories that these systems created. One of these was the notion that to be a slave was to be African but to be an indentured labourer was to be Indian. However, there were Indian slaves just as there were African indentured labourers, and work by Marina Carter (Carter 2006) demonstrates the extent to which recruitment of indentured labour in South Asia drew on pre-colonial Asia-centred slave networks.

A further articulation between different systems of forced or semi-forced labour has emerged from recent work which seeks to integrate land-based migrant labour systems with oceanic forms of migration. In the case of southern Africa, this work has explored how the seafaring corridor of the southeast African littoral created a zone in which adventurous migrants could extend their reach (Finch-Boyer 2014). Another theme has been to use the port city to calibrate the land-based migrant labour regimes with exclusionary immigration controls. As Andrew MacDonald (MacDonald 2007) has argued in his history of Durban as port, the 'logic of the compound' meets that of the 'port of exit' (33).

These zones of forced migration across land and sea hold out important consequences for non-Western creolisation. Especially from an Indian Ocean perspective, the work emerging from Africanists has shown much creolisation to be conscripted and something which complicates more sentimental or easy ideas of Indian Ocean cosmopolitanism (Becker and Cabrita 2014; Simpson and Kresse 2008).

In some cases, these studies of maritime labour have been calibrated with work on infrastructural assemblages (Anderson and Peters 2014; Anim-Addo 2011), part of a postcolonial Latourian trend. Historical geographer, Anyaa Anim-Addo (Anim-Addo 2011) examines such assemblages in her analyses of the Royal Mail Packet Service in the Caribbean and its use of coaling stations, which relied largely on bonded labour. Indeed this theme of coal stations has become an important focus in understanding steam-driven empires (Gray 2014). The demise of steam and the rise of the turbine engine has likewise focused attention on oil and, as Tim Mitchell (Mitchell 2011) has so famously argued, its longer-term role in shaping the politics of the American empire and the post-World War II global dispensation. These themes of energy have become increasingly important in linking both oceans, especially apparent in the explosion of work on fuel or energy humanities (Wenzel et al. 2017), which is in turn linked to questions of ecology and waste.

Arc 2: sub-imperial configurations

Another type of arc pertinent for our purposes is the band of sub-Antarctic islands that circle the pole. This insular system is generally considered as discrete from the equatorial archipelagos of the Indian and Atlantic oceans. Semipolar as opposed to tropical, uninhabited as opposed to inhabited (if in some cases through slavery and indenture), the two systems occupy different academic domains. Yet, there are good reasons to draw them together since both functioned as strategic stepping stones in the larger story of global resource colonialism.

As with broader arcs of European imperial rule, islands were central proxies in the Antarctic story – markers of exploration and discovery, strategic staging posts, sites of experiments in sovereignty and science and nodes of invisible labour to sustain these prestige projects of what became the 'Antarctic Club' of nations and whose Antarctic involvement marked them as 'white' (Dodds 1994; Van der Watt 2012). The imagination that informed these developments was not that different from the ideologies dominating the penal assemblages of the Indian Ocean carceral archipelagos: possession, conquest of nature, environmental colonialism and racialisation through geography.

While much of this island stockpiling was driven by European nations, one striking feature of the Antarctic story is the involvement of regional powers as sub-imperial forces. Argentina, Chile, Australia, New Zealand and to a lesser extent, South Africa, all constructed themselves as key players with historical and strategic rights to the southern polar world, a story in which islands played an important role. Antarctic politics enabled the emergence of a 'southern hemispheric empire,' a commonwealth of science in which the legatees of British and Spanish imperial authorities found common cause (Dodds 1994; Van der Watt 2012).

While long obscured by anti-colonial nationalism, sub-imperialism as a theme is becoming more important, especially as a way of trying to understand the divisions and fissures within particular countries and within and across the global south. Most well-known has been work on India as a sub-empire, a hub from which other regions were governed and from which soldiers, police and indentured labour were sent to diverse destinations (Blyth 2003; Metcalf 2007). As work by Antoinette Burton (Burton 2012) and Jon Soske (Soske 2009) has demonstrated, India's imperial attitudes persist into the present. South Africa has also recently come to be studied as a sub-imperial power (with its colony South West Africa / Namibia and its Antarctic island outstations, which fall under South African sovereignty) (Henrichsen et al. 2015). This sub-imperial emphasis is designed to critique the teleological anti-apartheid, nation-focused logic of South African historiography. As a way of knowing and an enduring system of knowledge that persists long after the demise of colonialism, imperial structures persist in a post-apartheid context through a logic of insiders and outsiders, the civilised and the barbarian, useful citizens and criminal surplus.

Arc 3: inter-imperial configurations

As area studies has started to loosen, the notion of area and region itself has become more capacious and mobile, and much work now routinely operates across imperial configurations and oceans. In her research on the Eastern Mediterranean, Ilham Khuri-Makdisi has examined the early twentieth-century workings of a radical socialist-inclined wing of the Arabic press, which unfolded across the Levant, Cairo and the Syrian diaspora in Brazil. Home to a significant Christian and Muslim Syrian diaspora, Brazil by 1922 hosted 95 Arabic periodicals, the highest number outside the Arabic-speaking heartland (Khuri-Makdisi 2010: 95). As she explains, the 'South American connection . . . played a key role in triggering the interest of

Arabic readers in socialism and anarchism in Beirut, Cairo, and Alexandria, as well as in the Americas' (2010: 52). Recirculated from Brazil back to these nodal cities in the Middle East, these anarchist and socialist ideas were in turn relayed from the Eastern Mediterranean into the Indian Ocean world, finding readers amongst communities of radicals especially in British India.

These sprawling textual networks created by the periodical press are critical in tracing global intellectual formations. Certainly until the rise of the telegraph and even beyond that, a vast periodical network girdled the globe, enabled by a textual honours system in which periodicals which exchanged copies were free to cut and paste from each other with attribution. This simple, unofficial, informal system crossed languages, religions and empires. Known as the exchange system, it needs to be understood as a truly demotic form of world literature. Obviously acts of translation (however loosely one construes that term) were central to the propagation and spread of this system, especially in a context where periodicals in the colonial world were almost routinely in more than one language. These networks created new intellectual geographies configuring the Eastern Mediterranean, Brazil and the Indian Ocean as Ilham-Makdisi shows, or projecting South Africa and India as a continuous intellectual space as Gandhi's *Indian Opinion* did. These intellectual filaments were also reinforced by travellers and sailors who took ideas and print culture with them. As John Maynard (Maynard 2005) has demonstrated, African American seamen passing through Australian ports passed Garveyist ideas on to Aboriginal wharf labourers who in turn introduced a Garveyist strand into Aboriginal political thought.

In her recent work, *Muslim Cosmopolitanism in the Age of Empire*, Seema Alavi (Alavi 2015) considers the intellectual cusp of the Ottoman and British empires, following a group of Muslim 'runaways', who fled British India in the wake of the 1857 mutiny-rebellion and made their way into the Ottoman world. Travelling on Naqshbandi Sufi networks forged in the thirteenth century, these emigres encountered religious scholars in Medina and Mecca from the British, Dutch and Ottoman empires. Drawing on technologies of steam, print and telegraph, they sought 'to forge Muslim unity across the Indian Ocean and the Mediterranean world so as to set up an alternate cultural imperium that would challenge the Western dominance in the region' (Alavi 2015: 213/10007).

In discussing her method, Alavi speaks of 'biography as the archive for writing world history' (Alavi 2015: 252/10007). Following the itinerant careers of individuals illuminates larger intellectual formations. One such case study is Chris Lee's discussion (2010) of the South African intellectual, Alex La Guma's international odysseys. Politically active in the ANC and the Communist Party within South Africa, La Guma went into exile in 1966. His career took him across Africa, Latin America and Asia both as an ANC representative and as a member of the Permanent Bureau of Afro-Asian Writers based in Cairo. Across his travels, he espoused a view of the anti-apartheid struggle as part of a larger anti-imperial movement and as a plank in tricontinental thinking. La Guma wrote prodigiously on his travels but is remembered today mainly as a South African writer, his larger tricontinental odysseys and texts fallen from view.

These latter arcs I have touched on are not strictly speaking oceanic, and once one moves away from the ocean, there are of course a host of 'arcs' one could draw out – the spread of global texts and cultural forms, whether Mao's *Red Book*, the telenovela, Indian cinema, theosophy or, as Ronit Ricci (Ricci 2011) has demonstrated, the *Book of One Thousand Questions*, which travelled from the Middle East to South and Southeast Asia.

But what if we want to make oceanic questions more central?

Heading out to sea

We now shift our rudder and head off for the open sea, in a section that is necessarily speculative and experimental and sketches out some of the directions in which post-humanist 'blue cultural studies' (Mentz 2009) is unfolding.

One place to start such a discussion is with Gaston Gordillo's strong version of post-human oceanic thesis (Gordillo 2014): 'to examine geo-physical forces in terms of their own materiality and rhythms, without reducing them to their social appropriations by human societies.' He continues,

> The ocean's spatiality forms an immense void not because it is empty but, on the contrary, because it is a positive presence that is a productive and disruptive multiplicity of intensities, singularities, and rhythms: a vortex that voids (interrupts, negates, disrupts) the spatiality of human mobility on land.
>
> (Gordillo 2014)

As Leslie Eckel suggests, such a view of the ocean necessarily implies an obliteration of 'all certainties belonging to those who attempt to write [the oceans] into history' (Eckel 2014). Jed Esty makes a similar point in relation to the Atlantic. A shift to a more thoroughly oceanic register would mean that 'the histories of slavery and diaspora [would no longer be] the sine qua non of the new matrix – an oceanic (dis)organization of space [would be].' He continues,

> If an oceanic logic is displacing a territorial logic as part of the 'archaeological turn in the humanities,' is that project any longer anchored in a recognizable geography (or hydrography) that warrants the name Atlantic? And, finally, without its African slave-diaspora core, will the broader, more neutrally oceanic formulation of the matrix lose the traumatic force of its association with a history of absences and specters.
>
> (Esty 2008: 107)

Such post-human oceanic models hold out radical implications across the disciplines. Yet, given that the field has hardly taken shape, it is difficult to know how this radical potential will unfold. As I've indicated earlier, Lindsay Bremner's work (Bremner 2015) offers generative possibilities, as does the scholarship from oceanic historical geographers, like that from Anyee Anim-Addo quoted earlier (2011). Charne Lavery (Lavery 2015) is currently working on an 'undersea' project, charting how we might imagine the depths of the Indian Ocean.

Interestingly literary studies has been one domain in which the impossible epistemology of the sea has been debated. Caribbean theorists have long furnished us with a tradition of thinking about the imperial ocean hydropoetically. Whether through ideas of tidalectics, the haunted ocean, or the sovereignty of the drowned, these thinkers have offered a rich range of ideas for thinking with and through water. One recent excursion in this domain is Elizabeth DeLoughrey's contemplation (DeLoughrey 2010) on the 'heavy waters of [Atlantic] ocean modernity' and the waste that it produces both in the forms of drowned slave lives and in the current militarised pollution of the Atlantic on whose seabed rest several nuclear reactors and warships.

In her analysis of oceanic narrative, Eckel proposes a method of reading, namely to answer the question that resounds through 'The Rime of the Ancient Mariner,' namely 'What is the ocean doing?' She suggests we examine how ocean narratives mirror 'the strong currents and blank zones of the waters they travel' (Eckel 2014: 130).

Yet, what do all of these larger frameworks and developments mean for African studies?

Africa as constitutive locus

A key challenge is to think about Africa between oceans, empires, areas and hemispheres. One long-standing problem in placing Africa in an oceanic framework is that of erasure. Seen from the black Atlantic, Africa has long featured as symbolic background. From the Indian Ocean side, Africa has a marginal presence compared to India. Put between the two oceans, it is as if the continent becomes a backdrop with the slave diaspora forced out into the Atlantic arena while indentured labourers enter from the Indian Ocean side. It also seems that the only people to ever leave Africa are slaves.

We need to think of Africa as a constitutive locus in global circuits of intellectual and cultural production. From the black Atlantic perspective, there has been a long-standing tradition of scholarship which foregrounds African intellectual energies in transnational circuits (Thornton 1998). Recent examples include Monica Popescu's account of late seventies Angola as a site which configures Cuba, anti-apartheid intellectuals and the Soviet Union (Popescu 2014). Victoria Collis-Buthelezi has discussed Africa as a destination for Caribbean intellectuals and travellers who migrated to Cape Town using the space of the British empire (Collis-Buthelezi 2015).

Equally important have been recent accounts of Africans who have travelled into the Indian Ocean, reversing the map of apparently one-way movement from South Asia to Africa. Whether African Protestants who travelled to India under the aegis of the International Missionary Council (whose number included Albert Luthuli) (Erlank 2009) or South African Indians travelling to different Indian Ocean destinations (Dhupelia-Mesthrie 2012), African intellectuals (and exiles) travelling to India or African soccer players in India, these outward journeys nuance our understandings of the intellectual projects that emerged between African and Indian scholars, one example being DDT Jabavu who visited India in 1949 for the World Pacifist Congress.

Tsitsi Jaji's *Africa in Stereo* offers productive ways to animate African intellectual work within the networks of diaspora. The metaphor she chooses is that of stereo-sound systems, which operate 'on the principle of minute temporal delays in the signal received by each ear, mimicking the way that in an acoustic space sound from any given direction arrives at one side of our heads milliseconds before it reaches the other side' (Jaji 2014: 12). She extends this metaphor to encompass the ways in which South African, Senegalese and Ghanaian music and media have incorporated African American traditions in a broader pan-African (small 'p') project.

Extending this idea of the stereo, we might think of Africa in the 'acoustic' space of both oceans receiving intellectual sounds and traditions from both directions, not always entirely aligned, with some lag and dissonance. One thinks for example of the apparently synced ideals of tricontinentalism, Afro-Asian solidarity and Bandung. Similarly there have been longstanding links between African-American and South Asian intellectuals whether du Bois's novel *Dark Princess*, the Dalit-Panthers or the Gandhi–Luther King connection.

Yet, at the same time, the lag between the incoming signals can be considerable, producing jarring dissonance. Antoinette Burton (Burton 2012) has explored the idea of 'Africa' in India that took shape in a contradictory legacy of imperial hierarchies of brown over black, on the one hand, and in anti-colonial ideals of Afro-Asian solidarity on the other. Understanding and excavating these frictions are critical to producing robust histories of the global south. Or, as Burton observes, 'racial difference and conflict [are] full-bodied dimensions of the postcolonial condition in all its worldly, combative variety, and that . . . resist conscription by narratives of overcoming, salvation and redemption as well as of solidarity per se' (Burton 2016: 7).

Another generative topic would be African epistemologies of the sea. One project in this regard would be to link up ideas of water/ocean spirits around the continent taking in ocean djinns in the Arab peninsula and East Africa, Nguni ideas of ancestors and the ocean on the south-eastern littoral and then the circum-Atlantic idea of Mami Wata. As the rich scholarship on Mami Wata indicates, this figure and her various instantiations carry contradictory charges (protection, destruction; fidelity, fickleness; fertility, death) and could be read as attempts to figure an impossible epistemology of the ocean. Appropriate for our purposes is the multiple cultural traditions that she encompasses. As Henry Drewal has indicated, these include 'African water spirits, European mermaids and snake charmers, Hindu gods and goddesses, and Christian and Muslim saints' (Drewal 2008).

Another dimension of such ocean epistemologies could be the idea of Africa as a source of healing technologies which gain power as they cross the water. Helene Basu's work (Basu 2008) on Siddis (communities of African descent) in India demonstrates that while this group generally erase their African ancestry, in settings where healing power is required, this African provenance is underlined. Related examples include East African respect for 'Arab' ritual specialists whose powers are augmented through their passage over the ocean or the power of ritual specialists in the African diaspora. A related example may be the Afro-Brazilian Umbanda spiritual traditions which have migrated to Portugal and have shaped new forms of religious activity (Saraiva 2007).

At the same time, this project might push us to think about those societies that are not seafaring, pre-colonial Southern African being one example. This emphasis is important – the rush towards oceanic studies presents the danger that maritime mobility becomes seen as normative, thereby rendering some societies oceanically 'other.'

Conclusion

As oceanic scholars grapple with how to combine the strengths of traditional maritime study with the urgency of ecological and environmental themes, Michael Pearson's work will remain a model and an inspiration. His scholarship has long operated both above and below the waterline and will continue to inspire future generations of scholars. He has created enough intellectual ozone to keep us going for some time.

References

Alavi, Seema. 2015. *Muslim Cosmopolitanism in the Age of Empire*, Cambridge, MA: Harvard University Press.

Allen, R.B. 2014. *European Slave Trading in the Indian Ocean, 1500–1850*, Athens, OH: Ohio University Press.

Anderson, Clare. 2000. *Convicts in the Indian Ocean: Transportation from South Asia to Mauritius, 1815–53*, London: Palgrave Macmillan.

Anderson, Clare. 2012. *Subaltern Lives: Biographies of Colonialism in the Indian Ocean World, 1790–1920*, Cambridge: Cambridge University Press.

Anderson, J. and K. Peters. 2014. "A Perfect and Absolute Blank: Human Geographies of Water Worlds," in J. Anderson and K. Peters (eds.), *Water Worlds: Human Geographies of the Ocean*, London: Ashgate: 3–19.

Anim-Addo, A. 2011. "'A Wretched and Slave-Like Mode of Labour': Slavery, Emancipation, and the Royal Mail Steam Packet Company's Coaling Station," *Historical Geography*, 39: 65–84.

Basu, Helene. 2008. "A Gendered Indian Ocean Site: Mai Mishra, African Spirit Possession and Sidi Women in Gujarat," in Helene Basu (ed.), *Journeys and Dwellings: Indian Ocean Themes in South Asia*, Hyderabad: Orient Longman: 227–54.

Becker, Felicitas and Cabrita, Joel. 2014. "Introduction: Performing Citizenship and Enacting Exclusion on Africa's Indian Ocean Littoral," *Journal of African History*, 55(2): 161–71.

Blackmore, Josiah. 2002. *Manifest Perdition: Shipwreck Narrative and the Disruption of Empire*, Minneapolis: University of Minnesota Press.

Blyth, R.J. 2003. *The Empire of the Raj: India, Eastern Africa and the Middle East, 1858–1947*, London: Palgrave Macmillan.

Boelhoewer, William. 2008. "The Rise of the New Atlantic Studies Matrix," *American Literary History*, 20(1–2): 83–101.

Borutta, Manuel and Sakis Gekas. 2012. "A Colonial Sea: The Mediterranean,1798–1956," *European Review of History: Revue européenne d'histoire*, 19(1): 1–13.

Bowen, H.V. 2012. "Britain in the Indian Ocean Region and Beyond: Contours, Connections, and the Creation of a Global Maritime Empire," in H.V. Bowen, Elizabeth Mancke and John G. Reid (eds.), *Britain's Oceanic Empire: Atlantic and Indian Ocean Worlds, c. 1550–1850*, Cambridge: Cambridge University Press: 45–66.

Braudel, Fernand. 1949. *La Méditerranée et le Monde Méditerranéen a l'époque de Philippe II*, Paris: Colin.

Bremner, Lindsay. 2015. "Fluid Ontologies in the Search for MH370," *Journal of the Indian Ocean Region*, 11(1): 8–29.

Burton, Antoinette. 2016. *Africa in the Indian Imagination: Race and the Politics of Postcolonial Citation*, Durham: Duke University Press.

Carter, Marina. 2006. "Slavery and Unfree Labour in the Indian Ocean," *History Compass*, 4(5): 800–13.

Cohen, Ashley L. 2017. "The Global Indies: Historicizing Oceanic Metageographies," *Comparative Literature*, 69(1): 7–15.

Collis-Buthelezi, Victoria J. 2015. "Caribbean Regionalism, South Africa, and Mapping New World Studies," *Small Axe*, 19(1(46)): 37–54.

DeLoughrey, Elizabeth. 2010. "Heavy Waters: Waste and Atlantic Modernity," *PMLA*, 125(3): 703–12.

Drewal, Henry John. 2008. "Mami Wata: Arts for Water Spirits in Africa and Its Diasporas," *African Arts*: 60–82, Summer.

Dhupelia-Mesthrie, Uma. 2012. "Cultural Crossings from Africa to India: Select Travel Narratives of Indian South Africans from Durban and Cape Town 1940s to 1990s," *South African Historical Journal*, 64(2): 295–312.

Dodds, Klaus-John. 1994. "Creating a Strategic Crisis Out of a Communist Drama? Argentine and South African Geo-Graphs of the South Atlantic," *European Review of Latin American and Caribbean Studies/Revista Europea de Estudios Latinoamericanos y del Caribe*, 56: 33–54.

Eckel, Leslie Elizabeth. 2014. "Oceanic Mirrors: Atlantic Literature and the Global Chaosmos," *Atlantic Studies: Global Currents*, 11(1): 128–44.

Erlank, Natasha. 2009. " 'God's Family in the World': Transnational and Local Ecumenism's Impact on Inter-Church and Inter-Racial Dialogue in South Africa in the 1920s and 1930s," *South African Historical Journal*, 61(2): 278–97.

Esty, Jed. 2008. "Oceanic, Traumatic, Post- Paradigmatic: A Response to William Boelhower," *American Literary History*, 20(1–2): 102–7.

Finch-Boyer, Heloise. 2014. "Southern African Port Towns and the Shaping of Indian Ocean Cosmopolitanisms in the Early 19th Century," paper presented to a workshop, Durban and Cape Town as Indian Ocean Port Cities: Reconsidering Southern African Studies from the Indian Ocean, Centre for Humanities Research, University of the Western Cape, 11–14 September.

Gordillo, Gaston. 2014. "The Oceanic Void," available at http://spaceandpolitics. blogspot.com/2014/04/the-oceanic-void.html (accessed 2 January 2017).

Gray, Steven. 2014. "Black Diamonds: Coal, the Royal Navy, and British Imperial Coaling Stations, Circa 1870–1914," PhD Thesis, University of Warwick.

Harms, R., B.K. Freamon and D.W. Blight (eds.). 2013. *Indian Ocean Slavery in the Age of Abolition*, New Haven: Yale University Press.

Harries, Patrick. 2013. "Negotiating Abolition: Cape Town and the Trans-Atlantic Slave Trade," *Slavery & Abolition: A Journal of Slave and Post-Slave Studies*, 34(4): 579–97.

Henrichsen, Dag, Giorgio Miescher, Ciraj Rassool and Lorena Rizzo. 2015. "Rethinking Empire in Southern Africa," *Journal of Southern African Studies*, 41(3): 431–5.

Hofmeyr, Isabel. 2013. "African History and Global Studies: A View from South Africa," *Journal of African History*, 54(3): 31–49.

Horden, Peregrine and Nicholas Purcell. 2006. "The Mediterranean and the New Thalassology," *The American Historical Review*, 111(3): 722–40.

Jaji, Tsisti Ella. 2014. *Africa in Stereo: Modernism, Music, and Pan-African Solidarity*, New York: Oxford University Press.

Khuri-Makdisi, Ilham. 2010. *The Eastern Mediterranean and the Making of Global Radicalism, 1860–1914*, Berkeley: University of California Press.

Lee, Christopher J. 2010. "Tricontinentalism in Question: The Cold War Politics of Alex la Guma and the African National Congress," in Christopher J. Lee (ed.), *Making a World After Empire: The Bandung Political Moment and Its Afterlives*, Athens: Ohio University Press.

Lavery, Charne. 2015. "Indian Ocean Depths: Cables, Cucumbers, Consortiums," paper presented at a conference, Indian Ocean Energies, University of the Witwatersrand, 23–26 July.

Lewis, Martin. 1999. "Dividing the Ocean Sea," *The Geographical Review*, 89(2): 188–214.

Macdonald, Andrew. 2007. "Strangers in a Strange Land: Undesirables and Border-Controls in Colonial Durban, 1897-c.1910," MA thesis, University of Kwa-Zulu Natal.

Maynard, John. 2005. " 'In the Interests of Our People': The Influence of Garveyism on Rise of Australian Aboriginal Political Activism," *Aboriginal History*, 29: 1–22.

McPherson, Kenneth. 1998. *The Indian Ocean: A History of People and the Sea*, New Delhi: Oxford India.

Mentz, Steven. 2009. "Toward a Blue Cultural Studies: The Sea, Maritime Culture, and Early Modern English Literature," *History Compass*, 6(5): 997–1013.

Metcalf, Thomas R. 2007. *Imperial Connections: India in the Indian Ocean Arena, 1860–1920*, Berkeley: University of California Press.

Mitchell, Timothy. 2011. *Carbon Democracy: Political Power in the Age of Oil*, London: Verso.

O'Reilly, William. 2004. "Genealogies of Atlantic History," *Atlantic Studies*, 1(1): 66–84.

Pearson, Michael N. 2003. *The Indian Ocean*, London: Routledge.

Popescu, Monica. 2014. "On the Margins of the Black Atlantic: Angola, the Second World, and the Cold War," *Research in African Literatures*. Special Issue on *Africa and the Black Atlantic*, 45(3): 91–109.

Ricci, Ronit. 2011. *Islam Translated: Literature, Conversion, and the Arabic Cosmopolis in South and Southeast Asia*, Chicago: University of Chicago Press.

Saraiva, Clara. 2007. "African and Brazilian Altars in Lisbon – Some Considerations on the Reconfigurations of the Portuguese Religious Field," in Nancy Priscilla Naro, Roger Sansi-Roca and David H. Treece (eds.), *Cultures of the Lusophone Black Atlantic*, London: Palgrave Macmillan: 147–58.

Simpson, Ed and Kai Kresse (eds.). 2008. *Struggling with History: Islam and Cosmopolitanism in the Western Indian Ocean*, New York: Columbia University Press.

Soske, Jon. 2009. "'Wash me Black Again': African Nationalism, the Indian Diaspora, and Kwa-Zulu Natal, 1944–1960," PhD thesis, University of Toronto.

Stanziani, Alessandro. 2014. *Sailors, Slaves and Immigrants: Bondage in the Indian Ocean World, 1750–1914*, London: Palgrave Macmillan.

Stern, Philip J. 2007. "Politics and Ideology in the Early East India Company-State: The Case of St Helena, 1673–1709," *The Journal of Imperial and Commonwealth History*, 35(1): 1–23.

Thornton, John K. 1998. *Africa and Africans in the Making of the Atlantic World 1400–1800*, Cambridge: Cambridge University Press.

Tinker, Hugh. 1974. *A New System of Slavery: The Export of Indian Labour Overseas, 1830–1920*, London: Oxford University Press.

Toussaint, Auguste. 1966. *History of the Indian Ocean*. Translated by June Guicharnaud. London: Routledge and Kegan Paul.

Van der Watt, Susanna Maria Elizabeth. 2012. "Out in the Cold: Science and the Environment in South Africa's Involvement in the Sub-Antarctic and Antarctic in the Twentieth Century", PhD diss., University of Stellenbosch.

Wenzel, Jennifer, Patricia Yaeger and Imre Szeman (eds.). 2017. *Fueling Culture: 101 Words for Energy and Environment*, New York: Fordham University Press.

Part II

CASE STUDIES

3

THE KAKATIYAS, MOTUPALLI AND THE SOUTHERN BAY OF BENGAL LINKAGES

Radhika Seshan

While Michael Pearson did not, in his works, ever directly use the words, the notions of place and space are part of many of his writings. For example, when he talked of 'how far inland' one had to go to get away from the smell of the sea, the notion of both place and space is clear (Pearson 2014: 66). Rila Mukherjee has examined his ideas regarding littoral societies in particular in detail (Rila Mukherjee 2017: 11–12) and, in the process, highlighted the ways in which he looked at littoral societies and spaces. What is meant by space and place? The political geographer John Agnew said that there are three fundamental aspects of place: place as location, place as locale and the sense of place (Agnew 1987). Fernand Braudel, as is well known, predicated his works upon the 'recognition of place as locale, upon places as connected settings, [and] upon place consciousness' (Withers 2009: 637–58). I do not propose to go into the entire debate on the meaning of place and space and the various philosophical questions that have been raised about space and place; rather, my concern here is with the notions of space as location and locale and then questions of whether these are addressed in some inscriptions of South India. Further, I would go into the territoriality and networked connections as expressed through the inscriptions and the ideas of locality and locale that they throw up.

The starting point of this paper is the notion of the *tinai*, the eco-zones that are to be found in the Tamil Sangam literature. There were five *tinai* – the fertile plains along the rivers, the coasts, the lower hills, the higher slopes of the hills and the arid barren lands. Each tinai was identified with a flower, a particular kind of people, and an emotion (for example, the hills were identified with the *kurinji* flower and with the hunting tribes of the area, as well as with the idea of spring or sometimes virginity). They thus clearly indicate a sense of the ordering of geographical and physical space and also, to some extent, of locating individuals. In the literature of that time, there was a further division visible in the poetry, of *akam* (inner) and *puram*

51

(outer). Can we perhaps term this also as a way of ordering space, from the point of the individual rather than the community? What is more significant is that the entire corpus of what is today known as 'Sangam literature' was re-organised from about the eighth century CE, during the initial period of Chola rule. A question that has to be asked is why the need was felt to re-organise the literature and what kinds of 'spaces' were being defined, in addition to the places themselves.

Chola inscriptions have been extensively studied – earlier (early in the twentieth century in particular) from the point of view of political history and chronology and later, for their economic value, for many of them talk of grants of land and administrative issues. Implicit in both is a sense of ordered space – ordered by reason of being within the Chola kingdom and governed by the existence of the king and the appurtenances of empire. It is to be remembered that inscriptions were both a political and an economic record, for they recorded grants of different kinds – of land, revenue, and taxes; by or to temples; and by or to individuals. What notions of space and place do they assert, and how have these notions been, either overtly or covertly, continued in later, non-inscriptional writings? Equally important, how, and to what extent, were such ideas/descriptions/notions continued in non-official inscriptions[1] – specifically those of the merchant guilds? Let me, therefore, start with a few inscriptions. (The inscriptions are to be found in different volumes, including *South Indian Inscriptions* and *Annual Report on South Indian Epigraphy* [Aiyer 1937].)

One of the first inscriptions that I focus on here is the one that records the establishment of the guild of the *Ainurruvar* – the '500.' The claim that they constantly make in their inscriptions is that they are the *'tisaiayirattiainnurruvar'* – the 'five hundred who go in a thousand directions.' How are these 'thousand directions' to be defined? Even if they are merely a literary exaggeration, there has to have been some idea of both directions and location, of the starting and end points and multiple off-shoots of that. Can this be called a sense of territoriality? Or is this a way of asserting identity through locality and location, giving, in the process, a sense of time, space and place and thus a kind of territorial assertion? It is noticeable that this inscription clearly says that the 'mahajans' and 'mahas-vamins' of the city of Aihole in Karnataka came together to establish the guild; why, in a landlocked city, was it necessary to talk of a thousand direc-tions, and where were these – on land alone, on land and sea, and if the lat-ter, then which sea? Later inscriptions of the 500 mention their activities in Southeast Asia, and we know that the Southeast Asian connection was one that had long been familiar to merchants of South India. Another question that I could perhaps pose here is, can this be called territoriality or a kind of pre-modern 'cosmopolitanism'? (Coller 2010: 447–70).

Another question that I would ask is on 'territoriality' and place. As mentioned, John Agnew identified three fundamental aspects of place: as location, as locale and as the sense of place (Agnew 1987). Can we see any or all of these in the inscriptions? In this sense, the inscriptions definitely give us a sense of location, for all of them are very specific in the ways in which they define where they are. Some of the inscriptions which talk about the guild setting up a village as an *erivirapattinam*, a fortified village, are replete with details about the village, the kinds of walls that were built and the money assigned for its upkeep, as well as some information about the route on which the village lay. Obviously, one would have to ask why a fortification was necessary on that particular route; but more significant is that the route itself is not clearly defined, as though everyone knew it, and so there was no need to define it further. So, can it be asked if this is indicative of a shared sense of territory, where routes did not need to be defined, only spaces did, because these spaces were being consciously altered? Y. Subbaruyulu (Chevillard et al. 2004: 583–94) has mentioned an inscription from Camuttirāpatti, which records that a big assembly, comprising the '18-*bhūmi* and *nānātēci*' and the 500 'of the town called *Paniyanatu*' along with a subordinate group called '*nammakkal*' (he then goes into a list of the members of the subordinate group) decided to make the town an *erivirapattinam*. Two groups were involved in this transaction – the 500, often called the 'Five Hundred of the eighteen *bhumi/visayam*, also known as the *padinenvisaya*,' and the local people. Once again, there is here a sense of belonging, both to the larger world of commerce and the locality itself. This is an inscription that Subbaruyulu has dated to 1050; another of 1090 also refers to the *padinenvisaya* (Karashima and Subbarayulu 2002: 57–61). Other inscriptions are equally specific in their defining of the amounts being assigned, as *pattanapagudi*, share of the village, or *maganmai*, toll or entry tax (see for example Champaklakshmi 1996: 320). Again, there is the implication that while amounts were specified, where the goods came from or where they went to did not need to be mentioned.

At the height of their importance, the *Ainnuruvar* claimed that they traded in the '18 *pattinams* [ports], the 32 *velarpuram* [perhaps coastal towns, but involved in the coastal trade alone rather than overseas trade] and the 64 *kadigaitāvalam* [periodic fairs]' (SII VII: No. 442). A similar inscription talks of the 500 as being the protectors of 'the four quarters, the 18 towns, the 32 *velarpuram* and the 64 *ghatikasthanas*' (ARSIE 256 of 1912). Nor was this restricted to the trade guilds, for in later times, there is mention of a guild of weavers, who were divided into four *tisainadus*, 18 *kilainadus* and 72 *nadus* (ARSIE 300 0f 1909–10). Were these merely symbolic numbers, or did they speak for a sense of territory, that, while not geographically located, was still familiar enough to not require any specific explanation? (An interesting, though unrelated fact is that, in the seventeenth century, the number '72' started being used much more extensively, so that the fort of Madurai was supposed to have 72 bastions, each supported by 72 *palayams* [Sathianatha Aiyar 1924]). By the fourteenth century, trade organisations were deeply entrenched into local institutions and were intrinsic to the economy of South India. It has been suggested that the external policy of the Cholas was considerably influenced by mercantile interests, so that their wars in South Karnataka can be seen as an attempt to establish control over the main trade routes between Karnataka and Tamil Nadu, while the attacks on Sri Lanka and Srivijaya, far from being mere plundering raids, can perhaps be viewed as commercial ventures, designed to encourage trade with those areas where pockets of Tamil merchants already existed (Champaklakshmi 1996: 213). Rooted in the locality, they yet had connections across the regions, through the previously established networks of contact. Can we then argue that it is in this century that we begin to go beyond 'region' and 'location' to the broader areas of 'territoriality' and 'networks'?

Similar questions can be raised with reference to the 500 outside India, in the inscriptions in Southeast Asia in particular. What are the points of reference in those inscriptions? Do they indicate a different kind of familiarity but a shared one, nonetheless? Also, who was involved in these trade networks? In the period when the guilds were of prime importance, we do not get much detail on specific groups that were participants in the trade across the Bay of Bengal. However, we do have the famous inscription regarding the Buddhist Vihara at the port of Nagapattinam (Singh 2014: 52–3), which clearly indicates the connections between two regions, Kadaram and Nagapattinam. Later sources do make frequent mention of the Muslim merchants involved in the trade, who are termed[2] 'chulias' and 'klings.' With reference to the former, Barbara Watson Andaya (Om Prakash 2012; Andaya 2012: 305–36) has pointed to research that has linked the word *chulia* to 'Cholamandalam,' the Coromandel. The word *kling* is derived from the older 'Kalinga,' the Odisha coast, but by the seventeenth century, it was also, like *chulia*, used to refer to Muslim merchants of the Coromandel Coast. Here is a different way of marking identity which, through naming, indicates location as well. At the same time, they point to the networks of contact across the Bay of Bengal.

Notions of space, place and territory exist, but we need to try to understand them in the context of both the activities of the guilds and the empire within which they were functioning. It is possibly significant that the guilds themselves began to be more localised as the Chola Empire declined and became more associated with the local, rural bodies (the *chitrameliperiyanadus*), but we perhaps need to study them again, from a different perspective.

What were the networks of the eastern Indian Ocean emanating from the peninsula? How ancient were these networks, and how long did they continue? The antiquity has been well established through archaeology, as seen in, for example, the excavations at Arikamedu and other places along the coast, which indicate some contact with the Roman world. Some continuity of contact from this coast may also be seen in the shore temple at

Mamallapuram (better known as Mahabalipuram) and the establishment of that port by Mahendravarman, the Pallava king.

While these are undoubtedly important, far better known are the linkages established and maintained during the Chola period. But something that needs to be pointed out is that much of this research focuses on the Coromandel Coast, and later in the medieval period, when the northern part of the Coromandel Coast and the Andhra Coast became much more visible, there is often a sense of this area having come up out of nowhere. Obviously, this cannot be the case. Therefore, what I am exploring here is the connections of this part of the Indian coast to the Bay of Bengal trade.

Can one really say that the Cholas were the first and the last to try to gain access to and control over the linkages of the region? It would probably be true to say that they were the first and the last to deliberately, as part of state policy, make such an attempt by consciously and carefully developing a trans-sea presence, in Sri Lanka and Srivijaya (Sastri 1955; Kulke 2010), but this is not to say that other state systems did not try to promote the connection in various ways. It is for this reason that I will now move to focus on the Kakatiyas of Warangal, often seen as a quintessentially land-based and land-oriented kingdom. While I will be mentioning a number of inscriptions, I will specifically focus on one, possibly the most famous one, the Motupalli inscription of 1244–1245.

The Kakatiyas seem to have begun as subordinates of the Chalukyas of Kalyani but became independent rulers around the middle of the twelfth century, when Rudra I came to power (1158–1195). It was at this time that the fort of Warangal was expanded and strengthened and the place became the capital of the kingdom. While Rudra seems to have conquered much of present-day Andhra Pradesh and Telengana, his successor, Mahadeva, went further west into the Deccan, to attack Devagiri. It was in the reign of the next king, Ganapati, that the Kakatiyas became a major power in the Deccan. The Kakatiyas continued to rule much of the Andhra/Telangana region until the middle of the fourteenth century.

During the reign of Ganapati (1199–1262), inscriptions mention that the Kakatiya power expanded to include the coastal regions of Andhra. The king then sent his generals to capture the city of Kancipuram and thereafter adopted the title of *samudrapati*. Another feature of the period is the use of the word *samudramu* to describe large tanks, which were located in the interior, nowhere near the ocean. The Motupalli grant belongs to this period. Should we not see this as significant?

The Motupalli grant refers to the place as *Dēśyūyakkondapattana* and makes, in the *prasasti*, mention of the war that he waged against Kalinga. It then goes on to talk about the trade

> by the merchants who deal in gold, elephants, horses and precious articles who were granted fixed amount of compensation for facing

great risk of storms and ship-wrecks at the time of voyage as against the practice of confiscation of gold by the earlier kings.

(Murthy 2011: 220–4)

This inscription was termed *abhaya-sasana*, an 'edict of assurances,' and was inscribed on a pillar set up at Motupalli. The inscription further compares this pillar to a 'staff of justice' (Murthy 2011).

The inscription makes some things very clear. First, there was trade by sea, and this trade carried with it multiple risks not found on land. Second, this trade was not new, and it was profitable enough that the king could think of giving compensation. Third, earlier kings often confiscated the gold that the merchants had rather than compensating them for their trouble in going overseas for trade. It is this last which is particularly interesting, for in the seventeenth century, both the English and the Dutch, in any treaties with the local rulers, made specific mention of their right to salvage the goods off any ship of theirs which may be wrecked on the part of the coast that a particular ruler governed. In other words, they claimed that they had the right over the ship, even if wrecked, and the fact that this clause was specifically written down indicates that this was not the common practice. Can one then draw a parallel between the statement in the Motupalli grant and the clauses inserted some five centuries later?

Almost exactly one century later, one of the local chiefs of the area, one Annapota Reddi, renewed the Motupalli grant. The fresh grant first 'permitted the merchants of Motupalli who traded with distant islands and coast towns to stop at their will in their homes at Motupalli and to leave them for other places.' It abolished duties on gold and silver and stated that merchants 'were allowed the liberty to sell their goods brought from other shores to anybody under any conditions and to carry in exchange to other countries any goods they chose.' While further saying that taxes were to be the same as earlier, this inscription also specifically said that cloth was not to be detained in the warehouses (ARSIE 601 and 602 1909). The similarity in the language of this to the earlier inscription, about merchants travelling to 'other shores' and the implications about both the risks and the benefits from such travel, are clear.

Other inscriptions reinforce both the importance of the sea and the merchants. One inscription refers to an administrative division of the kingdom, named 'Vela-nadu,' and makes specific mention of Dvipa, located 'at the confluence of the Krishna with the sea' (Murthy 2011: 189). This is the place that later came to be known as Divi Island. European accounts of the seventeenth century mention this as an island which was at the mouth of the Krishna River and was the point at which ships bound for Masulipatam had to anchor.[3] Motupalli also seems to have been part of this *nadu*, for there is another inscription which describes Motupalli as a *Velanagara* – a 'mercantile town located on the sea shore' (Murthy 2011: 193).

What I am trying to argue is that one needs to look at both the language and symbolism of the inscriptions, as well as the content. Motupalli remained an important port of call for the merchants of (apparently) different parts of Southeast Asia as well as of India, and the coast was well known to the Arab merchants. The grant of Annapota Reddi very specifically mentions the 'Turuska' among the merchants who came to Motupalli and seems to imply that they too were permitted to buy houses and reside in the town. The term 'Vela-nagara,' meaning 'a mercantile city on the sea-shore,' that was used to define Motupalli does not indicate that it was a new word or one that was little used.

Other inscriptions testify to the networks of trade in the kingdom. For example, one, of the reign of Ganapati, records the gifts by the merchant guilds dealing 'with the five kinds of metals' – the *panchalohālabehara-muadedinakharamu*; the guild dealing with perfumes – the *gandhaaśesa-nagaramu*; and the *santa-nagaramu*, the guild dealing with (probably) the *santhai*, the local markets (Murthy 2011: 376–7).

The merchant guilds were an important part of the economy of South India, and studies have focussed on the larger guilds, the Ayyavole and the Manigramam. But from this inscription, guilds, meaning thereby associations of merchants, dealt with specific products. This clearly indicates a considerable degree of specialisation and also the existence of a market in which such specific products could be sold. It is these networks that one needs to remember when talking of continuities.

Motupalli was definitely an important port, but it should be remembered that a port is necessarily inseparable from its hinterland. Networks are those that link the hinterland and the foreland, and it is the existence of such networks that determines the continued existence or otherwise of a port. The Cholas, it has been said, expanded into those areas in which the Ayyavole guild traded, and therefore, they first expanded into the Karnataka region and then into Sri Lanka and Southeast Asia. Even if, in the Kakatiya inscriptions, we do not find mention of these guilds, there are clearly guilds that were operating. Geographically, the Kakatiyas were very well located, in that through this kingdom, access was possible both to the west coast and to the southeastern and southwestern coasts of India. As old as the Roman networks, these routes are rather less studied, but from the fifteenth century onwards, we have travel accounts, such as those of Niccolo Conti and Athanasius Nikitin, which clearly identify the routes across the peninsula. Motupalli itself was no longer an important port when these travellers came to India; its place had been taken by ports such as Masulipatnam. Still later, in the seventeenth century, Jean-Baptiste Tavernier went into detail about the route from Surat to Masulipatnam, and from the seaward side, in the same century, we have the account of Thomas Bowrey.

The account of Marco Polo, also of the thirteenth century, gives us a little more on the role of trade in the Kakatiya world. He says,

> When you leave Maabar and go about 1000 miles in a northerly direction you come to the kingdom of Mutfili. This was formerly under the rule of a King, and since his death, some forty years past, it has been under his Queen' (Rudramma, who ascended the throne on the death of her husband, Ganapati).
>
> (Yule 1871, 1903: 295)

Elsewhere, Marco Polo talks about the system of justice that prevailed, especially with regard to debts and their collection, for he says,

> 'If application for payment shall have been repeatedly made by a creditor, and the debtor puts him off from time to time with fallacious promises, the former may attach his person by drawing a circle around him, from whence he dare not depart until he has satisfied his creditor, either by payment, or by giving adequate security. . . . Should he attempt to make his escape, he renders himself liable to the punishment of death, as a violator of the rules of justice'. However, it is one too clear whether this is specific to the Kakatiya kingdom, or more generally to different parts of south India.
>
> (Masefield 2003: 366).

For Marco Polo, while the most important feature was that this was the kingdom from where diamonds were procured, what was also noteworthy was that in that kingdom were 'made the best and most delicate buckrams, and those of highest price; in sooth they look like tissue of spider's web.

> (Yule 1871, 1903: 296)

Hermann Kulke has argued that 'Through its Indian and foreign Muslim trading communities, India's ports became more directly linked with the "international" Muslim trade in the Indian Ocean' (Kulke 2010: 14). If, as he has said, the tenth century saw the rise of three powerful dynasties in Asia – the Fatimids in Egypt, the Song in China and the Cholas in India, then perhaps, for the thirteenth century, one can postulate the rise of powerful regional kingdoms, which were based on the networks established earlier but were, from the point of view of political economy, more localised. Such local networks would then mean that the prosperity of a port was dependent on the politics of the interior and thus give credence to the hypothesis put forward by Sinappah Arasaratnam in the late 1980s, where he said that the prosperity-decline curve of ports on the Coromandel Coast was linked not to geography but to the politics of the interior (Arasaratnam 1986). Where earlier diplomacy, through warfare or missions, had been the norm, now, it was merchants and merchant guilds, operating at more regional and local levels, but still bolstered by the state. Noboru Karashima has pointed out that the largest number of inscriptions referring to guilds, particularly the *ainurrurruvar*, are to be found in Tamil Nadu in the tenth century, but in the eleventh and twelfth, there are far more of the same guild to be seen in Karnataka, as well as in the other areas conquered by the Cholas. By the thirteenth century, guild inscriptions had declined, to be replaced by an increase in *pattanapagudi* inscriptions – something that Karashima has linked to the 'loss of state support' in that century and the replacement of this support by 'powerful Local organizations' (Kulke 2010; Karashima 2010: 152–3).

To go back to the question asked at the beginning, what were the networks, and how long did they last? What is clear is that by the time of Ibn Battuta, Motupalli was not particularly important, but the coast was well known. The continuity of networks was with the entire coast, and at different times, different ports were of importance. Can we trace the shift in the people involved in the mercantile networks of the southern Bay of Bengal but in the continuity of the contacts in themselves? Maybe we need to look at the inscriptions and the travel literature once again for this kind of information. A further point that therefore needs to be highlighted is that, when one is talking of networks, one cannot stop at the coast. The coastal or oceanic networks were part of the hinterland networks, and the prosperity of one was reflected in the trade of the other. Thus 'continuities' need to be seen in not just oceanic or coastal trade but also in the sourcing of the products for that trade and their dissemination in the interior. What I am therefore arguing is that networks need to focus on hinterlands as well as inter-port dynamics.

Notes

1 What I have in mind here is some of the later (seventeenth-century) literary sources, specifically a Telugu late Bhakti work, named the *Ekanatha Ramayana*, which used both tinais and the Chola kingdoms as defining the area in which his poems were to be read and which ended up being preserved in the Saraswati Mahal Library, Thanjavur.
2 I should say here that I have not been able to look at the *prasastis* of those inscriptions, only at a summary of their contents.
3 In these records, Divi is often described in terms similar to Swally Marine near Surat, as the point of disembarkation, before goods had to be transported over land to the city itself.

References

Agnew, John. 1987. *Place and Politics: The Geographical Mediations of State and Society*, Boston and London: Allen and Unwin.
Aiyar, Sathianatha, R. 1924. *History of the Nayaks of Madura*. Humphrey Milford: Oxford University Press. Reprint 1991. Delhi: Asian Educational Services.

Aiyer, K.V. Subrahmanya (ed.). 1937. *South Indian Inscriptions*, Madras: Government Press: vol. VIII.

Andaya, Barbara Watson. 2012. "A People That Range into All the Countries of Asia: The Chulia Trading Network in the Seventeenth and Eighteenth Centuries," in Om Prakash (ed.), *The Trading World of the Indian Ocean, 1500–1800*, New Delhi: Pearson Education: 305–36.

Annual Report on South Indian Epigraphy. 1887–1967. Madras: Government Press. Various volumes, 1896 onwards.

Arasaratnam, S. 1986. *Merchants, Companies and Commerce on the Coromandel Coast, 1650–1750*, New Delhi: Oxford University Press.

Champaklakshmi, R. 1996. "Developments Within: Urban Processes in the Early Medieval Period A.D. 600–1300," in *Trade, Ideology and Urbanisation*, New Delhi: Oxford University Press: 203–310.

Chevillard, Jean-Luc, et al. 2004. *South Indian Horizons: Felicitation Volume for Francois Gros on the Occasion of His 70th Birthday* (Publications Du Department D'Indologie: 94). Pondicherry: Institut Francais de Pondicherry.

Coller, Ian. 2010. "East of Enlightenment: Regulating Cosmopolitanism between Istanbul and Paris in the Eighteenth Century". *Journal of World History*, 21(3): 447–70, September.

Karashima, N. 2010. "South Indian Merchant Guilds in the Indian Ocean and Southeast Asia," in Hermann Kulke, K. Kesavapany and V. Sakhuja (eds.), *Nagapattinam to Suvarnadwipa: Reflections on the Naval Expeditions to Southeast Asia*, First Indian Edition, New Delhi: Manohar: 135–57.

Karashima, N. and Y. Subbarayalu. 2002. "Goldsmiths and Padinen-vishayam: A Bronze Buddha Image of Nagapattinam," in Noboru Karashima (ed.), *Ancient and Medieval Commercial Activities in the Indian Ocean: Testimony of Inscriptions and Ceramic Shards*, Report of the Taisho University Research Project 1997–2000, Tokyo: Taisho University: 57–61.

Kulke, Hermann. 2010. "The Naval Expeditions of the Cholas in the Context of Asian History," in Hermann Kulke, K. Kesavapany and V. Sakhuja (eds.), *Nagapattinam to Suvarnadwipa: Reflections on the Naval Expeditions to Southeast Asia*, First Indian Edition, New Delhi: Manohar: 1–19.

Masefield, John (ed.). 2003. *Travels of Marco Polo*, New Delhi: Asian Educational Services, Reprint.

Mukherjee, Rila. 2017. "Revisiting Michael Pearson's Indian Ocean Littoral," *Asian Review of World Histories*, 5(1): 9–30, January.

Murthy, S.S. Ramachandra (ed.). 2011. *Inscriptions of the Kakatiyas of Warangal*, Bangalore: Indian Council of Historical Research, Southern Regional Centre.

Om Prakash (ed.). 2012. *Trading World of the Indian Ocean, 1500–1800* (Vol. 3 Part 7 of the *History of Science, Philosophy and Culture in Indian Civilization*). Chennai: Pearson Education India.

Pearson, M.N. 2014. "Indian Ocean Port-Cities: Themes and Problems," in Rila Mukherjee (ed.), *Vanguards of Globalization: Port-Cities from the Classical to the Modern*, New Delhi: Primus: 63–77.

Sastri, K.A.N. 1955. *The Colas*, Madras: University of Madras.

Singh, Upinder. 2014. "Gifts from Other Lands: Southeast Asian Religious Endowments in India," in Upinder Singh and Parul Pandya Dhar (eds.), *Asian Encounters: Exploring Connected Histories*, New Delhi: Oxford University Press: 45–61.

Withers, Charles W.J. 2009. "Place and the 'Spatial Turn' in Geography and in History," *Journal of the History of Ideas*, 70(4): 637–58, accessed through Project Muse, 31 July 2012.

Yule, Henry (trans. and ed.). 1871, 1903. *The Book of Ser Marco Polo, the Venetian*, London: J. Murray.

4

REGIONAL IDENTITIES, MARITIME NETWORKING AND ISLAMIC CONVERSIONS IN FIFTEENTH-CENTURY JAVA

Kenneth R. Hall

> The land of Java has become more and more renowned for its purifying power in the World;
> It is only India and Java that are noted for their excellence as fine places . . .
> And so constantly all kinds of people come from other countries in countless numbers . . .
> Namely India, Cambodia, China, Yawana [Vietnam], Champa, the Carnatic [South India] and so on, . . . sailing on ships with merchants in large numbers,
> Monks and priests in particular – when they come they are given food and are happy to stay.
>
> (*Nagarakertagama*, 83.2–4)[1]

Consistent with the Hindu-Buddhist perspective of the Old Javanese fourteenth-century chronicle poem's opening statement, the *Nagarakertagama*'s author asserts that Java's continued patronage of Indic religion was vital to its continuity in an increasingly destabilizing 'global' world in which only India and Java – as they remained dedicated to Hindu-Buddhist virtues – were stable civilisations. The passage highlights Java's external 'knowledge networking' contacts over its international marketplace exchanges, including the intellectual dialogue facilitated by 'monks and priests' who travelled on merchant ships and established residency in stable Java. Here Java is presented as India's wealthy peer as well as contented (as Java is said to have food to spare) with less focus on Java's material prosperity than its 'purifying [spiritual] power' and the consequent superior quality of its culture. It is notable that the citation pairs Java with India as one of the two 'excellent' Asian cultural centres, as China is relegated to the longer list of linked 'material' trading societies that follows.

Consistent with the scholarship of Michael Pearson that contrasts the variety of historical Indian Ocean networked relationships, especially those between coastlines and hinterlands, this study addresses this assertive self-image of Java's cultural accomplishments with focus on the Majapahit era's legacy to its successors. Majapahit Java was the culmination of early Java predecessor courts that had been productive, internally focused and upstream-based central and east Java wet rice cultures. The Majapahit polity linked the prior agriculturally productive and Hindu/Buddhist court base in Java's upstream to its downstream, notably as this inclusive upstream-downstream extended into the Java Sea network of regional coastal ports and market-places and subsequently into the Straits of Melaka region to its west and the eastern Indonesian archipelago to its east. Numbers of local Islamic conversions were one consequence of this maritime externalisation. This gradual embrace of Islam, documented in Java's new fifteenth- and sixteenth-century Islamic-era poetic and chronicle literature, provides opportunity for the cross-reference and comparison of Java's prior Hindu-Buddhist era literature, as the new regional Islamic chronicle sources (e.g., the *Hikayat Raja-Raja Pasai, Hikayat Banjar* and *Sejarah Melayu*) provide more substantive address to Java's contemporary extended Indian Ocean linkages as well as external perceptions of fifteenth- and sixteenth-century Java.

The Majapahit court's variety of records, as confirmed in contemporary regional, Chinese, Middle Eastern and the first Western sources, attribute Java's 'golden age' as consequential to the initiatives of Majapahit's chief-of-state Gajah Mada (r. 1329–1364), who campaigned to incorporate Majapahit into the regional maritime realm of *Nusantara*, which included the inclusive 'islands between' Sumatra in the western and New Guinea in the eastern Indonesian archipelago. According to Majapahit's 1365 *Naga-rakertagama* (*Desawarnana*) court chronicle, Gajah Mada pledged to forgo '*palapa*,' worldly pleasures, such as the consumption of special foods, spices, or beverages; extensive religious activity; and sexual relations until he had achieved this goal.

Scholars debate Gajah Mada's achievement of this literary claim; most agree that except for its Java, Bali and Madura core territories, Majapahit's wider authority is better characterised as a sphere of political, commercial and cultural influence and periodic and uneven control over these strategic regions and ports-of-trade in the Indonesian archipelago. Similar to the Chinese dynastic fleets of the Yuan and Ming eras, Majapahit's state ships periodically sailed to archipelago port polities to receive tribute and proclamations of submission to Majapahit's 'superior' command but also marketed Java products for profitable primary and secondary regional and international commodities. Java's importance as the economic and cultural hub of the archipelago region from the fourteenth to the sixteenth centuries was due to its productive rice economy, social and political stability, cultural achievements and dominant networked ports-of-trade that were the region's strategic bases. According to the era's regional literature, there was always the potential of a Majapahit military/naval intervention to sustain regional marketplace stability. This made possible the international marketing of eastern Indonesian archipelago spices, the pepper production of Sumatra and southern Borneo and Java's rice exports, batik cotton textiles and a variety of craft products (notably Java ironwork) for wide regional consumption.

The precise nature of Majapahit's 'empire' remains the source of controversy against the *Nagarakertagama* court text's claim that Majapahit was a prominent empire consisting of 98 tributaries, stretching from the Straits of Melaka to the eastern Indonesian archipelago, although the earliest versions of the southeast Borneo polity's *Hikayat Banjar* affirms the evolving polity's emulation of Majapahit Java culture. Most scholars have portrayed this assertion of Majapahit's declaration of international authority as representing no more than Majapahit's sphere of influence, inclusive of regions that acknowledged Majapahit's regional interests and Majapahit's sustaining role as a vital political and commercial intermediary connecting secondary Southeast Asia regional merchants and producers with international traders. Others assert that this self-proclamation was no more than a statement of contemporary geographical knowledge rather than a documentation of Java's regional sovereignty. There is no doubt, however, that Majapahit Java-based fleets periodically visited many parts of the archipelago on Majapahit diplomatic and commercial missions. In the *Negarakertagama*, 'ambassadors' were said to have obtained formal regional submissions to Majapahit, and in return, Majapahit ships maintained the stability of a largely open regional trading system. The splendour, regional presence and overall authority of the Majapahit court led many regional rulers to send it tribute in much the same way as they periodically dispatched tribute to contemporary Ming China's court.[2]

Majapahit's trading prominence paired with its role as a regional cultural centre to provide Majapahit with a powerful sanctioned base to stand against defiant regional rulers. The east Java-based mixed maritime and agricultural kingdom, in contrast to the prior upstream central Java polities, did in fact establish especially close trading and cultural links with pepper suppliers in Sumatra and the spice-producing regions in Indonesia's eastern archipelago. Thus Majapahit's contemporary textual assertions that it was a regional 'empire' grounded in arbitrary regional inclusion rather than institutionalised centrality was truthful, as regional literature acknowledges local emulation of Majapahit's cultural achievements and wider marketplace connections rather than acknowledging submission to its political authority, as in reality Majapahit never had affective administrative power outside its Java, Bali and Madura core.[3]

IDENTITIES, NETWORKING AND CONVERSIONS

Majapahit, Straits of Melaka and Java Sea regional identities c. 1500

By the end of the fifteenth century, the Javanese, Balinese, Malays and other populations who shared the Straits of Melaka and Java Sea collectively defined themselves in reference to the inspired leadership of the fourteenth- and fifteenth-century east Java-centred Majapahit polity. In the quotation from the *Nagarakertagama* that begins this chapter, the more distant centres of civilisation are distinguished from those populations in the Majapahit 'core' in or near the Straits of Melaka and Java Sea region, as this core was considered to be in Majapahit's sphere of influence in contrast to those on the periphery that were not. Fittingly the poet author of the *Nagarakertagama* calls his work the *Desawarnana*, 'a description of the regions.' This characterisation of the Majapahit realm as a collation of diverse regions is significant; the epic poem highlights the supreme state minister Hayam Wuruk's (r. 1350–1389) visits to the regions of the Java countryside around 1360, as this paired with reciprocal regional diplomatic missions to the Majapahit court that confirmed local submissions to Majapahit's regional authority. The court text asserts that the Majapahit monarch's detailed Java travels confirmed his ancestral ties and celebrated each region's importance as an integral part of his realm's core. Having confirmed the monarch's Java base, the chronicle proceeds to describe the Majapahit monarch's wider band of authority that stretched beyond *Yawabumi*, 'the land of Java,' to include *Nusantara/dwipantara*, 'other islands,' and *Desantara*, 'other countries,' on the state's periphery (13.1–15.3). Not only was *Yawabumi* under the Majapahit monarch's direct rule, but *Nusantara*, the wider regions of the Indonesian Archipelago and the Malay Peninsula were understood to be submissive to his protection and overlordship more out of respect than because of Majapahit's physical presence.[4]

Thus it was logical in the minds of the fourteenth- and fifteenth-century poets, chroniclers and their audiences, both courtiers and commoners, that previous King Kertanagara (r. 1268–1292) should have sent a naval expedition to the Melaka Straits and the Malay Peninsula (*Malayu*) to rightfully assert his regional sovereignty as the straits and the peninsula were thought to be within Majapahit's territorial core.[5] According to surviving fifteenth-century literary sources, though King Kertanagara technically sent this naval expedition to claim wives from his regional subordinates, his real intent was to confirm local rulers' affirmations of their subordinate position in his Java-based state's political and cultural orbit – conceptualised as an inclusive Indic *mandala* polity in which 'satellite' subordinates orbited the political centre. Thus, *Nusantara* was the physical core space where the sequential Majapahit monarchs had direct political interests but not omnipotent control (see Figure 4.1). The *Desantara* were even more

65

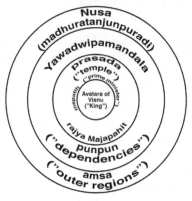

The Concept of the Majapahit Polity according to the Tuhanam Inscription (1326)

The Concept of the Majapahit Polity according to the Nagarakertagama (1365)

Figure 4.1 Two contemporary Java literary conceptions of the Majapahit Java Mandala State

Source: Kenneth R. Hall, *A History of Early Southeast Asia, Maritime Trade and Societal Development, 100–1500*, Lanham, MD: Rowman and Littlefield, 2011, 254 (253–286). The graphic of the Mandala State is adapted from the unpublished original by permission of Hermann Kulke.

distant and lay beyond the conceptual *mandala* state core. Many of these 'countries' were Southeast Asian polities with which Majapahit had diplomatic and cultural exchanges as indicated in the following *Nagarakertagama* passage:

> The above [inclusive *Nusantara*] are the various regions protected by His Majesty; on the other hand, the Siamese of Ayutthya and also of *Dharmanagari* [Nakhon Si Thammarat on the Malay Peninsula], *Marutma* [Martaban, Burma/Myanmar, a lower Burma Bay of Bengal coastline cultural and commercial centre], *Rajapura* [Ratburi, southwest of modern Bangkok], as well as *Singhanagari* [Singhaburi, north of Ayutthya on the Chaophraya river], Champa, Cambodia, and *Yawana* [Vietnam] are always friends (15.1).[6]

A parallel view of the inclusive Southeast Asian region and Majapahit authority is found in the following reference to Majapahit in the fourteenth-century *Hikayat Raja-Raja Pasai*, the first of the Malay-language court chronicles reporting on the Straits of Melaka region in the fifteenth century:

IDENTITIES, NETWORKING AND CONVERSIONS

> The (Majapahit) Emperor was famous for his love of justice. His empire grew prosperous. People in vast numbers thronged to the [capital] city. At this time every kind of food was in great abundance. There was a ceaseless coming and going of people from overseas territories that had submitted to the [Majapahit] monarch, to say nothing of places inside Java itself. Of the districts on the coast, from the west came the whole of the west, from the east came the whole of the east. From places inland right down to the shores of the Southern Ocean the people all came for an audience with the "Emperor," bringing tribute and offerings. . . . The land of the Majapahit was supporting a large population. Everywhere one went there were gongs and drums being beaten, people dancing to the strains of all kinds of loud music, entertainments of many kinds like the living theatre, the shadow play, masked-plays, step-dancing, and musical dramas. These were the commonest sights and went on day and night in the land of Majapahit.[7]

In this and other contemporary regional Malay-language *Hikayat* chronicle accounts, the nearby 'overseas' territories are said to be subject to Majapahit, both culturally and economically, if not politically, as the listed areas are comparable to those enumerated in the *Nagarakertagama*'s detailed conception of an inclusive maritime *Nusantara* Southeast Asia. According to this confirming external chronicle, Majapahit's notional domain spread from Samudra-Pasai at the northeast end of the Straits of Melaka to the Banda Islands on the eastern end of the Java Sea.

However, an opposing characterisation was offered by the retrospective seventeenth-century *Hikayat Banjar* chronicle of the then-prominent southeast Java Sea Kalimantan/Borneo southeast coastline pepper port of Banjarmasin, which reports Majapahit's late fifteenth-century demise:

> Majapahit became more and more chaotic. Everyone fled from the capital and some went to Bali, others to [the commercial port-polities at] Tuban, Madura, Sidayu, Sandang, Demak, Pajang, or Kudus.[8]

Significantly this and other Malay language chronicles of island Southeast Asia that are contemporary to or post-Majapahit literary sources collectively assert that their rulers had ancestral or diplomatic ties to the royal family of Majapahit.[9] None of the post-Majapahit sources claimed to be Majapahit's direct heirs; instead, they referenced previous Majapahit diplomatic exchanges to legitimate their territorial rights on the basis of their

Majapahit networked linkage. Collectively among these secondary ports, there was a common veneer of admiration, awe, and grudging respect for Majapahit's power. Yet despite their homage to the Majapahit and its legacy, the local chronicles also made the contradictory assertions that their populations were always more astute than those of Majapahit. They only lost battles against Majapahit when attacked by Majapahit's numerically superior fighting forces or when Majapahit was assisted by the capable populations of other islands. Never were Majapahit forces said to be victorious because of their superior battlefield skills, courage, knowledge or divine guidance.

For the most part, the Malay chronicles are positive in reference to Majapahit's past, as a Majapahit linkage was vital to local assertions of legitimacy. Regional chronicle accounts are generally consistent with the *Nagarakertagama* court text in portrayals of Majapahit's political and cultural accomplishments. Subsequent newly prominent archipelago polities following Majapahit's late fifteenth-century fall claimed their legitimacy based in their past Majapahit linkage, as this confirmed local and regional authority.[10]

By contrast, the *Babad* chronicle literature of Java's post-1500 Islamic courts presents a generally negative view of their Majapahit predecessors.[11] For example, according to the seventeenth-century *Babad Tanah Jawi*, Panembahan Senapati, the first ruler of Majapahit's successor central-Java-based Mataram polity, claimed descent from Brawyaya VII (r. 1489–1517), the last ruler of Majapahit, as other regional leaders of the post-Majapahit era similarly validated their legitimacy by claiming their rightful continued authority. However, the Javanese *Babad* Islamic court literature follows in admitting that Majapahit's legacy was tarnished, because the last Majapahit monarch Brawajaya was morally and physically polluted, having suffered from venereal disease. His infection was cured, and the royal bloodline (and thus Brawajaya's Mataram heirs) physically and spiritually cleansed when Panembahan Senapati slept with a Wandanese slave girl who had been brought to Java by his soon-to-be queen. The new wife was the daughter of the king of Champa (central and southern Vietnam), one of the nine countries outside Nusantara said by the 1365 *Nagarakertagama* to have always been in friendly relations with Majapahit.[12] Around 1600, according to the *Babad*, the great-great-great-grandson descended from this union was the founder of the Muslim Mataram realm (1582/87–1755) based in Kota Gede (on the southern edge of modern-day Yogyakarta) in west central rather than east Java.

The *Pararaton*, a product of the transitional fifteenth-century east Java-based countryside, is a pre-Islamic state document that is critical of Majapahit's overly external relations as one reason for its demise, in contrast to the fourteenth-century court's *Nagarakertagama*, which celebrated Majapahit's wide regional networking as foundational to its success. In the notable previously discussed episode in the *Pararaton*, which precedes the composition of the *Nagarakertagama* but claims to have been excluded from that account, possibly because this was read as reflecting negatively on the reign of King Hayam Wuruk (1350–1389), who was celebrated as the pinnacle of Majapahit's sovereignty. As reported, the *Nagarakertagama*'s author was a Buddhist priest, whose account had focused on King Hayam Wuruk's righteous conduct as appropriate to the Indic *Dharmasastra* tradition of dutiful kingship. From the *Nagarakertagama* author's perspective, the Majapahit rulers' moral purity had drawn outlying regions, including those beyond Java's shores, to participate in Majapahit's sanctified regional sovereignty.

In other words, the exemplary ethical character of Majapahit's monarchs was said to have made them *cakravartins*, 'universal monarchs,' who ruled by moral example rather than by physical force. The later Majapahit court lay at the centre of a 'circle of kings' (*mandala*), drawn into the orbit of Majapahit by the brilliance of its Java-based realm. This representation was conceptualised in Majapahit's state emblem (see Figure 4.2), which featured an encircling and radiant star.[13]

In contrast to the *Nagarakertagama*'s self-celebrated pacifism, the subsequent late fifteenth-century *Pararaton* enumerates Majapahit's aggressive initiatives, alluding not to Majapahit's adherence to the classical Indian *Dharmasastra* ('dutiful service') tradition but to the *Arthasastra* ('self-service'), which advocated military activism rather than passivity and forgiveness as the basis of a successful monarchy.[14] In the *Pararaton*'s fifteenth-century revisionist narrative, Majapahit had engaged in deliberate efforts to subordinate neighbouring rulers and therein physically incorporate their realms into Majapahit's polity. Thus, as an example, the *Pararaton* recorded a major battle between Majapahit and the ruler of the Sunda Straits regional passageway between Java's northern and Sumatra's southern coastlines.[15] According to this account, the Sundanese launched a maritime expedition against Majapahit in 1357. While the Sunda ruler's original intent was said to have been peaceful, as the flotilla of ships were escorting the Sundanese king and his daughter to Majapahit, where she was to be presented in marriage as a means of sealing a formal alliance with the Majapahit king. However, Majapahit's monarch refused to accord her a rank as queen that would have made the two kings of equal status. Upon hearing this, the Sundanese were so enraged that they launched a naval attack that sailed up the east Java Brantas River to attack the Majapahit court. Their attack failed, as they were defeated at downstream Bubat by Majapahit forces commanded by Majapahit's chief minister Gajah Mada.[16]

The attack by the Sunda ruler and the response by Majapahit's court is consistent with the patterns of competition among the riverine-system-based island Southeast Asian realms of the fourteenth to sixteenth centuries. The Sunda Straits ruler was said to have controlled the strategic riverine systems on both the Java and Sumatra sides and from these strategic locations was a serious commercial and military rival to Majapahit's wider interests in the western Indonesian archipelago. Thus, the Sunda naval expedition

Figure 4.2 Fifteenth/sixteenth-century Majapahit Emblem of State, Jakarta National Museum

Source: Photograph by author

sailed up the Brantas River to negate Majapahit's rivalry and in doing so lay exclusive claim to its Sunda Straits interests. According to subsequent Java literary sources, the Sunda monarch's failed attack on Majapahit resulted in Majapahit's reciprocal naval initiatives against challenging west Java and south Sumatra polities and therein asserted its Sunda Strait coastline interests.[17]

The attack on the Sunda Straits region was not immediate, but twenty years later, in 1377, Majapahit sent a major punitive expedition against Palembang, another longstanding competitor in the Melaka and Sunda Straits region, as Palembang had been the base of the strategic southeast Sumatra-based Srivijaya thalassocracy, and followed with attacks on Straits of Melaka regional ports at Jambi, Temasik (Singapore Island) and the Malay Peninsula.[18] This set in motion a series of regional transitions that resulted in the temporary closure of these Melaka and Sunda Straits–based polities. Intriguingly, the successors of the Palembang-based rulers, who would eventually re-establish themselves at Melaka in the late fourteenth century, traced their legitimacy to Majapahit. According to the fifteenth-century *Sejarah Melayu* Melaka court chronicle, the establishment of the Melaka portpolity allegedly received Majapahit's blessing. According to this usually trustworthy Malay chronicle account, the ruler of Majapahit had married the daughter of the king of the port polity of Tanjungpura (modern-day Pontianak on the southwest coast of Borneo/Kalimantan), brother of the ancestors of Melaka's rulers, in a marriage that theoretically made Melaka and Majapahit of equal stature. In the *Sejarah Melayu* story, Sultan Mansur Syah of Melaka subsequently sailed on a diplomatic mission to Majapahit to negotiate a marriage to a Majapahit princess and in successfully doing so, received Majapahit's recognition of his sovereignty over the southeast Sumatra coastline, as at that time, Majapahit retained control of the Jambi and Palembang ports on the southern end of the Melaka Straits.[19]

Bali provides an additional example of Majapahit's regional legacy in the self-conscious retrospective memories of its neighbours. Accordingly in the Majapahit court's *Nagarakertagama* account, King Kertanagara conquered Bali in 1284 (42.1). However, fifty years later, a second invasion was necessary, because, according to the *Nagarakertagama*:

> The king of Bali was evil and base –
> He was attacked with an army, broken and completely crushed;
> Every kind of evil-doer was fearful and made off quickly
>
> (49.4)[20]

Historians normally assume that Majapahit's chief minister, Gajah Mada, led Majapahit's 1343 reconquest of Bali.[21] However, the *Nagarakertagama* is vague on this point, briefly stating that

> [Gajah Mada] . . . had been [the king's] companion in bringing about an increase in Java's [regional] power in the past. In Bali and Sadeng [north coast central Java] was the proof of his success in defeating his enemies.
>
> (70.3)[22]

As for the Balinese perspective, there are two textual traditions that relate Bali's Majapahit connections, both late eighteenth-century compilations of earlier texts that record the origins of Bali's Gelgel Dynasty (fourteenth through seventeenth centuries). The first of these, the *Usana Jawa* poetic text credits military commander Arya Damar, not the chief minister Gajah Mada, as the leader of Majapahit's 1343 expedition:

> The kingdom of *Bedahulu* (Bali) was subjected by the kingdom of Majapahit because of the astuteness of the great *patih* [state minister] Gajah Mada. . . . The kingdom . . . was destroyed through the strength of Arya Damar who succeeded in carrying out all that he had vowed to achieve.[23]

The *Usana Jawa* text adds that Arya Damar had to return to Bali some time later to again subdue Majapahit's rivals. The Balinese *Babad Dalem* account connects Bali with Majapahit not because of Bali's conquest by Majapahit but because of the resettlement of numerous Majapahit nobles in Bali following Majapahit's sixteenth-century demise. The *Babad Dalem* records the appearance of Majapahit's royal regalia and weapons, notably magical *kris* daggers that arrived on the island subsequent to Majapahit's fall, as these spiritually empowered Bali's kings.[24]

Majapahit and Java's first Muslim sultanate

Western scholars writing about the Indonesian archipelago's history conveniently break Javanese history into two eras: Hindu-Buddhist and Islamic.[25] Despite the many continuities of the Majapahit legacy into the Islamic era, this division is generally justified on the grounds of two major changes in the local documentation from the transitional period. To begin, there was a linguistic transition. As political supremacy shifted from Hindu-Buddhist kingdoms to Islamic sultanates, the use of Old Javanese and the residual bilingual use of various Indic languages generally disappeared from contemporary documents. Second, the local literary sources suddenly began to acknowledge the presence and prominence of Muslims at the centre of regional polities. Prior to 1500, the Majapahit sources generally do not acknowledge the practice of Islam, nor did they address the development of the contemporary initial Islamic states on Java's north coast. Instead, they summarised the pre-Islamic past and speculated on Java's future while reflecting on the practices of the still active Saivite Hindu and Buddhist religious sects.[26]

By contrast, the post-1500 Javanese literature not only expressed an Islamic perspective, but it also suggested continuity between the new Islamic states and the Javanese culture that preceded them.[27] Islamic civilisation became prominent in coastal Java in the fifteenth century, and by the sixteenth century, there were several well-established north Java coast Islamic port polities that displaced Majapahit as the transitional centres of authority in Java's history. The fifteenth and sixteenth centuries were therefore a critical period of transition, as coastal port polities on Java's north coast welcomed an assortment of maritime diaspora, notably multi-ethnic traders from India, China and the archipelago world, who found Islam appealing at a time when the most prominent Indian Ocean sojourners were already identifying with this 'new' faith.[28]

This chain of initial conversions, which were most likely trade-related, was initially slow to develop. A Muslim merchant diaspora had already begun to appear as Southeast Asia–based regional tributary mission delegates to China's court by the eleventh century. Yet the first notable conversions of a Southeast Asian port polity did not occur until the thirteenth century, when Samudra-Pasai's monarch declared his northeast Sumatra port a sultanate. Java's initial Islamic port polities did not exist until the fifteenth century. However, Muslims were present in upstream Java by the fourteenth century, and in the sixteenth century, the transition to Islamic states appears to have been due to the ease of Islam's initial synthesis with Javanese traditional culture.

In the view of historians, Southeast Asia's Islamic conversions were for the most part not spiritually motivated but rather trade-related, as embracing Islam helped attract Muslim traders from farther west to do business in Java's port polities, bringing increased trade revenues to the local monarchs who were now co-religionists. In this view, the Southeast Asian rulers were actively seeking to attract Muslim traders, who by the thirteenth century were becoming preeminent in the international route between the Middle East and Southeast Asia. Local conversions implied a favourable religious environment for the traders and also assured local acceptance of the universal Islamic moral code, at least as this applied to commercial transactions – and possibly personal ones as well. Significantly, it was the coastal port polity elites who were the first converts to Islam, and only later did upstream hinterland populations join them. The upstream populations, by contrast, seem to have had little initial incentive to accept Islam, since their community membership was already satisfied by reference to non-Islamic traditions. Eventually, however, upstream conversions to Islam took place through the agency of downstream rulers, who sought to encourage local acceptance of Islam as a means of expanding and legitimizing their own authority while also increasing the flow of inland produce to their downstream ports.[29]

The motives for conversion remain open to question. Was the initial patronage of Islamic merchants and local conversion to Islam only a token gesture meant to derive economic benefits? Was conversion also related to Islam's political potential for linking the diverse upstream and downstream population clusters into a common socio-political entity? Or was the conversion motivated more by genuine spiritual commitment than by practical mundane goals? In addition, paralleling the earlier transfer of Indic traditions to Southeast Asia, there are questions of the mode by which Islamic conversion took place. Did the sojourning merchants' international connections make them capable of transmitting Islamic culture directly, or did they merely create the social and commercial networks into which religious teachers could move? In other words, did the traders provide more than mere deck passage for ritual specialists and pilgrims, or were they merely forerunners of the latter? More generally, in exactly what ways did merchant sojourners and downstream-based maritime diaspora facilitate the cultural dialogues that became the basis for Southeast Asia's selective localisations of Islam?[30]

Generally, historians have been reluctant to see merchant sojourners as sources of cultural transmission – neither Buddhist, Hindu nor Islamic – and they tend instead to credit these transitions to the knowledgeable 'wise practitioner' priests, monks and scholars who took passage alongside the traders.[31] But one can also argue that on these prolonged voyages and during the monsoon layovers, it would have been possible for literate merchants, priests, monks, and scholars to share in common recitations and discourse on the sacred religious texts as a means to pass time. In the earliest age, Hindu and Buddhist manuscripts were foundational to these sojourning literate textual communities, just as the *Qur'an* and *Hadith* were core Islamic conversion and religious-community-defining texts. Merchant diaspora who associated with the Muslim, Buddhist, Indic and Chinese cultural realms also had connections that undoubtedly offered opportunities for cultural brokering. In the time of Majapahit, not long after these initial merchant-settlers had established a functional community in Java, Muslim scholars arrived in the region and founded Java's first mosques on northern Java's coastline, therein legitimizing the new downstream portpolities' existence. This is analogous to events in the earlier eras, when the consecration of Indic Hindu and Buddhist temple complexes confirmed the presence and legitimacy of Java's early upstream Indic religious communities.[32]

Whatever the underlying reasons, the post-1500 Java literature suggests a less abrupt transition to Islam than might otherwise appear to be the case. The year 1527 is commonly cited as the date when a coalition of Muslims from the Java north-coast-based polities ended Majapahit's existence. Nevertheless, the local literatures suggest that the fifteenth century actually laid the foundation for Java's Islamic future, due to the contacts in this period between the remnants of the Majapahit kingdom and the new Islamic Java coastline port polities at Demak, Japara, Gresik, Banten, Cirebon and Tuban. This post-1500 literature viewed the late Majapahit period not as an era in which Java's society became compartmentalised between competing religious factions, as might be expected, but rather as one in which Javanese society was successfully localizing Islam into the cultural mainstream in a rapidly changing era in which Java was aggressively engaged in the maritime realm beyond its shores, with transitional economic, societal and cultural consequences.[33]

Muslim gravestones and inscribed stones at Trawulan, adjacent to the site of the east Java Majapahit court, provide support for these themes of continuity. They indicate that Muslims already resided at the court by 1368 and that several high-ranking members of the court were practicing Muslims.[34] The abrupt absence of Islamic tombstones dated after 1475, combined with the details of a 1486 inscription, suggest there may have been an abortive coup in 1478 (the date given in the inscription), followed by a backlash against Muslim presence at the court. Since this Muslim community at the court would likely have had significant ties to the coastline resident trading diaspora, any moves to suppress Islam by the post-1478 court would have paralleled the efforts of Java's reigning kings to restrict foreigner diaspora to Java's north coast rather than granting them open access to the Java upstream.[35]

Collectively, these court tombstones, post-1500 Javanese literature and several non-Java fifteenth- and sixteenth-century written sources suggest that the fifteenth century was an era of significant transition in Java, just as it was elsewhere in the Southeast Asian region. Notable among these written sources are the Malay chronicle literature of the Melaka Straits region (e.g., the *Hikayat Raja-Raja Pasai* and *Sejarah Melayu*); the record of the Chinese scribe Ma Huan, who visited Java as a member of a Chinese expedition in 1416 commanded by the Muslim eunuch admiral Zheng He; and the report of the Portuguese scribe Tome Pires, who visited Java's north coast in 1513.[36]

The sixteenth-century *Kidung Sunda* text offers the earliest literary reference to Islam in Java literature. This maritime community source recounts the story of the Sunda Straits king's daughter who travelled to Majapahit in 1357 to become Hayam Wuruk's bride. This story may be remembered in connection with the *Bubat* incident recounted earlier in this chapter but from the Sundanese (Sunda Straits, west Java/south Sumatra) perspective.[37] According to this text version, the Sunda wedding party was massacred by Majapahit troops. Paralleling somewhat the previous *Pararaton*'s Javanese language account, the *Kidung Sunda* relates that upon its arrival the Sunda delegation was received with insufficient dignity and ceremony.

Accordingly, the Sunda king's chief minister attempted to rectify this injustice by sending an embassy to Majapahit's chief minister Gajah Mada at the nearby Majapahit court. On their way to the court, and this is a significant departure from the *Pararaton* account, the Sunda dignitaries are said to have come upon the *Misigit Agung*, or Grand Mosque. There is no other written or archaeological evidence of a Grand Mosque in the vicinity of Majapahit's court. However, as noted, there are numerous Muslim tombstones near the court site dating from this period, making it likely that there was indeed at least one if not more Islamic communities meeting somewhere near the court.[38]

The previously noted *Hikayat Raja-Raja Pasai* Malay chronicle from the contemporary northeast Sumatra coastline port polity also reports the existence of Muslim communities at the centre of the Majapahit realm. The Samudra-Pasai account relates that after Majapahit's conquest of Samudra-Pasai in the mid-fourteenth century, captives were taken to Majapahit Java where they were 'allowed to settle.' These were Muslims, 'and that is why there were so many holy graves in the land of Java at the time when Pasai was conquered by Majapahit' in the mid-fourteenth century.[39]

The regional Malay language sources differ, however, on the degree to which the new Islamic rulers drew on non-Muslim ancestry to validate their sovereignty. The Samudra-Pasai chronicle, for example, roots the legitimacy of Samudra-Pasai's monarchs in the Middle East. By contrast, the *Hikayat Banjar*, representing the southeastern Borneo pepper port polity that was well-established at Banjar by the late sixteenth century, traces its monarch's legitimacy to both Samudra-Pasai and Majapahit bloodlines. Highlighting the fourteenth-century tie between Java and Samudra-Pasai, the Banjar chronicle represents Samudra-Pasai to be the then cradle of Southeast Asia's Islam – and the source of the eastern Indonesian archipelago (southeast-Kalimantan-based) Banjar's Islamic tradition – while also acknowledging that during its foundational era, Samurda-Pasai had been subject to Majapahit's sovereignty. According to the Banjar chronicle's retrospective account, Majapahit's rulers were never intolerant of Islam. Instead, the Majapahit ruler was said to have encouraged the settlement of a permanent Muslim community within the capital city – as a way to appease his Samudra-Pasai princess bride by gifting that community carte blanche to support their conversions of other regional residents to Islam:

> The King of Majapahit, Dipati Angrok, sent ten ships to bring a princess of Pasai to marry him, but who after the marriage was given a separate house. She had a son, following which her brother came to Majapahit to visit. Homesick, she wouldn't let her brother leave, so he settled nearby the court. The local inhabitants of this community soon wished to convert to Islam; the Majapahit king had no objections, and said: 'Tell Bungsu that he may convert to Islam anyone who wishes – whether from the capital or the villages.'[40]

However, there is a great deal of difference – in this and other era court texts – between permitting a minority Muslim community to form at the political centre and legitimating widespread state elite conversions to Islam.[41] Discussion of the importance of this transformative conversion of archipelago Hindu-Buddhist state elite to Islam and its consequences follows.

Majapahit and the rise of Java's Islamic states

Java's Islam, its initial downstream Islamic states, chronicles and adaptive traditions developed a unique religious and cultural tone, often drawing explicitly on Java's Hindu-Buddhist Majapahit roots. Java's post-Majapahit polities projected themselves as Islamic at first glance, yet their rulers and subject populations synthesised the new religion's fundamental tenets while retaining substantive Javanese traditional customs that were rooted in the culminating Hindu-Buddhist Majapahit era. For example, Java's newly converted Muslim court elite continued to dress in *batik* cloth consistent with longstanding Javanese fashion, rather than the counter-example of the populations of the Malay regions of the western archipelago, who adopted distinctively Islamic dress.[42]

In the case of Java, as in most of the Indonesian archipelago, rather than wholesale Islamic cultural transitions in the fifteenth-century, the period was characterised by a renewal of Java's upstream commitment to most of its pre-Islamic values. One can speculate that had Java's coastal communities predominated in the foundational fifteenth-century transitional era, Java might have developed a cultural style similar to the fundamentalism of Aceh on the northern Sumatra coast, where the elite of that prominent coastal centre had consciously cultivated linkages with Islamic communities and the Islamic cultural patterns in India and the Middle East.[43] Instead, Java's traditional landholding elite favoured their longstanding rural-based ways of life over those of the internationally engaged Java coastal ports, which, like Aceh, readily converted to Islam. The new Muslim elite were taking a foundational move to sustain their international commercial networking and urban residencies that distinguished them from the traditional populations of Java's rural hinterlands.

Unlike Aceh, the early Java Islamic portpolities embraced only the required basics of Islam, what Javanese called 'the essence of Islam,' and were selective in their use of new Islamic vocabulary and a 'foreign' lifestyle. They maintained the cultural and artistic legacies of the Majapahit period and compartmentalised traditional religious ritual and that of Islam.[44] Notably upstream Javanese Muslims were drawn to Islamic ritual rather than the study of Islamic doctrine and *Shari'a* jurisprudence. Their fifteenth-century Straits of Melaka neighbours were more thorough in their embrace of Islam and the Quran. Java's new Islamic elite placed emphasis on Islamic ritual that made the transition to Islam 'fit' with pre-existing Javanese and wider eastern Indonesian archipelago cultural and ritual practices.[45]

Despite the tendency to maintain a good deal of Javanese cultural tradition, local embrace of Islam certainly brought cultural challenges. As an example, new Islamic Javanese literature drew on historical traditions that linked contemporary polities back to Islam's seventh-century Middle Eastern origins. Conversion to Islam embedded the Javanese in trade networks that linked Java to the major international port polities of the Straits of Melaka, the South China Sea and the eastern Indonesian archipelago, where they traded and socialised with Middle Eastern, African, South Asian and Chinese Islamic diaspora, some of whom were permanent residents, while others made seasonal stopovers in Southeast Asia's ports. According to the *Nagarakertagama*'s author, all of the significant regional ports-of-trade enumerated in the text were in regular contact with fourteenth-century Majapahit.

Javanese cultural traditions showed great resilience during this transformative era. This was said to be consequent to the local conversions made by the agency of nine divinely empowered *wali sanga* ('saints') who arrived by sea to convert Indonesian archipelago residents to Islam. Contemporary tales of these saints' regional activities, a mixture of legitimizing myth and fact, assumed focal prominence in Javanese conversions to a localised Islam that was based on a mix of Javanese Islamic and pre-Islamic historical traditions. The *wali sanga* followed in the footsteps of the *wuku*, the Hindu, Buddhist, or indigenous *resi* clerics whom the fifteenth-century *Tantu Panggelaran* archipelago Islamic text credited with the founding of Java's rural *mandalas* ('shrines').[46] These nine Muslim saints were notionally comparable to the nine Indic *Lokapalas* of pre-Islamic tradition who guarded the eight quarters of the world as well as its centre.[47]

As such, the *wali sanga* were manifestations of much older Java historical-tradition, rooted in the classical Javanese texts (such as the *Nagarakertagama*) that attributed the founding of new religious centres to the agency of spiritually-empowered Hindu and Buddhist clerics. It was to be expected, therefore, that the Javanese should attribute the establishment of the new Muslim communities to the activities of figures like the legendary *wali sanga*, and subsequently Islamic foundational saints arrived by sea to be celebrated both in popular ritual and post-conversion literature. Even today, the *wali sanga* Javanese 'saints' are readily acknowledged as empowered intermediary divines who are charismatic intermediaries in Javanese Islamic tradition and known for their tolerance of mixed local and Islamic textual traditions.[48]

Most of the *wali sanga* came from outside Java. For example, as noted, the first *wali sanga* had a Champa (central Vietnam coastline) origin. According to tradition, Princess Putri Cempa (of Champa) married the king of Majapahit, Bra Wijaya.[49] She had two nephews, who are described as the 'sons of an Arabic man of religion.' The elder of these nephews, the most senior of the *wali sanga*, became the *imam* of the mosque at the then prominent north Java coast port city of Gresik. Meanwhile, the younger Raden Rahmat of Ngampel Denta would become the most senior ancestor and spiritual leader of the then strategic Surabaya east Java-based port polity and eventually the most senior of the *wali sanga*.[50]

As reported, the stories about these founding Muslim saints have a uniquely Javanese flavour, effectively rooting Javanese Islam in pre-existing Javanese culture. This style contrasts with the less rarefied self-concepts of the Malay polities to the northwest, such as Melaka and Aceh, whose rulers considered themselves 'Helpers of the World and of the Religion,' because of their 'possession of the law' (*mempunyai*). By contrast, Java's rulers were understood to be 'God's Shadow,' a concept that has mystical resonance consistent with notions employed in earlier Javanese polities. Like the previous Hindu-Buddhist monarchs, legacy Javanese Muslim rulers continued to access the supernatural, except that in place of reciting Sanskrit *mantra*s and paying respects to Indic and local deities, they accessed Islam's immense supernatural energy through recitations of Arabic verse and the practice of Islamic ritual.[51]

These changes were nevertheless significant, and they were discussed in both local and foreign sources. Tome Pires, writing from Portuguese Melaka around 1511, provided the initial European records of Java's Islamic states. His commentary is especially useful in distinguishing those contemporary regional societies that were Muslim and those that were not.[52] New chronicle and literary traditions from this same early sixteenth-century era provide additional historical details about the new Islamic states.

Two of the most useful remnants of these transitional Islamic textual traditions are the Malay chronicle literature known as *Hikayat* (e.g., the *Hikayat Raja-Raja Pasai*) and the *Babad* poetic Islamic chronicles of Java. When speaking of the transition to Islam, the Malay chronicle literature focuses on events that converted and transformed former animistic rulers into good Muslims,[53] while the contemporary Javanese literature highlighted miracles and mystical experiences that empowered those same rulers. The *Hikayat Raja-Raja Pasai*, the earliest of the Malay chronicles, tells the story of how Southeast Asia's first sultan Merah Silu converted to Islam at the end of the thirteenth century. According to the local chronicle, the Prophet visited Merah Silu in a dream and either spit or urinated into his mouth. Merah Silu awoke from this dream miraculously circumcised and able to recite the entire *Qur'an*. Shortly thereafter, a Muslim scholar dispatched from Mecca arrived to fulfil the prophecy made centuries earlier by Muhammad himself. The Muslim cleric arrived in Sumatra shortly after Merah Silu's dream, and on his arrival, he was vested with the appropriate symbolic regalia of civil authority, which the scholar had carried with him from Mecca, and immediately thereafter Merah Silu proceeded to institute Islamic law throughout his realm.[54]

In contrast to the Malay chronicles' emphasis on the Islamisation of particular rulers, the seventeenth-century *Babad Tanah Jawi* chronicle poem from Java – which is the culmination of earlier *Babad* literature – highlights the miracles and mystical experiences that empowered Java's Muslim rulers. In addition to transferring empowerment, these collective experiences created partnerships between rulers and priests/Islamic scholars, provided connections to the historical legacy of prior Javanese polities and transferred legitimacy from previous polities to the new Islamic courts. While these chronicles note legacy connections with earlier centres of Islamic scholarship and ritual, what is especially noteworthy is the literary preoccupation with rooting Islam firmly in pre-Islamic local traditions. Unlike the foundation stories of the Malay chronicle literature, Java's Islamic foundation myths do not focus on a Middle East institutional link but on the agency of the nine Java saints (*wali sanga*).

In the late fifteenth and early sixteenth centuries, these saints had come to Java, independently of each other, from various regions of the world, bringing the new faith and collectively initiating Islamic scholarship and worship.[55] Under the guidance of these saints, rulers and populations of the Hindu-Buddhist polities gradually came to accept Islam.[56] Rather than grounding their legitimacy in political and religious descent from Mecca, Java's Islamic courts considered themselves successors to the Majapahit legacy, and stories of the *wali sanga*–linked conversions were essential to self-representation. In contrast to the Malay language stories, in the Java conversions there were no citations of divine intervention, nor were there miraculous signs of conversion – such as Meru Silu's overnight circumcision. Instead, the *wali sanga* are portrayed performing miracles that so impressed Java's courts and their elite that the Java elite were gradually drawn into religious partnerships with the saints' spiritual and political projects.

This can be illustrated by reference to stories detailing Demak's founding and eventual victory over Majapahit. Demak was one of several port-polity trading centres that had evolved on Java's northwest coast, and by the sixteenth century it had distanced itself from among its competitors to become the then ritual centre of Javanese Islam.[57] Demak's origin myth focuses on the story of Raden Patah, known as 'the visitor.' A member of Southeast Asia's multi-ethnic maritime diaspora, Raden Patah was born at Palembang in Sumatra to a Chinese diaspora woman whose bloodlines drew in part from the Majapahit royal lineage. Raden Patah was thus descended from both the Majapahit court and the Chinese Muslim diaspora communities that from Yuan Dynasty times had been sojourning in the Sunda and Melaka Straits and were seasonal residents of Java's north-coast ports. Raden Patah settled in the north Java coast port of Gresik, which was largely populated by Chinese merchant diaspora. Then in the first quarter of the fifteenth century he moved to Demak, where he became immeasurably wealthy.[58] In the second half of the fifteenth century Majapahit's monarch appointed him Demak's governor, because of his commercial and personal prowess and also his royal blood. As at that time the Majapahit court declined Raden Patah asserted Demak's autonomy, as 1478 is the traditional date of his founding the Demak sultanate.[59]

The subsequent passage of power from Majapahit to Demak and other Islamic successor states is collectively recorded in the seventeenth-century *Babad Tanah Jawi*, as introduced earlier. Composed during the 1613–1645 reign of Sultan Agung at the central Java-based Mataram realm, the *Babad* is the culminating text in Java's early Islamic literary development. In contrast to the Hindu/Buddhist *Nagarakertagama* and the *Pararaton*, the *Babad Tanah Jawi*'s notion of legitimate order focused not on elaborate court-centred rituals but rather on the passage of political authority along

IDENTITIES, NETWORKING AND CONVERSIONS

the royal bloodlines to one who was spiritually empowered and morally just.[60] Instead of rooting Mataram legitimacy in connections to the Prophet or to Mecca, the *Babad* places emphasis on Mataram's legitimate succession from the kings of the Majapahit Hindu-Buddhist kingdom, detailing the shift in authority from Majapahit to Mataram and other Islamic successor states in a passage of power from the Majapahit king to his sons.

The portion of the *Babad Tanah Jawi* addressing this transition begins with the account of a Majapahit military campaign against the Muslim-dominated Giri north coast portpolity, which had failed to submit to Majapahit's sovereignty. The account begins as follows: Prince Brah-Widjaja [king of Majapahit] heard the report that many people submitted to Giri. Patih [chief minister] Gaja Mada was then sent out to march against Giri. The Giri population got into a tumult and fled to the palace. At that moment the *sunan* [ruler] of Giri was busy writing and became frightened when he heard of the enemy's arrival, [and that they] intended to destroy Giri. He threw down the pen with which he was writing and prayed to God. The thrown-down pen changed into a *kris*, which of its own accord proceeded to the attack. Many from [Majapahit] died in battle. Those remaining fled back to[Majapahit].

In other words, when Majapahit's forces attacked, the Giri ruler had been absorbed in 'meditative writing,' most likely working on his Arabic calligraphy. This dedication echoed the meditative rituals (*tapas*) ascribed to rulers in earlier periods. In the Old Javanese literary tradition, it was by such actions that rulers achieved *sakti*, 'divine empowerment,' and thus became 'one with the Lord.'[61] According to the account, the Giri ruler was unwilling to risk his life in battle, but the divine intervened, and a *kris*, a spiritually empowered dagger, defeated the Majapahit army.

Later, the divinely empowered *sunan* ('ruler') of Giri died and was succeeded by his less empowered son. During the son's reign, Majapahit was able to conquer Giri. However, even in defeat, Giri was magically protected, for when the Majapahit victors attempted to steal the body of the deceased ruler, the result was another glorious victory for the Muslim polity. Following its eventual subjugation of Giri, Majapahit's monarch sent his two sons with a troop of soldiers to retrieve the body of the deceased *sunan*, as possession of the body would deprive Giri of its magical/divine power. This task should have been easy, as the grave of the recently buried *sunan* was merely guarded by two cripples. Majapahit's soldiers commenced digging, but when they reached the coffin, they were possessed and fell to the ground. So the cripples were ordered to dig instead. This time, the coffin was opened, but the result was not what the soldiers had expected:

> [When] the soil in the grave had been excavated the boards with which the coffin had been closed were taken away . . . countless number of bees came out of the grave, flew upward and filled the

[sky]. . . . Then they attacked the [Majapahit] troops . . . [and then the Majapahit capital]. Prince Bra-Widjaja [Majapahit's monarch] and his army left the capital and fled far away, because they did not consider themselves capable of resisting the attack of the bees.

Having driven off the soldiers, the bees returned to Giri. Majapahit's armies never again threatened Giri, which renewed its previous prosperity. As for the two cripples, because of their faithfulness in guarding the gravesite, they were miraculously cured and released from the magical spell that had debilitated them.

The astonishing powers associated with the *sunan* of Giri also play a role in the next tale, which focuses on the transfer of power from the Majapahit monarch to an immediate descendant who had converted to Islam. This portion of the story begins in the north Java coastline port polity of Bintara, where one of the sons of the Majapahit monarch had taken up residence and converted to Islam. This son subsequently refused to perform an annual ritual recognizing his father's sovereignty.[62] Concerned about this slight but desiring a peaceful resolution, the Majapahit monarch dispatched another of his sons to reason with his brother. Raden Patah, the Prince of Bintara, informed his visiting brother that – although he respected their father – he could not perform the ritual of submission, because he had converted to Islam and Islam 'does not permit a Muslim to pay his respects to an infidel.' Hearing this, the envoy joined his brother's cause. The two descendants of Majapahit subsequently forged an alliance with other north Java coast Muslim portpolities, and they were also joined by several *wali sanga* who added legitimacy to this holy alliance and ritually sanctified it. Thus united, the confederacy seized the Majapahit court (*kraton*), with the two brothers in the lead.

It is at this point that the story explicitly acknowledges the legitimate transfer of power. The Majapahit ruler is said to have witnessed his defeat from his lookout tower (*panggungan*) above the court's public reception area (*alun-alun*) immediately outside the royal compound. When he saw Raden Patah, Prince of Bintara, seated on his throne, which rested on the magically empowered mat (*pagelaran*) that was symbolic of the realm's authority, he ascended to heaven with the remainder of his troops, content to leave his polity in the hands of his rightful heir. However, the transition was not without dire omens, for

At the same moment that [the Majapahit ruler] ascended to heaven, something like a ball of fire was seen that came from the [Majapahit] palace, [and] looked like a bolt of lightning and sounded like terrible thunder, which fell down [on Bintara, the port polity of the offending son].

IDENTITIES, NETWORKING AND CONVERSIONS

This divine retribution was interpreted as indicating that either the Majapahit throne or its seizure was tainted.[63] Consequently, rather than immediately accepting the alliance's encouragement that he should declare himself Java's new ruler and claim his rightful possession of Majapahit's authority 'due him as his heritage,' Raden Patah had the *sunan/prince* of Giri sit on the Majapahit throne for forty days, 'to make the traces left by an infidel prince disappear.' This forty days of purification, and the number forty in general, had strong predecessors in the Abrahamic Judeo-Christian-Islamic tradition. Noah dealt with a forty-day flood (itself an act of purification) in the Old Testament; in the New Testament, Christ spent forty days meditating and resisting temptation in the wilderness, and in the *Qu'ran*, Muhammad devoted forty days in a cave meditating, denying satanic temptations and receiving divine inspiration before he embarked on his ministry.

The story continues with Raden Patah, now purified and carrying the legacy of Majapahit, shifting his base from east Java to Demak on the central Java northern coastline.

> When the forty days during which the throne was purified had passed, the *sunan* of Giri transferred the princely dignity to Raden Patah. Raden Patah now was prince of Demak and reigned over the whole of Java under the name Senapati Djimbun Ngabd'ur-Rahman Panembahan Palembang Saidin Panatagama. . . . All the Javanese were submissive and embraced [his authority as also] Islam. Then it was agreed to erect a mosque in Demak. The *walis* [saints] divided the work among themselves. All were not ready. Only the *sunan* of Kali-Djaga lagged behind; his task was not yet done because he was just making a pilgrimage [to Pemantingan]; on his return to Demak the mosque would be erected. In preparation for his return Sunan Kali-Djaga [newly re-empowered because of his pilgrimage] hastily collected a few chips that he tied together. That night the chips transformed into a column [that became the foundational element of the new mosque]. The next day . . . the mosque was erected, in the year 1428. The longitudinal direction of the mosque pointed to the *kaaba* in Mecca.
>
> *(Babad Tanah Jawi)*

Collectively, these summary transition stories stressed the transfer of power not to upstart rulers but to the descendants of appropriate Javanese with royal genealogy who had converted to Islam and then united with the divinely-inspired *walis*. Even so, the new Muslim rulers did not possess sufficient empowerment in themselves to directly take on civil authority. Instead, in submission to the divine, they proceeded to ritually cleanse the old east Java infidel court of its Hindu-Buddhist desecrations and therein shifted authority to a new spiritually empowered Islamic centre in east Java.

Only then could the supernatural mosque at Demak become the spiritual centre of the Javanese Islamic community – now centred in central Java.[64]

The *Babad* episodes openly draw from previous literary conventions, though perhaps not from commonly accepted belief, holding that Java's kings could become invisible in times of crisis.[65] Such an episode appears in the eleventh-century Javanese *Arjunawiwaha kakawin*, wherein the human lord Arjuna accompanies the heavenly nymph Suprabha, his future wife, to the court of his demon opponent. There, his female companion, Suprabha, seduces the morally vulnerable chthonic spirit, while the celestially empowered Arjuna, who is invisible to all but Suprabha, secures the vital information that he needs to defeat the demon and save humankind.[66]

Another appears in the fourteenth-century *Nagarakertagama*, where it is implied that King Kertanagara, facing death when his *kraton* was invaded by Kadiri's forces in 1292, became invisible or, as the chronicle states, 'was released into the realms of Siwa and Buddha, [and thus] returned to the abode of the Buddha.'[67] Yet another incidence appears in the previously cited fifteenth-century *Pararaton* episode, which reports the popular tradition that the king of Kadiri, facing defeat at the hands of Majapahit's alliance became invisible and disappeared from the earth. The diverse Java religious traditions took different approaches to the possibilities implied by invisibility. For example, according to the fifteenth-century *Panji Margasmarakidung* poem, when the Kadiri court fell to the Majapahit alliance around 1300, the Kadiri court's monarch magically disappeared as his forces were defeated by Majapahit's army. The assumption of the subsequent *Panji Margasmara* authors, consistent with the previous *Pararaton* and the *kakawin* Javanese literary traditions, was that the Kadiri monarch had become a divine. By contrast, in stories reported in the *Babad Tanah Jawi*, the invisible Mataram monarch later reappeared in his court, consistent with the Islamic belief that he was merely a divinely empowered human rather than a divine himself.[68]

Textual communities in pre-1500 Java: a concluding overview

Thus, the realm characterised in the stories of the variety of post-Majapahit Islamic literary sources are much the same as those depicted in the traditional pre-Islamic Java Hindu-Buddhist-era literary sources. It is a Javanese world, indeed a Javanese textual community, which is peopled with an established set of symbols, powers, meanings and spiritual entities. This community recorded its ideals and realities in texts and then used those texts to define its past, present and future socially, economically and politically. These historical sources collectively expressed the values approved and expected of its community leaders (or at least the values expected of its leaders whether or not they were deserved). These literary sources also expressed the social mores and standards governing relations both within and beyond the community.

Java textual communities conceived of key individuals who possessed a combination of religious, philosophical and mystical experiences that derived from commonly understood mythological and supernatural beliefs, which were rooted in an animistic past overlaid with Hinduism and Buddhism and later Islam. So important were these collective beliefs to the Javanese community that even the highly educated defined themselves with reference to the mystical and supernatural. It was commonly accepted, furthermore, that ghosts, devils and other Java spirits possessed the power to aid or hurt wider humanity. These spiritual forces were not thought of as absolute good and evil opposites but rather as having the capacity to ensure success or lead to failure.

Throughout the Java centuries, there continued to be a parallel substratum of mysticism officiated by local *resi* clerics. This ritualised Javanese mysticism remained aloof from the Hindu, Buddhist and Islamic textual communities, regarding traditional oral tradition as superior and possessing the 'true secrets' to salvation and other desired communal values. Combining a strong sense of mythology with a deeply-rooted animism encouraged belief in personal superiority and invulnerability; this mystical tradition nevertheless drew on a different sense of time and place than that of the West. In the Javanese way of thinking, all that existed had its own qualities and its own course through time. Events did not occur by accident but were due to the coincidence of multiple cycles of days, months and years in the Javanese calendar.[69] Even a person's existence was thought to be cyclical, emanating from a point of harmony and returning to a point of symmetry, regardless of what occurs in the middle.

However, it should be noted that the evolution of Javanese culture was not a mere matter of an exchange of Indian Ocean regional ideas. Indeed, this study has explored the effects of the twin forces of external contact and internal development, as evidenced in the progressive evolution of Java's textual and oral traditions. The views collectively expressed by the local populations in their temple iconography, inscriptions, chronicles, literary texts and archaeological remains suggest that by the end of this transitional era from Hindu-Buddhist monarchies to Islamic sultanates, and from previous upstream agricultural societies to global marketplaces, Java villagers, lords and monarchs were collectively participants in a common discourse that defined the organisation and meaning of their world and the types of authority appropriate to it. Though their regional networks were partially enabled by gifts, conquests, constructions and economic alliances, ultimately there was common societal participation in a hierarchical system that was intimately related to the rituals and ceremonies that originated with or were validated by past and present courts. All members of this society were collectively potential reciprocal participants in the offerings made and ceremonies performed on their behalf by lords and/or clerical ritual specialists.[70]

Many other aspects of the traditional Javanese religious mind-set went well beyond formal devotion to the celestial divine and instead embraced traditional animism. Whether under the spiritual guidance of an Indic priest, a Buddhist monk, an Islamic cleric or a local *resi* spiritual intercessionary, it was common for Javanese to practice fasting, prayer and meditation (*tapa, shahada*) in hopes of acquiring ascetic or supernatural power (*sakti, siddhi, kasekten*) that, in theory, one's personal powers might even equal those of the gods. These still common beliefs and practices in Java have mixed Indic, Muslim and local roots, drawing on the *Mahabharata* and *Ramayana* epic tales and India's popular *Pancatantra* moral fables and later on Sufi Islamic texts in their localised versions and elaborations.

In the Indic-inspired traditions, Java's rulers were descended from the gods and received *wahyutjakaraningrat*, godlike empowerment. The monarch was in one sense the gods' representative on earth and in another was himself a god who was temporarily mortal (an *avatara*) but who would return to his divine state at death. Similarly, whether as a *bodhisattva* in the Buddhist tradition or a *wali sanga* 'saint' in the Javanese Islamic tradition, the monarch achieved purity in his secular existence in order to transition to the next. Thus, the monarch not only focused on his own spiritual fortunes but also devoted himself to assisting his fellow humankind in their quest for earthly prosperity and a propitious life after death.

Furthermore, since a monarch spoke on the behalf of the gods, what he spoke could be nothing other than the truth, and whatever he did, even if questionable to the human mind, it was always right, since a monarch's actions were part of a divine plan. For this reason, the various titles and names bestowed by the monarch were symbolic statements that the recipients partook in the divine by means of their relationship to the monarch. In theory, the monarch ultimately delivered his subjects from suffering in this world that they might enter the glory of eternity, and to merit royal favours was to participate at least partly in the achievement of that goal.

According to Java religious texts, various material goods – both local and from abroad – were incorporated into royal and religious rituals and then redistributed to participants and witnesses as appropriate to their ritual status. Rulers and ritual specialists possessed the knowledge and provided the authority and prestige to back this system of material symbolism, through their participation in periodic ritualised redistributions in which elites and commoners demonstrated their subordination to their monarchs and clergy by their acceptance of symbolic beneficence. The most successful rulers rewarded loyalty and ability with recorded material or symbolic gifts and accordingly protected their collective followers from the misfortunes of this world and the destructive retributions of the chthonic and celestial universes.

Yet, at least in the inscriptions and chronicles, the monarchs were not directly punitive toward those who failed to participate in royal initiatives, for such was the assumed relationship between ruler and the supernatural that, if the monarchs did not punish wrongdoers, the divine would. Thus, to reject royal authority was to expose oneself to the unpredictability of natural forces, fate, external threat and retribution by the spirits and the divine. The monarch was said to have cosmic hegemony over life and death and, in theory, unlimited omnipotence, and the ruler passed some of this on to those who assisted in his community leadership. By their participation in religious and secular ritual practices and court ceremony, the monarch's networked subordinates shared in his link with the supernatural and thus mutually affirmed the status hierarchy implicit in the communal system and replicated the monarch's gifting in their outreach to their local dependents.

Revisionist scholarship has redefined traditional literacy as being more than the transmission of knowledge in print or script and instead embraces the notion that knowledge of the written word in traditional religious and secular texts did not necessarily translate into readership. But the alternative knowledge transfers based in traditional textual transmission in oral recitations or in dramatic, musical and dance rituals allowed the illiterate and semi-literate public to share these written texts in communal reading sessions, religious ceremonies and dramatic and musical performances.[71]

Thus contemporary scholars study regional written texts, inscriptions and iconographic portrayals of texts at temples in Java and wider maritime Southeast Asia, as these have emerged from rich pre-print literary written and oral traditions. Long-standing oral renditions of texts continued in both formal and informal settings, as the initial texts were widely sung, read and performed, adding to the text body movements, facial expressions, languages, musical traditions and contextual practices that connected the pre-printed literary forms – notably *lontar* palm leaf texts that remain the source of oral recitations. Against the Western notion that literary consumption was done through private reading and study, in Java and elsewhere in contemporary Southeast Asia, there is still a range of performing arenas from households to wider public spaces (including television) that connect performance and other representations of textual matter in ways that allow variable consumption of sacred texts and historical chronicles. This continuity of the oral drama, dance and pre-print traditions prevents the written text from being fixed, as multiple reading, recitation and consumptive practices encouraged personal appropriations that still shape Southeast Asia's popular literary marketplace.

In sum, this study is based in a comparative study of the distinctive knowledge transfer characteristics of Java's evolving literary traditions – from the culminating Hindu-Buddhist era of dynastic sovereignty portrayed in the fourteenth-century *Nagarakertagma* chronicle during the formative years of the Majapahit court to the fifteenth-century *Pararaton*, which characterises the Majapahit court during its decline. From the late fifteenth century, the transition to Islamic sultanates is recorded in the *Babad* literature initiated by the new downstream Islamic courts. These innovative Islamic texts legitimised the transition of dynastic power from Java's upstream wet-rice agricultural centres to its subsequent downstream multi-cultural Islamic port-of-trade marketplaces that had regular international engagements. The multiple north coast Islamic port-polity marketplaces superseded the power of the previous upstream courts as portrayed in the seventeenth-century *Babad* chronicle poems composed by Islamic clerics at the original downstream sultanate courts. Eventually, downstream courts were displaced by the new Mataram sultanate court in the productive central Java upstream near modern-day Yogyakarta, which was nearby the earlier foundational centres of Javanese Hindu-Buddhist spiritual and textual tradition at Prambanan and Borobudur.

This study has examined the tensions of network and hierarchy intersections in Java, consequent to Java's evolution from an agricultural economy to one substantively engaged in international trade and the consequent transitions in political authority as these linked with Java's religious evolutions from local spirit worship to Hindu-Buddhism and subsequent Islam. Herein, early Java society benefited from networked upstream-downstream agricultural network commodity flows, as later Java ports-of-trade would depend on the exchanges of a variety of local and international products and knowledge transfers in their downstream marketplaces and courts.

While in previous scholarship, I have focused on the knowledge transfers related to the Indonesian archipelago's role in international maritime trade relative to the movement of goods and people, which enhanced regional networking – as this influenced the strategic placement of political and economic centres,[72] this study has considered the importance of networked literary flows as recited, studied and performed consequent to Java's religious transition from Hindu-Buddhism to Islam. Herein, religious change was a factor in the destabilisation and challenge to Java's early societal hierarchy that was based in Hindu-Buddhist theology. One can argue that Java's transition from a generally steady rice-based agricultural society to one of mixed economic pursuits, coincident to Java's evolving role as a major marketing centre in the vibrant eastern international maritime trade network, was a substantive factor in Java's acceptance of Islam.

Islam had its origin in the cosmopolitan trading societies of the Middle East and was not based in a definitive agricultural social order. Hindu-Buddhist knowledge networks were foundational to Java's evolving wet-rice socio-economy that supported early state-building based in localisations of Indic conceptions of a consistently ordered agrarian public. Java's initial ritualised upstream courts were inadequate to sustain Java's transition to a new marketplace-oriented society that was more open to social mobility, and subsequent Java society fragmented. New downstream courts embraced

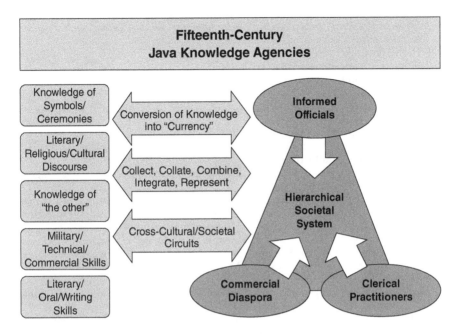

Figure 4.3 Java knowledge agencies, c. 1500

Islam, a 'marketplace faith' with significant ideational linkage to internationalism (symbolised in the egalitarian pilgrimage to Mecca as the culminating Islamic worship experience with subsequent hierarchical religious consequences) over provincialism provided the opportunity for resolution of Java's post-Majapahit-era societal fragmentation. Herein, this study has focused on the kinds of structures and intersections that characterised Java in the 1400–1600 era, as summarised in the concluding following flow chart (see Figure 4.3), which highlights the pivotal role of three knowledgeable intermediary agencies (informed officials, commercial agents and religious clerics) as 'wise practitioners' in Java's fifteenth-century era of societal transition.

Notes

1 Stuart O. Robson, *Desawarnana: (Nagarakertagama) by Mpu Prapanca*, 85 (Leiden, Netherlands: KITLV, 1995); Robson, "Thailand in an Old Javanese Source," *BKI*, 153.3 (1997): 434.
2 Louise Levathes, *The Treasure Fleet of the Dragon Throne, 1403–1433*, 99, 104, 118ff, 120(New York: Oxford University Press, 1994); J.V.G Mills, trans., *Ma Huan, Ying yai sheng lan (The Overall Survey of the Ocean Shores First Published in 1451)* (Cambridge: Cambridge University Press for the Hakluyt Society, 1970).

3 Lydia Kieven, *Following the Cap-Figure in Majapahit Temple Reliefs: A New Look at the Religious Function of East Javanese Temples, Fourteenth and Fifteenth Centuries*(Leiden: KITLV, 2013).

4 Hermann Kulke, "Epigraphical References to the 'City' and the 'State' in Early Indonesia," *Indonesia* 52 (1991): 3–22.

5 This expedition is mentioned in the *Nagarakertagama* (41.5) and in the subsequent *Kidung Harsa-Wijaya*, as discussed in Ann R. Kinney, *Worshipping Siva and Buddha: The Temple Art of East Java*, 124, 157 (Honolulu: University of Hawaii Press, 2003).

6 Robson, *Nagarakertagama*, 34.

7 A.H. Hill, "The *Hikayat Raja-Raja Pasai*, The Chronicles of the Kings of Pasai," *JMBRAS* 33.2 (1960): 161.

8 J.J. Ras, *Hikayat Bandjar: A Study in Malay Historiography*, 424–5 (The Hague: Martinus Nijhoff, 1968).

9 A. Teeuw, "Hikayat Raja Pasai and Sejarah Melayu," in *Malayan and Indonesian Studies*, edited by J. Bastin and R. Roolvink, 222–34 (Oxford: Oxford University Press, 1964); R. Roolvink, "The Variant Versions of the Malay Annals," *BKI* 123 (1967): 310–29; and S. Supomo, "The Image of Majapahit in Later Javanese and Indonesian Writing," in *Perceptions of the Past in Southeast Asia*, edited by Anthony Reid and David Marr, 171–85 (Singapore: Heinemann Educational Books (Asia), 1979).

10 J.J. Ras, "Sacral Kingship in Java," in *Fruits of Inspiration*, edited by Hermann Kulke et al., 373–88 (Groningen, The Netherlands: Egbert Forstein, 2001).

11 M.C. Ricklefs, *Seen and Unseen Worlds in Java, 1726–1749: History, Literature, and Islam in the Court of Pakabuwana II*, 5–16 (Honolulu: University of Hawaii Press, 1998); Supomo, *loc. cit.*

12 Roderich Ptak, "From Quanzhou to the Sulu Zone and Beyond: Questions Related to the Early Fourteenth Century," *Journal of the American Oriental Society* 113 (1993): 269–94; Roderich Ptak, "The Northern Trade Route to the Spice Islands: South China Sea-Sulu Zone-North Moluccas (14th to Early 16th Century)," *Archipel* 43 (1992): 27–56.

13 Kinney, *Worshipping Siva and Buddha*, 218, figure 197; John N. Miksic and Endang Sri Hardiati Soekatno, eds., *The Legacy of Majapahit* (Singapore: National Heritage Board, 1995), notably the cover photo of Majapahit royal symbol.

14 Thomas R. Trautmann, *Elephants and Kings, an Environmental History*, 261–97 (Chicago: University of Chicago Press, 2015); Michael Charney, *Southeast Asian Warfare, 1300–1900*, Handbook of Oriental Studies, South-East Asia, Section 3, vol. 16 (Leiden: Brill, 2004).

15 O.W. Wolters, "A Few Miscellaneous Pi-chi Jottings on Early Indonesia," *Indonesia, 36* (October 1983): 46–62, Ithaca, New York: Cornell University Press, 1983, 60, n. 54.

16 Hall, *History of Early Southeast Asia*, 275–80.

17 Kenneth R. Hall, "The Early Historical Texts, Breaking into Them and Breaking Out of Them: A Case Study of the Old Javanese Pararaton," in *Texts and Contexts in Southeast Asia, Part 2*, 1–18 (Yangon, Mynamar: Universities Historical Research Center, 2003).

18 Derek Heng, *Sino-Malay Trade and Diplomacy from the Tenth Through the Fourteenth Century*, 72–110 (Athens, OH: Ohio University Press, 2009); Derek Heng, "State-Formation and Socio-Political Structure of the Malay Coastal Region in the Late Thirteenth to Early Fifteenth Centuries" (2018); Rila Mukherjee, "The Indian Ocean world of Srivijaya" (2018).

19 O.W. Wolters, *The Fall of Srivijaya in Malay History*, 113–14 (Kuala Lumpur: Oxford University Press, 1970).

20 Robson, *Nagarakertagama*, 59.

21 George Coedes, *The Indianized States of Southeast Asia* (Honolulu: University of Hawaii Press, 1968), 234, citing N.J. Krom, *Hindoe-Javaansche Geschiedenis*, 391 (The Hague: Nijhoff, 1931); and the *Nagarakertagama*. Slametmuljana, *A Story of Majapahit*, 61 (Singapore: Singapore University Press, 1976).

22 Robson, *Nagarakertagama*, 76.

23 Helen Creese, *In Search of Majapahit: The Transformation of Balinese Identities*, 8 (Monash: Centre for South and Southeast Asian Studies, 1997).

24 Creese, *In Search of Majapahit*. A Javanese nobleman, Sri Aji Kresna Kepakisan, the grandson of a Brahmin, was installed as the Majapahit's vassal monarch (*raja*) of Bali based at Samprangan in the Gianyar regency. Subsequently In the next generation the seat of the *raja* moved to Gelgel in the Klungkung regency, which became a strong semi-independent regional court. When Majapahit collapsed Gelgel became the heir to classical Javanese civilization. Hans Hägerdal, "Bali in the Sixteenth and Seventeenth Centuries; Suggestions for a Chronology of the Gelgel Period," *Bijdragen tot de Taal-, Land- en Volkenkunde* 151 (1995): 101–24. See Kenneth R. Hall, "The Initial Acceptance of Islam in Southeast Asia," *JESHO* 44 (2001): 198–219, on the Majapahit legacy in fifteenth-century Samudra-Pasai; and Kenneth R. Hall, *Java's Evolving Military History in the 10th–15th Centuries: Evidence of Contemporary Iron Imports as Documented in Shipwrecks, Epigraphy, and Literary Records* (Hong Kong: Hong Kong City Museum, 2018).

25 G. Coedes, *The Indianized States of Southeast Asia* (Canberra: Australian National University Press, 1975); D.G.E. Hall, *History of South East Asia* (London: Macmillan & Co. Ltd., 1955); M.C. Ricklefs, *A History of Modern Indonesia* (Bloomington, IN: 1981).

26 Several of these involved new practices that had arisen in the fifteenth century. These included the new Saivite ritual known as 'The Night of Siwa' (A. Teeuw et al., *Siwaratrikalpa kakawin*, 19–23 (The Hague: Bibliotheca Indonesica, 1969) which was borrowed from Vijayanagara, the most prominent political centre in southern India at that time. In Teeuw's view, the initiation of this ritual not only reflected Java's strong south Indian (Keling) ties, but also reasserted traditional Indic ritual in the face of new Islamic developments. As previously noted, the *Nagarakertagama* (canto 93) reports a south Indian connection – see Robson's commentary, p. 148. Robson asserts that *the Rama Keling*, the Javanese version of the Malay *Hikayat Seri Rama*, is a product of the fifteenth century and reflects Java and Melaka's south Indian connections [Stuart Robson, "Java at the Crossroads, Aspects of Javanese Cultural History in the 14th and 15th Centuries." *BKI* 137(1981): 284–5]. These, as well as the *Serat Menak Amir Hamzah*, which is a standard in the repertoire of the Javanese *wayang golek*; and the *Kidiung Aji Darma*, which may have been written at the fifteenth-century Majapahit court [G.W.J. Drewes, *The Romance of King Angling Darma in Javanese Literature*, 45–7 (The Hague: Bibliotheca Indonesica, 11, 1975); L.F. Brakel, *The Story of Muhammad Hanafiyyah, A Medieval Muslim Romance* (The Hague: Bibliotheca Indonesica 16, 1977), all reflect the complicated cultural connections between the fifteenth- and sixteenth-century Javanese, Malay, and south Indian cultural realms.

27 Anthony Day, "Islam and Literature in South-East Asia," in *Islam in South-East Asia*, edited by M. B. Hooker, 130–59 (Leiden: Brill, 1983); H.J. de Graff and T.G. Th. Pigeaud, *Islamic States in Java, 1500–1700* (The Hague: Martinus

Nijhoff, 1976); G.W.J. Drewes and L.F. Brakel, *The Poems of Hamzah Fansuri* (Dordrecht: Foris, 1986); T.G. Th. Pigeaud, *Literature of Java: Catalogue Raisonne of Javanese Manuscripts in the Library of the University of Leiden and Other Public Collections in The Netherlands*, 3 vols. (The Hague: KITLV, 1967–1997); M.C. Ricklefs, *A History of Modern Southeast Asia, c. 1300-Present*, 49–52 (Bloomington, IN: Indiana University Press, 1981); M.C. Ricklefs, "Babad Sangkala and the Javanese Sense of History," *Archipel* 55 (1998): 125–40.

28 See Pierre-Yves Manguin, "The Merchant and the King: Political Myths of Southeast Asian Coastal Polities," *Indonesia* 52 (1991): 41–54, on the sea trade residents on Java's north coast in the sixteenth century.

29 Pierre-Yves Manguin, "The Amorphous Nature of Coastal Polities in Insular Southeast Asia: Restricted Centers, Extended Peripheries," *Moussons* 4 (2002): 73–99.

30 Elizabeth Lambourn, "From Cambay to Samudra-Pasai and Gresik – the Export of Gujarat Grave Memorials to Sumatra and Java in the Fifteenth Century," *Indonesia and the Malay World* 31 (July 2003): 221–80; Elizabeth Lambourn, "Tombstones, Texts, and Typologies – Seeing Sources for the Early History of Islam in Southeast Asia," *JESHO* 52.2 (2008): 252–86.

31 Tansen Sen, *Buddhism, Diplomacy, and Trade, the Realignment of Sino-Indian Relations, 600–1400* (Honolulu: University of Hawaii Press, 2003).

32 Kenneth R. Hall, "Ritual Networks and Royal Power in Majapahit Java," *Archipel* 52 (1996): 95–118; Kenneth R. Hall, "Ritual Transitions and Kingship in Fifteenth-Century Java: A View from the Candi Panataran Complex," in *Structure and Society in Early South India, Essays in Honour of Noboru Karashima*, edited by Kenneth R. Hall, 276–312 (New Delhi: Oxford University Press, 2001).

33 Anthony Johns, "From Buddhism to Islam: An Interpretation of the Javanese Literature of the Transition," *Comparative Studies in Society and History* 9 (1966–1967): 40–50.

34 The tombstones date 1376, 1380, 1407, 1418, 1427, 1458, 1467 (2), 1469 and 1475; 1458 has an inscriptional reference to Putri Cempa; 1407, 1427, 1467 and 1475 belong to one family. The earliest of the tombstones of court aristocrats bear the Majapahit court's sun symbol, which is accompanied by the guardian-deities of the nine sacred directions, as the entitlement of a court elite. For comparison with similar entitlements of Straits of Melaka court elite, see Heng, "State-Formation and Socio-Political Structure of the Malay Coastal Region."

35 "Petak Inscription of 1486"; J. Noorduyn, "Majapahit in the Fifteenth Century," *BKI* 134.2–3 (1978): 244–53.

36 Geoff Wade, "The Zeng He Voyages: A Reassessment," *Journal of the Malaysian Branch of the Royal Asiatic Society* 78.1 (2005): 3–58; Geoff Wade, "Early Muslim Expansion in South-East Asia, Eighth to Fifteenth Centuries," in *The New Cambridge History of Islam Volume 3: The Eastern Islamic World, Eleventh to Eighteenth Centuries*, edited by David O. Morgan and Anthony Reid, 366–408 (Cambridge: Cambridge University Press, 2010); A. Cortesao, *A Translation of the Suma Oriental of Tome Pires, an Account of the East from the Red Sea to Japan. Written in Malacca and India in 1512–1513* (London: Hakluyt Society, 1944).

37 More on the episode can also be found in Robert Wessing, "Á Princess from Sunda, Some Aspects of *Nyai Roro Kidul*," *Asian Folklore Studies* 56 (1997): 317–53; also Robert Wessing, "Spirits of the Earth and Spirits of Water: Chthonic Forces in the Mountains of West Java," *Asian Folklore Studies* 47 (1988): 43–61; and Robert Wessing, "*Sri* and *Sedana* and *Sita* and *Rama*: Myths

and History in West Java," *Asian Folklore Studies* 42 (1990): 235–57, relative to the localizations of the Indic tradition in west Java.

38 The notion of a collective "resident" Islamic community contrasts to the alternative of assorted individual Muslims who were contracting their services to the court. Minimally one would expect that the Muslim population at the court would gather for Friday prayers, but there is no record thereof. See Robson, "Java at the Crossroads," 278; and Jan Wisseman Christie, "Javanese Markets and the Asian Sea Trade Boom of the Tenth to Thirteenth Centuries AD," *JESHO* 41.3 (1998): 364–78, who makes the case that Java courts traditionally treated "foreigners" as individuals dependent on the court, to limit their potential to form collectives and to especially limit their interactions with the Java countryside.

39 Hill, "*Hikayat Raja-Raja Pasai,*" 159.

40 J.J. Ras, *Hikayat Bandjar, a Study in Malay Historiography*, 419 (Gravenhage: Nijhoff, 1968). See also J.J. Ras, "The Panji Romance and W. W. Rasser's Analysis of the Theme," *BKI* 129 (1973): 411–56, as he explores the role of the *Panji* tales in the transitional localizing of Majapahit court culture in downstream southeast Borneo/Kalimantan.

41 Heng, "State-Formation and Socio-Political Structure of the Malay Coastal Region."

42 In the Western Archipelago, local dress changed with the Islamic conversions. Muslim men began to wear pants or trousers, and women began to cover their breasts. In Java, traditional tailored men's and women's skirts, robes, coats, shirts, and jackets became popular among the elite. Most of such stylized cloth was made from imported textiles, because of their high quality and general availability, but also because of continuing fears that locally produced cloth was spiritually possessed; popular belief held that cutting imported cloth rather than locally woven textiles minimized personal danger. M. Gittinger, *Spendid Symbols: Textiles and Traditions in Indonesia*, 28–31 (Washington, DC: The Metropolitan Museum of Art, 1979); see also Kenneth R. Hall, "The Textile Industry in Southeast Asia, 1400–1800," *JESHO* 39.2 (1996): 87–135; and Kenneth R. Hall, "The 15th-Century Gujarat Cloth Trade with Southeast Asia's Indonesian Archipelago," in *Gujarat and the Sea*, edited by Lotika Varadarajan, 439–66 (Greater Noida: Darshak Itihas Nidhi, 2012).

43 Leonard Andaya, "Aceh's Contributions to Standards of Malayness," *Archipel* 61 (2001): 29–68.

44 Soemarsaid Moertono, *State and Statecraft in Old Java: A Study of the Later Mataram Period, 16th to 19th Century* (Ithaca, NY: Cornell University Southeast Asia Program, 1968).

45 M.C. Ricklefs, *The Seen and Unseen Worlds in Java, 1726–1749* (Honolulu: University of Hawaii Press, 1998). My Gadjah Mada University faculty colleagues in 2003–2004 debated these points. In parallel to that earlier period focal in this study, contemporary Javanese have been most attracted to those aspects of the 20th-century Islamic renewal movements that focus on ritual (what my colleagues refer to as "Arabizing") rather than on the intellectual traditions of "international Islam." Rather than focusing on the ideas, or what some Muslims call the "essence" of Islam, most Javanese devotees focus primarily on the observance of the rituals themselves, including such things as devotedly praying five times a day, taking the *Haj*, observing *purdah*, and diligently observing the month of Ramadan. See John Bowen, "Islamic Transformations: From Sufi Doctrine to Ritual Practice in Gayo Culture," in *Religion in Indonesia*, edited by Rita Kipp and Susan Rogers, 113–35 (Tuscan, AZ: University of Arizona Press, 1992), who develops parallel themes relative to more northern Sumatra society. It is also

notable that in the early 2000s, there were strong political sentiments against proposals to ground civil society more deeply in international Islamic orthodoxy, viewing such moves as a betrayal of Javanese Islam, selling out its ritualized traditions and community to the intellectualism of "international" Islam.

46 As may be remembered, these *mandalas* were Indic-inspired religious communities whose shrines were administered by a local *resi* ritualist; and in the 15th century, these communities and shrines were playing an especially prominent role in Javanese popular religion.

47 See for example the incorporation of the nine Lokapalas in the Majapahit court's sun symbol, as they connect the sun source to the receptive society.

48 For example, just before the month of Ramadan begins, Javanese Muslims still make pilgrimages to the graves of the *wali sanga*, both as acts of religious devotion and spiritual cleansing and as opportunities to mystically bond with the *wali sanga*.

49 That the princess was an actual person is documented by her gravestone, dated 1458, at the Tralaya Majapahit court site.

50 George Coedes, *The Indianized States of Southeast Asia*, 217 (Honolulu: University of Hawaii Press, 1968), reports an even earlier Champa contact: the Cham king Jaya Simhavarman III married a Javanese princess named Tapasi at the beginning of the 14th century. Furthermore, in 1318, a Cham king was defeated by the Vietnamese and thereafter took refuge in Java (Coedes: 229). Early Cham connections, not all of them Islamic, are confirmed in the Nagarakertagama, as reported earlier, as well as in the Java *Babad* sources. The *Sejarah Melayu* documents the marriage of a Cham king to a Javanese princess when it speaks of the end of the Cham kingdom, after the Chams were widely scattered following their defeat by the Vietnamese around 1471. In this chronicle account, two sons of the Cham king escaped; one went to Aceh and the other to Melaka. The Cham refugees were received in Melaka by Sultan Mansu (1459–1477), who told them to embrace Islam, which they did – there is no evidence of their prior conversion. See, however, Pierre-Yves Manguin for evidence of early Cham Islamic communities as these relate to the early Cham-Javanese ties in Manguin, "L'introduction de l'Islam au Campa," *BEFEO* 66 (1979): 255–69; also Anthony Reid, "Chams in the Southeast Asian Maritime System," in *Charting the Shape of Early Modern Southeast Asia*, edited by Anthony Reid (Singapore: Institute of Southeast Asian Studies, 2000), 39–55; and Rie Nakamura, "The Coming of Islam to Champa," *JMBRAS* 73.1 (2000): 55–66.

51 Peter Riddell, *Islam and the Malay-Indonesian World: Transmission and Response* (Singapore: Horizon Books, 2001); A.H. Johns, "On Qur'anic Exegetes and Exegesis," in *Islam: Essays on Scripture, Thought, and Society*, edited by Peter Riddell and Tony Street, 3–49 (Leiden: E. J. Brill, 1997).

52 Cortesao, *The Suma Oriental of Tome Pires (1515)*, II, 166–200; see also Ma Huan's account of the "Java Coastline and the Majapahit Realm c. 1430," in *Ying-yai Sheng-lan, the Overall Survey of the Ocean's Shores*, translated by J.V.G. Mills, 86–97 (London: Cambridge University Press, 1970); A.H. Hill, "The Chronicles of the Kings of Pasai," *JMBRAS* 33.2 (1960): 116–19; Kenneth R. Hall, "Upstream and Downstream Unification in Southeast Asia's First Islamic Polity: The Changing Sense of Community in the Fifteenth Century Hikayat Raja-Raja Pasai Court Chronicle," *JESHO* 44.2 (2001): 198–229.

53 Heng, "State Formation and Social Structure."

54 A.H. Hill, "The Chronicles of the Kings of Pasai," *JMBRAS* 33.2 (1960): 116–19.

55 M.C. Ricklefs, "Six Centuries of Islamization in Java," in *Conversion to Islam*, edited by Nehemia Levtzion, 100–28 (New York: Holmes and Meir, 1979).

IDENTITIES, NETWORKING AND CONVERSIONS

56 The best summary of this conversion process is in Jean Gelman Taylor, *Indonesia: Peoples and Histories*, 21 (New Haven: Yale University Press, 2003).

57 These Islamic north coast ports replaced Tuban, which had been Majapahit's preeminent port. In the *kakawin* and *kidung* literature, this was the place from which naval expeditions departed, and it was also the place visited by the diplomatic missions of foreigners and the place where assorted foreign merchants arrived and departed. See Pierre-Yves Manguin, "The Vanishing Jong: Insular Southeast Asian Fleets in Trade and War (Fifteenth to Seventeenth Centuries)," in *Southeast Asia in the Early Modern Era, Trade, Power, and Belief*, edited by Anthony Reid, 197–213 (Ithaca, NY: Cornell University Press, 1993); Pierre-Yves Manguin, "Trading Ships of the South China Sea, Shipbuilding Techniques and their Role in the History of the Development of Asian Trade Networks," *JESHO* 36 (1994): 253–80.

58 Anthony Reid, "The Rise and Fall of Sino-Javanese Shipping," in *Charting the Shape*, edited by Anthony Reid, 56–84 (Singapore: Institute of Southeast Asian Studies, 2000).

59 See S. Supomo, "From Sakti to Shahada, the Quest for New Meanings in a Changing World Order," in *Islam: Essays on Scripture, Thought, and Society*, edited by Peter Riddell and Tony Street, 232–4 (Leiden: E. J. Brill, 1997), on the magical roots of Demak. There is an alternative tale of its founding based on a conversion myth that attributes its origin to the intervention of the *wali sanga* who support the shift of power from Majaphit to Demak, because Raden Patah has been empowered by the Divine.

60 M.C. Ricklefs, "A Consideration of Three Versions of the *Babad Tanah Djawi*, with Excerpts on the Fall of Madjapahit," *BSOAS* 35.2 (1972): 285–97; Rickelfs, "The Evolution of *Babad Tanah Jawi Texts*," *BKI* 135 (1979): 443–54.

61 S. Supomo, "From Sakti to Shahada, The Quest for New Meanings in a Changing World Order," 219–236. See especially 230–236, in which Supomo discusses the transition of the pre-Islamic Javanese sense of meditative empowerment (*sakti*) to an understanding of supernatural energy (*kasekten sahada*) that is achieved by reciting Arabic verses, which had become the alternative to invoking Hindu and Buddhist deities using Sanskrit *mantras*.

62 This formal acknowledgement of the primary ruler's sovereignty is still practiced annually at the Yogyakarta court. At the end of the month of Ramadan, the Sultan of Yogakarta receives his family members and other courtiers in a ritual that culminates in the proclamation of loyalty by the courtier from a kneeling position, with one's head placed in the lap of the Sultan, and the verbal request that the Sultan forgive his loyal subjects for their various sins during the past year. A parallel ritual is carried out in Muslim families, where at the end of the month of Ramadan, family members return to their homes and in hierarchical order – males in order of their birth followed by daughters (married daughters before unmarried daughters) and then grandchildren by age (males before females) – approach their father on their knees, lay their heads in his lap, admit their sins from the past year, and ask for their father's forgiveness. This annual ritual is taken very seriously and is a powerful symbolic statement that renews and celebrates the family. My Indonesian friends have told me that their willingness to participate in this ritual is an important means of resolving family differences. In several cases in which the parents and their child had not been on speaking terms, even for years, the willingness of the child to participate in this annual ritual and the parent's reciprocal ritual proclamation of forgiveness was sufficient to clear the issues of the past and reopen the parent-child relationship without further discussion.

63 This episode has a Tantric Buddhist foundation. The thunderbolt, the symbol of Tantric power, could represent the retribution of the Indic gods, a statement of their continuing capacity to inflict harm and symbolically denoting their termination of their prior partnership with the Javanese people and specifically with the Majapahit court.

64 Kenneth R. Hall, "European Southeast Asia Encounters with Islamic Expansionism, Circa 1500–1700: Comparative Case Studies of Banten, Ayutthaya, and Banjarmasin in the Wider Indian Ocean Context," *Journal of World History* 25.2-3 (2014): 229–62.

65 Such a capacity for invisibility in times of crisis is a literary convention if not a widely accepted belief that was a common attribute of Java's kings, as was the case in the *Negarakertagama* account of the fall of the Kadiri's court to Majapahit's forces at the end of the thirteenth century.

66 Stuart Robson, ed. and trans., *Arjunawiwaha: The Marriage of Arjuna of Mpu Kanwa* (Leiden: KITLV, 2008).

67 *Nagarakertagama, 43.5, 44.1* (Robson, 56).

68 Stuart Robson, "Notes on the Early Kidung Literature," *BKI* 135 (1979): 300–22.

69 See J. Noorduyn, "Some Remarks on Javanese Chronogram Words: A Case of Localization," *BKI* 149 (1993): 298–317; Shelly Errington, *Meaning and Power in a Southeast Asian Realm* (Princeton: Princeton University Press, 1989).

70 In the *Bharatayuda kakawin*, lords were those who "partook of the garden," in contrast to commoners who were too earthbound to effectively enjoy its beauty. Commoners could only grasp for the physical possession of one of the court's flowers, which would shortly wither and die. Unlike humankind, these physical objects of worldly beauty could not pass on to another realm of existence. See also A.M. Barrett-Jones, *Early Tenth Century Java from the Inscriptions, a Study of Economic, Social, and Administrative Conditions in the First Quarter of the Century*, 59–90 (Dordrecht: Foris Publications, 1984).

71 Ilicia Sprey, "Indic Model and Javanese Adaptation: The Evolution of *Wayang Kulit* (Shadow Puppet) Theatre in Indonesia from 'Pre-History' Until the Sixteenth Century," 405–420; and Kenneth R. Hall, "Knowledge Networks, Literary Adaptations, and the 'Sanskrit Cosmopolis' in Fifteenth Century Java," in *India and Southeast Asia: Cultural Discourses*, edited by Anna L. Dallapiccola and Anila Verghese, 361–404 (Mumbai: K. R. Cama Oriental Institute, 2017).

72 Kenneth R. Hall, "Indonesia's Evolving International Relationships in the Ninth to Early Eleventh Centuries: Evidence from Contemporary Shipwrecks and Epigraphy," *Indonesia* 90 (October 2010): 15–46.

5

BROKERS AND GO-BETWEENS WITHIN THE PORTUGUESE STATE OF INDIA (1500–1700)

Amélia Polónia

Empire-building depends on regional and central powers, and the role of traditional monarchies and modern states in the construction of overseas empires is undeniable. Such empires, in terms of administrative control and military organisation, required complex logistics and substantial financial capacity, not readily available to individuals or isolated groups. The complex systems produced and coordinated by central powers often depended on informal networks based on cooperation from individuals and non-state actors. Therefore, historians must explore the performance of the latter working in favour of, or even sometimes against, government policies and procedures to understand informal ways of building overseas empires. Global interactions based on self-organizing networks becomes essential for our understanding of those dynamics that transcended political, religious and economic frontiers.

> There is a growing consensus that most of the European empires overseas were profitable and successful due to the intervention of individuals or groups of individuals engaged in the common good of the social and economic networks they served. More often than not, these self-organized, trans-imperial, cross-cultural networks imposed serious challenges to State, Church and Monopolistic institutions, since they were the source of most of the illegal and contraband transactions world-wide, but they were also the ones that within, or in collaboration with the institutions actually became agents of empire building.[1]
>
> (Antunes and Polónia 2012)

The case of the Jesuits in Japan emerges as symptomatic of this trend: agents of institutionalised networks, ruled by the Roman church and one of the most powerful and well-structured religious orders of the time, introduced in the East by the Portuguese crown itself, they were part of the formal setup of empire building. Nonetheless, their presence in Japan depended frequently on cooperation with local landlords. A process of cultural assimilation and widespread behaviour of cheating and defection – to the Portuguese crown, to the Portuguese merchants and to the Japanese landlords – is visible.

Jesuit presence in Japan, even if traditionally accounted for from a religious point of view, involved political, economic and cultural patterns going beyond their performance as missionaries. Priests and representatives of the Portuguese crown, as well as brokers between Japanese, Portuguese and Chinese and dealers and intermediaries between the Canton, Macau and Nagasaki trades, answering to their own logic rather than to those of Rome or Lisbon, the Jesuits in Japan are a case in point for those studying colonial empires from the other side of the mirror. The analysis of their performance is based on two approaches: one theoretical, setting the basis of the theories from which the analysis will be undertaken; the other empirical, contextualizing their performance in Japan within the overall framework of the Portuguese presence in the East and Far East.

Theoretical framework: new theories on empire building

European historiography associates analysis of colonisation in the Early Modern Period (1400–1800) with the 'empire building' process in the overseas expansion of the Portuguese, Spanish, British and French crowns or by the Dutch and British monopolistic companies as the main lever in the process. The analysis of European empires is predominantly associated with state policies and institutions; the historical outcomes of early modern empires are usually focused on central power tactics and imperial rivalries, monopolies, warfare strategies and political disputes between colonisers. This perspective leads to three main consequences.

First, they focus on central power strategies, and exclude how individuals and groups of individuals contributed to historical dynamics, at times to an even greater extent than the central power itself. Second, the few existing analyses based on networks deal mostly with institutionalised, formal connections – political, religious or economic – excluding those acting within an informal and non-institutionalised space. Third, they disregard the active influence of the agents, societies and civilizations of contact in Africa, Asia and America, thus ignoring local inputs to colonial dynamics.

Even though a relevant number of studies has already gone beyond this perception regarding Asia and particularly the Indian Ocean, such as by Sanjay Subrahmanyam (Subrahmanyam 1990a, 1990b, 1993, 1996a, 1996b,

2004), Michael Pearson (Pearson 1976, 1998, 2005), or James Boyajian (Boyajian 2008), much still remains to be done. Such perspectives[2] are in fact the subject of more recent research, through the lens of a dynamic European and non-European historiography. The idea of 'informal empires,'[3] the basic concept of this chapter, as a means to underscoring the informal ways in which European overseas dominium was built during the First Global Age, presents an alternate theoretical approach to empire-building dynamics.

Simultaneously, networks became a central concept in this vision, and network reconstitution methods become a core procedure in the analysis of early modern globalisation. Researchers now focus their attention on informal, trans-imperial and cross-border networks rather than on more formal ones resulting from central power strategies, the latter by nature national and promoting rivalry rather than cooperation. This historiographical trend falls in line with the emerging revisionist writing where Francesca Trivellato's *The Familiarity of Strangers* (Trivellato 2009) or Xabier Lamikiz's research on Spanish merchants and overseas networks (Lamikiz 2010) are pioneers.

This trend also follows the path set by recent historiographical approaches deriving from inputs from theories on cooperation applied to history. This was developed by the international and interdisciplinary research project-DynCoopNet, supported by the European Science Foundation's TECT (The Evolution of Cooperation and Trade) programme.[4] The strategy and work plan of this research programme, aiming to establish the agency of self-organising commercial networks over various temporal scales, became a major tool to re-evaluate worldwide dynamics from a new individual-centred perspective.

However, to fully understand the mechanisms of cooperation, it is important to acknowledge that cooperation does not take place only among individuals or informal networks. Individual actors and informal networks do not always act against formal powers such, as the crown or the state. Cooperation between individuals and the state is often a decisive means of empire building. According to theoreticians of cooperation, this phenomenon is described as 'a behaviour which provides a benefit to another individual and which is selected because of its beneficial effect on the recipient' (West et al. 2007: 416). Economic definitions of cooperation focus on two fundamental characteristics. One defines cooperation as the collective action of individuals aiming to share a certain task that is lucrative for all participants (Jesus and Tiriba 2009: 80). The other sees cooperation as a social process where individuals, groups and institutions act in a concerted way to reach common goals. Economic approaches, in this sense, focus not only on economic characteristics of cooperative relations (cost vs. benefit) but also on the social attributes of partners and their relations (Ribeiro 2015: 25–7). This behaviour is driven by goals, expectations and motivations implying collective or

AMÉLIA POLÓNIA

dyadic interaction between individuals (Axelrod 1984: 6). Even if the game thus established has inevitable social implications, individual motives and beliefs are the basis of cooperation.

Besides theories of cooperation, self-organisation theories are also useful tools for a more accurate understanding of the dynamics under scrutiny. Self-organisation is seen as a process where some form, order or coordination arises out of the interactions between the components of an initially disordered system. This process is assumed to be spontaneous: it is not directed or controlled by any agent or subsystem inside or outside the system. Self-organisation occurs within, and is studied in, a variety of physical, chemical, biological, social and cognitive systems. An author who connected the principles of self-organisation with functioning world systems is political scientist George Modelski. He stressed the connection of the dynamics of self-organisation with the concept and dynamism of world system evolution (Modelski 1990, 2000; Modelski et al. 2008). According to him, 'dynamic physical, biological and social systems evolve in such ways that order increases so that several parts are mutually adapted in what are evolutionary processes' (Modelski n.d.). The large-scale processes of the world system, as well as evolving human social organisation, may be seen as self-organising. Powered by a set of influential mechanisms, self-organisation is a critical feature of the world system (Jantschs 1980).

The other connotation of self-organisation lies in the realm of so-called evolvability: the capacity of certain groups, areas or ensembles to produce spontaneous order, mostly when on the edge of chaos (Modelski n.d.). According to this understanding, one needs to highlight not only the features of disruption and unsettlement occurring in stressful periods but also the creative and positive aspects of reorganisation and the greater inclusiveness of larger harmonies. Modelski sees them as a necessary component of the world system and a factor in world system functioning.

One could apply the same theoretical principles to the world system of the First Global Age. The worldwide economic framework produced during this period is, in fact, full of examples of cooperation and self-organisation: that national, international and intercontinental trade networks existed is well known; inter-confessional trade between Catholics, Protestants and Jews is well documented; worldwide transference of goods and capital was based on cooperation patterns, as was the overall communication system; and an active transference of news and information was a major pillar of cooperation in those days. In this process, trust and reputation became valuable, and gossip was a mechanism of both advertisement and warning. In all of them, commoners – mainly pilots, seafarers, captains, shipmasters and merchants – were key elements of the system, as were crown officers or missionaries.

To discuss the evidence underlying these assumptions, we will focus on the Portuguese presence in the East, first at a general level, looking for global processes of cooperation, then from a micro-approach centred on the actions of the Jesuits in Japan as managers of empire building.

Informal networks in Portuguese overseas expansion

It is undeniable that the first global routes, involving all oceans and continents, were created by the Iberian empires. The Portuguese were the first, in a European context, to initiate this movement and create regular maritime routes making exchange possible at a global level. While the Portuguese projection over the world is well known, what is lesser known are the reasons and rationale to explain the take-off and performance of a small, peripheral country enabling it to take leading positions in building and maintaining long-term imperial dynamics. Can only state policies be the answer?

Role of the state and individuals in building up Portuguese overseas settlements

There is a historiographical consensus that the Portuguese crown launched the overseas expansion, but is this really true? The conquest of Ceuta in 1415, seen by Portuguese historiography as the first step in the imperial expansion, was an initiative of King John I. But this episode is also regarded by renowned Portuguese historians as the last episode in the process of the Christian Reconquest of the Iberian Peninsula, rather than as the first step towards modern geographical expansion. Moreover, it depended on the contributions of individual agents forced to commit financial, military and naval means to the operation (Thomaz 1994: 44–102).

It has also been proved that some of the processes of geographical discovery, shipping and colonial settlement were not, in fact, led by central players in the Portuguese monarchy, such as Prince Henry, the so-called 'Navigator,' but were the result of a multiplication of individual initiatives and casuistic achievements later incorporated into central power strategies. From the first, in terms of the juridical organisation of colonial spaces, the Portuguese crown often relied on private individuals to whom powers of settlement, military defence and trade affairs were delegated. The model of hereditary captaincies implemented in the Atlantic archipelagos and later in Brazil is a case in point. Even when the state sought to centralise overseas territorial administration, as was the case from 1542 with the establishment of the *Governo Geral* (General Government) in Brazil or the creation of the *Estado da Índia* (the State of India), these were never able to exclude or avoid informal interventions of private parties.

The administrative model aimed for both a monopolistic spice trade system and effective control over all agents travelling to the East – officials, military personnel, adventurers or members of religious orders. It aimed to provide the state with control over the overall processes taking place from the East to the Far East. But this was not what actually happened. A definition of the Estado da Índia by Luis Filipe Reis Thomaz shows clearly that the presence of the Portuguese in the East went far beyond the control of the Estado da Índia. According to him,

> The State of India in the 16th century designated not a well-defined geographical space, but a collection of territories, establishments, assets, individuals and interests that were administered, managed or governed by the Portuguese crown in the Indian Ocean and neighbouring seas, and the coastal territories from the Cape of Good Hope to Japan.
>
> (Thomaz 1994: 207)

In general terms, this points to interests that were officially governed by the crown, but it does not coincide with the much broader notion of 'Portuguese Expansion in the Indian Ocean,' which also covers non-official modes of settlement, developing regardless of the state and, in some cases, even against the state. Thomaz stresses the importance of the sub-colonisation phenomena – the creation of smaller colonies from the main colonies – which escaped central control in both administrative and economic terms. These colonies proliferated throughout the Indian Ocean at Pattani (Southern Siam); Nagapattinan; Saint Thomas of Mylapore (Coromandel Coast) and most particularly at Macau.

It is widely acknowledged that, with regard to Japan, the Portuguese crown delegated religious, political, cultural and commercial authority to the Jesuits on whom the success of Portuguese relations with Japan depended. Neither the crown nor the viceroyalty had any role in this expansion and consolidation, as they did not interfere with the final outcomes of the process, which ultimately led to the expulsion of the Portuguese from Japan in 1639 after the expulsion edict directed toward missionaries in 1614 (Coutinho 1999). The availability of contacts and interactions between Europe, particularly Portugal, and the East and Far East depended in fact on the regular operation of formal and informal networks. Among the formal and institutional Portuguese networks in the East, there were, in the first place, all the administrative, financial and military structures which represented the State of India, including a wide range of officers – viceroys, judges, clerks, bailiffs, captains, tax collectors and notary officers. The institutional framework provided by the missionary activities of the Franciscans, Jesuits, Dominicans and even Benedictines and, later on, Augustinians should not be forgotten either.[5] These organisations, together with the ecclesiastical networks sustained by the structures of the bishoprics founded in the overseas territories and integrated into the Portuguese *Padroado* in the East or ruled by the Portuguese crown, provided flows of information and goods.

The municipalities,[6] emulating the same model in Portugal, constituted other nodes within a structural network responsible for the organisation of the Portuguese presence overseas. Last, but not least, the framework provided by the *Misericordia* Houses, civil confraternities duplicating and emulating the organisation of their metropolitan counterparts and present in the Portuguese colonial settlements, should also be considered (Bethencourt 2010; Sá 2010). These institutions provided not only spiritual and social assistance to Portuguese settlers and their descendants but also ways of transferring news, goods and money.

Besides these providing formal and institutional networks, individual connections among agents also have to be considered. The crown, keeping detailed records, intended to control all departures from Lisbon to the East. Only individuals licenced by the crown were entitled to travel to India. The law further restricted European settlers by acknowledging only three categories of legal residents in Asia: soldiers, *casados* or married men, estimated at about two thousand circa 1600 (Boyajian 2008: 32), and clergymen, including priests and missionaries. In addition, the law put further restrictions on certain groups. It barred all foreigners from Asia and persons suspected of unorthodox beliefs, including the Portuguese New Christians, descendants of former Jews forcefully converted. Women were also strictly forbidden from travelling to the East.

The reality was, however, far from that stipulated by the law. With regard to Jews and New Christians, their presence in the East, especially in Goa, has been well-documented from the early decades of the sixteenth century. The first known reference to flows of illegal immigration by New Christians to India dates from 1519, and this phenomenon resulted in the promulgation of crown legislation to control such immigration (Baião 1949: 17–18). They tended to increase from the 1530s onwards, and available documentation corroborates their geographic dispersal, including destinations such as Goa, Cochin and Hurmuz, as well as Cambay, Bassein, Chaul, Cape Comorin, St. Thomas of Mylapur, Bengal, Pegu, Tenasserim, Melaka, Siam, the Moluccas and even Japan and China (Cunha 1995: 26). Their number, power and influence, especially in the business world, is corroborated by a letter to the king by Dr. Jerónimo Dias, dated 1539, from Goa, in which he noted,

> And they are here in no small numbers in this city and in Your Highness' other settlements and fortresses and they are very harmful. Those who are here are involved in all sorts of contracts and trade and other activities because everything is in their hands . . . (f.15v). All these carracks come over here full of those unauthorised and clandestine men. We do not believe that Your Highness is aware of this because they bribe everyone with gifts and money and bypass

all the restrictions that might have been imposed in these matters by Your Highness.[7]

The same can be said about women. Among those who departed overseas, a clear distinction has to be made between those who left under royal orders, or were even driven by the crown, and surreptitious and illegal departures. Indeed, women boarding ships, mostly to India, about whom we have more information, were targeted by civil and religious convictions. The legal constraints can be highlighted by the 1524 Vasco daGama resolution, according to which any woman found on board without royal permission would be publicly flogged and banished to one of the hunting grounds of Africa, even if married. Her husband would be placed in irons and forced to return to Portugal, and the captains of the ships who assisted them or did not surrender them to authorities would lose their salaries[8] (Correia 1862: III, 21).

Although, because of both lack of sources and the sub-register practice, as their presence was mostly illegal and disguised, it is not possible to measure with any accuracy their proportional presence on board on the different maritime runs, but one can surmise women's presence on board would be minor – exceptional and counter-productive – but constant. More so, their performances as colonisers depended on their prior travel overseas.

Unauthorised individuals, besides those sanctioned by the crown, entered thus the cosmopolitan Eastern universe. Portuguese authorities could barely control these flows. They acted individually or within informal networks, often depending on active collaboration with local populations and trade agents. We can include within this group the 'lançados' (so called because they were scattered all over Asia) – individuals who left Portuguese-controlled settlements to trade freely and who sometimes became renegade mercenaries and corsairs at the service of neighbouring Muslim states. According to an estimate by Anthony Disney, native princes from the Malabar Coast to Bengal employed as many as five thousand 'lançados' in the early seventeenth century (Disney 1978: 21; Boyajian 2008: 33).

This was a very mobile population, searching for new opportunities and risking the unknown to achieve major profits. They had an active role in the building of a visible Portuguese presence in the East and were in fact responsible for some of the first Portuguese contacts with the expanding frontiers of the Eastern world. One of them, Fernão Mendes Pinto, trader, soldier, pirate and adventurer,[9] is taken as being responsible for the first contacts with Japan, much as Jorge Álvares, with a similar profile, is credited as the first Portuguese explorer to have reached China and Hong Kong. They emerge, thus, as active agents of initial contacts and responsible for the permanence of Portuguese presence in Asia even after the empire's decline.

It is in fact urgent to recognise that declining Portuguese dominion was not just a result of strong competition from other European powers but also of evolving local contexts involving changing power equilibria and economic priorities of Asian landlords. In fact, the interference of new European players was no more than a catalyst for the strong reaction of local landlords to Portuguese presence and activities. The Dutch, French, and British were as critical to the failure of the Portuguese State of India as were the Xá Safavid, the Nayaka kings of Tanjavur and Madurai (Subrahmanyam 1993) or the policies of Toyotomi Hidehoshi or Tokugawa Ieyasu in Japan. Likewise, the taking of Melaka, Ceylon, Cranganor, Nagapattinam, Cochin, Coulam and Cannanore by the Dutch was no more decisive for the withdrawal of the Portuguese Estado da India than the loss of Hurmuz to the Xá Abbas in 1622; the losses of Siriam (1612), Hugli (1632) and the Canara ports (1654); or the loss of Nagasaki and the final expulsion of the Portuguese from Japan in 1639.

Additionally, the Portuguese crown's loss of dominion in the East and Far East did not correspond to an equivalent loss of protagonism on the part of Portuguese agents. Their presence was still resilient on the Malabar Coast, the Bay of Bengal and the Far East. During the seventeenth century, the Portuguese reaffirmed their presence on the Coromandel Coast at Porto Novo (New Port) to circumvent the loss of Nagapattinam to the Dutch. In St Thomas of Mylapore, a Portuguese community was officially reassembled after the loss of the settlement, as was also done in Hugli, where a Portuguese presence is again noticed in 1660. The same pattern was replicated in Ayutthaya in Siam, where, in 1684, an organised community guided by Jesuit priests was still in place, maintaining prominence despite the successive presence of the Dutch, British and French.

A statement by one of the administrators of the VOC to the rulers of the United Provinces in 1658 upon the taking of Ceylon, summarises the Dutch perception of this resilience:

> The greater number regard India as their fatherland, thinking no longer of Portugal; they trade thither little or not at all, living and enriching themselves out of the treasures of India, as though they were natives and knew no other fatherland.
>
> (Corn 1997: 203)

Charles Corn, author of *The Scents of Ede*, notes further,

> Despite having been ousted from the Spice Islands and losing their monopoly to the Dutch, the Portuguese were scattered in pockets throughout Asia.... [T]he Portuguese ... were unique among European colonizers of the Far East in their ability to involve themselves deeply in the social and cultural lives of the Asian peoples among whom they did retain a foothold. ... Ironically, if any European tongue was the language of merchant intercourse, even in Batavia, it was Portuguese, much to the displeasure of the Dutch, who had

overridden the Portuguese in matters of trade but made little effort
to regard local cultures sympathetically.

(Corn 1997: 203)

Regardless of the reasons, the disappearance of Portuguese official
presence in the East in the seventeenth century did not apply to the same
degree to Portuguese agents. The role of the Portuguese 'casados,' men who
had been encouraged by official policies to marry local women, is widely
acknowledged as an essential element of permanent settlement and as factor
of rootedness. Their skill as intermediaries and translators; their knowledge
of trade circuits, monetary and political systems and their cultural backgrounds were, in fact, of significant value for local rulers and the next generation of Europeans.

The resilience of the Portuguese in Macau and Timor throughout the seventeenth and eighteenth centuries right at the core of Dutch and British influence, provides additional proof of the availability of Portuguese agents as
individuals to maintain networks of trade and the capacity for cooperation.
This leads us to a discussion of the performance of self-organised networks.
These networks were not created after the loss of Portuguese primacy in the
Eastern world but were already in place during the State of India's golden
age. The difference between the power of the State of India, its institutions
and representatives and that of private entrepreneurs can be sustained with
financial indicators. Financial demands were repeatedly imposed on Portuguese municipalities and particularly on the Goa city council to prepare
royal armadas and armies for the defence of the State of India, much as
private loans were requested from and provided by local entrepreneurs and
businessmen in Goa at a time when the official budget of the State of India
was depleted and representatives of the Portuguese crown were unable to
militarily respond to European and local attacks (Miranda 2015).

While the official presence of the Portuguese crown in the Indian and
the Pacific Oceans was collapsing from the end of the sixteenth century
onwards, private business, even when led by crown representatives, kept
running successfully, going as far as to deal with formal enemies of the Portuguese crown. During the seventeenth century, in times of declared crisis,
the depletion and bankruptcy of the royal treasury did not in any way correspond to the situation of private entrepreneurs. This leads us to the main
focus of our discussion: individual initiatives and self-organised and informal networks as main factors in globalisation.

Self-organising trade networks in the East

Portuguese and European historiography describe Portugal's commercial
expansion as being based on monopolistic strategies headed by the crown.
It is true that the crown imposed some monopolies, as it is also true that

monopolistic systems led to the primacy of state policies to the detriment of individual initiatives. But in the Portuguese case in the fifteenth and sixteenth centuries, this monopolistic model can only be identified in what concerns the Mina gold trade and the spice trade on the Cape Run. James Boyajian notes that from the inception of the Cape trade, its architects – the king of Portugal and the Portuguese nobility – conceived of the enterprise as a royal monopoly with concessions to nobles who served the king in Asia and in other military posts. Private trade in Asia was an afterthought, and the king erected barriers to its growth. Portuguese law strictly regulated embarkations in Lisbon, the only port authorised to launch vessels bound for India (Boyajian 2008: 29).

This being so, a huge area of participation remained open for business initiative. Only the spice trade and the silver and gold trades were crown monopolies. Private entrepreneurs were able to act as intermediaries in inter-Asian trade and were authorised to carry in the carracks heading for Lisbon a considerable number of products – silks, porcelain, furniture, textiles, tapestry, precious and semi-precious stones and perfumes, as well as slaves for personal service – with enormous possibilities for profit.

Even strict monopolistic policies regarding spices were not able to totally exclude individual initiatives. In fact, they frequently coexisted. We are not referring only to smuggling, which is an illegal and parallel flow of merchandise and capital, but also to internal mechanisms authorised by the state itself which allowed for the presence of single agents in monopolistic circuits. In Portugal, in 1560, at the height of the spice trade, only 60 per cent of the products was handled by the crown. The remaining 40 per cent was traded by individual agents with the crown's permission, as has been proved by Vitorino Magalhães Godinho (Godinho 1987: III, 43–80).

Something parallel seems to have happened in the ports of the Coromandel Coast concerning the Eastern and Far-Eastern traffic. It is important to keep in mind that from the administration of Lopo Soares de Albergaria onwards, the Bay of Bengal was an area of great opportunity for merchants, mercenaries and corsairs. Even when official missions were intensified and a fleet (which ceased to operate in the 1530s) was instituted to patrol this maritime space, individuals, interlopers and even outsiders were active in it. Extortion, bribery, deception and piracy emerged as by-products of the Portuguese presence in the Bay of Bengal and on the Coromandel Coast, where official Portuguese control was negligible (if not non-existent) and where important shipping and trade networks intersected, linking Mylapur and Nagapattinam with Melaka (Thomaz 1999).

These tendencies were all the more conspicuous in the case of the trade routes in maritime Southeast Asia and the Far East. First acting as an extension of the Cape Route and as a means of provisioning carracks waiting for spices in Cochin, these routes gradually achieved autonomy, the Portuguese playing the role of intermediaries in a vast and heterogeneous inter-Asian regional trade. Their advantages included their capacity to transport large cargo loads and the heavy artillery they carried on board. These meant an intimidating dominion of the seas.

These agents on the move included 'casados' (the only term applied in the sources to merchants who were not acknowledged as such in the East), officers and missionaries travelling through a network of posts spreading from the western coast of Africa to Japan, together with a considerable number of other informal agents, such as seafarers, soldiers and adventurers. The long waiting period between the arrival and the departure of the Cape Route carracks, the fact that crews and garrisons were only paid for the time spent on board or during conflicts, in addition to the delay in paying wages, increased desertion figures. These men were also driven by the opportunities offered by privateering, by employment in missions for local rulers or by promising trade opportunities with unprecedented profit rates. The overlapping of administrative, military, fiscal, religious or sailing activities with overseas trade is a historically proven fact and has numerous implications. The nobleman/merchant, the clergyman/merchant (Polónia 2007: I, 285–495, II, 269–275, 2001: II, 297–310), whether secular priest or missionary, or the sailor/merchant are in this context dominant social types. The ultimate example of this is the trade monopoly the Jesuits held in Japan, a matter to which we will return.

From these patterns rose the agency of powerful informal networks – the real dynamics of the Portuguese presence in the East. Luís Filipe Thomaz was one of the first Portuguese historians to stress the meaningful outputs of these dynamics in studies complemented by analytical perspectives and empirical evidence provided, among others, by Anthony Disney (Disney 1978, 2009); and James Boyajian (Boyajian 1993, 2008).

In the East, the operations of trans-imperial and cross-border networks were undoubtedly in place. They were essential for the running of the Cape Route and for the provisioning of the armadas, depending on local markets, even for labour force recruitment to guarantee what would become even more important to the sustainability of Portuguese presence in the East: their role as intermediaries in inter-Asian trade. The complexity of this agency can be found in the twenty-seven routes that, c. 1570, radiated from Goa, Melaka and Macao. These included routes from Goa to Hurmuz, Mozambique, Ceylon, Moluccas, Coromandel, the Bay of Bengal and Melaka; from Melaka to Siam, Macau, Japan, Burma, Moluccas and Bandas; and from Macau to Japan, Indonesia, Siam and Timor (Russell-Wood 1993: 32). In their quest for cinnamon in Ceylon, cloves in the Moluccas, nutmeg and mace from Bandas, luxury goods such as sandalwood from Timor, silk from China or lacquer from Pegu or simply as transporters of textiles, rice and wood, the Portuguese became mediators in a vast range of inter-cultural contacts.

The Portuguese in Japan: the role of the Jesuits

The presence of the Portuguese in Japan should be understood within this global framework and be analysed on these lines (Polónia 2013). The evolution of Portuguese contact with Japan is well known. In 1543, the Portuguese arrived in Japan. Two men, one probably Fernão Mendes Pinto, trader and adventurer, were passengers on a Chinese ship that landed at Tanegashima Island. The Portuguese were keen to trade with Japan. At a time when trade between China and Japan was affected by conflicts and warfare due to a number of incidents involving Wokou piracy in the South China Sea, Portugal assumed the role of intermediary between the two countries.[10] The protagonism of individual agents, the first contacts mediated by third parties – in this case a Chinese crew – and the role assumed by the Portuguese brokers adapting to the favourable conditions this particular juncture offered them are all factors in the functioning of self-organised networks.

Besides acting as traders in the China-Japan trade, the Portuguese brought new products to Japan: tobacco, sweet potatoes, clocks and guns. The introduction of European guns was to play a major role in Japan's political evolution. In a context of a generalised civil war within a feudal political structure, with power disputed among local landlords, expertise in handling European rifles offered military leaders an obvious advantage. Geoffrey Parker (Parker 1996: 140, 201) showed how this factor led a profound military revolution as armies rapidly established rifle corps able to guarantee permanent shooting. This appropriation of European rifles by Japan is further proof of individually-based dynamics of cooperation. No confrontation strategy led by a state could provide the enemy with the military superiority such as that given to the Japanese through the use of the rifle. The drafting of treatises on how to handle the new weapon, the ability to mass produce it and the development of new military tactics based on rifle brigades comprise key elements of an acculturation process and technical transfer based on individual exchanges. These contributed to a dynamic of globalisation not only of products and trade but of technology and knowledge as well.

The *namban-jin* (the southern barbarians), as the Japanese called the Portuguese, centred activities on the island of Kyûshû and created a business settlement in Nagasaki by 1571. Kyûshû was a peripheral area of Japan, far from the capital Miyako, and less affected by the war. The Jesuits would later be in charge of the administration of the Nagasaki settlement by decision of the local Christian landlord, Bartolomeu Sumitada.

Kyushu's position, in relation to the Portuguese empire in Asia, was similarly peripheral, both with regard to the headquarters of the State of India, Goa, and the major shipping routes controlled by the Portuguese. Located on the edge of Eastern Asia, where official Portuguese presence had not yet been established except at Macau, their presence in Japan could survive only through individual contacts and the performance of self-organised networks involving Portuguese, Chinese and Japanese merchants. Informality and adaptation were the two main traits of such networks, which involved the purchase of Chinese merchandise, mainly silk, at Cantonese fairs, their transportation to Macau and their final transfer to Japan.

Some formal structures were to be introduced into this framework by the Jesuit missions. In 1549, Jesuit missionaries, led by Francis Xavier, arrived in Japan, intent on founding missions and converting the Japanese to Christianity. Their mission of widespread evangelisation impacted most on Japan, spreading throughout its territory by establishing permanent missions. In 1551, Francis Xavier travelled to the capital, Miayko, to gain a foothold in Japan's political centre (Hall 2003: 312–16), and in 1554, Fernão Mendes Pinto, temporary Jesuit member, was sent by the viceroy as ambassador to the Daimyo of Bungo (Costa 1989: 110–11).

The Jesuits were led to engage in political infighting within Japan from which they sought to obtain the support of local landlords and reap benefits. It seemed to work, at least in the first decades of the Jesuit presence, with Christianity being accepted or at least tolerated among other confessions, and they were able to increase the number of their missions. The fact that by 1588, there were more than 150,000 baptised Japanese was a clear indicator of Jesuit success. They sought to implement in the Far East the same strategy they had followed in Europe and the East: the conversion of elites, which then resulted in mass conversions of Japanese subjects (López-Gay 2000: 103–16; Sousa 2007: I, 45–53). With the Jesuits, religion, politics and ultimately trade became a structural trend emulating a well-known shift in Portuguese overall expansion.

If, at the beginning of their presence in Japan, the involvement of Jesuits in local political battles, generalised civil wars and the fragmentation of local power proved to be beneficial to their aims and goals, in the long run, this same strategy, became risky and excessively invasive of Japanese political balances. These were even classified as acts of duplicity and treason and ended up working against the Jesuit presence in Japan, contributing to the first anti-Christian edict signed by Toyotomi Hideysohi in 1587, the edict of expulsion of the Jesuits from Japan in 1614 and, ultimately, the edict of expulsion of the Portuguese in 1639.

Behaviours of cooperation, deception and desertion have to be considered in order to understand the overall framework within which Jesuit status evolved in Japan.

During the period of Portuguese presence, Japanese warfare was radically changed by the introduction of handguns and cannons, as noted. The victories of Oda Nobunaga are well-known. After learning how to use the new weapons, he captured the port of Sakai in 1569, achieving victory at Nagashino in 1575. By the time he was assassinated in 1582, Nobunaga controlled central Japan. Toyotomi Hideyoshi continued the work of reuniting Japan. In 1587, he subdued the southern island of Kyushu, and by 1590, he had conquered eastern Japan. Tokugawa Ieyasu, his general, seized power and pursued the reunification of Japan under a strong political and military power (Hall 2003: IV, 40–95, Sousa 2007: I, 123–225).

In the context of unification, the Jesuits meant division in not only religious terms but also a politically ingenious rising power that was intellectually skilled and goal-oriented. It seems that their political manoeuvring was no longer tolerated by the new, centralised power regime. Accusations of generalised persecutions by these agents of a new confession, the Christian faith, against some priests, local populations and their customs and the destruction of temples and idols served as additional reasons to expel the Jesuits. The terms of their involvement in trade, to which we will return, only added to this animosity. Moreover, if they had been useful to local landlords as intermediaries and brokers since their arrival at the end of the sixteenth century, their presence became less determinant at a time when other brokers, offering the same services for less involvement, attempted to infiltrate Japan. First, the Spanish tried to circumvent the Portuguese; then the Dutch appeared as a serious alternative to the Portuguese monopoly as merchants and missionaries, if indeed the two functions could ever be separated in the case of the Jesuits. This leads us to the analysis of the merchant networks in place and the role played by the Jesuits.

Introduced by local agents, namely Chinese pilots exploiting traditional trade channels and opening new ones, Portuguese traders, adventurers, mercenaries and outsiders penetrated a new region and contributed to consolidating, in the second half of the sixteenth century, one of the most profitable and rewarding trade routes of the time: that connecting Melaka to China and China to Japan. This traffic, at first maintained on a smuggling basis, provided the Portuguese with an advantageous position in inter-Asian trade, which they monopolised for almost a century. Their cargo capacity and their weapons superiority added to internal political circumstances in the Far East and guaranteed the Portuguese a universe of opportunities.

Co-operation was an essential feature. In fact, from the beginning, the Portuguese had crossed unknown waters with the assistance of native pilots. The Portuguese arrived in the Indian Ocean, led from Sofala to Calicut by a local Muslim pilot, Ahmad Ibn Majid (Velho 1999). They tapped local navigational knowledge: Arab, Gujarati, Javanese and Malay pilots staffed Portuguese voyages from Malabar to Ceylon, Melaka, the Sunda Islands, Java, Moluccas, Sumatra and Siam, much as Chinese pilots were frequently used for the Melaka-Macau-Japan run (Russell-Wood 1993: 15).

Macau was a major hub in this traffic. It was by the time of the first contacts with Japan a merchant republic not yet under the Portuguese State of India. Through individual initiatives, the city went quickly from an unknown, marginal place to a pivotal point in the Far Eastern maritime trade routes. We have already noted that trade dynamics were mainly created by self-organising networks led by marginal agents and outsiders of the Portuguese empire in the East. Beginning as a hub for smuggling, Macau evolved into a merchant republic ruled by the Leal Senado,[11] the main municipal structure, under the authority of the captain who ran the Goa-Macau route. Indeed, Macau began as a territory in which the state was only represented by the captains-general of the Goa route to Japan. Only in 1623 did Macau have a resident captain of its own.

When Portuguese mediation between China and Japan through Macau went beyond an illegal and irregular parallel circuit to become a regular maritime trade route, the king appropriated this route by royal provision, assigning it to noblemen as reward for services rendered (Cooper 1972). Macau's local merchants had to negotiate freights with the carrack captains, according to pre-established rates defined by their wealth. Taken as beneficial to some of the richest traders, the ecclesiastical administrator of the territories of Macau, China and Japan, Melchior Carneiro, a Jesuit himself, tried to better organise the attribution of freights in the 1570s. He included the Jesuits in this proposal as supervisors of a new model of trade, based on a contract with fixed amounts (the *contrato de armação*), in which the participation of smaller traders as well as the Misericordia houses and other non-lucrative institutions, like the Jesuits themselves, would be included. Later on, identical patterns tended to be organised in Nagasaki to which the main cargoes were shipped and free trade was replaced by the 'pancada' contract (i.e., the overall silk cargo would be sold at a fixed price in order to avoid speculation). Again, the Jesuits, in the person of João Rodrigues Tçuzzu, became the main regulators of the system, Rodrigues being nominated as representative of Tokugawa Ieyasu. Mediators between Portuguese and Japanese traders, the Jesuits also acted as brokers and agents for Japanese landlords. This position would allegedly benefit their own interests, since they were themselves involved in trade with significant cargo amounts. These loads were integrated in their own shares, negotiated through third parties and resulted from their position as brokers and trade agents for the more prominent daimyos, from whom they received silver to buy merchandise at Cantonese fairs on their behalf. It should be noted that the silver trade was illegal and forbidden by Portuguese royal edicts, treated as a matter of high treason in Macau, where religious excommunication was imposed on offenders. The prohibition was intended to avoid increasing opportunities for smuggling by direct trading avoiding the monopolistic run from Macau to Japan. If we remember that Jesuits were also authorised to include extra portions of merchandise on the carracks because of the 'armação' contract and that their shares increased significantly over time, it is possible to understand the leading role of the Jesuits in this official trade.

Also, in the correspondence sent to Rome and in reports by the order's visitors, allegations rose of Jesuits participating in a parallel trade outside of both the yearly trade route and the 'pancada' system in Japan. It was proved they sold silk in parallel markets outside of Nagasaki, where they could get better prices (Sousa 2007: II, 333–425). Well connected with local traders, belonging to a network operating within the overall Portuguese 'Padroado,' able to obtain credit to use in financial and commercial speculation and with their extensive knowledge of the Japanese language, economy and markets, the Jesuits were in a privileged position and took advantage of this, acting as traders and brokers as much as missionaries.

It should be noted that their participation in this trade was both against the general principles of their ecclesiastic status, which required vows of poverty, and against their own internal regulations. Special edicts were required from the general of the Jesuit Order, in Rome, the pope, and the king in order to proceed with the subsequent legitimation of a practice in place which was illegal and profitable. The Jesuits were able to obtain them all after a persistent intransigence from the general of the order in the 1560s and 1570s. The pope's sanction, which gave them formal authorisation to trade between Macau and Japan, only dated from 1582, but it formalised a practice that had long been in place. The justification for this apparently exceptional status was given on the basis of practical theology, according to which the benefits of trade were essential to missionary activity, official funding from the church and the crown being insufficient or irregular to provide for the needs of an ever-growing number of Jesuit foundations and dependencies in Japan. Religion justified trade (Sousa 2007: II, 362–395). Christianisation justified profit. Their religious status and apparently non-profitable intention justified all kinds of privileges, and the Jesuits became the main silk traders on the Macau-Japan maritime trade route in the 1580s. The parallel participation of the Jesuits in illegal trade, involved in silver imports to Macau and China and the delivery of cargoes on illegal ships in an underground trade that ran parallel to crown carracks, is documented in numerous records. Besides the trade led by the company, allegedly to guarantee the Japanese missions, the agency of individual Jesuits, both European and Japanese, should be acknowledged within the frame of a totally illegal flow of merchandise and money moving significant amounts of merchandise.

Besides this trade, another domain deserves further consideration; this was the reason for repeated discussion in the correspondence with Rome: the involvement of Jesuits in the Japan slave trade. A twofold perspective is visible. On the one hand, the Jesuits condemned human trafficking and asked the Portuguese king to prohibit slave trade in Portuguese settlements in the Kyûshû area. This was conceded by King Sebastian in 1570. On the other hand, Gaspar Coelho, vice provincial of the company in Japan, stated that the Jesuits were accused of colluding in the slave trade through the issuing of licences to slave traders, ensuring that the Japanese slaves they traded in had been acquired according to legal conditions (Sousa 2007: II, 461). Even if it is not clear if Jesuits were involved in human trafficking, the company had indirect responsibilities in the implementation and organisation of slave trade networks, which came to have a wider impact on local populations than the previous networks in place (Sousa 2007: II, 507–530).

This intense involvement and the strong position achieved by the Jesuits in trade circuits involving Japan was subject to heated debate at the time and strongly criticised at several levels. They were, in fact, targeted by merchants affected by Jesuit expertise and privileges, as well as by local landlords who used Jesuits as trade intermediaries but suspected their duplicitous behaviour. It is in this context that the expulsion of João Rodrigues from Nagasaki in 1610, by order of the city's governor, should be understood. Additionally, other ecclesiastical agents, other religious orders and the king himself disapproved of them. Philip III promulgated edicts in 1607, 1609 and 1610 forbidding Jesuit trade in Japan. However, the prohibition never had any formal effect and was revoked by July 1611 under the contention that the Jesuits were not provided with regular and sufficient funding like the other Eastern missions. Trade became the basis for the implementation of Christianisation and missionary activity in Japan (Sousa 2007: II, 413–14). Regardless of the reasons, it is impossible to separate religion from trade when considering Jesuit presence in Japan. Fr. Sebastian of San Pedro, a Franciscan who wrote a defamatory treaty on the Jesuits, explained that the Jesuits' Nagasaki religious house was known as the customs house and the 'House of Contratación,' the same designation given in Seville to the house which administrated the entire Spanish trade to America under crown rule![12]

The activities of the Jesuits in Japan shed light on another dimension of our discussion: the interference of trans-imperial networks in this overall framework. After the 1570s, with the regular arrival of the Manila galleons from America and the reinforcement of Spanish colonial presence in the Philippines, boundaries between actions of Portuguese and Spanish colonisers and traders were more difficult to ascertain. If under the law, no Spanish person could interfere or set up establishment in Portuguese settlements, the reality was quite different. Macau was a hub where merchants of diverse nationalities and confessions crossed activity and business.

In the first place, an active movement of ships was established connecting Manila and Macau. From Macau, the Spanish tried persistently to reach China, Melaka and Japan. Even if the municipal power of Macau, the Loyal Senate, reacted officially to Spanish presence, there are also accounts whereby they refused to punish Spanish captains, shipmasters or traders who had disobeyed the law. Moreover, the Castilian Domingos Segurado had obtained from the Portuguese João da Gama the captaincy of the carrack in charge of the Macau-Japan route, thereby acquiring jurisdiction over Macau's subjects (Sousa 2007: II, 346–7). Several trips were illegally and jointly organised and provisioned with mixed capital by Portuguese and Spanish subjects from Macau to China and Japan. On their way to China, these ships were trailed by British vessels in order to determine whether they were legitimate. Portuguese pilots, attracted by high wages, were part of Japanese crews, manoeuvring ships against the policy of closure of Japanese ports and maritime trade, and they were followed in this by the Japanese. Asian crews and armadas, whether Japanese, Chinese or European, were usually multi-national. The Portuguese did as much with the Castilian ships, where they were not only sailors but also pilots and captains. Repeated Castilian expeditions were organised from Manila to China and Japan, just as Portuguese expeditions were organised heading to Manila. One of them was even put together by the captain of Cochin himself. Indeed, this was not a marginal activity led only by outsiders; itoften involved central personalities of the official presence.

The issue of loyalty to the Portuguese crown or to Portuguese interests is another topic under revision. T'ien Tse Chang, in his work on *Sino-Portuguese trade* (Chang 1934: 104), showed how Portuguese traders living in Japan married daughters of prominent Japanese traders, becoming defenders of Japanese trade interests rather than Portuguese in a trend which can be seen on the West Coast of Africa as well.

Last but not least, it was not only lay agents who were active in the constitution and maintenance of trans-imperial and cross-border trade networks. The Castilians used mainly religious agents to penetrate Portuguese settlements in Malacca, China and even in Japan.[13] China is a case in point: from 1575 onwards, Augustinians, Dominicans, Franciscans and Jesuits mediated systematic efforts by Castilians to penetrate this territory and to initiate trade relations, with immediate reactions from the Portuguese traders, representatives and clergy (Sousa 2007: II, 344). Under the dynastic union between Spain and Portugal from 1580 to 1640, the two realms had one king.

I cannot end this chapter without focusing on a last relevant topic: Jesuit missionary activity and acculturation processes in Japan. I do not intend to review the evangelisation tactics followed by the Jesuits or analyse their acculturation processes. However, I cannot disregard the individual interactions taking place between European and Japanese Jesuits as brothers and auxiliary personnel of the Jesuit missions. This leads to another area of research, inter-culturality, an additional dimension of globalisation.

The aforementioned specificity of the Jesuit mission in Japan; its uniqueness with regard to the main centres of authority of the Portuguese empire in the East, its sporadic contacts with Portuguese merchants coming from Macau once a year, its marginality regarding the main epicentres of evangelisation, its peculiar status within the Portuguese 'Padroado' in the East – all worked together to make the Jesuits dependent on internal conditions in Japan. This circumstance raised a number of problems along with advantages, since Jesuit missionary activity was not associated with a foreign political power intent on imposing itself over Japan.

The Jesuits depended thus, simultaneously, on the protection and welfare of the daimyos and on cooperation and assistance from local agents.

In what concerns evangelisation, a twofold strategy applied: adoption of the Buddhist system of the 'dógicos,' or dojucus, who acted, not as priests, since they did not take vows, but as co-operators and even as assistants in the domain of catechisation, and formation of an indigenous clergy by the admission of Japanese as members to the company. Their number, in both cases, increased over time, and the dependency of European Jesuits on these elements became crucial to the mission's sustainability (Costa 1989: 17–47).

The decision to enforce the constitution of a local clergy was always under scrutiny and debate. From correspondence and reports, it seems that even as European Jesuits in Japan defended their position, it aroused strong reaction from the institutionalised hierarchy in Rome. The massive establishment of local clergy was still exceptional in the overall framework of the Portuguese Padroado regarding the Jesuits, whose selection criteria were, even in Europe, very strict.

The need to follow a different policy in Japan increased from 1587 onwards and particularly in 1614, when European missionaries were expelled. By then, the Jesuits understood that the maintenance of Christianity in Japan depended on the activities of indigenous priests. The number of ordinations then increased even though Jesuits would often return, disguised as merchants and sailors, to their previous domain of activity (Costa 1989: 17–47, Sousa 2007: I, 6–30).

Although the Jesuits admitted and implemented the ordinations of local priests and depended on a significant number of 'dógicos,' or dojucus, for their activity, criticism toward them, a certain incomprehension of their habits and a permanent claim as to their lack of discipline and obedience prevail in Jesuit letters. An unavoidable Eurocentric position and incomprehension of the daily habits and psychological profiles of local collaborators is present in the majority of letters from the 1580s onwards. There are other statements that project a sense of superiority on the part of the Japanese, parallel to a clear admission that the European Jesuits depended on them for evangelisation, for cultural contacts and for political relations, because of their knowledge of the language, the culture and local politics.

In 1587, Pedro Ramon, a Jesuit priest, wrote,

> I have dealt with them already for ten years and each day I am more surprised and I state (if one can make this comparison without being odious), that these people here are much better than in Europe, and this without a shadow of doubt.[14]

This is not, however, the prevalent vision at a time in which Jesuits were already persecuted.

The 'acomodatio' concept, which is a policy of total integration of Japanese indigenous priests in the company, does not seem to have worked; on the contrary, a sense of European superiority, local difficulty to accede to higher positions in the hierarchy, formal claims and the use of political play by Japanese priests in order to circumvent the difficulties felt in the missions and use of political pressure to achieve their aims led to internal tension. The written testimonies repeatedly reflect the overall mechanisms of cooperation: collaboration, deception and duplicity occurred on a daily basis. The frequent abandonment of the mission by *dojucus* and Japanese priests was a sign of this lack of accommodation (Sousa 2007: I, 77–104).

Inter-culturality worked both ways and seemed to be more effective with the European Jesuits, as acculturation was a major and inevitable trend in the presence of the Jesuits in Japan. They tended to adapt to the local environment in ways incomprehensible to the company's European visitors. The latter were even to doubt who were the converted: the Japanese to Christianity or the Jesuits to Japanese culture! Language, cuisine, the architecture of Jesuit houses and churches, clothes, daily schedules, the nature of self and corporal punishments toward third parties[15] all seemed more Japanese than European (Loureiro 2010: 155–68; Costa 1989).

Conclusion

Some ideas may now be highlighted. In the first place, colonisation in the East was a complex and multidimensional process which, in its economic, cultural, ethnic, linguistic and even environmental implications, had more to do with activities of individual agents crossing all kinds of frontiers: linguistic, cultural, geographical, political and religious, rather than with the functioning of formal national empires. Our analysis illuminates the build up of the globalisation processes. These were based on cooperation, while formal empires presented themselves as more disposed to mechanisms of imposition. We must accept and acknowledge the informal ways of empire building frequently running against imperial interests. Empires by themselves had little to do with globalisation.

In the second place, mechanisms of globalisation can be better understood if one looks at the other side of the mirror and searches for mechanisms of cooperation (which involved also ways of deception, desertion and competition) operating among informal individual networks. Authority and verticality were more fluid than in formal structures, and communication flows persisted, crossing frontiers sometimes against the formal and institutionalised rules that agents were expected to comply with.

Third, Portuguese overseas expansion as a whole is quite expressive of the ways in which individual agents and self-organised networks worked in favour of the building and maintenance of a polyhedral overseas empire. They were essential to it; their path not only followed crown policies and desideratum but also reflected their own goals, aims and strategies.

Understanding Portuguese empire building and collapse implies understanding the manner in which agents interacted within and outside the boundaries of the formal empire.

Last, but not least, the case study of the Jesuits in Japan gives us an example of how these networks operated and interacted in the First Global Age. Official agents both of the church and the Portuguese crown, the Jesuits operated by themselves in an adaptive process where their decisions and strategies had more to do with Japanese and East Asian constraints, demands and opportunities than with the official framework of a faraway Portuguese eastern empire or Catholic ecumenism. Religion, politics and trade were inextricable domains of individual agency. With the Jesuits, missionary activities, as well as political and economic performance, have to be understood in the framework of different networks that intermingled in a disentangled way, including lay and ecclesiastical Portuguese, Japanese and Chinese agents. Imposition, negotiation and adaptation weaved a web of global interactions between Europeans, Japanese and other Asians, on which thorough reflection and research is essential to fully appreciate the dynamic, open, complex, non-linear system which characterised the First Global Age.

All these analyses would not be possible without the seminal work and historiographic trail of Michael Pearson and his views on how the Portuguese interacted within the Indian Ocean and beyond. A vivid and warm acknowledgement of his graciousness, along with his overwhelming generosity as a historian sharing knowledge and wisdom with his followers, among which the author of this chapter is included, will never be eloquent enough.

Notes

1 Antunes, Cátia; Polónia, Amélia – Introduction to the session: *Beyond Empires: Self Organizing Cross Imperial Networks vs Institutional Empires, 1500–1800*, available at http://www2.iisg.nl/esshc/programme, accessed 2 February 2012.

2 Perspectives addressed for instance by Charles Boxer's copious bibliography on the Portuguese empire: Boxer 1969, 1985, 1986, 1978; by J. Parry: Parry 1971; by John Elliot and others concerning the Spanish empire: Elliot 2006, 2009; by Henry Kamen: Kamen 2002, or in a vast body of works on the British empire: Lawrence 1994, Lloyd 1996.

3 See for instance the roundtable "Building Informal Empires," in *The Pursuit of Empire: The Dutch and Portuguese Colony of Brazil, 1621–166*. Workshop (Leiden University, 10–11 November 2011).

4 DynCoopNet – "Dynamic Complexity of Cooperation-Based Self-Organizing Commercial Networks in the First Global Age," approved by TECT ("The Evolution of Cooperation and Trading") – Program EUROCORES (European Collaborative Research) – European Science Foundation *(Ref. 06-TECT-FP-004)*.

5 See, on this matter: Ames 1989, 2000; Boyajian 1993, 2008; Broeze 1989; Prakash 1998; Prakash and Lombard 1999; Santos 1999; Sousa 2007; Subrahmanyam 1995; Thomaz 1994; Xavier 2007.

6 On the dynamic interactions of a crown leadership with judicial and municipal institutions in Europe and overseas, see Hespanha 1994; MacLachlan 1988; Major 1960; Owens 2005; Phelan 1967; Shennan 1986.

7 3 December 1539 – Goa (TT.CC. I Parte, Mç. 66, doc. 47, fl. 15–16), published in CUNHA 1995: 253.

8 The bishop of Goa, Ferdinand, in a letter written to the king, at a later date to 1532, recognizing that many women are taken on the royal ships and vessels with the knowledge and consent of the commanders themselves, states, "And so his Majesty will be served if the captains do not bring in their ships and galleons, single women, as they do, as the matters of war and places where they are claim for virtuous works and for confessions rather than to get involved with them, which is the cause for some ships being lost, as they are." Cf. REGO1950: II, "Carta de Goa, 1532", Correia 1862: III, 21.

9 Fernão Mendes Pinto (1509–1583) sailed from Portugal on 11 March 1537 bound for India. According to his own testimony in *Peregrinação*, Mendes Pinto claimed to have been shipwrecked, captured, and sold into slavery 16 or 17 times. The accuracy of his records are somewhat doubtful, the reality was a frequent mixture with fantastic and heroic narratives in his biography. He arrived in Malacca in 1539 and worked for the captain of the fortress there as an emissary to the kingdoms of Sumatra and Malaya. He then went to Patani on the east side of the Malay Peninsula and started a thriving business trading with the Thais in Bangkok. Robbed by pirates, he and his partners got revenge by becoming pirates themselves. He then traded along the coast of Indochina. He was shipwrecked on the coast of China and sold as a slave to work on the Great Wall of China. He became involved in the Burmese-Thai wars and wrote the first European account of Burmese politics and history. From Thailand, Mendes Pinto made his second trip to Japan, where he landed in the port of Kagoshima. On his departure, he brought back a Japanese stowaway whom he handed over to St. Francis Xavier in Malacca and thus inspired Xavier's effort to travel to Japan and Christianize the inhabitants. Sometime during these years in Asia, Mendes Pinto had accumulated a large fortune. He was a wealthy merchant when he made his third voyage to Japan in 1551, where Francis Xavier was installed at the court of one of the feudal lords of southern Japan. He gave Xavier the money to build the first Christian church in Japan. Cf Albuquerque 1994: II, 904–6; Almeida 2006; Polónia and Capelão 2018.

10 This overview can be found in numerous books. See, for all: Subrahmanyam 1995: 141–9; Bourdon 1949; Hall 2003: IV, 302–72; Costa 1995: 119–30.

11 *Leal Senado* – Portuguese for Loyal Senate, the seat of Macau's government.

12 Sebastian de San Pedro – Tratado (1617). Biblioteca de la Real Academia de Historia. Cortes 566, fl. 31. Quote by Sousa 2007: II, 416, note 264.

13 Philip II ended the monopoly of evangelisation of Jesuits in Japan, authorising the activity of other religious orders in Japan, through the Castilian Padroado. In 1600, Pope Clement VII, through the brief *Onerosa pastoralis* authorises the entrance of other religious orders in China and Japan through the Portuguese 'Padroado.'

14 Letter from Pedro Ramon to the General Priest Claudio Acquaviva, from Yqizzuqi, 15 October 1587 in *Arquivum Romanum Societatis Iesu, Collection Japonica and Sinica*, 10II. Fls. 282f-285v. Cit Sousa 2007: I, 85.

15 Arquivum Romanum Societatis Iesu, Collection Japonica and Sinica, 2, fl. 165. Cit. Sousa 2007: I, 74.

AMÉLIA POLÓNIA

References

Albuquerque, Luís de (dir.). 1994. *Dicionário da Expansão Portuguesa*, Lisboa: Círculo de Leitores: vol. II.

Almeida, António Fernando. 2006. *Fernão Mendes Pinto, um aventureiro português no Extremo Oriente: contribuição para o estudo da sua vida e obra*, Almada: Câmara Municipal de Almada.

Ames, Glenn Joseph. 1989. *The Estado da India: 1663–1677. Priorities and Strategies in Europe and the East*. Lisbon: n.p.

Ames, Glenn Joseph. 2000. *Renascent Empire: The House of Braganza and the Quest for Stability in Portuguese Monsoon Asia, c. 1640–1683*, Amsterdam: Amsterdam University Press.

Antunes, Cátia and Amélia Polónia. 2012. *Introduction to the Session: Beyond Empires: Self Organizing Cross Imperial Networks vs Institutional Empires, 1500–1800*, available at http://www2.iisg.nl/esshc/programme (accessed 2 February 2012).

Axelrod, Robert. 1984. *The Evolution of Cooperation*, New York: Basic Books.

Baião, António. 1949. *A Inquisição de Goa. Tentativa de História da sua Origem, Evolução e Extinção*, Lisbon: n.p.

Bethencourt, Francisco. 2010. "Configurações políticas e poderes locais," in Francisco Bethencourt and Diogo Ramada Curto (eds.), *A Expansão Marítima Portuguesa, 1400–1800*, Lisboa: Edições 70, 207–64.

Bourdon, León. 1949. *Les Routes des Marchands portugais entre China et Japon au milieu du XVIé. siècle*, Lisbon: Gráfica Lisbonense.

Boxer, Charles. 1969. *The Portuguese Seaborne Empire, 1415–1825*, London: Hutchinson.

Boxer, Charles. 1978. *The Church Militant and Iberian Expansion, 1440–1770*, Baltimore: Johns Hopkins University Press.

Boxer, Charles. 1985. *Portuguese Conquest and Commerce in Southern Asia, 1500–1750*, London: Variorum Reprints.

Boxer, Charles. 1986. *Portuguese Merchants and Missionaries in Feudal Japan, 1543–1640*, London: Variorum Reprints.

Boyajian, James. 1993, 2008. *Portuguese Trade in Asia Under the Habsburgs, 1580–1640*, Baltimore: Johns Hopkins University Press.

Broeze, Frank (ed.). 1989. *Brides of the Sea: Port Cities of Asia from the 16th–20th Centuries*, Kensington: New South Wales University Press.

Chang, T'ien Tse. 1934. *Sino-Portuguese Trade from 1514 to 1644: A Synthesis of Portuguese and Chinese Sources*, Leyden: Brill.

Cooper, Michael. 1972. "The Mechanisms of the Macau-Nagasaki Silk Trade," in *Monumenta Nipponica*, Tokyo: University of Sophia: vol. XXVII, n. 4.

Corn, Charles. 1997. *The Scents of Eden: A History of the Spice Trade*, New York, Tokyo and London: Kodansha International.

Correia, Gaspar. 1858–1866. *Lendas da Índia*, Lisboa: Academia Real das Sciencias, VIII vols.

Costa, João Paulo Oliveira e. 1989. *O Japão e o Cristianismo no Século XVI. Ensaios de História Luso-Nipónica*, Lisboa: Sociedade da Independência de Portugal.

Costa, João Paulo Oliveira e. 1995. *A descoberta da Civilização japonesa pelos Portugueses*, n.p.: Instituto Cultural de Macau, Instituto de História de Além Mar.

Coutinho, Valdemar. 1999. *O fim da presença portuguesa no Japão*, Lisboa: Sociedade Histórica da Independência de Portugal.

Cunha, A. 1995. *A Inquisição no Estado da Índia: origens (1539–1560)*, Lisbon: Arquivos Nacionais-Torre do Tombo.

Disney, Anthony R. 1978. *Twilight of the Pepper Empire: Portuguese Trade in Southwest India in the Early Seventeenth Century*, Cambridge, MA: Harvard University Press.

Disney, Anthony R. 2009. *The Portuguese in India and Other Studies, 1500–1700*, Farnham: Ashgate.

Elliot, John H. 2006. *Imperios del Mundo Atlantico. España y Gran Bretaña en America (1492–1830)*, Madrid: Taurus.

Elliot, John H. 2009. *España, Europa y el Mundo de Ultramar (1500–1800)*, Madrid: Taurus.

Godinho, Vitorino Magalhães. 1987. *Os descobrimentos e a economia mundial*, Lisbon: Presença, III vol.

Hall, John Ehitney (ed.). 2003. *The Cambridge History of Japan. Vol. IV: Early Modern Japan*, Cambridge: Cambridge University Press.

Hespanha, A.M. 1994. *As Vésperas do Leviathan: Instituições e poder político – Séc. XVII*, Coimbra: Almedina.

Jantschs, Eric. 1980. *The Self-Organizing Universe: Scientific and Human Implications of the Emerging Paradigm of Evolution*, New York: Pergamon.

Jesus, Paulo de and Lia Tiriba. 2009. "Cooperação," in *Dicionário Internacional da Outra Economia*, Coimbra: Almedina.

Kamen, Henry. 2002. *How Spain Became a World Power, 1492–1763*, London: Penguin.

Lamikiz, Xabier. 2010. *Trade and Trust in the Eighteenth Century Atlantic World: Spanish Merchants and Their Overseas Networks*, n.p.: The Royal Historical Society, The Boydell Press.

Lloyd, T.O. 1996. *The British Empire 1558–1995*, Oxford and New York: Oxford University Press.

López-Gay, Jesús. 2000. "Métodos misioneros en el Japón del siglo XVI," in *A Companhia de Jesus e a missionação no Oriente: actas do colóquio internacional*, Lisbon: Brotéria, Fundação Oriente: 103–16.

Loureiro, Rui. 2010. "Turning Japanese? The Experiences and Writings of a Portuguese Jesuit in the 16th Century Japan," in Lachaud Dejanirah Couto e François (dir.), *Empires Eloignés*, Paris: École Française de l'Extrême Orient: 155–68.

Maclachlan, Colin M. 1988. *Spain's Empire in the New World: The Role of Ideas in Institutional and Social Change*, Berkeley and Los Angeles: University of California Press.

Miranda, Susana Munch. 2015. "Elites urbanas, negociação política e fiscalidade no Estado da Índia (1614–1640)," in Susana Truchuelo García, Roberto López Vela y Marina Torres Arce (eds.), *"Civitas": expresiones de la ciudad en la Edad Moderna*, Santander: Editorial de la Universidad de Cantabria, 2015: 275–98.

Modelski, George. 1990. "Is World Politics Evolutionary Learning?" *International Organization*, 44(1): 1–24.

Modelski, George. 2000. "World System Evolution," in R. Denemark, J. Friedman, B. Gills and J. Modelski (eds.), *World System History: The Social Sciences of Long-Term Change*, New York: Routledge: 24–53.

Modelski, George. n.d. "Self-Organization in the World System," in *Encyclopedia of Life Support Systems (EOLSS): Developed Under the Auspices of the UNESCO*, Oxford: Eolss Publishers, available at www.eolss.net.

Modelski, George, Tessaleno Devezas and William R. Thompson (eds.). 2008. *Globalization as Evolutionary Process: Modeling Global Change*. Abingdon and New York: Routledge.

Owens, J.B. 2005. *"By My Absolute Royal Authority": Justice and the Castilian Commonwealth at the Beginning of the First Global Age*, Rochester: University of Rochester Press.

Parker, Geoffrey. 1996. *The Military Revolution: Military Innovation and the Rise of the West, 1500–1800*. Cambridge and New York: Cambridge University Press.

Parry, J. 1971. *Trade & Dominium: The European Overseas Empire in the Eighteenth Century*, London: Phoenix Press.

Pearson, Michael N. 1976. *Merchants and Rulers in Gujarat: The Response to the Portuguese in the Sixteenth Century*, Berkeley: University of California Press.

Pearson, Michael N. 1998. *Port Cities and Intruders: The Swahili Coast, India, and Portugal in the Early Modern Era*, Baltimore, MD: Johns Hopkins University Press.

Pearson, Michael N. 2005. *The World of the Indian Ocean, 1500–1800: Studies in Economic, Social, and Cultural History*, Burlington, VT: Ashgate.

Phelan, John L. 1967. *The Kingdom of Quito in the Seventeenth Century: Bureaucratic Politics in the Spanish Empire*, Madison: University of Wisconsin Press.

Polónia, Amélia. 2001. "Evangelização e comércio. A figura do eclesiástico mercador," in *Estudos em homenagem a João Francisco Marques*, Porto: FLUP: 297–310, vol. 2.

Polónia, Amélia. 2007. *Expansão e Descobrimentos numa perspectiva local. O porto de Vila do Conde no século XVI*, Lisboa: INCM: II vols.

Polónia, Amélia. 2013. "Self-Organized Networks in the First Global Age: The Jesuits in Japan," *The Bulletin of the Institute for World Affairs Kyoto Sangyo University*, (28): 133–58, February.

Polónia, Amélia and Rosa Capelão. 2018. "Introdução," in Fernão Mendes Pinto (ed.), *Peregrinação*. Lisbon: Círculo de Leitores (*Colection "Obras Pioneiras da Cultura Portuguesa*): 21–85, vol. 19 (this is the overall Introduction to the critical edition of Peregrinação).

Prakash, Om. 1998. *European Commercial Enterprise in Pre-Colonia India*, New York and Cambridge: Cambridge University Press.

Prakash, Om and DenysLombard (eds.). 1999. *Commerce and Culture in the Bay of Bengal: 1500–1800*, New Delhi: Manohar.

Ribeiro, Ana Sofia Vieira. 2015. *Early Modern Trading Networks in Europe: Cooperation and the Case of Simon Ruiz*, London and New York: Routledge.

Russell Major, J. 1960. *Representative Institutions in Renaissance France, 1421–1559*. Madison, WI: University of Wisconsin Press.

Russell-Wood, A.J.R. 1993. *A World on the Move: The Portuguese in Africa, Asia, and America, 1415–1808*, New York: St. Martin's Press.

Sá, Isabel dos Guimarães. 2010. "Estruturas eclesiásticas e acção religiosa," in FranciscoBethencourt and Diogo RamadaCurto (eds.), *A Expansão Marítima Portuguesa, 1400–1800*, Lisbon: Edições 70: 265–92.

Santos, Catarina Madeira. 1999. *Goa é a chave de toda a Índia. Perfil político da capital do Estado da Índia (1505–1570)*, Lisbon: CNCDP.

Shennan, J.H. 1986. *Liberty and Order in Early Modern Europe: The Subject and the State, 1650–1800*, London and New York: Longman.

Sousa, Lúcio Manuel Rocha de. 2007. "O Japão e os Portugueses (1580–1614). Religião, política e comércio," Unpublished PhD diss., Porto: II vols.

Subrahmanyam, Sanjay. 1990a. *Improvising Empire: Portuguese Trade and Settlement in the Bay of Bengal, 1500–1700*, New Delhi: Oxford University Press.

Subrahmanyam, Sanjay (ed.). 1990b. *Merchants, Markets and the State in Early Modern India*, New Delhi: Oxford University Press.

Subrahmanyam, Sanjay. 1993. *The Portuguese Empire in Asia, 1500–1700: A Political and Economic History*, London and New York: Longman.

Subrahmanyam, Sanjay. 1995. *O império asiático Português, 1500–1700. Uma história política e económica*. Lisboa: Difel.

Subrahmanyam, Sanjay (ed.). 1996a. *Institutions and Economic Change in South Asia*, New Delhi: Oxford University Press.

Subrahmanyam, Sanjay (ed.). 1996b. "Merchant Networks in the Early Modern World," in *An Expanding World*, Aldershot: Variorum Books: vol. 8.

Subrahmanyam, Sanjay (ed.). 2004. *Land, Politics and Trade in South Asia*, New Delhi: Oxford University Press.

Thomaz, Luis Filipe R. 1994. *De Ceuta a Timor*, Lisboa: Difel.

Thomaz, Luis Filipe R. 1999. "Portuguese Control Over the Arabian Sea and the Bay of Bengal: A Comparative Study," in Om Prakash and Denys Lombard (eds.), *Commerce and Culture in the Bay of Bengal, 1500–1800*, New Delhi: Manohar; Indian Council of Historical Research: 115–65.

Trivellato, Francesca. 2009. *The Familiarity of Strangers: The Sephardic Diaspora, Livorno, and Cross-Cultural Trade in the Early Modern Period*, New Haven and London: Yale University Press.

Velho, Álvaro. 1999. *Roteiro da primeira viagem de Vasco da Gama à Índia*, Porto: FLUP.

West, S.A., A.S. Griffin and A. Gardner. 2007. "Social Semantics: Altruism, Cooperation, Mutualism, Strong Reciprocity and Group Selection," *Journal of Evolutionary Biology*, 20(2): 415–32.

Xavier, Ângela Barreto. 2007. *A Invenção de Goa. Poder imperial e conversões culturais nos séculos XVI e XVII*, Lisbon: ICS.

6

SOUTH ASIAN SETTLERS AT BATAVIA IN THE SEVENTEENTH AND EIGHTEENTH CENTURIES

Ryuto Shimada

In 1619, the Dutch East India Company (*De Vereinigde Oost-Indische Companie*: hereafter VOC) set Batavia to be the most important centre for administrative control of the company in Asia. This city was a typical example of a European colonial city in Southeast Asia established in the early modern period. It was developed by the Dutch Company, and after the collapse of the VOC in 1799, Batavia became the colonial capital of the Dutch East Indies under the control of the government in the Netherlands. As the key station of the Dutch colonial control, Batavia continued to be governed by the Netherlands as a colonial city until the Japanese army invaded the Dutch East Indies and changed the name of Batavia to Jakarta in 1942 at the time of World War II. After the defeat of the Japanese army, Jakarta became the capital of the Republic of Indonesia. By and large, the case study of Jakarta is an example of a colonial city established in the early modern period that continued to grow up until now. In fact, we know several present-day mega-cities in maritime Asia, such as Manila, Kolkata and Mumbai, whose establishments went back to the early modern period. Thus, this research on the history of Batavia during the early modern period is going to contribute to a more comprehensive understanding of the early modern European colonial cities in Asia.

First, in the case of Batavia during the early modern period, the city was of importance as the central administration post in Asia for the VOC. The VOC was established in 1602 for trade between Europe and Asia. The initial purpose of the establishment was to obtain Asian products, such as pepper and other spices, for the European market in exchange for silver supplied to Asia from the Netherlands. Such Euro-Asian trade was a fundamental business of the VOC, and for this business, the VOC needed a central trade-handling post in Batavia, where the company collected Asian products and dispatched them to the Netherlands. Besides the Euro-Asian trade, Batavia was also the key station for the intra-Asian trade of the VOC. The company had numerous trading posts in maritime Asia from East Asia through Southeast Asia and South Asia to West Asia, and by connecting these trading posts, the VOC was engaged in the intra-Asian trade as well. In short, Batavia was crucially important for both types of business – Euro-Asian trade and intra-Asian trade.

Not only for the historical study of maritime trade, Batavia is also an attractive objective for the study of the history of cross-cultural relations. This early modern colonial city had a typical feature of multi-ethnic societies. European people were politically the majority governing the city, yet they were simply a minority in terms of population size, even if the mestizos were included in the number. In contrast, Asian slaves accounted for half of the total population of Batavia, and there were Asian settlers, including Chinese, Malay and *Moor* people, in the city. In addition, it is curious that Javanese people and Sundanese people were not in the city in principal. This is due to contracts with the local kingdoms, which were afraid of the outflow of their people to the Dutch territory around Batavia, although it is not true that none of these local people lived in Batavia. Sometimes, they moved into Batavia, and sometimes they had to be included as a population of Batavia alongside the expansion of the Dutch territory.

It is a key point for the historical analysis of Batavia in the age of the company that the population in Batavia was composed not only of Dutch and European immigrants and their descendants but also of Asian immigrants and their descendants. In other words, almost all of the population of Batavia had origins in immigrants and their descendants. The VOC had a plan to develop the city, but there was a shortage of immigrants from the Netherlands, thus Asian immigrants were necessary. To promote the immigration of Asian people, the VOC granted autonomy to Asian citizens to a certain degree according to their ethnicity.

When the VOC began to establish the city of Batavia in 1619, the high government of Batavia appointed Souw Beng Kong (Bencon) *kapitan*, which was the official title of the person in charge of the Chinese community at Batavia, as he was head of the Chinese community. Under the Chinese *kapitan*, the Chinese community enjoyed a certain autonomy. He held civil trials among the Chinese people in those cases in which neither the company's servants nor non-Chinese people were concerned. In the course of time, the Chinese group obtained a much higher degree of autonomy from the so-called *major* system, while other Asian ethnic groups, such as the *Moors*, came to obtain the privilege of autonomy. In addition, the governance of the city of Batavia was done not directly by the VOC but by the city council. The members of the city council included Chinese and other Asian people, as well as servants of the VOC and European free citizens. Batavia was a typical colonial city in the early modern period, where multi-ethnic people lived together in peace, and for this purpose, ethnic autonomy to some degree and the division of living areas within the city were realized.

Keeping in mind this multi-ethnic character of the city, this chapter sheds light on the Moor people in Batavia during the seventeenth and eighteenth centuries. While there are ample previous studies available on the Chinese community of Batavia (Blussé 1986), less attention has been paid so far to the Moor people at Batavia. In fact, the definition of Moor is not so clear in the case of Batavia. Therefore, the main aim of this chapter is to make clear as to who the Moor people were. First, the chapter gives a survey of previous studies on the *Moors* in Batavia. Second, the population of *Moors* at Batavia is investigated. Through quantitative survey, not only the trends of the *Moors* but also their social structure, such as family formation, are made clear. Third, the chapter focuses on the occupations of the *Moors*. Fourth, it highlights their autonomous system at Batavia, which was granted by the authorities of the VOC.

Previous studies

It is obvious that less attention has been paid so far to the Moor people at Batavia. Even when previous studies mentioned them, it was on a small scale with a few lines to a few pages of explanation at the longest. In comparison, there are ample of previous studies on Arab immigrants from Hadhramaut and their descendants since the nineteenth century (van der Berg 1886; Jonge 2000).

Indonesian history experts often consult the works of Thomas Stamford Raffles. He published *The History of Java* (1830), where gave an explanation of the Moor people as follows: Moor people were indigenous setters from the Coromandel Coast and the Malabar Coast to Java. They had been powerful before the establishment of the Dutch monopoly. Yet, at the beginning of the nineteenth century, their trade was no longer as important. Their trading ships came to Sumatra, Penang and Malacca from Coromandel but not so often to Java (Raffles 1830: Vol. 1 83). In short, *Moors* were the immigrants and their descendants from the Coromandel Coast or Malabar Coast. They were engaged in trade with Java and South Asia, but at the beginning of the nineteenth century, their trade was limited to Sumatra, Penang and Malacca. In contrast, regarding *Khója*, Raffles explained that *Khójas* meant the indigenous people from the Coromandel Coast (Raffles 1830: Vol, 2 168). To sum up, Moor referred to immigrants from Coromandel or Malabar, while *Khója* was an immigrant from the Coromandel, as far as we follow the definition given by Raffles.

However, F. de Haan, in his *Oud Batavia*, published in 1922, gave a much more comprehensive and accurate explanation of the Moor people at Batavia. The key points are as follows: First, *Moors* had lived in the *pekojan* since 1633, which is now the Arabian district. Second, *Moors* were different from Arabian people. This distinction was made clear legally in 1828. Third, the term Moor initially meant a Muslim immigrant from Kalinga on the Coromandel Coast. Fourth, the words of *Moren en Jentieven* are often seen in historical records. Fifth, Muslims from the Malabar Coast were also called *Moors* at Batavia. Sixth, *Khója* initially meant the merchants from Gujarat. Seventh, the Moor *kapitan* was appointed in 1753. Moreover, the Moor *major*, a position one rank higher than *kapitan*, was appointed in 1774 (Haan 1922: Vol. 1 486–7).

According to de Haan, Moor people were immigrants and their descendants from the Coromandel Coast and the Malabar Coast, and without question, they were Muslims. However, *Khója* initially referred to merchants originating from Gujarat. This explanation was different from that given by Raffles, but in short, not only *Moors* but also the *Khója* were Muslim merchants coming from Coromandel, Malabar or Gujarat.

As the study by de Haan has been cited frequently so far and obtained a position of high reliability, this definition of Moor was basically accepted on a large scale. For instance, Huur de Jonge fundamentally succeeds the definition by de Haan and explains that *Khója* was initially used for the immigrants from Gujarat, and later this word included the immigrants from Coromandel and Malabar and that the terms of *Khója* and Moor were exchangeable in terms of meaning (Jonge 2000: 143–4).

By the way, F. W. Stapel, who contributed to the development of the research by consulting the archives of the Dutch East India Company in the twentieth century, made a glossary of the special terms seen in the records of the VOC when he edited a summary of the general missive of the high government at Batavia to the Netherlands for publication. In his glossary, he gave an explanation of Moor as follows: Moor was a general term to refer to Muslims, especially in Southwest Asia. It came from *Mouros* in Portuguese. *Getieven*, in contrast, referred to Hindu people in South Asia, and it was an oppositional term to Moor (Stapel 1943: 589–91). Generally speaking, there is nothing different from the definition by de Haan.

In any case, the term of Moor meant the Southwestern Muslim in the documentation of the VOC, according to previous studies that were analysed.

Population of the Moor people

The high government of Batavia annually drew a report of the population of Batavia according to ethnicity. In 1632, for example, the total population amounted to 8,060. Among them, the VOC employees accounted for 1,730. European free citizens were numbered 638; Chinese people 2,390; emancipated Asian/Portuguese slaves (*Mardijker*) 495; Japanese people 83; and other slaves 2,724 (Raben 1996: 86). This population data suggested that there were no Moor people at Batavia in that year, although *Moor* employees of the VOC or *Moor* slaves may have existed there.

Table 6.1 shows the population of Batavia in 1699. The total population of Batavia in this year amounted to 71,599, and among them, around 22,000 people lived in the walled city and the others in the suburban area. In regard to the *Moor* people, the *Moor* and *Getieven* population in the walled city amounted to 330 and the *Moors* in the suburban area to 945. Seventy years later, in 1769, the total population grew to 130,281, as seen in Table 6.2. Among them, *Moor* people amounted to 354 in the walled city and 1,377 in the suburban area.

These data allow us to make the following observations: First, these South Asian immigrants tended to live in the suburban areas. This is because *Moor* people moved to and lived more tightly together in the present-day *Pekojan* area in the first half of the seventeenth century. Second, most South Asian immigrants were Muslims, and thus the shares of the Hindu Gentiles (*Getieven*) were smaller than those of Muslims (*Moor*).

In the early nineteenth century, the urban area of Batavia expanded, especially to the south. Furthermore, the urban area no longer meant simply the space of the walled city. In this way, the *Pekojan* area was included within the urban area, and the *Moors* in *Pekojan* were counted in the category of the urban population. Take an example of the population data in 1835 as shown in Table 6.3. In that year, the city of Batavia in total had 252,188 people, while 66,264 people lived in the urban area and 185,924 people lived in the suburbs. The *Moors* and the Arabs amounted to 564 in the urban area and only 7 in the suburban area. The total population rose in general from the first half of the seventeenth century to the early nineteenth century. However, the population of *Moor* people rose in the seventeenth and the eighteenth centuries but from the eighteenth century, declined. In fact, the *Moor* population moved as follows: 447 people in 1691; 2,975 in 1701; 487 in 1710; 477 in 1720; 453 in 1730; 712 in 1740; 774 in 1750; 984 in 1760; 1,465 in 1770; 937 in 1780; and 853 in 1790.[1] The *Moor* population rapidly increased in the late seventeenth century, and it reached around 3,000. However, it soon decreased and then stagnated around five hundred people. In the 1740s, it rose again, yet it declined throughout the second half of the eighteenth century.[2]

The ratio of males and females provides an interesting fact. Take the data of 1774 for an example. In that year, 1,528 *Moor* people lived in the suburban area of Batavia. Among 1,528, male adults amounted to 481 and female adults to 418, while there were 322 boys and 307 girls. Both gender ratios of adults and children were almost even. This observation implies that *Moor* people lived in Batavia forming families with children.

While *Moor* people in Batavia were immigrants from the Indian subcontinent, as seen earlier, Arab immigrant numbers increased in Southeast Asia, especially from Hadhramaut from the second half of the eighteenth

Table 6.1 Population of Batavia in 1699

	European	Mestizo	Mardijker	Chinese	Moor/Gentile	Malay/Javanese	Gentile
Urban	1,783	670	2,407	3,679	330	277	–
Suburban	475	507	5,515	4,395	–	–	945
Total	2,258	1,177	7,922	8,074	330	277	945

	Malay	Ambonese	Bugis/Macassrese	Balinese/Javanese	Slave	Total
Urban	–	–	–	260	12,505	21,911
Suburban	2,222	719	6,045	15,549	13,216	49,688
Total	2,222	719	6,045	15,909	25,721	71,599

Source: Raben (1996: 309, 323)

Table 6.2 Population of Batavia in 1769

	European	Mestizo	Mardijker	Chinese	Moor/Gentile	Malay/ Javanese	Moor
Urban	1,271	861	898	2,220	354	646	–
Suburban	388	363	4,306	26,064	–	–	945
Total	1,659	1,224	5,204	28,284	354	646	945
	Gentile	*Malay*	*Ambonese*	*Bandanese*	*Bugis*	*Macassrese*	*Butonese*
Urban	–	–	–	–	–	–	–
Suburban	180	1,404	227	113	4,274	3,461	328
Total	180	1,404	227	113	4,274	3,461	328
	Mandarese	*Sumbawanese*	*Timorese*	*Balinese*	*Javanese*	*Slave*	*Total*
Urban	–	–	–	–	–	9,163	15,413
Suburban	757	579	97	13,398	35,917	21,635	114,868
Total	757	579	97	13,398	35,917	130,798	130,281

Source: Raben (1996: 316, 330)

Table 6.3 Population of Batavia in 1835

	Christian/ In-lander	Chinese	Moor/Arab	Slave	Total	Jew
Urban	2,889	41,283	18,262	564	3,266	66,264
Suburban	439	170,821	14,250	7	407	185,924
Total	3,328	212,104	32,512	571	3,673	252,188

Source: ANRI: Batavia 338/3 bijlage 1

century. It could be possible that the Arab immigrant population increased also in the case of Batavia, yet it was not until the nineteenth century that the category of Arab was separated from the category of *Moor* in the Dutch documentation. The National Archives of the Republic of Indonesia (*Arsip Nasional Republik Indonesia* [ANRI]) hold some population statistics of Batavia during the nineteenth century. As far as these population statistics are concerned, it was in 1821 that the category of Arab became separated from that of *Moor*.[3] Already in 1858, the number of Arab people in Batavia was larger than that of *Moor* people, as there were 595 Arab people and 292 *Moor* or Bengali people in 1858.[4]

The population of *Moor* people had already declined in the middle of the nineteenth century, and Arab people became more important. The quarter of *pekojan* of Batavia had been a district of *Moor* people during the seventeenth and eighteenth centuries, yet now in the nineteenth century, it became a sort of Arab quarter in turn.

Occupations of the *Moor* people

There were two types of *Moor* people in Batavia in the seventeenth and eighteenth centuries. One type concerned the *Moors* who settled in Batavia and were engaged in trading business, while the other type was in connection with the employees of the VOC.

The first type of *Moor* merchants were engaged in maritime trade as well as in the commerce within the city of Batavia. According to George Bryan Souza, throughout the eighteenth century, the maritime trade was conducted by *Moor* traders between Batavia and Nagapattinam, which was the key port city of the VOC on the Coromandel Coast (Souza 1986: 133, 137). In addition, when the VOC sold commodities in Batavia to important merchants, some *Moor* merchants were permitted to join the auction. For example, four *Moor* merchants (i.e., Mohonmeth Mira Dauwt, Mahometh Lebe, Assan Nina Dauwt and Aboe Bakar Dauwt) were recorded as *Moor* merchants permitted to join the auction in 1750 (Chijs 1888: 646).

The other type of *Moor* merchants were sailors employed by the VOC. The Dutch company employed Asian people as sailors for the company's vessels. The form of the employment was similar to that of lascars, who were Asian sailors employed by the English East India Company (Jaffer 2015).

A major group of Asian sailors employed by the VOC were the Gujarati *Moor* sailors, and most of them were Muslim, although a recent study demonstrates that the category of *Moor* sailors under the VOC included Asian-originated Portuguese sailors (Rossum 2014: 220–4). In such a case, these Asian-originated Portuguese sailors were additionally mentioned as the so-called *Toepas* in Dutch records of lists of sailors whose identity was Portuguese but who had Asian blood. This suggested that most *Moor* sailors were Muslims.

Dutch documentation of the VOC offers several kinds of information on *Moor* sailors. From the seventeenth century, *Moor* sailors had been employed by the VOC. Initially, the VOC employed many Asian sailors together with European sailors. Besides *Moor* sailors, there were Javanese and Chinese sailors employed, and in many cases, their salary was pre-paid at the beginning of the contract of employment (Rossum 2014). For the VOC, the cost of employing Asian sailors was lower than for European sailors. Keeping the difficulty in communication in mind, the VOC was willing to employ Asian sailors.

However, according to the study by Van Rossum, the Gentlemen XVII, the most important decision-making body for the Dutch company in the Netherlands, prohibited them from employing Muslim sailors on the VOC vessels in the 1710s (Rossum 2012: 43). But the problem of a shortage of staff became clear in the course of time. When Gustaf Willem van Imhoff was appointed the governor-general in 1743, he restarted the employment of *Moor* sailors because of the shortage of sailors. This is probably due to the shortage of Chinese sailors after the Chinese revolt and massacre at Batavia in 1740.

A group composed of less than ten Gujarati *Moor* sailors were managed and led by a Muslim boatswain *sarang* (literally coming from *sarhang* in Persian). The proclamation of the VOC at Batavia dated on 24 March 1775 referred to a regulation of provision of foodstuff for *Moor* sailors at work on board, as follows:

The monthly provision of foodstuff for a *Moor* sailor was 50 lbs. (1 Dutch lb. = 495 g) of rice, 1 lb. of sugar, 1 lb. of tamarind, 1 lb. of salt, 2.5 lbs. of dried fish, 3 cans of arrack and other foodstuff valued at two guilders and eight stuivers.

In contrast, the same proclamation mentioned the regulation of provision of foodstuff for European sailors: A European sailor was monthly provided with 40 lbs. of rice, 10 lbs. of beans, 2 lbs. of salted fish, 2 lbs. of pork bacon, 4.5 cans of arrack, 4 packs of olive oil, 0.5 can of Asian vinegar, 2 lbs. of sugar, 2 lbs. of tamarind, 3 lbs. of salt, 1 can of Cape wine and other foodstuff valued at two guilders and eight stuivers (Chijs 1891: 931–2). In general, provision of foodstuff for a *Moor* sailor was less than that for a European sailor, but interesting points can be found when comparing particular foodstuff. While pork bacon was not provided for *Moor* sailors, more salted fish was offered to a *Moor* sailor than to a European sailor. In addition, the alcoholic drink of arrack was provided to *Moor* sailors although they were Muslims.

By the way, *Moor* sailors went to several places in Asia by working on board of vessels of the VOC, and this situation allowed *Moor* sailors easily to work for their particular private trade. When they were on board, they were permitted to be accompanied by some belongings, and thus it was possible for them to make a private business by bringing a set of merchandise to the destination and selling it. This kind of private business was a serious problem for the VOC, not only with *Moor* sailors but also European sailors. In fact, the high government of Batavia prohibited this kind of private trade for European employees as well as for *Moor* employees (Chijs 1891: 25). This prohibition, in other words, suggested a broad existence of private trade by sailors.

Moreover, the Dutch company employed not only *Moor* sailors but also *Moor* staff. *Moor* staff were engaged in construction of small boats at the shipyard in the port of Batavia. These small boats were used for transporting the cargo between the warehouses on the land and the Dutch vessels anchored at the port in the Bay of Batavia (Rossum 2012: 44).

Autonomy of the *Moor* people at Batavia

Moor residents in Batavia were granted a sort of autonomy, especially the *Moor* citizens engaged in their own business. First, their houses were concentrated in a specific district. As de Haan mentioned, during the early decades of the seventeenth century, *Moor* people resided near the Cannel of *Moor* in the western section of the walled city of Batavia (de Haan 1921: 486). However, in 1633, most *Moor* people were compelled to move outside of the walled city except for some of the rich. It was the *Moor Kwartier* that they moved to, and it was located close to the western wall of the city. The quarter is currently the so-called *pekojan* in Indonesian, and it had several old mosques established in the seventeenth and eighteenth centuries, such as Masjid Al-Anshor, which was established in 1648 thanks to the *waqf* by Muslim immigrants from the Malabar Coast in the southwestern part of the Indian subcontinent. In addition, there are still Masjid Kampong Baru and Masjid An-Nawir in this quarter. The former was established in 1748, and it became the Friday mosque for the Muslims from British India in the nineteenth century, while the latter was constructed in 1760, when Sayyid Abd Allah b. Husayn Aydarus was invited (Heuken 2007: 192–2).

In regard to the autonomy, *Moor* people were granted a sort of autonomy next to the Chinese people. In May 1753, Aboe Bakar was appointed the first *kapitan* of the *Moor* group (Blussé and Dening 2018). He can be considered Aboe Bakar Daut, a *Moor* born at Batavia as seen in the proc-lamation of the VOC at Batavia dated on 9 July 1751. Afterward, he was promoted (Chijs 1889: 72) to the *major* of the *Moor* group in 1774. With this appointment, the high degree of autonomy of the major system was granted to the *Moor* group next to the Chinese society in the seventeenth century (Chijs 1891: 867). At this time, Abd Allah Dauwd was appointed *kapitan*, and Patan Mochamat Nina was *luitenant*, which was a position next to the *kapitan*.

Furthermore, the VOC granted another privilege to the *Moor* people at Batavia, that is the establishment of the hospital specifically for *Moor* peo-ple in 1751.[5] At this hospital, *Moor* people were privileged to enjoy the service at half of the normal cost. However, this *Moor* hospital was closed in 1785 because of the fourth Anglo-Dutch War between 1780 and 1784. In this war, the VOC's vessels and trading posts in maritime Asia were attacked by the British. The war was put to an end in 1784, but the Dutch were heav-ily defeated, and the VOC lost various sorts of commercial bases in South Asia. Trading posts in the island of Ceylon and around the Malabar Coast were captured by the British. In addition, the VOC lost the trading post at Nagapattinam, which was the main trading post on the Coromandel Coast. Besides the loss of trading posts in South Asia, the VOC lost many vessels and suffered from the shortage for business after the war. As the VOC was actively engaged in Euro-Asian trade as well as intra-Asian trade before the war, the shortage of vessels seemed to be a possible catastrophe for the VOC. Because of the shortage of vessels and the stagnation of the trading business of the VOC, the necessity of offering advantages to *Moor* people became less, and it was not so necessary to employ *Moor* sailors either. Therefore, the *Moor* hospital was closed within the short period of around three decades (Bruijn 2009: 117).

Conclusion

Batavia, present-day Jakarta, was one of the early European colonial cit-ies in Southeast Asia. It was established in 1619 by the Dutch East India Company, and it was the place where the VOC had their main key station in Asia. While European people were in the minority in terms of popula-tion, many Asian immigrants lived there. Though there were ample previous studies on Chinese immigrants in Batavia during the seventeenth and eight-eenth centuries, there are a few studies available that focus on South Asian immigrants into Batavia.

Keeping this condition in mind, this chapter aimed to provide a prelimi-nary analysis of the South Asian Muslim immigrants in Batavia during the VOC period. This chapter firstly gave a discussion of the terminology of *Moor* people in the Dutch documentation of the VOC in Batavia; through the analysis of previous studies, it was made clear that this term refers to South Asian Muslim settlers in Batavia. It is clear that this word refers to Muslim people in the texts of the VOC at Batavia, although it ranged according to the contexts. In the case of Batavia's Dutch records, this word refers to the Muslim people originally coming from South Asia.

Second, it offered a demographic investigation of South Asian Muslims in Batavia. Then it highlighted the general feature of South Asian Muslim families in Batavia and mentioned that a specific district was formed in Batavia for *Moor* people in the seventeenth century. The population of the Moor people rose from around 1740 and reached its peak around 1770. However, it decreased in the late eighteenth century. It finally declined in the first half of the nineteenth century, while the Arab immigrant population increased in turn. Generally speaking, *Moor* people at Batavia formed families with children.

Third, the chapter focused on their occupation. They were engaged in maritime trade as well as inland commerce in the city. Some of the *Moor* people were employed by the VOC as sailors. These sailors were mainly Gujarati Muslim sailors working on the Dutch company's vessels. Some *Moor* people also worked at shipyards to construct small vessels for the use of the VOC at Batavia.

Moor people were privileged by the VOC Batavia to have 'self-governance,' with *kapitan*s and *majoor*s appointed by the high government of the VOC at Batavia. Their status of autonomy was high-ranked, next to the Chinese community's, in the second half of the eighteenth century. In addition, the VOC offered a special hospital for *Moor* people at that time. However, the population of South Asian Muslims began to decrease, while the VOC began to lose its power in South Asia in the 1780s when the VOC was defeated by the British in the Fourth Anglo-Dutch War.

In a nutshell, the existence of *Moor* people in Batavia during the early modern period was unique. Fundamentally, for the VOC, the Moor people were significant in the following two points: First, the *Moor* people were one of the key sources for manual labor. In fact, the VOC utilised the *Moor* people as sailors for their vessels and as constructors of small boats in Batavia. They could meet the demand for manual labor, as the VOC suffered from a shortage of such labourers.

Second, the *Moor* people had a sort of character of competitiveness, like the Chinese. From the establishment of the city of Batavia, the VOC heavily relied on overseas Chinese in terms of sources of manual labor, as entrepreneurs for inland industry and as traders for coastal trade and for domestic trade within the city. To avoid a heavy dependence on overseas Chinese, the VOC was willing to promote immigrants from South Asia and gave privileges to the Moor people at Batavia. In order for this European colonial city to exist peacefully, the VOC had to maintain a multi-ethnic society.

Notes

1 Nationaal Archief (National Archives of the Netherlands (NA)): Archief van de VOC (VOC) 1489, 1642, 1767, 1916, 2117, 2482, 2752, 2972, 3252, 3562, 3870.
2 NA: VOC 3391.
3 Arsip Nasional Republik Indonesia (National Archives of Republic of Indonesia (ANRI): Arsip Batavia (Batavia) 338.3.
4 ANRI: Batavia 350.2.
5 ANRI: Hoge Regering 613, p. 160 (Generaleresolutie: 16 februarij 1751).

References

Blussé, Leonard. 1986. *Strange Company: Chinese Settlers, Mestizo Women, and the Dutch in VOC Batavia*, Dordrecht: Foris Publications.

Blussé, Leonard and Nie Dening. 2018. *The Chinese Annals of Batavia, the Kai Ba LidaiShiji and Other Stories (1610–1795)*, Leiden and Boston: Brill Academic Publishers.

Bruijn, Iris. 2009. *Ship's Surgeons on the Dutch East India Company: Commerce and the Progress of Medicine in the Eighteenth Century*, Leiden: Leiden University Press.

Haan, F. de. 1922. *Oud Batavia*. 2 Volumes. Batavia: G. Kolff.

Heuken, Adolf S.J. 2007. *Historical Sites of Jakarta*, seventh edition, Jakarta: Cipta Loka Caraka.

Jaffer, Aaron. 2015. *Lascars and Indian Ocean Seafaring, 1780–1860: Shipboard Life, Unrest and Mutiny*. Rochester: Boydell Press.

Jonge, Huur de. 2000. "A Divided Minority: The Arabs of Batavia," in K. Grijns and Peter J.M. Nas (eds.), *Jakarta-Batavia: Socio-Cultural Essays*, Leiden: KITLV Press.

Raben, Remco. 1996. "Batavia and Colombo: The Ethnic and Spatial Order of Two Colonial Cities 1600–1800," unpublished PhD thesis, Leiden University.

Raffles, Thomas Stamford. 1830. *History of Java*, second edition, London: John Murray.

Rossum, Matthias Van. 2012. "A 'Moorish World' Within the Company: The VOC, Maritime Logistics and Subaltern Networks of Asian Sailors," *Itinerario: International Journal on the History of European Expansion and Global Interaction*, 36(3).

Rossum, Mattias Van. 2014. *Werkers van de wereld: Globalisering, arbeiden interculturele ont moetingentussen Aziatischeen Europesezee lieden in dienst van de VOC, 1600–1800*, Uitgeverij Hilversum: Verloren.

Souza, George Bryan. 1986. *The Survival of Empire: Portuguese Trade and Society in China and the South China Sea 1630–1754*, Cambridge: Cambridge University Press.

Stapel, F.W. (ed.). 1943. *Pieter van Dam's Beschryvinge van de Oostindische Compagnie*, derdeboek's, Gravenhage: Martinus Nijhoff, 1943.

van den Berg, L.W.C. 1886. *Le Ḥadhramout et les colonies arabes de l'archipelindien*, Batavia: Imprimerie du Government.

van der Chijs, J.A. (ed.). 1888, 1889, 1891. *Nederlandsch-Indisch Plakaatboek, 1602–1811*, Zesdedeel, Batavia: Landsdrukkerij.

7

PHYSICIANS, SURGEONS, MERCHANTS AND HEALERS

Production, circulation and reconfiguration of knowledge in eighteenth-century Portuguese India

Fabiano Bracht

This chapter analyses the evidence contained in historical sources of the eighteenth-century Portuguese empire regarding processes of the construction, circulation and reconfiguration of medical knowledge in South Asia. The main hypothesis is that the inherent social structure of the Portuguese empire was deeply influenced by racial and social interactions that involved Portuguese and local agents in a dynamic of shared production and the circulation of knowledge.

Throughout the early modern era, the city of Goa, located on the western coast of India, was the nerve centre of the Eastern Portuguese Empire. However, discussions concerning this subject matter must always encompass and contemplate a considerably broader geographical space. The designations 'extended Indian Ocean' or the 'East Indies' encompass the whole region that surrounds the Indian Ocean, where the circulation of vessels was greatly influenced by the monsoon regime (Bethencourt 1998: 250–69). In this sense, this chapter bears a great debt to Michael N. Pearson's work. He helped to consolidate, since the mid-1970s, the understanding that the Portuguese Empire, especially its eastern part, is to be seen as a dynamic cluster of localities and communities, mercantile or otherwise, each extremely lively and endowed with great transformative potential.

Since its dawn in the fifteenth century, the empire formed itself as a complex system of frontiers, one that would expand as the caravels reached farther and farther. The term *frontier* is frequently employed by historians with a specific function. As defined by Peter Burke (Burke 2009), a frontier is not necessarily a place; it can be regarded as the limits of a cultural encounter in which both sides are clearly defined but, at the same time, conditioned by specific factors and endowed with a selective permeability of historical dimensions. Although this is a valid concept, it must be broadened to fit the present study for two main reasons.

First, since human cultures do not exist dissociated from their surrounding environment, a frontier's permeability dynamics are strongly affected by variables related to the physical surroundings in which they occur (Bracht 2013). Second, among the factors influencing the production of knowledge in the field of natural philosophy and some of its correlated fields – such as medicine and pharmacy – throughout the early modern era, few exerted greater influence than the large variability of ways in which intercultural relations were established (Raj 2010: 10–11) in the expansion of colonial empires (Pratt 1992: 6). Colonial territories, in terms of knowledge-circulation, may be defined as frontier regions – mobile, dynamic and mutable in nature – but also as borders with established boundary limits often difficult to overcome. In its metaphorical sense, a frontier may also be understood as a territory of dispute, where new cultural standards are forcibly moulded as each side gains, or loses, terrain. In terms of knowledge production, the term *frontier* attains a meaning akin to Richard White's own definition (White 2001); White states that a series of interactions and intersections of social and economic natures occur in a given geographical and temporal space. With this very metaphorical space in mind, the point where intercultural exchanges take place would be the site of clashes between

> imperial or state regimes and non-state forms of social organization, a rough balance of power, a mutual need or desire for what the other possesses, and an inability of one side to commander enough force to compel the other to do what it desired.
>
> (White 2001: XII)

In this sense, continuous processes of permutation, appropriation and re-signification take place, profoundly influenced by the eventual degree of disequilibrium that exists between the opposing forces positioned at the frontier complexes. In this kind of process, we frequently observe that '*force and violence are hardly foreign to the process of creating and maintaining a middle ground, but the critical element is mediation*' (White 2001: XII). By 'mediation,' I do not allege that there is any kind of isonomy in the relationship between the sides; I do, however, mean that there exists some reasonable cause in supposing that – as an interpretative possibility – the coloniser is not always able to obtain that which he covets, in the same manner that the colonised resists and always strives to concede the bare minimum.

The idea that conflict and the need for mediation were also processes inherent to knowledge production in colonial environments became widely regarded as valid. Knowledge creation – through exchange and negotiation – embeds itself inside the *contact zone*, the *locus* of the colonial encounters, the space in which peoples geographically and historically separated come into contact with each other and establish ongoing relations, usually involving conditions of coercion, radical inequality, and intractable conflict.

(Pratt 1992: 6)

Knowledge production in colonial environments, far from being a direct outcome of understanding, emerged from conflict but also from mutual interests, through sensitive processes of negotiation. The congruences – or parallels – common points of interest that stemmed from these processes were, to a great extent, the result of an incomplete understanding of the other being, nevertheless, a continuous process of *'mutual and creative misunderstanding'* (White 2001: XII). This concept, *'creative misunderstanding,'* has become the keystone in recent understandings on knowledge production in colonial universes (Cook 2013). I shall attempt to demonstrate how knowledge production – mainly concerning medicine, pharmacy and natural philosophy – in Portuguese India can be, in a sense, a good example of that type of process.

Among physicians and pundits: evidence of a conflicting coexistence

The first Portuguese authorities in India quickly realised that local physicians and healers – *Panditos*[1] (Pundits) as they were called by the Portuguese – were, naturally, much more keenly informed in the arts of tending to tropical maladies (Pearson 2001a: 401–19) than their European counterparts. One may find a multitude of evidence regarding the influence of *Ayurvedic* medicine in the manner in which European physicians absorbed and apprehended knowledge on remedies and diseases in the Indian subcontinent (Walker 2002: 74–104). In part due to difficulties of a lack of physicians and also the scarce availability of effective remedies in the treatment of diseases encountered in the East Indies, a great number of physicians, apothecaries, surgeons, herbalists and natural philosophers contributed to the development of knowledge on plants, animals and diseases through teaching Indian medicine. This occurred in two ways. The first and more frequent was through the many *Vaidya* or herbalists and apothecaries of Indian origin who worked at hospitals for Portuguese authorities (Walker 2002: 74–104). Information was largely absorbed through the daily observation of these professionals. The second one, less frequent yet highly important, consisted of dialogues between European practitioners and their Indian counterparts, leading to a subsequent exchange of information. Several physicians, apothecaries and even Portuguese merchants were able to establish extensive contact networks from which they received, eventually through material compensation, information concerning the healing properties of a panoply

139

of local drugs (Pearson 1996: 20–41). It is plausible that the networks were not constructed and maintained without expending considerable amounts of energy, verbal exchange, negotiation and effort from both sides.

As for the Europeans, those who were successful in their enterprise were ushered into a very selective universe, entry to which may have come at the expense of favours, services or even monetary compensation. In a manuscript comprising more than 100 pages and 82 medical recipes employed in the *Hospital Real* (lit. 'Royal Hospital'), one is informed that, in that period, there were *'in this city of Goa alone, more than eighty masters or Pandits'* (BNP – COD 2102). These, according to its author, João dos Reis, were not keen on sharing their recipes and knowledge.

In 1696, when João dos Reis wrote his book of recipes, his criticism was directed at Indian physicians: those *Panditos* who never pursued their studies at a European institution and yet worked at the *Hospital Real*, prescribing remedies and directly competing with the few Portuguese practitioners (BNP – COD 2102). The *Hospital Real*, an institution which was initially under the control of Portuguese physicians, slowly became the central 'battleground'; a catoptric object of the colonial society's own contradictions but also one that was increasingly sustained by an Indian workforce. Over the course of the seventeenth and eighteenth centuries, the difficulties of meeting imperial demands made it increasingly common for practitioners born and educated in the colonies to be granted licences to practice medicine and surgery and work in the production of remedies (Lopes 1996:121–122). The immense lack of human resources in the empire was one of the reasons behind the apparent sense of urgency in which reforms in education and medicine production were passed and implemented since the fifth decade of the eighteenth century.

Almost a century after João dos Reis voiced his disapproval of the huge number of *Panditos* who directly competed with Portuguese specialists, we find that, in Goa, competition was no longer an issue. That is, around the 1780s or perhaps even earlier, there were no physicians working in Portuguese India who received higher education at university or even any surgeon educated in Europe (Bastos 2010b: 61–79). The situation changed very little up until the end of the eighteenth century. In 1799, the governor and general captain of the State of India, Francisco António da Veiga Cabral da Câmara (1733–1810), wrote to Rodrigo da Sousa Coutinho, at the time the secretary of state of the Marine and the Overseas Territory, informing him that

> currently, in this State, there is not any Portuguese Physician who have studied at the University of Coimbra, and those working at the Hospital as well as others in this city, none of them studied with method, so that they have to be considered as practioners.
>
> (HAG – Monções do Reino, vol. 271)

There was also a lack of medical schools, although metropolitan professionals had filled this deficit by sporadically lecturing on the subject since the seventeenth century; this fact was a constant source for re-vindication from local Portuguese and Indian elites (Pearson 2001b). Albeit under Portuguese authority, the majority of the physicians, surgeons and apothecaries in Portuguese India were Indians. And although licences to practice were only granted to Christians, many non-Christian professionals went against Portuguese regulations and practiced their craft. In practice, the state had long been incapable of exercising its control in an effective manner on activities connected to the assistance and treatment of the ill, and this inability was greater when it came to the manufacturing and distribution of remedies (Pearson 2001b; Bastos 2010b: 61–79).

After expansion that effectively tripled the size of the territory under Goan control in the years leading up to 1788, the sheer numeric disequilibrium between Christians and Hindus led to the latter being largely favoured, rendering ineffective most policies that aimed at regulating professionals in any branch of traditional medicine. Nevertheless, issues regarding public health were at the centre of priorities of the secretariat of state of the Marine and the Overseas Territory. One of the motives was the urgent need to provide satisfactory medical and surgical treatment to the numerous troops, especially officials, a necessity of utmost importance given the period of constant tension between Goa, its neighbours, the Maratha Empire and the Kingdom of Mysore, headed by the Sultan Fateh Ali Khan Sahab Tipu (1750–1799). The situation was grievous, especially because of the impossibility of the Portuguese kingdom and other colonial territories, like Mozambique, to contribute to the war effort in an adequate manner. Goan troops were faced daily with adversities wrought by constant skirmishes; misfortunes that comprised not only wounds inflicted by battle but also maladies that severely ailed them. As there were no readily available replacements for soldiers afflicted by wounds and ailments, those who were put out of commission had to be swiftly treated in order to return to battle as soon as possible. This was always a challenge for physicians, surgeons and apothecaries. Even the Pombaline reforms of auxiliary regiments and battalions of *sipaios* (sepoys), mostly comprising native soldiers, did little to mitigate Goa's difficult situation (Avelar 2012).

Besides the severe shortage of soldiers, the Goan population suffered tremendously from diseases. For the imperial administration, India never was the easiest of territories to support in terms of medical aid and care. Mortality rates of Europeans, slaves and local populations were the highest in the empire. Goa is located in a plain full of swamps that, while adequate to rice farming, was equally propitious for the proliferation of disease-ridden – especially, malaria-ridden – mosquitoes. Aside from this ailment, other illnesses affected the local population. The deadliest among these was *Mordexim*, which some researchers have identified as cholera

(Pearson 2001: 401–19). As the *Hospital Real* was since the sixteenth century an institution devoted to the care of Portuguese individuals – especially those of the highest ranks in the imperial hierarchy – several institutions rose in Goa and its vicinity to tend to local needs. These institutions were as varied as the stratifications in Goan society were complex.

Information on the existence of such institutions dates back to the sixteenth and seventeenth centuries. The *Hospital Real* was located on the *Cais de Santa Catarina* (lit. 'Saint Catherine's wharf'), close to the *Mandovi* river. At the turn of the seventeenth century, there was yet another hospital in Goa; this institution, the *Hospital dos Pobres* (lit. 'Hospital of the Poor'), or *Hospital da Gente da Terra* (lit. 'The People of the Land's Hospital'), cared for the local population in general. However, from the sixteenth century, other hospitals that tended to the general public appeared, such as *Hospital de Todos-os-Santos* (lit. 'All Saints' Hospital), *Hospital de São Lázaro* (lit. 'Saint Lazarus' Hospital'), *Hospital da Piedade* (lit. 'Hospital of the Piety'), or the *Hospital da Cidade* (lit. 'City's Hospital'). Some of the aforementioned facilities existed simultaneously, operating in different buildings. As time went on, there were mergers, such as the annexation of the *Hospital da Piedade* by the *Hospital de Todos-os-Santos* in 1707, thenceforth named *Hospital da Piedade e de Todos-os-Santos* (lit. 'Hospital of the Piety and All Saints'), which apparently was also known as *Hospital dos Pobres*. The sources of income for these institutions were diverse as well. Besides the *Irmandade da Misericórdia*, which financially supported the *Hospital de Todos-os-Santos*, the city itself also invested in caring for the sick, paying for operations at the *Hospital da Piedade* and at the *Hospital da Cidade* itself. Over the course of the seventeenth century, municipal assistance maintained the *Hospital da Piedade*, as the *Irmandade da Misericórdia* managed the *Hospital de Todos-os-Santos* (Bastos 2010a). With the effective merging of these institutions at the dawn of the eighteenth century, the two dimensions of assistance – public and ecclesiastical – were also subjected to a merger. The *Hospital Real* was still operating but mostly as a military hospital for Portuguese military personnel. There were other minor hospitals – often mere infirmaries – spread throughout villages that were part of parishes (Lopes 2006: 119–22). Moreover, since the sixteenth century, the establishment of health-care facilities was a part of the strategy of conversion of the local population to Christianity (Županov 2008: 269). Because of the multiplicity of agents operating in those hospitals and the fact that these spaces did not stand isolated from the aforementioned conflicts – feuds characteristic to colonial Goa itself – Cristina Bastos's lines concerning the coexistence of these institutions are an enlightened interpretation of the reality within Goa's hospitals:

> Goa's colonial hospitals concentrated not only episodes and practices of treatment, healing, cure, death, rescue, redemption,

encounter, and experimentation, but also the histories of inclusion, exclusion, occupation, power balance and capacity of negotiating or to decide.

(Bastos 2010b: 68)

Because of ever-increasingly unhealthy conditions, the place where the State of India's capital was originally established was slowly but surely deserted by its own population. By 1775, the population of Goa was reduced to one-tenth of what it had been at the twilight of the sixteenth century, and the majority of the administrative services were transferred to the nearby Panjim. Goa would still be the capital of the State of India, albeit in title alone, until 1843, although it was by then long abandoned, referred to as *Velha Goa* (lit. 'Old Goa') (Bastos 2010b: 68).

During the major part of the early modern period in Goa, assistance to the sick was performed by two very heterogeneous groups. The first of these comprised physicians, surgeons, apothecaries, herbalists and healers of Indian origin, partially or totally instructed in their own traditions. In bigger numbers, these specialists worked in a more distributed manner amongst non-Christian natives but also amongst Portuguese, Indo-Portuguese and Luso descendants. The majority of these individuals were Hindu, more focused on communities in which the Christian population was a minority – or even non-existent – mainly in the newly conquered territories (Lopes 1996). Christians in the most remote villages occasionally sought them out. Muslim physicians, in contrast, are rarely mentioned, either in sources or in historiography. This specific group was heavily persecuted by the authorities during the colonial period; the references to *Hakim* were more frequent in the sixteenth century, but they decreased, although not disappearing entirely, at the end of the seventeenth century (Pearson 1996: 20–41). The second group comprised agents with European education, many intimately involved with religious orders. All orders would virtually participate in one stage or another of health care and assistance, from the Dominicans and the Franciscans to the Augustinians, although, up until 1760, the Jesuits were the most active of all the orders in these spheres (Županov 2008: 263–300). After the expulsion of the Society of Jesus, the Brothers Hospitallers of Saint John of God assumed an ever-increasing role in health matters.

Although these groups can be described separately, the same cannot be said of the universe of knowledge shared among them. Since the sixteenth century, physicians, surgeons and apothecaries of European origin absorbed as much information as they could on uses, techniques and medical knowledge of Asian provenance (Pearson 1996: 20–41, 2001: 401–19). This path was also traversed by their Indian counterparts, through the *contact zone* between the selectively permeable borders established among the two universes now co-existing in the same sphere. Indian physicians, herbalists and healers began sharing and employing techniques, remedies and conceptual approaches introduced by Europeans (Pearson 1996: 20–41, 2001: 401–19). Both sides influenced each another. With the suppression of the Society of Jesus after 1760, the number of local practitioners of medicine, pharmacy and surgery increased even more in relative terms. The kingdom, through its colonial representatives, annually granted a large number of licences to professionals of various fields linked to the sphere of health care. Nevertheless, the extreme degree of insalubrity still posed grave problems to the local administration and ruined institutions; the *Hospital Real*, in particular, was the recipient of constant criticism levelled at it by representatives of the crown and other agents. In 1783, the naturalist Manuel Galvão da Silva vividly described his impressions of the conditions of the Hospital Real de Goa:

> I have been observing, Sir, that almost every day in this hospital dies those people from the fleet, which were in good conditions, despite have bear'd the heavy malaise of the long journey; I do not know the true cause, because I was always out of this city; however, I can certify Your Excellence that the same hospital and its healers will kill every single one His Majesty sends to this lands. The hospital, instead of being well ventilated, illuminated, and have the proper cleanliness, it is a dungeon full of bars, gates, and oyster panes, where the air never has free access: the terrible odour exhaled by a pipe that comes from inside the building and goes straight near the sea prevents any ship of anchoring there. There is in this Hospital a section, called house of the weaks, and doomed are those who enter there; not because they could not live anymore; but for the helplessness in which they are left; and the terror that kills them briefly. The so named Physicians are uneducated men, whom never knew, not even by name, what is Medicine, and amongst them the most famous, if one wants to be medicated, needs to be closed in his office to not get drunk.
>
> (AHMB – Remessa 387)

Accounts of the *Hospital Real's* deficient sanitary conditions were considerably frequent from the seventeenth century. Portuguese authorities often considered the lack of Europe-educated professionals as the main factor responsible for the widespread sanitary problems experienced by the State of India. In fact, Indian physicians were still looked upon with distrust in the eighteenth century – not unlike the distrust in Indian professionals manifested by João dos Reis in 1699. This is a veritable sample of the hostile environment of open conflict that affected social relations in the field of health care. It is plausible to think that this had more to do with the racial, social and religious contradictions that existed within colonial societies than with the Portuguese accepting – or not – Indian healing practices. Since the sixteenth century, European physicians, upon arrival in India, were keen to adopt many of the syncretic practices developed by professionals since Garcia da Orta's time, as well as present practices, such as, for instance, the recipes illustrated by João dos Reis. These practices were common among the majority of Indian physicians, both Christian and non-Christian, over the course of the eighteenth century. Hence, there was a much more complex process of the validation of knowledge on the part of the authorities at Goa and in the metropolis.

Although there were numerous local physicians, surgeons and apothecaries operating in several institutions, the colonial authorities sent constant requests to the crown for people qualified enough to lecture on medicine and surgery. These entreaties were not exactly new; they had been a frequent affair since the end of the seventeenth century. The requests were granted numerous times; however, no systematic procedure concerning the resolution of the problem was ever put into effect (Bastos 2010b: 61–79). On April 20, 1785, in order to respond to the pleas of the governor of the State of India, Minister Melo e Castro ordered the military surgeon Francisco Manuel Barroso da Silva to move to Goa to assume the post of chief surgeon. Barroso da Silva's commission was teaching surgery and anatomy, as well as managing the establishment of a botanical garden (ABD).[2]

Once he arrived in Goa, Francisco Manuel began working with a team of physicians, nurses and apothecaries of Indian and Portuguese lineage. Because of local factors, the arrival of a surgeon from the kingdom did little to change the dynamics of work at the Hospital Real. Often viewed as inadequate in the treatment of local maladies, the arrival of remedies imported from Europe was conditioned by the rhythm of monsoons. Medicines frequently arrived in a degraded state or were even purloined over the course of a trip. Pharmacies at Goan hospitals were always filled to the brim with useless substances – expired or in an advanced state of deterioration (Bastos 2010b: 61–79). As one would expect, these factors had an impact on the price of medicines, making them virtually inaccessible to most of the population. Another factor must also be taken into consideration: Goan markets offered a large variety of local remedies sold by herbalists and prescribed by local physicians or healers.

Still, there was a demand for European medicines. There was a considerable dynamic of production of remedies in Goa at the time. Until 1760, the Jesuit Pharmacy was an important production centre, which, in turn, was highly profitable to the society's priests, although they were not formally allowed to profit from such gains (Walker 2007: 569–79). Indeed, since the sixteenth century, an environment of shared production of therapeutic knowledge emerged in Goan territory, encompassing not only Goan substances and local knowledge but also those substances that circulated within imperial market networks.

Concerning available human resources, Portuguese India developed an interesting particularity which directly impacted on social relations in the medical profession. The colonisers' initial idea was to abolish the caste system because of its ancestral connection with the Hindu faith; in practice, what transpired over the course of centuries was the result of disputes and accommodations through which Indian elites could aspire to the best of both universes. Indians, mainly those belonging to the Brahmin and Charodo castes, which adopted the Christian faith, maintained their social statuses, castes and ancestral properties. Through converting to the Catholic faith, they were also inducted into the chain of benefits that the colonial administration reserved for those who obeyed – at the very least in appearance only – the rules imposed upon the territory by Christianity (Lopes and Matos 2006: 15–70).

Many among the converted became important Christian activists. But social transformation of this magnitude was not a linear process; nor was it devoid of conflicts. The converted Indian elites, while aiming at obtaining the best of both worlds, also found themselves embroiled in a conflict on two fronts. On one side, there were the racial barriers imposed by the colonial administration; on the other, there was the distrust of the elites and communities of non-converted individuals (Xavier and Županov 2015: 15–41). In a sense, they also faced the worst of the two universes. But, in their constant search for a balance that would never materialise, this clash also produced the characteristics intrinsic to knowledge production. They were able to develop a great variety of strategies and establish negotiation channels (Xavier and Županov 2015: 15–41). Among these, we find the practice of medicine and the healing arts (Lopes and Matos 2006: 15–70; Bastos 2010b: 74). The Charodos dedicated themselves mainly to activities concerning letters and commerce, particularly from the beginning of the nineteenth century onwards. In the eighteenth century, the Goan Brahmins held medicine to be one of their favourite activities (Bastos 2010b: 74).

Around 1794, the chief physician of the State of India was a Goan Catholic Brahmin, whose family had long adopted the Christian religion and nomenclature (Walker 2016: 161–92). Ignácio Caetano Afonso apparently maintained himself in the highest medical post in Portuguese India for over ten years up until his death in 1798, without ever having to study medicine as taught in European universities. The official correspondence of the State of India reveals that Ignácio Caetano Afonso was a pupil of the Portuguese Luís da Costa Portugal, his predecessor, who trained other professionals when he occupied the post of chief physician (Walker 2016: 161–92). Through Timothy D. Walker's analysis of the aforementioned correspondence (Walker 2016: 161–92), one can infer that Ignácio Caetano's education in medicine was not limited to his old master's lectures on the subject. The Brahminic tradition in the practice of medicine was beyond the reach of local colonial authorities. Ignácio Caetano drew from the knowledge imparted to him by several other masters – *Panditos*, Brahmins, Catholics and physicians renowned among local communities.

In the quality of chief physician, Ignácio Caetano was also tasked with the evaluation of those who aimed at practicing medicine in any part of Goan territory. In 1795, Queen Maria wrote three times to Cabral da Câmara, the Governor and General Captain of the State of India, authorizing students examined by Ignácio Caetano to practice medicine. They were Camilo do Rosário de Sá e Noronha,[3] Agostinho Salvador Clemente[4] and José Caetano Lobo.[5] The first two resided in the village of Lutulim, and the last hailed from Sirulá parish. All served in the Hospital Militar (lit. 'Military Hospital') for some time. Although there is no mention of any of them belonging to the Brahmin caste, they were Indians, not of Portuguese descent. This means that there were mechanisms of reproduction of medical knowledge that were – in part, at least – under the direct control of individuals born and raised in India.

The knowledge that these professionals possessed is itself a token of what has been stated at the outset: a syncretic blend emerged comprising local and European elements, combined with substances that were part of the myriad products in circulation within the empire. In theoretical terms, in order for them to operate within the hospitals, they were probably judged as being up to the standards of the European authorities. In terms of efficiency, although complaints about the practices of Eastern physicians were commonplace, documentary sources suggest that, in the eyes of the authorities, these individuals were as competent as expected. This bipolarity is not the least surprising; it was an integral part of the dynamics between local authorities and the central power. The governor, Cabral da Câmara, praised Ignácio Caetano immensely, although he would always remark that the latter did not attend university (Walker 2016: 161–92).

Circulating agents, circulating knowledge

In 1794, while acceding to a request by Martinho de Melo e Castro to Cabral da Câmara's predecessor, Francisco da Cunha e Meneses (1747–1812), Ignácio Caetano composed a small document with information concerning four medicinal roots that were used by the Hospital Real's staff. The manner in which the document was composed – *Descripçoens e Virtudes das raízes medicinaes, que de Lisboa se recomendão ao IL^{mo} e Exmo Sor Gov^{or} e Capitão Gen^{al} Francisco da Cunha e Menezes, 1794*[6] (lit. 'Descriptions and Virtues of the medicinal that were requested by Lisbon to His Excellency, the Illustrious Governor and General Captain Francisco da Cunha e Menezes, 1794') – suggests that the requested information was to precisely identify the substances mentioned in the report. Indeed, there were descriptions of four roots, *Pau Cobra* or *Hampaddu*, *Mongus* root, *João Lopes Pinheiro* root and *Calumba* root. The news of their use reached Lisbon through the complex networks that kept the imperial government informed about the natural potentialities of the empire. As was common, appropriate diligences were requested. Once it arrived in Goa, the requisition was brought before the chief physician. A large part of the circulation of knowledge followed this very route, and many times, the academic purposes of such knowledge was merely secondary.

Although the news of their use emerged from Goa, none of the afore-mentioned roots were from Portuguese India. The *Pau Cobra* and the *Mongus* roots were exported from Ceylon, and the *João Lopes Pinheiro* and the *Calumba* roots were brought in from Mozambique. In addition, these substances were not new to imperial medical networks. Ignácio Caetano himself noted that if the authorities wanted to learn more about the roots' virtues, they should refer to the pharmacopoeias of João Curvo Semedo (1716) and Manoel Rodrigues Coelho (1735) and asserted that these two works contained more detailed information than he himself could ever supply.[7] A relative disharmony between the information that the minister solicited and what the chief physician supplied is noticeable. Although Ignácio Caetano did comply with what was expected of him – he sent information concerning these four roots – the information was not in the expected format. This would lead one to believe that each was preoccupied with his own specific reality and there were distinct perspectives regarding what type of information was relevant on both sides of the dialogue. However, this was not the last time that both parties exchanged correspondence on this matter; several years later, new inquiries on the subject from Lisbon would arrive in Goa (Walker 2016: 161–92).

In 1799, in order to comply with the previous year's request, new descriptions were prepared. Ignácio Caetano had passed away the previous year (Walker 2016: 161–92), and the information, written in the form of a report and sent to the then minister, Rodrigo de Sousa Coutinho, elaborated on the aforementioned roots, along with seven additional substances. This time, the enquiry was passed on to the chief surgeon, Francisco Manuel Barroso da Silva, who had been previously sent to India to lecture on surgery and anatomy. The new list also contained information on plants from various parts of the empire, and this time, it related that this information was obtained from local physicians and herbalists. Moreover, aside from the chief surgeon, the document was also signed by three of the aforementioned local physicians. When the document was sent to Lisbon, the governor felt obligated to declare that although these professionals were doctors with licences, none among them had attended a university – not even Francisco Manuel Barroso da Silva, for he was merely a surgeon.[8]

I must point out an interesting aspect regarding the social issue in the validation of produced knowledge. Although the texts were penned by the chief surgeon and three additional Goan physicians working at the Hospital Militar, the veracity of the information was countersigned by José Caetano Pacheco Tavares, then secretary general of the State of India.[9]

Even though no single substance cited in the documents was unknown in Europe by then, the information concerning their precedence and use would still be viewed as incomplete up until the end of the eighteenth century. In Goa, research on these subjects resumed. In correspondence exchanged with the Real Museu da Ajuda (lit. 'Royal Museum of Ajuda') in 1800, the Cirurgião-Mor, Barroso da Silva, compiled more complete information regarding the *João Lopes Pinheiro* root – or, better yet, the root of the *Tefoleira* tree.[10] In the document regarding the aforementioned remedy – for years used in India and Europe alike and known as being originally from Mozambique – there are some pieces of information that allow us to better understand the routes that a plant or a medicinal product could traverse within imperial networks. After several years of research on this very substance, Barroso da Silva was successful in unveiling some of the mysteries surrounding its origin.

> João Lopes Pinheiro, as far as I could know, was a Portuguese who came to Azia in the company of a group of Jesuit priests and passing through Mozambique observed a Kaffir, from Manica, who used to cure diverse maladies only by using roots, trees, bushes and fruits; one of the Jesuits came to him once with a dysentery which was taking him to the grave. The man gave him, several times a day, a root smashed in water, sometimes with milk, curing the priest in just a few days. Observing after, other cures of the same nature, he asked other Kaffirs in seek for knowing the root by himself, starting to using it with great success in the cure of various infirmities and earning a considerable amount of money and giving the root his own name. I am not informed about in which year those things happened, and it is impossible to know, except at the expense of hard work consulting the Jesuit's papers which are in such a bad condition kept in Her Majesty's Archives; nor does this seem to me to be essential.[11]

Still according to Barroso da Silva's enquiry, several years later, the same João Lopes Pinheiro established himself in Goa as a merchant, where he continued to amass fortunes by marketing the aforementioned root. Meanwhile, his stay in the State of India's capital was cut short because

> as soon as he could, he moved on to Dutch Batavia, and with the aforementioned roots continued to make prodigious cures, and in this city gave a portion of them to a certain Dutch Lady, with instruction for its use, and the said Lady, moving to Europe, shared with it with Gassbios, instructing him on its application.[12]

Although the matter of the Dutch acquiring that root for free was called into question in a later passage, Barroso da Silva affirmed that that was indeed the case – rising from a man named João Lopes Pinheiro, a merchant responsible for the dissemination of a remedy of African origin throughout Asia and then throughout Europe. In fact, this route makes sense. The *João Lopes Pinheiro* root was referred to by this name in Portuguese pharmacopoeias from 1760, when it was cited in the third edition of the *Pharmacopea Tubalense* penned by Manoel Rodrigues Coelho.

After this brief history of the remedy in question, I now turn my attention to the ensuing issue – the extensive analysis of its applications and uses, mainly in Goa, in order to fill in the blanks, so to speak, in the literature concerning it. The major interest was its application in treating dysentery and *Mordexim*, ailments that prompted the concern of the medical community, but also its application as a potent febrifuge.

Over the course of his investigations, Barroso da Silva concluded that there ought to be various species of the bush from which the root was extracted, and these species were native to various regions along the Indian Ocean. Sebastião Dalgado, author of the *Glossário Luso Asiático*, published in Coimbra in 1919, classified the *João Lopes Pinheiro* root with plants from the *Todalia* genus – identified in the eighteenth century by Linnaeus and Lamark (Dalgado 1919: 382). With the available data, it is not possible to assess the precision of Dalgado's association; nevertheless, one must note that some of the plants belonging to that genus are currently used as source of medicines of herbal provenience in Eastern Africa and Southern Asia.[13] It is also plausible that the roots, diffused throughout Asia and Europe, were extracted from various different species of the same genus. The circulation of drugs was a long-reaching process, and drugs were transported outside of the official networks – a fact that hinders efforts of tracking and pinpointing them. In Barroso da Silva's account, we find important evidence concerning the establishment of informal networks serving as pathways for the circulation of knowledge. Regarding the information that he uncovered, including the therapeutic applications of the *João Lopes Pinheiro* root, he declared that

> These knews were comunicated to me by Paulo Lopes, a Goan born man devoted to the study of Medicine, who lived in Mozambique for almost 50 years. . . . He said have known João Lopes Pinheiro three years before the Jesuit's extinction, which was in 1760, at the same time of the publication, in Europe, of the Pharmacopoeia Tubalense, in which the said root is mentioned, and it is difficult to believe that in such a few time those information could have arrived in Europe. Therefore, I assume that, in Europe, the Lopes Pinheiro Root was knew many years before, perhaps informed by João Lopes himself.[14]

As the author himself suggested, the complete chronology of knowledge circulation is difficult to unravel; nevertheless, there are important aspects.

First, and regardless of the problems related to concrete dates, one can surmise that there was some swiftness to the process of knowledge transmission. The aforementioned information was circulated throughout Mozambique, Goa and the Dutch colony of Batavia in Indonesia in a surprisingly quick fashion. Upon arrival in Europe, the knowledge was readily processed – the fact that the said knowledge figured in some of the publications of 1760 can attest to this. One must keep in mind that travel through the Indian Ocean was always subject to the monsoons' annual cycles, which means that all circulation obeyed the monsoons' pendulous and biannual rhythm. The same criteria applied to communications with Europe.

The plant's trajectory itself – undertaken by different people – attests to the transformative properties of knowledge-circulation noted by James Secord (Secord 2004: 654–72). The root would have impressed João Lopes in Mozambique around the fifth decade of the eighteenth century, or some years prior to that, after he witnessed local healers using it to heal patients. Also, one must not overlook the fact that a Jesuit priest supposedly let himself be treated by a local inhabitant with it, attesting to its curative potential. João Lopes negotiated the information with the men who originally possessed the aforementioned knowledge that the merchant deemed important. I assume that, during the negotiation process, the locals only transmitted that which they found pertinent. Who could say how much they had concealed? One must also be mindful of the fact that there were linguistic barriers and dissimilar conceptions of nature, disease and cure that might have prompted them to negotiate. In the *contact zone*, the re-signification performed was one that allowed for inclusion of the remedy in the European universe of knowledge.

Upon arriving in India, João Lopes Pinheiro found the very same root there. Or was it a different species? Nevertheless, a new re-signification took place; the knowledge was passed on to local physicians, apothecaries, herbalists and healers. The *João Lopes Pinheiro* root began to be sold in Goan markets, associated with new names and meanings. How many people were involved in this process? To this end, it is also important to mention that João Lopes Pinheiro, the most likely disseminator of the remedy, was mentioned as a merchant but never as a physician, surgeon, apothecary, or pharmacist, which would suggest he possessed some degree of training or a licence. As negotiator, he circulated beyond the borders of the Portuguese Empire and throughout the Dutch colony of Batavia. It is unlikely that he had gone there without prior knowledge or contact with local agents. Perhaps he had Portuguese – or Goan – contacts there? Nevertheless, we know that he was ultimately successful in selling his products in Europe, assuming that he had in his stock more than just the aforementioned root, and he even had one of them described in a very effective advertising platform: a pharmacopoeia. To complete the process of circulation, when new information regarding the *João Lopes Pinheiro* root was sent to Europe by the Indian physicians working at the Hospital Real,[15] among them Ignácio Caetano Afonso, the chief physician, they validated the information they had sent by turning to a European medical authority, pointing to the contents of the *Pharmacopea Tubalense*.

Final considerations

Because of the centralising model of imperial administration, which barred the colonies from founding and having their own institutions of higher education or even their own press, the circulation of both qualified professionals and knowledge was strictly conditioned by the metropolis's limited capacities. In Asia, that entailed that circulation was conditioned by the dubious communication networks of the Route of India, which had a less-than-optimal flow. At the same time, in strategic terms, Asian colonies were relegated to the background over the course of the eighteenth century; we can clearly see this by comparing them to the colonies on the Atlantic Coast. This had a considerable impact on the circulation of almost everything, from goods and people to knowledge between India and Europe. One of the outcomes of that process was, for instance, the establishment of mildly dynamic circulation patterns involving the diverse parts of the Eastern Empire – mainly India and Mozambique – and also other parts along the Indian coastline, including several colonies under the control of rival European nations. This was a fundamental factor in the specific case of the various medicinal drugs, among them the *João Lopes Pinheiro* root, analysed in this chapter.

The documents concerning this prodigious root (or *roots*, perhaps?) supply important information on how chains of production, extension, reconfiguration and circulation of knowledge worked in a simultaneous fashion and in a manner encompassing both official chains and informal networks. Interpenetration and the permeability of these networks, and of the border environments themselves, demonstrate how difficult the identification of the outlines of both can be. Historians tend to typify their characters, simplifying them to make their analyses more manageable, attempting to define their roles as agents belonging to one side or another. However, the very same characters frequently show us how social environments can be extremely nuanced. Even if the 'João Lopes Pinheiro' we find described in Barroso da Silva's writings did not exist, the plausibility of the narrative is nevertheless a basis for unravelling the degree of complexity in studies on the circulation of people, remedies and knowledge in the extremely diversified environment of the colonial universe.

Abbreviations

HAG   Historical Archive of Goa
BNP   National Library of Portugal (Biblioteca Nacional de Portugal)

AHMB   Natural History Museum Archive / Bocage Museum Archive, Lisbon
ADB   Historical Archive of Braga
ANTT   *Torre do Tombo* National Archive, Lisbon

Notes

1 The term *Pundit* is of Sanskrit origin, although it is found in the majority of the languages of the Indian subcontinent and originally meant 'sage,' 'professor,' or 'philosopher.' It was a title used to refer to individuals with a higher education. Oftentimes, those dubbed as *Pandit* were Brahmins; this caste was intimately linked to the practice of Ayurvedic medicine and to the knowledge of medicinal drugs. In Portuguese writings since the sixteenth century, the term *Panditos* is applied in an almost exclusive manner to the *Vaidya* physicians, who practiced a distinctive type of traditional medicine – a branch of healing practices which not only incorporated in itself the empirical experience of millions of years of medical practice but was also indubitably influenced by *Ayurveda*'s ancestral principles and by Muslim systems.
2 ADB – Reference Code: PT/UM-ADB/FAM/FAA-AAA/001525.
3 ANTT – Junta da Real Fazenda do Estado da Índia, Livro 62, Documento n° 32.
4 ANTT – Junta da Real Fazenda do Estado da Índia, Livro 62, Documento n° 216.
5 ANTT – Junta da Real Fazenda do Estado da Índia, Livro 62, Documento n° 306.
6 HAG – Monções do Reino, vol. 265.
7 HAG – Monções do Reino, vol. 265.
8 HAG – Monções do Reino, vol. 265.
9 HAG – Monções do Reino, vol. 265.
10 AHMB – Remessa 388a.
11 AHMB – Remessa 388a.
12 AHMB – Remessa 388a.
13 Information about the medicinal use of the *Todalia* genus is available at the *JSTOR Global Plants*. http://plants.jstor.org/compilation/Paullinia.asiatica.
14 AHMB – Remessa 388a.
15 HAG – Monções do Reino, vol. 265 e 271.

References

Avelar, Pedro. 2012. *História de Goa: de Albuquerque a Vassalo Silva*, Alfragide: Texto editores.
Bastos, Cristiana. 2010a. "Hospitais e sociedade colonial. Esplendor, ruína, memória e mudança em Goa," *Ler História*, (58): 61–79.
Bastos, Cristiana. 2010b. "Medicine, Colonial Order and Local Action in Goa," in Anne Digby, Ernst Waltraud and Projit B. Muhkarji (eds.), *Crossing Colonial Historiographies: Histories of Colonial and Indigenous Medicines in Transnational Perspective*, Newcastle: Cambridge Scholars Publishing: 185–212.
Bethencourt, Francisco. 1998. "O estado da Índia," in Francisco Bethencourt and Kirti Chaudhuri (dir.), *História da Expansão Portuguesa. Vol 2, Do Índico ao Atlântico*, Lisboa: Círculo de Leitores: 250–69.
Bethencourt, Francisco and Diogo Ramada Curto. 2010. "Introdução," in Francisco Bethencourt and Diogo Ramada Curto (eds.), *Expansão Marítima Portuguesa, 1400–1800*, Lisboa: Edições 70.

Boxer, Charles Ralph. 2011. *O Império Marítimo Português 1415–1825*, Lisboa: Edições 70.

Bracht, Fabiano. 2013. "Bagas ardentes e remédios para tudo: uma história da peregrinação das plantas americanas nos séculos XVI e XVII," M.A. Thesis, Universidade Estadual de Maringá, Maringá.

Burke, Peter. 2009. *Cultural Hybridity*, Cambridge: Polity Press.

Cook, Harold. 2013. "Creative Misunderstandings, Chinese Medicine in 17th Century Europe," in Daniel T. Rodgers, Bhavani Raman and Helmut Reimitz (eds.), *Cultures in Motion*, Princeton, NJ: Princeton University Press: 215–40.

Cortesão, Jaime. 1996. *A Política de Sigilo nos Descobrimentos*, Lisboa: Imprensa Nacional-Casa da Moeda.

Crosby, Alfred W. 2011. *Imperialismo Ecológico: a expansão biológica da Europa, 900–1900*, São Paulo: Companhia das Letras.

Dalgado, Sebastião Rodolfo. 1919. *Glossário Luso-Asiático, Volume I*, Coimbra: Imprensa da Universidade de Coimbra.

Livingstone, David N. 2003. *Putting Science in Its Place Geographies of Scientific Knowledge*, Chicago: University of Chicago Press.

Lopes, Maria de Jesus dos Mártires. 2006. 'Vida Religiosa: princípios comportamentos e prática', in: Lopes, Maria de Jesus dos Mártires (Ed.). *O Império Oriental, Nova História da Expansão Portuguesa, vol. V, tomo 2*, pp. 100–133, Lisboa: Editora Estampa.

Lopes, Maria de Jesus dos Mártires and Matos, Paulo Lopes. 2006. 'Naturais, Reinóis e Luso-descendentes: a socialização conseguida', in:Lopes, Maria de Jesus dos Mártires (Ed.). *O Império Oriental, Nova História da Expansão Portuguesa,vol. V, tomo 2*, pp. 15–70, Lisboa: Editora Estampa.

Pearson, Michael, N. 1996. "First Contacts Between India and European Medical Systems: Goa in the Sixteenth Century," in David Arnold (ed.), *Warm Climates and Western Medicine: The Emergence of Tropical Medicine, 1500–1900*, Amsterdam: Editions Rodopi B. V.: 20–41.

Pearson, Michael N. 2001a. "Hindu Medical Practice in Sixteenth-Century India," *Portuguese Studies*, 17: 401–19.

Pearson, Michael N. 2001b. "The Portuguese State and Medicine in Sixteenth-Century Goa," in Pius Malekandathhil and Teotonio R. de Souza, *The Portuguese and Socio-Cultural Changes in India, 1500–1800*, Kerala: Fundação Oriente: 401–19.

Pratt, Mary Louise. 1992. *Imperial Eyes: Travel Writing and Transculturation*, London and New York: Routledge.

Raj, Kapil. 2010. *Relocating Modern Science: Circulation and the Construction of Knowledge in South Asia and Europe, 1650–1900*, Basingstoke: Palgrave Macmillan.

Secord, James A. 2004. "Knowledge in Transit,' *Isis*, 4(95): 654–72.

Thomaz, Luís F. Reis. 1994. *De Ceuta a Timor*, Lisboa: Difel.

Walker, Timothy D. 2002. "Evidence of the Use of Ayurvedic Medicine in the Medical Institutions of Portuguese India, 1680–1830," in A. Salema (ed.), *Ayurveda: At the Crossroads of Care and Cure*, Lisboa: Centro de História de Além Mar: 74–104.

Walker, Timothy D. 2007. "A Commodities Price Guide and Merchant's Handbook to the Ports of Asia: Portuguese Trade Information – Gathering and Marketing Strategies in the Estado da India (circa 1750–1800)," in Charles J. Borges and Michael N. Pearson (eds.), *Metahistory: History Questioning History*, Lisboa: Nova Vega: 569–79.

Walker, Timothy D. 2013. "The Medicines Trade in the Portuguese Atlantic World: Acquisition and Dissemination of Healing Knowledge from Brazil (c. 1580–1800)," *Social History of Medicine*, 3(26): 1–29.

Walker, Timothy D. 2016. "Global Cross-Cultural Dissemination of Indigenous Medical Practices Through the Portuguese Colonial System: Evidence from Sixteenth to Eighteenth-Century Ethno-Botanical Manuscripts," in Helge Wendt (ed.), *The Globalization of Knowledge in the Iberian Colonial World*, Berlin: Max Planck Research Library for the History and Development of Knowledge: 161–92.

White, Richard. 2001. *The Middle Ground: Indians, Empires and Republics in the Great Lakes Region, 1650–1815*, Cambridge: Cambridge University Press.

Xavier, Ângela Barreto. 2008. *A Invenção de Goa: Poder Imperial e Conversões Culturais Nos Séculos XVI e XVII*, Lisboa: Imprensa de Ciências Sociais.

Xavier, Ângela Barreto and Inês G. Županov. 2015. "Ser brâmane na Goa da Época Moderna," *Revista de História (São Paulo)*, 172: 15–41.

Županov, Ines G. 2008. 'Conversion, Illness and Possession: Catholic Missionary Healing in Early Modern South Asia', in: Guenzi, Caterina; Županov, Ines G. (Org.). *Divins remèdes: Médecine et religion en Inde*, pp. 263–300. Paris: Editions de LÉcole des Hautes Estudes en Sciences Sociales

8

INDIAN SEAMEN (LASCARS), SHIPBOARD LABOR REGIME AND THE EAST INDIA COMPANY IN THE FIRST HALF OF THE NINETEENTH CENTURY

Ghulam A. Nadri

In August 1801, the *Union*, an English East India Company ship, departed from Calcutta (now Kolkata) in Bengal for England. On its departure, it had 55 *lascars*, 4 servants and 7 sepoys (Indian soldiers) on board. On the way, it received 8 lascars from another ship (the *Suffolk*), which was stranded at St. Jacks Bay. Of the total 74 Indian crew on board, 28 died during the journey, and more than a dozen of those alive were ailing when the ship arrived in England in February 1802. Death and illness on board ships bound to Europe were not uncommon. Natural nautical hazards, such as shipwreck, diseases caused by bug bites or malnutrition and injuries during the performance of duty, which could not be treated in time, caused heavy loss of life among the ships' crews. What was unusual in the case of the *Union* was that many lascars allegedly died because of ill-treatment by the ship's commanding officers and because there was neither a surgeon nor medicine on board to treat the sick and wounded lascars. Upon arrival in England, authorities in London were informed of the brutalities and murders on board the *Union*, and an enquiry committee was set up, which investigated the matter.

Forty years later, in 1841, a private British ship, *David Scott*, was preparing to leave Calcutta for Mauritius when it ran into trouble. Some of the lascars on board were found sick and, therefore, unfit for the duties they were hired to perform during the voyage. Upon further enquiry, it was discovered that at least 30 of them were not proper sailors. They had been forcibly put on board by Ibrahim, the *ghatserang*. They had been allegedly press-ganged, which was in violation of the standard procedure of recruiting ships' crews. Upon their request and apprehending that sick and incompetent crew would

156

put the ship in hazard, the captain returned those 30 men to Calcutta. The Magistrate of Calcutta conducted an enquiry, took depositions from the returning lascars, prepared a report and recommended to the government measures to stop this malpractice. In response to a newspaper reporting on this matter, company authorities in Mauritius too carried out an enquiry when the ship arrived there and sent their reports to Calcutta.

What makes these two cases important and somewhat unique is that the first one led to a judicial enquiry in London by a committee appointed for that purpose and the second resulted in magisterial enquiries in Calcutta and Mauritius. Consequently, each of these cases generated a large number of documents in the form of reports, testimonies and depositions, which contain valuable information on lascars' lived experiences during the voyage and recruitment practices in India.[1]

The question, however, is whether the issues that these cases lay out are exceptions and happened only on these ships or they represent the norm. In other words, how representative are they of the treatment lascars generally received from European officers on board and of lascar recruitment practices in India. While these documents are significant and, using them, one can explore the legal and judicial dimensions of the cases, in this chapter, I use these sources to explore Indian sailors' lived experiences by analysing the dynamics of the labour regime and power relations on board European sailing ships, as well as to illuminate the structure of the labour market in Bengal, the role of the *ghatserang* and his social network, the professional backgrounds of lascars and the EIC government's take on these issues. It details the circumstances in which men were press-ganged and examines the role of local men and women involved in this process. Although we do not know much about their actual experiences, as of most other subaltern groups, the extant documents related with the affairs of the lascars on the *Union* and *David Scott* capture some important aspects of their lived experiences and provide intriguing insights into their lives and journeys from the labor market at home to uncharted waters of the Indian Ocean and beyond.

Historiographical context

In the literature on Indian maritime history, the significant role of sailors (lascars) in facilitating navigation and trade in the early modern and colonial periods is well recognised. However, the scholarship is primarily focused on issues related to sailors on shore and in ports at both ends of the journey. Consequently, the social and economic dynamics of the maritime labour market in Indian port cities, such as the role of local agents and colonial administration in the recruitment of sailors, and issues and implications of lascars' arrival and stay in London are fairly well covered (Fisher 2006: 21–45). There is a general assumption and acknowledgement among scholars that lascars were ill-treated on board European ships. But, beyond that, there is hardly any discussion and analysis of what the actual journey entailed, how lascars were treated during the journey on European ships and why the journey was so fraught with violence, deaths and desertion. Michael Pearson has for long advocated that scholars need to explore seamen's lived experiences aboard ships. In an interview with me in 2004, he said,

> I felt that most of the most recent books on the Indian Ocean were far too much concerned with trade, to the exclusion of other matters, and especially religion. And I felt they gave no impression of an actual nautical experience. Certainly, I would include the book Ashin Das Gupta and I edited in this category, as well as the very fine work by another dear friend, Sinnappah Arasaratnam. As to earlier histories of the ocean, the French scholar Toussaint's book seemed to me rather jumbled, and with far too much attention to land matters which had nothing to do with the ocean. Ken McPherson's book on the Indian Ocean was a fine synthesis, showing an impressive command of the secondary literature. But it was a bit pedestrian, with no hint of the actual maritime experience, as people have lived it over history.[2]

(Nadri 2004: 3)

Since then, however, many scholars have written about sailors and explicated the social, economic and political dynamics of the labour market in late pre-colonial and colonial India (Balachandran 1997, 2006; Ewald 2000; Fisher 2006; Nadri 2015). They have examined the role and agency of *ghatserang* (labour crimp) and the mechanisms of recruitment and supply of sailors to European ships (Balachandran 1997, 2006; Ahuja 2006; Fisher 2006). Their studies also explore the implications of British colonial conquests in India for the maritime labour market and the interplay of identity, race and political authority in the colonial period. Comparative analyses of Indian and European sailors with respect to their wages and provisions, terms of employment and work conditions have led to the view that colonial social engineering and racial differences between the two played an important role in determining the fate of Indian sailors particularly in the late nineteenth and early twentieth centuries. Often, the analysis turns into a discussion of the domination of European colonial merchant capital and subordination or submission of Indian labour and the ensuing hardships the latter were forced to go through. The reality, it seems, was more complex than this. More than race and racial discrimination, the market forces of supply and demand, competition among shipowners and the social/ethnic composition of the crew, as well as the monsoon-driven sailing seasons, played an important role in shaping the shipboard labour regime and the relationship between its various constituents. The analysis of lascars' nautical experiences in the early nineteenth century must, therefore, go beyond the binary between colonial domination and Indian subordination and take into account the role of market forces and the complex hierarchy through which power and authority were exercised aboard ships.

Although, sailors' lived experiences were almost always unpleasant, their lives became even more miserable in the late eighteenth and nineteenth centuries. During this period, the English East India Company (EIC) and private European shipowners employed a large number of lascars in Indian ports to man their ships. The nature of the relationship between lascars and their British/European employers changed considerably as the EIC consolidated its colonial government in India and as the demand for maritime labour increased because of an unprecedented expansion in shipping and maritime trade between India and Europe, as well as across the Indian Ocean and South China Sea. With the growing number of ships and voyages, the demand for lascars and other maritime workers rapidly increased. The market for this type of labour was not so elastic as to fully absorb the demand pressure. Labour contractors and European and Asian employers (shipowners) had to work through, as perhaps was always the case, a system of recruiting labour, which was based on contingency and ad-hoc arrangements. Employers' complaints about lascars' unfitness for the job and lascars' discontent due to insufficient provision and unhealthy and harsh living and working conditions on board have always been the characteristics of the Indian maritime labour market. With the political ascendancy of the EIC in India in the second half of the eighteenth century, measures were adopted to regulate the market and limit the role and power of local labour contractors. It is important to note that the call for such initiatives came from shipowners, who generally blamed the labour contractors for all kinds of malpractices, such as delay in supplying lascars, sending men on board who were unfit for the job and not paying advance salaries to them or their families. In March 1783, the EIC government in Calcutta passed a set of regulations which laid out a new recruitment process (HMS 190 (1783): 81–102). It fixed the monthly wages for lascars (six rupees for skilled lascars and four rupees for less skilled lascars), *serang*, *tindals* and other maritime workers (see Table 8.1) and advance salary (two to four months depending on distance); established a Marine Registry Office headed by a principal officer, the Registrar of Lascars; required all lascars to be registered with that office; and imposed fines for any non-compliance. This was the EIC's first major intervention in the labour market through legislation, and the intent was to free the recruitment process from the control of labour contractors (*seer serang* or *ghatserang*). The new regulations, however, failed to have the desired effect and were withdrawn a year after (Fisher 2006: 23–5, 32–4).

All that the colonial government's intervention in the labour market did was make the process even more complicated and impracticable. Michael

Table 8.1 Wages of native seafaring persons

	In time of peace	In time of war
Gunners	Sicca Rs. 25	Sicca Rs. 35
Carpenters	20	25
Caulkers	15	20
Sea Cunnies	12	15
Syrangs	15	20
1st Tendall	12	15
2nd Tendall	10	12
3rd Tendall	8	10
1st Lascars	6	7
2nd Lascars	4	5
Batta Lascars to ding their own provision	10	10
Cook (for the Captain)	12	15
Butler (for the Captain)	12	15
Officers' servants	6	8

Source: British Library, Home Miscellaneous, 190, p. 85

Fisher has rightly pointed out that 'when such modes of labour recruitment and service, historically common in the Indian Ocean, interacted with conditions and contexts brought from Europe, even more complications eventuated' (Fisher 2006: 25). Labour contractors continued to play their role in the market, and shipowners continued to depend on them for the supply of lascars. As is evident from the case of the *David Scott* (1841), shipowners were dependent on labour contractors and were not able to make them comply with the regulations and supply lascars suitable for the job. The latter, it seems, took advantage of the seasonality of the market and supplied incompetent and unfit labour to shipowners who were frantically recruiting lascars to man their ships in order not to miss the sailing season. What followed on board ships during the voyage was determined to an extent by how well the ship was staffed and how competent and capable the lascars were to carry out their responsibilities. In the nineteenth century, many ships on oceanic voyages were reported to be inadequately staffed. They were short of lascars, and the size of the crew shrank further during the journey, which left them unprotected against the hazards of the sea journey and increased the workload of the lascars remaining on board (HMS 501).[3] Much also depended on how competent and skilled the lascars were. As several of them were press-ganged, they had neither the will nor the competence to perform their duties. This, together with the harsh working conditions, insufficient provisions/food and unhealthy living conditions rendered the relationship between lascars and officers bitter and fraught with violence. Although this adversely affected everyone, lascars suffered the most, as they were at the bottom of the hierarchy. What the lascars on board the *Union* went through during the journey from Calcutta to England

INDIAN SEAMEN AND THE EAST INDIA COMPANY

is a testimony to a disaffected shipboard labour regime and a labour recruitment process which was fraught with malpractice and manipulations.

Lascar's lived experiences aboard the *Union*

The deck of a sailing ship was an arena in which the dialectics of expectations and disappointment, discipline and disorder, authority and resistance, as well as life and death played out. In 1801, lascars and other crew members aboard the *Union* were in this arena, and they went through all of these during the journey from Bengal to England. When several of them testified before the commission investigating the matter in London, they recounted their experiences and told the commission what they had witnessed or heard taking place on board during the voyage. Almost all witnesses, Indians and Europeans, stated that the captain of the ship, John Luke, and his chief mate, Plumb, treated the crew, particularly the lascars, brutally and inhumanely. They attested that many of those who died during the journey died because of severe beating, lashing and flogging by the chief mate and other officers and the lack of recovery thereafter. Many of those who survived the journey had a similar experience. John Moore, the boatswain of the ship, recounted how he was abused by his superiors. Once on board, he was not allowed to step out of the ship and go to Calcutta to claim his advance (two months' salary) from the recruiting agent. On another occasion, he was denied food for three days, which made him 'very low and weak and laid me under the disagreeable necessity of requesting the carpenter of the ship to steal some for me.' He also attested that on one occasion, the chief mate held him and shook him against the ship's side until 'blood gushed out of (his) mouth and eyes' (HMS 501: 10). The serang attested that the chief mate flogged and beat the lascars in a most cruel manner and that the captain ordered his chief mate to 'flog the men till he should see their back bones.' The commission quoted the serang as stating that 'the chief mate flogged the men like devil and told the serang that if ever any of the men went below he would give the serang two dozen lashes' (HMS 501: 6–7). The serang further stated

> that the chief mate took some of the men by the hair of their heads, pulled them down, beat their heads against the deck, and jumped upon them when down, that one man died three days after being so ill-treated and that the serang has now in his possession some of the teeth of three men which were beat out by the chief mate.
>
> (HMS 501: 8)

John Thomas, the *secunny* of the ship, testified before the committee and said,

> on the ship's departure from Bengal the whole crew were well and healthy, but did not remain so long from the Mates being continually

161

flogging and beating the men, which treatment caused much illness among them notwithstanding the men were continued to be punished tho' rendered unable to perform their duty, in consequence of which severity 26 or 28 men died on the voyage the major part of them from the aforesaid treatment by the officers of the ship.

(HMS 501: 18)

Not only lascars but their chiefs, such as the serang and tindal, were similarly treated inhumanely. According to John Moore's testimony, the first tindal was beaten so violently that 'he remained for some time in a very bruised state.' He further stated on oath that

Plumb took hold of one of the tindals, Balli (or Balla), by the hair of his head with one hand and beat him with the other and occasionally took up a stick and beat him with it also, until he was unable to stand; the said Balli often told me and his shipmates also, that he should never recover from such a severe beating; the aforesaid (Balli) died 4 days before we reached St. Helena.

(HMS 501: 14)

John Thomas too testified before the commission that Plumb twisted his (Balla's) hair with one hand and beat him and knocked him down with the other until he fell and that Balla died a few days after. On one occasion, John Thomas himself was beaten up with a stick (cane) by Captain Luke. In his deposition, John Thomas recounted, 'I was beat by Captain Luke when at the wheel he said "why dont you steer her small" he called to the boy to fetch his cane he broke it over me.' He also recounted that he saw the captain beating his steward, Peter Bell, on two or three occasions and once saw him beating the *secunny*, Yusuf (HMS 501: 52–3).

What precipitated this kind of violent physical assault on lascars? Complaining against insufficient food or unhealthy living conditions, which was deemed by the officers as indiscipline, and failure to come up to captain's expectations in performing their duties resulted in violence and brutality. Peter Bell, captain's steward, stated that the lascars were beaten up when they complained about food or want of water or rice (HMS 501: 20). According to John Moore's testimony, the first tindal was beaten up for not reeving the inner hailyard as promptly as the officers expected him to do. John Thomas told the commission that the chief mate, Plumb, beat a lascar (Boxee or Bakshi) so violently for not performing his duty that he died a few days after. He further observed that Bakshi was incapable of performing his duty because of a previous beating. Even European crews, such as the steward, boatswain and *secunny*, were ill-treated by their superiors for failing to perform their duties to the latter's expectations. Peter Bell received six to seven blows on his chest from the captain because two fowls were dead in the hen coop (HMS 501: 56). Friendships and camaraderie were not countenanced on board, and the officers ensured that no solidarity developed among lascars and other crews. John Moore himself was once punished for an alleged camaraderie and for making his shipmate, John Strum, drunk (HMS 501: 12). Shipmates were not even allowed to help the sick or wounded lascars. Peter Bell recounted that he was not allowed to give any when Balla, the tindal, was sick and asked him for some tea.

While some lascars had to go through this violent experience, most of them suffered from other hardships, such as insufficient food and unhealthy living conditions on board. On British ships, lascars received less expensive provision and less sleeping space than British sailors (Fisher 2006: 38). Lascars on board the *Union* slept under the forecastle, the forepart of the upper deck, which was almost always wet because of constant exposure to the sea water. Even the sick and wounded lascars had no place to rest or sleep other than that damp and dingy part of the deck, which minimized the chances of recovery. In his deposition, the serang described this situation in the following words.

> the whole of the lascars were birthed under the forecastle and that he believes that several of the men died in consequence of severe treatment and having no proper place to sleep in and the sick having only water when ill and their birth being often very very wet.
>
> (HMS 501: 7–8)

According to Bell's testimony, lascars after they received severe beating retired and slept under the forecastle, which was always wet. He recounted that a lascar, who had been beaten up and was unable to move from his wet birth under the forecastle became so 'nauseous and offensive' that he was brought up and placed in the forechains where he died or was thrown overboard.

British ships on oceanic voyages were required to have a surgeon and some medicine on board to treat the sick and wounded crew. The *Union* had neither a surgeon nor any medicine on board, and that aggravated the problem. Most of those who testified before the commission observed that if there had been a surgeon on board and medicine to treat the lascars, many would have been cured and more lascars would have survived the journey. According to the serang's testimony, in order to evade beating, lascars often 'hurt their feet and broke their shin.' For lack of treatment, they developed sores and other complications, which rendered them incapable to perform their duties properly (HMS 501: 33–4).[4] Remedial measures, such as serving bread mixed with rum and sugar, were not enough to treat them and save their lives. According to Peter Bell's testimony, there was a medicine box in the captain's cabin, but that was not for the lascars (HMS 501: 20). While some East

India Company ships complied with the regulation and had a surgeon on board, many others did not, and many private merchant ships made long-distance voyages without a surgeon. In their letter to the enquiry committee, the surgeons of the London Hospital, who treated the sick lascars, observed that 'humanity is called upon in behalf of seamen in general in merchant ships trading to distant ports without surgeons on board' (HMS 501: 34). The absence of a surgeon on board may have been the cause of a higher number of lascar deaths on many ships. In 1798, for instance, two EIC ships, *Gabriel* and *Calcutta*, sailed from Bengal for Britain, and 37 out of 99 lascars died on the former and 35 out of 88 died on the latter during the journey. Upon arrival in London, sick lascars were either treated on board by a visiting surgeon or were sent to a hospital. During March to May 1802, 20 lascars from the *Union* were admitted to the London Hospital, six of whom died. Similarly, 19 lascars from the EIC ship *Ganges* were admitted, seven of whom died (HMS 501: 35–6).

Food was another major issue, and it was, in some ways, at the core of the acrimonious relationship between lascars and officers. Lack of appropriate and sufficient food was the most common complaint lascars made against their officers. Lascars on the *Union* and other ships complained about the poor quality of food they received on board. Feeding the lascars on board European ships was a complicated issue because of the dietary restrictions many lascars observed. Officers claimed that lascars were given plenty of rice, vegetables, vinegar, mutton, beef and fish (dried fish or herring). In his letter to the enquiry committee, Captain Luke reported that lascars got mutton and fish alternately and unlimited quantities of rice, beer, vegetables, vinegar and so on. In his testimony, however, the serang told the committee that during the journey, the lascars had sufficient rice and lentil (*dal*) and two pounds of *ghee* (purified butter) per month but no fish, and he makes no mention of mutton or beef. Peter Bell, in his testimony, stated that the lascars complained about food and that they had neither fish nor meat throughout the journey. Upon arrival in the Thames, they got some sheep and Swedish herring in addition to rice for the crew on board. It is, however, not known if the lascars ate mutton. They certainly did not eat herring as the serang stated. Muslim lascars generally did not eat mutton or beef unless they themselves butchered the animal. It was, therefore, expected that when the ships arrived in London, live sheep were supplied on board for lascars. Some captains did not come up to this expectation. When asked about this, the captain of the *Perseverance* (the company ship, which had arrived from Bengal around the same time as the *Union*) stated that live sheep were not needed because there were 'so few lascars on board and none of them hesitating to eat fresh beef.' The surgeon who visited the *Perseverance* and observed the crew on board reported that the lascars complained about food, saying that they had only rice to eat and that too of an inferior quality. He further observed that lascars were starving, and if they ate mutton or beef, they ate only because of hunger. The captain, however, stated that the lascars never complained about food during the journey and said that if they complained to the surgeon, it was because the cook was sick and none on board was willing or able to take that position (HMS 501: 24–9).

Whether the lascars could eat meat and fish (fresh or dried) during the journey or in the London dockyard is not so significant. What is important is whether these items were on the menu and whether the captains and officers took an extra step to make sure that the food they served was in accordance with lascars' dietary restrictions and preferences. For instance, in the eighteenth century, the Dutch (VOC) employers were sensitive to the dietary habits of their Muslim sailors (*moorsezeevarenden*) and gave them fish instead of meat (Nadri 2015: 354). Given that lascars on European ships during this period were considered, as Michael Fisher calls it, 'a collective mass' and not as individual human beings, most shipowners or captains and officers on board did not take that extra step (Fisher 2006: 37). The only exception, it seems, was the inclusion into the meal of purified butter, which no lascar hesitated to eat. We now know that European ships employed lascars partly because that was unavoidable but mainly because it was cheaper than employing European sailors both in terms of wages and allowances, including meals and living spaces on board ships. It was not unusual then that lascars aboard ships lived uncomfortably and had less expensive meals consisting mainly of rice, lentils and *ghee*, which was just enough to subsist. Lascars were aware of their limits and knew that complaining about food was not going to make their lives any better. There were other bigger problems, such as beating and flogging and lack of care for and cure of sick lascars, which bothered them more than the food offered on board.

What befell on board the *Union* on her passage from Bengal to London shows how the shipboard labour regime functioned and reveals a disaffected relationship among its various constituents in the hierarchy, i.e., the captain and his chief mate, the European crew and subordinate officers and lascars and their Indian petty officers (tindal and serang). This was more or less the norm, and like the lascars aboard this ship, those on other British ships sailing between India and Britain had a similar, and in some cases even worse, experience. Nevertheless, it reflects the failure on both sides (lascars and officers) to come up to each other's expectations. The failure was primarily due to a flawed system of lascar recruitment, lack of accountability and the difference between British and Indian cultural contexts in which the meaning of labour and expectations from it varied widely. As mentioned earlier, how the shipboard labour regime functioned depended on how it was constituted, who the lascars were and how they were recruited. We do not know the circumstances in which lascars on board the *Union* were recruited; neither do we know who they were or what their professional backgrounds were. We also do not know what negotiations took place between them and the labour contractors or whether they had any prior knowledge of what serving on board a sailing ship entailed. But if an analogy can be drawn with what the lascars experienced when they were recruited for the *David Scott* in 1841, it may be argued that many lascars were involuntarily aboard the *Union* and had no skills, experience or even knowledge of the life or duties of a sailor. Their professional background, skills and experiences prior to the ship's departure determined to a large extent what they would experience during the journey.

'Press-ganged' lascars: the case of *David Scott*

In March 1841, *David Scott*, a British registered private merchant ship, was in Calcutta in the River Hugli preparing to leave for Mauritius. The ship's agent, Colvelle and Gilmore & Co. was asked to supply 69 lascars. The agency contracted the ghatserang, Ibrahim, to recruit lascars for the ship, which the latter did accordingly. At the muster roll before leaving the harbour, the officers found out that at least 30 of them were landsmen and unacquainted with the life or duties of sailors. Many of them were sick and, therefore, incapable to serve on board the ship. After further examination, they learned that they had been press-ganged and forcibly put on board. The captain decided to send those thirty men to Calcutta and complained to the magistrate about this. As a result, an enquiry was conducted into this matter, and depositions were taken from twelve of the returning men. It is evident from their testimonies that they were taken aboard the ship against their will and in a sort of tranquilised state, under false pretexts and promises and without any advance payment of four months' salary (Board's Collection 1998: 1–45). Of the 12 men who testified before the judicial authorities, six were peasants/cultivators, two were milkmen, one was a cook, one was a coachman, one was a *manji* (one who rows a boat) and one was a daily (*batta*) lascar. These men were either lured with money or false promises of employment or were detained by men who worked as sub-agents (*bhati-yara*) of the ghatserang. They were kept in confinement for several days and were given drinks or sweetmeats mixed with sedatives, like *bhang* (a sort of marijuana) or other narcotics. Once they were out of their senses, they were taken to the ship. Madho Behreh, in his deposition, stated that he was a milkman (cowherd) in Cuttack and had come to Calcutta to take a bath in the Ganges when Pheku approached him and promised to secure him a gardener's job. When he told Pheku that he was not a sailor (*khalassi*), two men forcibly took him to the ship at night (Board's Collection 1998: 12). Similarly, Kartik Kyburt recounted his experience with the enquiry officer in his mother tongue, which the interpreter translated as follows.

> I am a native of Tumlook (East Midnapur, Bengal) and used to cultivate, I know nothing of a seafaring life, I came to Calcutta

INDIAN SEAMEN AND THE EAST INDIA COMPANY

first says to bathe in the Ganges then says I came to take service as a Baboo's gwala (an Englishman's milkman). I was shipped on the Scott by a Bhatteeyara of Mutchoa Bazar I do not know his name, the serang who took me is on board the Scott. I got no advance except the cloth now on me. . . . I was taken by force, they fed me with something that made me drunk.

(Board's Collection 1998: 18–19)

These men were not only professionally diverse, but they also came from different regions and cultural zones. At least four of them (Govind Puddon, Abdollah, Koroon and Madho Behreh) were from Orissa, and another four (Mohamed Ali, Mirza Alfoo, Hassan Ali and Madho Ahir) came from Shahjahanpur, Farrukhabad and Kanpur in what is Uttar Pradesh today. The remaining four men (Abdollah or Ishmaji, Kartik Kyburt, Bimjee Mussalman and Najibullah) were from different districts of Bengal. According to Frederick Stanley, the ship's chief mate, among 34 lascars that the ghatserang sent aboard, there were Assamese, Chinese, labourers, coolies and other landsmen (Board's Collection 1998: 36). George Robson, the second mate, told the chief commissary of police in Mauritius that the men sent aboard by the ghatserang, Ibrahim, were from different trades and vocations, such as 'grooms, gardeners, tailors, milkmen, all landsmen' and 'totally unfit for sea service.' He further stated that when they were asked what induced them to come on board as seamen, they replied that

they had been made drunk by the ghautserang and his people, some of them tied hands and feet and put into carts and boats and that they were not aware that they were to form part of the crew for Mauritius.

(Board's Collection 1998: 40–1)

It is evident from these statements that many who were recruited to serve on board as lascars had no prior experience of a sailor. This was not unusual. After all, there were lascars of similar description on board British ships, and they were there unwillingly. What was unique about the *David Scott* was that the captain and the chief mate came to know of this in time and could send them back to Calcutta, which led to a judicial enquiry. It is, however, interesting that there were men aboard that ship who, having been press-ganged and put on board against their will, were able to serve as lascars and made it to Mauritius. The chief mate, Frederick Stanley, stated that when the ship was on her way to Mauritius, a young man came to him crying and saying that he was not a lascar and that he was kidnapped and sent aboard by the ghatserang. He recounted that the lascar, Hussain Khan, told him that he had come to Calcutta to meet with his uncle and then the ghatserang got hold of him and gave him a red cap, a knife, a rupee, a frock and trousers and also some drugs to smoke, after which he lost his senses and was taken to the ship (Board's Collection 1998: 41).

These instances of press-ganging reveal how flawed the lascar recruitment process in Bengal was. The captain and mates of the ship blamed the ghatserang for deceiving them. As George Robson, the second mate, told the judicial officer he was testifying before, he was

> acquainted with the villainous practice of ghat-serangs which is to kidnap any description of persons they can lay hold of, intoxicate them with drugs, and decoy away, and ship them on board as seamen, in order to pocket the greatest part of the advance made on account of the captain, thus practicing a double deception, upon the unfortunate individuals, as well as the captain of the ship.
>
> (Board's Collection 1998: 42)

Government officials, such as the magistrate of Calcutta and judicial officers in Calcutta and Mauritius, who conducted the enquiry, too held the ghatserang responsible for the deception and fraud in supplying lascars. They believed that by sending incompetent men on board, who were kidnapped and intoxicated, the ghatserang kept for himself the advance salaries he was paid by the captains or their agents. The measures that they proposed to the Government of Bengal sought to limit the role of ghatserang, much like the regulations of 1783. But this time, the Government of Bengal did not take any legislative action that would have satisfied the ship captains and officers.

Ghatserangs were not the only ones to be blamed for the flawed recruitment practices. Ship captains and officers were also partly responsible. To avoid paying salary and allowances for weeks and months before the ship's departure, they preferred a late delivery of lascars on board. They hired daily lascars (*batta* lascar, who were different from sea lascars) to serve on board as labourers and prepare the ship for departure. This had to do with the nature of the demand for lascars, which was always contingent on actual labour shortages on ships arriving in Calcutta. This was unlike the commodity market where advance buying was a common practice and where merchants and companies expected delivery of goods at the earliest opportunity. The demand for specific goods was known well in advance, and they were in a better position to place orders for them to their brokers and suppliers (Chaudhuri 1978: 305–11; Prakash 1998: 167–74; Nadri 2009: 123–4). There was, therefore, only a short window of time between arrivals and departures during which ships had to be staffed. As the captains competed and frantically tried to get lascars on board, the suppliers came under pressure. That the ship, *David Scott*, sailed up and down the river Hugli between Calcutta and Kejri (Kedgeree) collecting lascars at different places testifies to this very nature of the maritime labour market. In his testimony, John Stanley, the chief mate, gave a daily account of how the ship, *David Scott*, sailed down the river from Calcutta to Cooly Bazar and got 14 lascars on board and moved on to Culpee, where a few more seamen joined, and then it arrived at Kejri where it was still short of 50 lascars (Board's Collection 1998: 35–6). To fulfil their contracts, the ghatserangs gathered men from wherever they could, sometimes without regard to experience or ability and, at times, even unscrupulously forcing and coercing men to serve as lascars.

The magistrate's report alludes to an increased demand for lascars in the 1840s because of the Opium Wars and an expansion in maritime trade as the cause of what happened in the case of the *David Scott*. Certainly, the demand for lascars was high and the supply of indentured labour to British colonies elsewhere too must have had an adverse impact on the maritime labour market. But a supply of incompetent and inexperienced men to serve as sea lascars on board ships was a perennial problem and rooted in the long-established structure of the labour market. For instance, in the second half of the eighteenth century, EIC and VOC officials complained against labour contractors, ghatserangs, for supplying inexperienced and incapable sailors (Nadri 2015: 350–1, note 50). The East India Company's colonial government, despite several measures at different times in the early nineteenth century, could not solve the problem. Proposals and legislative measures, such as the regulations of 1783 and those suggested by the magistrate of Calcutta in 1841, to impose accountability on the concerned parties seemingly failed to dislodge the resilient older modes of lascar recruitment. This was primarily because the ghatserangs worked through a complex network of agents, contractors, sub-agents and a host of men and women, all of whom played a vital role in the process and had a share in the reward (advance money). In the age of sail, ghatserangs held a prominent position in the labour market similar to what brokers held in the commodity market for European merchants and companies.

Conclusion

What the lascars went through on the EIC ship the *Union* and in the process of recruitment for the ship the *David Scott* reveals the nature and working of the shipboard labour regime and the maritime labour market in the first half of the nineteenth century. Through an analysis of what transpired on these two ships, this chapter has illuminated the experiences that the lascars lived through on shore and during the journey. I have argued that the hardships and violence that they experienced was not unique to these ships but a common characteristic of the labour regime aboard ships and of the labour market. The disaffected shipboard labour relations resulted from failure on the lascars' side as well as on the captain's side to come up to each other's expectations (proper and satisfactory food, healthy living and working conditions, discipline and prompt performance of duty). This failure was not because of any racial arrogance of British officers or of lascars' moral or physical weakness and their inherent inability to do the job as some EIC directors believed (Fisher 2006: 38). Evidence from these cases does not show a racially informed hierarchy of power and authority aboard ships. European and Indian crew interacted freely and, at times, helped each other. Many European petty officers were treated brutally by their superiors as were the lascars. It is worth noting here that many European crew who testified before the enquiry commission empathised with the lascars and held the captain and the chief mate responsible for treating the lascars inhumanely. Using the evidence related to lascar recruitment for the *David Scott*, this chapter has illuminated the dynamics of the labour market. I have argued that labour relations on board a ship depended on how the ship was staffed, who the lascars were and how they were recruited. The chapter shows that the flawed system of lascar recruitment was responsible for the disaffected labour relations on board ships.

Notes

1 Home Miscellaneous Series (hereafter HMS) 501; Board's Collection 1998 (doc. no. 88668) 1841: 1–46.
2 'An Interview with Michael Pearson' by Ghulam A. Nadri. 2004. *Itinerario*, 28(3): 14. Recently, some scholars have paid close attention to cultural/religious processes in the Indian Ocean world (Green 2011).
3 The size of the crew aboard the *Union* with a 750-ton capacity was inadequate. The enquiry commission suspected that the stranding of the *Suffolk* at St. Jacks Bay was reportedly due to an insufficient crew.
4 In 1802, the surgeons in the London Hospital reported that they had received several lascars with sore feet ('mortification of the feet'), many of whom died in the hospital.

References

Primary sources

British Library, London, UK.
Board's Collection 1998 (doc. no. 88668). 1841. "Collection Relative to a Case of Illegal Private Impressment of Certain Natives of India as Lascars for the Ship David Scott," pp. 1–46.
Home Miscellaneous Series 190. 1783. "A Rule Ordinance and Regulation for Ascertaining and Fixing the Wages to Be Paid to the Native Seafaring Men Belonging to the Port of Calcutta and for Securing the Same to the Said Men as Also for the Better Providing the Ships and Vessels Navigating to and from the Said Port with Native Seafaring Men," Calcutta, pp. 81–102, 10 March.
Home Miscellaneous Series 501. 1802. "Report of the Committee of Shipping Related with the Ship," Union, pp. 1–134.

Secondary sources

Ahuja, Ravi. 2006. "Mobility and Containment: The Voyages of South Asian Seamen, 1900–1960," *International Review of Social History*, 51: 111–41.

Balachandran, G. 1997. "Recruitment and Control of Indian Seamen, Calcutta, 1880–1935," *International Journal of Maritime History*, 9: 1–18.

Balachandran, G. 2006. "Circulation Through Seafaring: Indian Seamen, 1890–1945," in Claude Markovits, Jacques Pouchepadass and Sanjay Subrahmanyam (eds.), *Society and Circulation: Mobile People and Itinerant Cultures in South Asia, 1750–1950*, London: Anthem Press: 89–130.

Chaudhuri, K.N. 1978. *The Trading World of Asia and the English East India Company, 1660–1760*, Cambridge: Cambridge University Press.

Ewald, Janet E. 2000. "Crossers of the Sea: Slaves, Freedmen, and Other Migrants in the Northwestern Indian Ocean, c. 1750–1914," *American Historical Review*, 105(1): 69–91.

Fisher, Michael H. 2006. "Working Across the Seas: Indian Maritime Labourers in India, Britain, and in Between, 1600–1857," *International Review of Social History*, 51: 21–45.

Green, Nile. 2011. *Bombay Islam: The Religious Economy of the West Indian Ocean, 1840–1915*, Cambridge: Cambridge University Press.

Nadri, Ghulam A. 2004. "Sympathetic "*Farangi*": An Interview with Michael Pearson," *Itinerario: International Journal on the History of European Expansion and Global Interaction*, 28(3): 6–17.

Nadri, Ghulam A. 2009. *Eighteenth-Century Gujarat: The Dynamics of Its Political Economy, 1750–1800*, Leiden: Brill.

Nadri, Ghulam A. 2015. "Sailors, *zielverkopers*, and the Dutch East India Company: The Maritime Labour Market in Eighteenth-Century Surat," *Modern Asian Studies*, 49(2): 336–64.

Prakash, Om. 1998. *The New Cambridge History of India, II.5, European Commercial Enterprise in Pre-Colonial India*. Cambridge: Cambridge University Press.

Part III

NEW HISTORIES

9

HAZARDS AND HISTORY ON THE WESTERN AUSTRALIAN COAST

The 'Pearling Fleet Disaster' of 1887

Joseph Christensen

Thomas Henry Haynes had two lucky escapes during his brief yet colourful career as a pearler and trader in the Eastern Seas, the maritime arena better known today as the Indo-Pacific. The first came in 1885 when a Sulu diver named Akalal ran amok aboard the brigantine *Sree Pas-Sair* just out of Makassar, striking Haynes with a hand lead and leaving him with a badly fractured skull requiring urgent if rudimentary surgery in Singapore (Streeter 1886a: 181–3). The second took place on his next pearling adventure, when he passed through a devastating tropical cyclone off the Northwest Coast of Australia. The 'Pearling Fleet Disaster,' as it came to be known, was announced to the outside world when the steamer *Australind* reached the regional port of Cossack, carrying Haynes as a passenger and with the dismasted *Sree Pas-Sair* under tow (see map, Figure 9.1). The storm had caught the pearling fleet in exposed waters off the Eighty Mile Beach, Haynes wrote at once to the colonial secretary of Western Australia, leaving fifty vessels damaged, scores of bodies floating in the sea and 'over five hundred men missing' (Haynes 1887a). His telegram caused a sensation throughout the colony. 'The number of lives lost is estimated at between four and five hundred including Europeans, Malays, Chinamen, and Aboriginals,' reported the main newspaper for the sprawling Northwest districts, leaving the settlers 'prostrated by the news of a catastrophe which threatens to surpass in every respect any other similar event in Australian annals' (*Victorian Express*, 30/4/1887: 4). The angst was no less pronounced in the capital of Perth, some 1,000 miles to the south. 'Never before,' remarked the *West Australian* newspaper (30/4/1887: 2), 'has there been anything approaching the catastrophe which overtook the pearling fleet last week . . . we can only hope that the loss of life may not prove to have been so extensive as at present we are left to infer.'

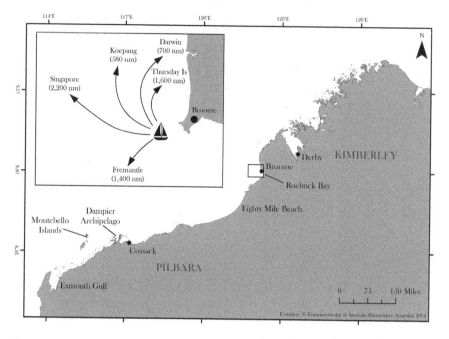

Figure 9.1 Map of Northwest Australia, showing locations mentioned in the chapter
Source: Prepared by the author

It was another three months before the full scale of the tragedy was laid bare. A police report numbered the fatalities at 140, a figure accepted ever since as the official death toll. Among these were 14 'white men' or Europeans, each named and their home port listed in the report. An additional 126 'coloured men' were also recorded as fatalities (Payne 1887a). This figure was reached by counting seven men for each of the 18 vessels known to have sunk; as we shall see, the true number of boatmen and boats lost in the cyclone was almost certainly higher. None of these non-whites was identified by name in reports on the incident. The *Western Mail* (7/5/1887: 28) conveyed a popular sentiment in its eulogy for the victims:

> No more dreadful disaster has, probably, occurred in the history of these colonies.... Although a large majority of the lives sacrificed are those of coloured races, there must be many deaths of those who will be mourned by our own kith and kin. Our earnest sympathy is with those who have suffered such sudden and unlooked-for bereavement.

This neatly captures the subalternity of those who provided the pearling fleets with its essential labour: 'Malays' from Singapore, Timor, the Sulu

Archipelago and many other places in between; Filipinos or 'Manilamen'; Japanese; Chinese; and Pacific or 'South Sea' Islanders. Although the losses turned out to be less than initially feared, the Pearling Fleet Disaster still ranks amongst the worst natural disasters in the first century of British settlement in Australia, and even if we accept the official figures, the cyclone of April 1887 remains today as one of the worst natural disasters in the nation's history (Christensen 2016: 290).

For Haynes, the disaster was also a prelude to what he regarded as the great legacy of his career – the founding of the port of Broome on Roebuck Bay not far from the Eighty Mile Beach (Haynes 1929). From a makeshift campsite and occasional watering place, Broome developed rapidly after April 1887 to become the headquarters of Western Australia's pearling industry and one of the largest pearling ports in the world. By 1915, when the half-century of British colonisation in the Northwest was commemorated, Broome was the largest of the region's towns, 'the continual coming and going of the pearling boats giving an air of activity,' its 'curious polyglot population' lending 'that flavour of the Orient which is inseparable from the search for pearls and pearl-shell, found only in the strange seas of tropical climes' (Battye 1915: 113–4, 132). This image lingered long into the twentieth century. It was 'the archetypical pearling port, with an exotic if hard life that was quite different in many respects from that lived elsewhere on the continent,' writes John Bach in his *A Maritime History of Australia* (1976; 238–9), where even in the 1950s 'one could feel in Broome that one was not really in Australia but in some community that Joseph Conrad might have created to weave one of his stories of the meeting of two cultures, one Eastern, one European.' Crucially, it was what Broome shared in common with other pearling ports that made it so unusual in an Australian context – a mixed-race community, pursuing a maritime industry of great antiquity, working their vast fleet of small boats according to the daily rhythm of the tides and the seasonal cycle of the monsoon (Christensen 2017: 256–63). The Australian adventurer Alan Villiers depicts similar scenes in *Sons of Sinbad* (1969: 350), his account of seafaring in the Arabian Gulf. Other comparable communities were once scattered widely across the Indian Ocean, from the Red Sea to the Palk Strait and the Gulf of Mannar and the waters of the Sulu and Celebes Seas (Reeves et al. 1988: 244). When Michael Pearson coined the term 'littoral society,' historians acquired a useful tool for describing such communities; 'we can go around the shores of an ocean, or a sea, or indeed the whole world, and identify societies that have more in common with other littoral societies than they do with their inland neighbours' (Pearson 2006: 353).

This chapter uses Pearson's approach to Indian Ocean history as a point of entry for revisiting the Pearling Fleet Disaster. In particular, it touches upon several inter-related aspects of his work. The first relates to the historical agency of natural or environmental hazards. Although Pearson pays close attention to the environment as a fundamental element in the ocean's history, his focus is on the long-term and cyclical forces of the monsoon, trade winds and currents. The hazardness of coasts (as place) and maritime lifestyles (as occupation) do not figure in this conception, as Rila Mukherjee (2017: 16) has observed; the shoreline may very well be 'subject to waves, currents, tides, tsunamis, floods and earthquakes,' yet 'incessant peril is not factored into Pearson's model.' It has been argued elsewhere that hazards bind the diverse societies and cultures of the Indian Ocean together through shared experiences of risk and adaptation (Bankoff and Christensen 2016: 1–6; Bose 2006: 102), and as Steven Schwartz demonstrates in his study of hurricanes in the Greater Caribbean (2015: xi), responses to extreme tropical weather provide a common organising theme for examining socially and culturally diverse meta-regions across extended periods of time. This is not only a question of environment but one that is also concerned with social relationships and boundaries, or 'connections not across and beyond the ocean, but inland' (Pearson 2003: 27). Greg Bankoff (2010: 1) writes that 'what makes a hazard into a disaster depends primarily on the way a society is ordered,' or, in other words, disasters are the product of social, economic or political factors that expose a community to danger. The marginal social status of Asian pearl divers and crews in late colonial Australia, evident in the anonymity of those lost in April 1887, is an important theme running through this chapter.

Another theme relates to Australia's place in Indian Ocean history. Like Kenneth McPherson before him, Pearson was at pains to draw his adopted homeland into his discussion of the ocean across long-term time scales. The attention he pays to Broome in his *The Indian Ocean* (2003: 271–2) is a case in point:

> In the 1890s copper helmets and canvas suits began to be used, and an influx of divers from Japan and the Malay area produced a boom in the 1880s and through to World War 1. Some 400 luggers were based in Roebuck Bay. In the off season, 3,000 divers congregated in Broome. . . . The valuable product was mother-of-pearl. Around 1900 Broome produced 80 per cent of the world's supply of this precocity. The trade declined in the 1920s and 1930s, and was dealt a fatal blow by the development in the 1950s of plastic.[1]

By necessity, however, it is only in the modern period that such examples arise, and even then, Australia occupies a position at the very margins of the ocean's history. As a group of colonies founded at the twilight of the age of sail, during the rise of Britain to global ascendency and with a clearly defined role in the imperial economic framework, the nation's trade within the ocean after the late eighteenth century was to a region that was itself undergoing the profound transformation of global integration, whilst

HAZARDS AND HISTORY ON THE AUSTRALIAN COAST

restrictions on immigration after the mid-nineteenth century were designed to maintain a British population by excluding the peoples and cultures of Asia. Yet as Pearson recognises, pearling, as one of the great maritime industries of Indian Ocean history, links Australia to the history of the ocean at large. The same can also be said for cyclones, which, as essential features of weather patterns in lands bordering tropical seas, occur widely across the ocean and its adjacent coasts (Qasim 1994: 30–40).

By exploring the Pearling Fleet Disaster, then, this chapter is also posing questions about approaches to, and the possibilities of, Indian Ocean history. To bring these questions together, the closing section considers a further aspect of Pearson's work. This is the distinction he makes, following Peregrine Horden and Nicholas Purcell in *The Corrupting Sea* (2000), between history of the ocean and history in it – that is, between an internal one using ocean-wide comparisons, or history *of* the ocean, and a history shaped by forces emanating from beyond the ocean, which comprises history *in* the ocean (Pearson 2003: 11–12; Hordern and Purcell 2000: 8; Vink 2007: 57). The disaster, I suggest, cuts across these distinctions, offering an example of how natural hazards might be considered as part of the 'deep structure' shaping the history of the ocean across the *longue durée*.

The disaster as fate

Much of the initial uncertainty had passed by the time the *Western Mail* (7/5/1887: 28) summarised the cyclone in this way:

> The first hasty rumours of the disaster that reached Perth were even more distressing than the authoritative reports subsequently received. Still the facts are calculated to appal the stoutest heart. If the terrible holocaust of victims has not been so serious as was at first reported, there is every reason to fear that the disaster has been attended with loss of life unparalleled in the history of Australian pearl fishing . . . the whole affair is inexpressibly sad and deplorable.

Even today, however, the precise scale of losses is uncertain. Four large 'schooners' (in practise, a storeship and tender ranging from around 20 to over 100 tons) were reported to have sunk: the *Dairymaid*, with its captain, four of its accompanying 'luggers'or diving boats and 32 Malay seamen; *Florence*, with 3 luggers and 20 men; *Lord Loftus*, with 1 lugger and 12 Malay seamen; and *Osprey*, with its captain, his son and seven Malay seamen. An additional 15 luggers (typically a small ketch of around 10 tons) were also listed; these were *Coocanut, Edith, Victoria, Lela, Le Grand, Maggie, Mary Ann, Theresa, Rose, Pearl, Rover, Ranger* and *Uno*, plus two unnamed luggers (Payne 1887a). But the official list is almost certainly

179

incomplete. Two luggers named *Charity* and *Faith* had not been sighted since leaving Darwin for the Northwest coast earlier in 1887 and seem likely to have perished in the cyclone, and a third lugger, *Ethel*, and an 'unnamed Japanese boat' appear not to have been counted in the police report (Cairns and Henderson 1995: 89–94). The official figure of 140 deaths is therefore likely to be an underestimate, as no allowance was made for the crews of the missing luggers nor for men swept overboard from vessels that rode out the storm.

All the same, this uncertainty is not surprising. In contributing through his telegram to misapprehensions over the scale of losses, Haynes unwittingly exposed the frailties of colonial administration in the northwest. There was as yet no permanent coastal settlement between Cossack and the port of Derby, and with pastoral expansion only just extending into the region inland of Eighty Mile Beach and Roebuck Bay, the disaster unfolded along a remote stretch of coast at the very frontier of settler society. Furthermore, when the first survivors reached Cossack, the resident magistrate for the Northwest districts was away overseeing the employment of Aboriginal labour on pastoral stations, and the town's only police officer was on leave. The colony's pearling inspector had meanwhile been blinded by lightning in the early stages of the storm. Against this backdrop, Haynes played a vital role not only in relaying reports of the disaster but in assisting the *Australind* to make a further search for survivors from the shattered fleet (Hicks 1887).

It was also the case that many of those feared lost were later found to have avoided the worst fate. The mate of the *Dairymaid* swam through the roughest of seas to another lugger and was rescued; a Pacific Islander was pulled alive from the water after clinging to wreckage for 12 hours; the schooner *Harriet* remained afloat and without loss of life, despite having all her diving boats swept from her decks and being thrown on her beam ends at the peak of the storm; the schooner *Mavis*, salvaged and refloated after striking a reef in Torres Strait less than two years earlier, survived again 'with bulwarks stove in and bowsprit badly sprung' (Hicks 1887); aboard the schooner *Annie Taylor*, also badly damaged, the captain's wife was found in the cabin neck-deep in water and holding a week-old infant above her head; and the lugger *Gypsy* eventually showed up at Cossack with its full complement despite being blown some 100 miles out to sea (Cairns and Henderson 1995: 89–94; Watson 1997: 25–6). When the list of 'White Men Lost' was announced, it transpired that only two Western Australians were among the deceased; 11 of the 14 men were listed as coming from Port Darwin, although many of these had come from Sydney before entering the pearling trade. Such facts went some way towards allaying the despondency that built up following the first reports from Haynes and others. 'It is a matter for much thankfulness that the blow to our West Australian pearling industry has been by no means as severe as at first was feared,' reported the *West Australian* (13/5/1887: 2). 'One by one, however, the missing vessels have turned up, and yesterday we were able to announce that the full number had reached port safely.'

Such statements assist in explaining the scale of the disaster. By 1887, the pearling industry on the northwest coast was made up of two distinct modes of operation. The first comprised the local vessels that survived the storm. These were known within the colony as 'swimming boats' because they employed naked or free divers, mostly Aborigines from adjacent areas, to harvest mother-of-pearl from the seafloor. This was a simple form of pearling reminiscent of pearl fisheries in the Arabian Gulf and southern India and had been practised in Western Australia with little modification since the mid-1860s (McCarthy 2006: 243–59). The remainder, including those vessels that bore the brunt of the disaster, comprised the so-called 'pump' or 'apparatus boats' that were equipped with modern 'diving dress,' which consisted of a rubber air hose, canvas suit, brass diving helmet and a hand-driven pump which supplied oxygen to divers below the sea. Also referred to as 'foreign boats,' these vessels had come from Thursday Island in Torres Strait – the historic centre of Australian pearling – Darwin, Singapore and even Sydney. Master pearlers like Haynes and his contemporary James Clark, one of the more entrepreneurial Torres Strait Islander pearlers, attached their apparatus boats to ocean-going schooners that could move freely across the Indo-Pacific. Known as 'floating stations,' their arrival had revolutionised the Western Australian industry by introducing the diving dress and, as a result, opening up vast new beds of mother-of-pearl shell in deeper waters previously inaccessible to local operations; the *Sree Pas-Sair*, Clark's *Mavis* and the ill-fated *Florence* had been among the earliest floating stations employed on the northwest coast (Mullins 2001: 3–7). After first appearing in 1884–85, this new mode of pearling developed quickly, as more apparatus boats arrived on the coast from Darwin and Torres Strait and established Western Australian pearlers began to adopt the technology. Whereas in 1885 there were only seven boats using the diving dress and more than 50 employed in free diving, by 1887, some 83 boats used the 'apparatus,' as opposed to only 15 'swimming' vessels (Bach 1955: 275; Smith 1887).

Yet these figures alone do not fully account for the pattern of losses. In hailing the survival of the 'West Australian' vessels, the press overlooked the fact that, for the remaining free-diving boats, the pearling season had officially concluded when the cyclone arrived. Regulations under the colony's *Pearl Shell Fishery Regulation Act* (1873) prohibited free diving between 1 April and 30 October, a measure designed to protect Aboriginal labour by allowing diving only when the temperature of the sea and air was sufficient to prevent hypothermia and alleviate the risk of respiratory diseases.

Although not every boat observed this requirement in 1887, for most, diving had indeed come to an end (Coppin 1947: 37–40). Furthermore, for the apparatus boats that continued to work beyond the start of April, the push into deeper waters left them more exposed to the extremes of tropical weather. Whereas the best free divers could reach perhaps seven fathoms, most went no further than five (that is, around nine to ten metres), meaning that vessels remained inshore and that safe anchorages at islands, mangrove creeks, inlets or natural harbours could be readily sought if a cyclone approached. Such precautions had been commonplace earlier in the 1880s, before the diving dress was introduced, when pearlers worked shallow waters around the Dampier Archipelago and along the coast westward to Exmouth Gulf (Brockman 2010: 57–8). By contrast, diving suits allowed men to work in depths of 20 fathoms or more (as deep as 35–40 metres) and onto grounds extending beyond 20 miles offshore. The rich banks off Eighty Mile Beach, only recently discovered by the fleet, lay far from the coast. The disaster was therefore a tragic demonstration of the dangers of working into such exposed waters.

If there is another factor that helps explain what took place during the disaster, then it is seamanship, or the skill of navigating in a storm. Knowledge of what action to take when a cyclone occurred could be the decisive factor determining the fate of any vessel. Experience had taught many pearlers to recognise that, if a safe anchorage could not be obtained, the best chance of survival was to slip the cable and attempt to ride out the storm at sea; the key was to keep a vessel head on into the wind, using sea anchors to slow its drift, working the pumps furiously and when necessary, cutting away the mast to prevent the ship being thrown onto her beam ends (Bartlett 1954: 242–54; Payne 1887b; Roe 1887). Yet in 1887, many in the fleet had little familiarity with the northwest coast or even with the waters off Darwin and Torres Strait, where cyclones also occur (albeit with a lower annual frequency than Western Australia). The local pearler Christopher Coppin witnessed the disaster aboard the *Jessie* and recounted how costly this inexperience could be. 'Scores of luggers sunk at their anchors, and many of the larger boats dragged their anchors and bore down on the luggers, swamping and sinking them.' Another 'big boat,' or schooner, sank right at her anchor. 'She was named "The Dairy Maid" and she was owned and sailed by a Captain French who had previously claimed that Australians did not know what a real cyclone was like – if they had been through what he had been through in some parts of the world, then they would know. I told him previously that if he stopped in the Northwest long enough he would probably alter his tone,' he recalled. 'One of the native boys told me later that he had seen one of the bigger boats in the ill-fated fleet furiously pushing against her anchor chain in the height of the storm. The chain tore a great hole in her and she sank with all hands in front of his eyes' (Coppin 1947: 39).

HAZARDS AND HISTORY ON THE AUSTRALIAN COAST

The disaster as turning point

What makes the Pearling Fleet Disaster particularly intriguing is the influence it has been credited with by historians. In an early study of the development of Australian pearling, Bach (1955: 31) suggests that the encounter with the April 1887 cyclone helped persuade many of the floating stations to depart Western Australia, setting the scene for the divergent development of the fleets based at Thursday Island and Broome from the 1890s on. He additionally suggests the disaster forced the exit of pioneering white divers through the loss of boats, equipment and lives, paving the way for the industry's near-total dependence on Asian divers and the political problems this created following the passage of the Commonwealth's *Immigration Restriction Act* (Bach 1955: 84). In her history of the industry, *Full Fathom Five*, Mary Albertus Bain links the disaster to the rise of Broome as a pearling port. Gazetted as a townsite in 1883, with a rough jetty erected by Haynes a couple of years later but still without permanent inhabitants in 1887, this watering point and occasional campsite on Roebuck Bay was transformed, she writes, 'following the disastrous cyclone of 1887, [when] a few bush camps, tents and sheds were erected by TI [i.e. Torres Strait] men anxious to repair damaged craft or salvage wreckage on 80 Mile Beach' (Bain 1982: 227). This marks the foundation of the port destined to become, by the early 1900s, the busiest settlement on the Northwest coast and one of the largest mixed-race communities in Australia.

Was the disaster a turning point in regional time? As both Bach and Bain also observe, attempts were certainly made to convert the sympathy generated by it into political currency for the industry. In early May 1887, Haynes wrote to Western Australia's colonial secretary,

> to bring [to] notice the critical position of a large number of the pearling masters here after the late disastrous storm and to draw . . . attention to the weight of both import and export duties being exacted by the Government.
>
> (Haynes 1887b)

This referred to a pre-existing grievance of the floating stations. Mobility and self-sufficiency were the hallmarks of their operation; the 'foreign' pearlers active along the coast since 1884 not only brought their own provisions with them but also sent their pearls and mother-of-pearl directly to markets overseas, thus avoiding customs duties and royalties levied in Western Australia (Haynes and Chippindall 1886). The colonial government had responded by introducing the *Pearl Shell Fisheries Special Revenue Act* (1886), which sought to regulate floating stations in the same way as established free-diving operators by enforcing licence fees and imposing duties on goods imported into the colony and excise charges on exports of shell. This was strongly opposed by the newcomers, who claimed the colony had no jurisdiction over operations taking place beyond the three-mile limit of its territorial waters, where the deeper beds they exploited lay (Bain 1982: 165–79). The disaster now forced matters to a head. When the colony 'passed the ordinance compelling ships with "foreign-going articles" to pay import duty on stores consumed afloat, a proceeding unique in Commonwealth history,' Haynes wrote to the colonial secretary,

> there was no member to represent the owners of these ships and none even to wage leniency towards them; neither has it hitherto been possible to make any combined representations to the Government on our own behalf as we have been separated by several hundred miles of water.

In light of the recent losses, he suggested 'that it is not an inopportune time to respectfully urge your Government either to repeal the late enactment regarding Import Duty or to abolish the Export Duty on the shells' (Haynes 1887b).

With others, including Clark, also vigorously opposed to the colony's regulations, it was not long before the entire industry was united in the case for reform. On 17 May 1887, a meeting held aboard the *Harriet* led to an agreement by all pearlers – that is, both the 'apparatus' and 'swimming' vessels – to petition Western Australia's governor with a request for relief. 'We the undersigned Pearl Shellers of the Nor: West Coast . . . have the honour to bring under your Excellency's notice the great loss sustained by us from the late Hurricane,' the petition read, 'with the object of respectfully requesting your Government to take off the export duty or Royalty on shell.' These losses amounted to some £20,000, it continued, leaving some pearlers completely ruined and others expecting not to recover for years (Haynes and Mcrae 1887). After the colony's Legislative Council rejected their appeal, a second petition was arranged and sent by Haynes to the secretary of state for Colonies in October 1887. His employer, the London jeweller Edwin Streeter, and Clark had each obtained legal advice questioning the validity of the 1886 act, so that the concept of territorial waters became the centrepiece of the industry's case. Floating stations were effectively foreign vessels working on the high seas, they argued, and were thus exempt from Western Australian regulations (Bain 1982: 175; Lehane 2014: 46–7). In August 1888, after considering the matter carefully, the secretary for state ruled in the industry's favour; the colony's regulations could not be applied to vessels operating beyond the three-mile limit, and hence, the 1886 act was unconstitutional (Bach 1955: 29).

This outcome embarrassed the Western Australian government, which, having embarked on a campaign for responsible government, needed to convince London it was capable of administering the vast, remote and thinly populated Northwest. Its response sealed Broome's future as the home port of the pearling industry. The colony had recourse to the newly established Federal Council of Australasia, which in early 1889, passed the *Western Australian Pearl Shell and Beche-de-mer Fishery (Extra-territorial) Act*. This legislation, along with a corresponding act covering Queensland, placed British-registered ships working on the high seas directly under jurisdiction of the respective colonies (Mullins 2001: 3). Later that year, the colonial secretary agreed to a compromise with the pearlers, reducing export duty by half in return for the fleet taking out licences under the new legislation (Powell 2010: 187–8). The other matter to be addressed related to customs. Since 1886, the floating stations had trans-shipped goods at sea from the *Australind* and other steamers sailing between Singapore and Western Australia. Smuggling, especially of liquor, was suspected to be widespread, representing both a loss to revenue as well as a harmful influence to Aboriginal peoples. The solution, worked out in September 1888, was to declare Broome a 'port of entry,' or official customs port. This would prevent trans-shipment at sea by providing shipping companies with a convenient port adjacent to the pearling grounds, forcing the pearlers into more regular visits ashore and thereby undermining the independence, and profitability, of the floating station system (Bach 1955: 30–1).

Broome, meanwhile, had continued to grow. In 1889, the town was selected as the Australian terminus for an undersea telegraph cable crossing the Timor Sea from Java, and together, the new telegraph station and customs house stimulated additional land sales and new buildings. In February 1890, when the pearling inspector reported that 'Roebuck Bay is the centre of the pearling industry having a fair harbour and a good place for repairing vessels,' it was evident that it was replacing Cossack as the fleet's base in Western Australia (Smith 1890). When the colony's first commissioner of fisheries, William Saville-Kent, visited in 1894, the transition appeared to be permanent. Broome, he reported to the Western Australian government, occupied

> a most important position with regard to the further development of the Nor'-West pearl and pearlshell fishery.... It represents, undoubtedly, the most convenient port throughout the grounds for the vessels of the pearl-shelling fleet to call for mails, stores and repairs, and for the transhipment and despatch of their cargoes of shell.

There was, he suggested, a growing tendency for the floating stations to be replaced by shore-based operations based permanently in Broome (Saville-Kent 1894). This was a welcome development to a government keen to support closer settlement and encourage small-scale capital, and it guaranteed a sympathetic reception to Saville-Kent's recommendation for the development of jetties and other shipping facilities. By the early 1900s, when the town was connected by a tramway to its harbour, it was one of the largest ports in Western Australia in terms of customs revenue, and as one parochial observer noted, 'outside Queensland, Broome is the only self-supporting tropical port in Australia' (Battye 1915: 114).

Yet neither Haynes nor Clark were present to witness Broome's rise or the shift to shore-based pearling that Saville-Kent foreshadowed. During 1888, Haynes had returned to England to marry, to lobby the Colonial Office on the question of territorial waters and to work with Streeter to form a new company, the Pearling and Trading Company, which aimed to develop the floating station system even further (Haynes 1929). In 1890, they purchased Clark's *Mavis* and its complement of luggers, but the Federal Council legislation and the taxes it introduced provided a compelling reason to leave, and in 1891, the company turned instead to the pearling grounds of the Aru Islands, in eastern Indonesia, across the Arafura Sea from Darwin (Mullins 2002: 26). Clark, meanwhile, returned to Torres Strait, having quickly rebuilt his losses in the disaster before selling out at a handsome profit to the Pearling and Trading Company. Bach would later credit the disaster as a factor in his departure, writing that

> the hurricanes of the North West coast probably helped Clark and others to make the decision. In April 1887, the fleets had suffered heavily from a blow . . . Clark himself admitted that the Western Australian grounds yielded more pearls, but said that the cyclones in that region were very dangerous, whereas the 'fretful' weather of the summer monsoon in Torres Strait could usually be avoided by making use of protecting shores and islands.
>
> (Bach 1955: 31)

This, however, almost certainly discounts the underlying economic motives. Mother-of-pearl prices fell sharply in the early 1890s, just as higher costs became a reality for the floating stations. The eastern Australian colonies had in the meantime slipped into severe economic depression, allowing Clark to re-invest his capital into pearling on favourable terms when the market began to recover a few years later. Clark would survive a second disastrous cyclone, the Bathurst Bay cyclone of March 1899, before deploying, like Pearling and Trading Company before him, the floating station system into the waters of the Dutch East Indies (Mullins 2002: 22–51).

The question of labour composition is also more complicated than Bach's analysis allows. There is no doubt that several of the white men lost in the disaster worked as divers, and it is equally the case that few white men replaced them. By 1901, when the new commonwealth's *Immigration Restriction Act* came into force, almost all diving was being carried out by Asians; only 6 of 236 divers were white, and 110 men altogether from a total of 1,680 engaged on the Northwest coast. In addressing the situation at the behest of the Commonwealth, a report by Broome's resident magistrate and sub-collector of customs dealt with the historical circumstances underpinning this dependence on foreign labour:

> Since the introduction of the diving apparatus in 1885 there have been altogether about 40 or 50 individual white divers. In the early years a good many of them worked their own luggers, the take of shell was then very large . . . but these fat years soon passed, and with them the white diver. Some retired on their earnings to shore businesses, others became pearling masters, mates and owners, or went back to Queensland; several were lost in the great blow of 1887 . . . a few got paralysed and had to give up diving.
>
> (Warton 1901: 8)

The disaster was therefore but one of several hardships facing divers. This view was later echoed by a Commonwealth Royal Commission into Australian pearling, which reported in 1916 'that diving for shell is not an occupation which our [i.e., white] workers should be encouraged to undertake. The life is not a desirable one, and the risks are great, as proved by the abnormal death rate amongst divers' (Bamford 1916: 6). The report quelled the contention surrounding the industry since 1901, ensuring it remained formally excluded from the White Australia policy.

The disaster as process

In pointing to the disaster's lasting influence, Bach and Bain confront a complex reality – that it was a momentous event during a period of far-reaching transformation in the pearling industry, if not the broader history of colonisation in Northwest Australia. It seems facile, however, to ascribe so much agency to a single event against the backdrop of a flourishing global trade in pearls and mother-of-pearl, the mobility of floating stations in the wider Indo-Pacific and a dynamic political milieu variously shaped by distant colonial and imperial governments and the imperatives of an emerging Australian nationalism. Their interpretations also reflect the bias towards the industry's political economy present in the archives (in this case, the records of Western Australia's Colonial Secretary's Office) and recapitulate the tendency for disasters to figure prominently in the memories of those who passed through them and thus become markers for the passage of time. As early as September 1887, the *West Australian* (28/09/1887: 2) was dismissing any lingering effects:

> Since the excitement over the terrible disaster which the first reports led us to believe had overtaken our Nor'-West pearling fleet died away amid the later and happier assurances of its comparatively insignificant effects, public attention has been little directed to the

affairs of this industry. And yet the business of pearl shelling has of late attained dimensions difficult to realise, and far exceeding anything known in its earlier and, as many still call them, its most prosperous days.

In fact, by the end of the year, a strong market ensured the industry recorded its highest revenue to date (Bach 1955: 282), hastening the transition to apparatus diving and further stimulating Broome's development.

This is not to suggest that the disaster was without lasting influence. Rather, its effects were subtler, being manifest in a process of adaptation to cyclone risk. The seasonality of free-diving, discussed earlier, was one of the most striking features of pearling in Western Australia when the *Sree Pas-Sair* first arrived off the coast in November 1884. Carrying a complement of Solorese and Sulu divers but not yet equipped with diving apparatus, the vessel had headed to Exmouth Gulf only to find the water was prohibitively cold. The episode is recounted in Streeter's *Pearls and Pearling Life*:

> Even in November the water in the Gulf was standing at 68° Fahr. [or 20°C], and the atmosphere at 72° Fahr., while all the boats were necessarily idle. Such cold water would be sufficient to kill men if they dived.

Haynes went instead to the Montebello Islands and worked there until January before returning to the Gulf, 'finding the water warm at last, and all the other pearlers doing well' (Streeter 1886a: 176).

This neatly summarises the situation that had prevailed since free-diving commenced in the late 1860s. Tropical cyclones form when the water temperature exceeds 26.5°C, leading in the case of the Northwest to a cyclone season that coincided closely to the diving season as prescribed under the *Pearl Shell Fishery Regulation Act* (1873). The arrival of the apparatus boats upset this pattern entirely. A diving suit and helmet protected its wearer against cold water, allowing diving in the winter months, when the state of the winds and tides was more favourable than during the summer monsoon. When the *Sree Pas-Sair* returned to Western Australia in 1885, equipped with diving apparatus, the intention was to work year-round. In September of that year, the pearling inspector found a fleet of apparatus boats working in Exmouth Gulf, before the swimming boats had yet to even sign on their divers for the coming season (Mayne 1885a).

This development had grave consequences for the industry. As referred to previously, apparatus boats were more vulnerable to cyclones because they worked in deeper waters, away from the sanctuary of the coast. The variable that determined if risk translated into disaster, however, was the unpredictability of extreme tropical weather. As a general rule, the cyclone season on the Northwest coast is well defined, running from the beginning of December to the end of March. Cyclones as early as November or as late as April are unusual, without being truly exceptional; in the first meteorological survey of Western Australian cyclones, covering the period 1872–1923, 10 per cent of all cyclones occurred in these months (Hunt et al. 1925: 9). By working in those months, the floating stations were tempting providence indeed. Haynes took this chance in 1885–86, interrupting his pearling only to visit Cossack for business or to re-provision from passing steamers (Streeter 1886b). Clark, with his experience at Torres Strait, was more circumspect following his arrival in May 1886. He wrote at the end of that year that 'the boats are dodging about now as these are the months when willyswillys or hurricanes come . . . not much shell will be obtained before March' (Lehane 2014: 40). The Darwin boats had departed Cossack in November 1886, although as their return voyage went past known shelling grounds, they too may have continued operating into the summer season (Mayne 1885b). But everyone on the coast was taken by surprise by the arrival of a cyclone in late April. As the *Western Mail* (7/5/1887: 28) reported, 'people were so unprepared for it, the season for such visitations having passed over without serious damage.'

If we put the losses to one side, then, the most tangible outcome of the disaster was to embed a cautious approach during the cyclone season. After April 1887, the fleet could only be insured 'at a rate that is almost a prohibitory one,' the pearlers claimed in their petition to the governor (Haynes and Mcrae 1887) and so a non-fishing season became firmly instituted to lessen risk in the industry. In December 1888, when only three swimming vessels remained active along the coast, the pearling inspector reported from Cossack that 'apparatus vessels had all left the grounds for the hurricane season and dispersed in various directions' (Smith 1888). In August 1889, when he reported again from Broome, it was clear where the bulk of the fleet had domiciled. 'When the hurricane season comes on (from end of November to April) I expect a number of the pearlers will lay their boats up here for repairs, and in that case there will be several hundred people staying on shore,' he wrote. 'At the present time there are about one hundred and fifty persons residing here, besides a large number of natives and I think police protection will then be necessary' (Smith 1889). By 1891, after a number of public houses had opened, Broome received its first police officer, gaol, and resident magistrate (Bain 1982: 223–30). By the turn of the century, the lay-up season had become a defining feature of the port. 'During the hurricane or "willie-willie" season (December to March), the fleets resort to some safe (comparatively) harbour, usually Broome,' the resident magistrate stated in 1901. 'Very little shelling is done at this time, and then only close at hand and when the weather is favourable.' During these months, the town's population swelled from around 500 to over 1,600, of which at least 1,500 were of the 'Asiatic races' (Warton 1901: 7). From a cultural standpoint, Broome had taken on the cosmopolitan character that was to define it within Australia deep into the twentieth century (Christensen 2017: 256–76).

The other implication of the lay-up season was to entrench the pattern of vulnerability demonstrated in April 1887. By 1901, the season was reported to run from 'December to March,' thus coinciding with the peak cyclone season (Warton 1901: 7). Every year, each master had to weigh up the same prospect – to delay coming into port or put out to sea early and so increase time on the pearling grounds or to exercise caution, lest an unusually early- or late-season storm bear down on the coast. Inevitably, more disasters followed. On 27 April 1908, a fleet of luggers was taken by surprise in the open waters off Eighty Mile Beach, leading to 117 deaths and 44 vessels sinking. A second cyclone in December 1908 caught a group of luggers at Lagrange Bay, not far from Roebuck Bay, resulting in 50 deaths and the loss of 39 vessels. A particularly early cyclone on 19 November 1910 again caught the fleet working near Roebuck Bay, sinking 34 luggers and costing 40 lives. Finally, on 27 March 1935, a cyclone at the very start of the season wreaked a path of destruction through waters north of Broome, resulting in an official death toll that narrowly eclipsed that which had been recorded in 1887 (Christensen 2016: 287–94). In Broome's cemetery, monuments commemorate the Japanese, Malay and Chinese victims of these disasters, a striking counterpoint to the anonymity of those lost in 1887. In conforming to a pattern established at the very foundation of the town, these memorials also underscore the importance of the original disaster. Broome may have since been visited by many cyclones, but none had quite the same impact as its first.

The disaster in history

The Great Depression dealt the pearling industry a hard blow, before the interruption to global trade during the Second World War and the rise of plastics and cultured pearls after it ensured its decline became terminal. Yet Broome's exotic image lingered on even after its fleet of luggers had ceased carrying Asian divers and crew along the Northwest coast. When Bach romanticised the town as a cultural melting pot in 1976, he was merely echoing other writers and travellers of the mid-twentieth century. Henrietta Drake-Brockman, visiting in 1946, was one of them; 'there clung still to Broome some indescribable quality of languor and romance not to be found at any other place I have visited in Australia' (Drake-Brockman 1963: 32). Ernestine Hill anticipated them both. 'From November to April, when the luggers come in for haven from the hurricane, Broome is filled with polyglot,' she wrote in *The Great Australian Loneliness*. But as 'a patch of the Orient in Australia, and its only port of pearls,' she could also sense the uncertain future facing the town. 'To-day the lustre of the town is a little dim,' Hill described at the start of 1935; 'its population has been reduced from 6000 to 1000 and its fleet from 400 to 50 ships' (Hill 1963: 41–61).

In time, however, the town was remade by the growth of tourism and pearl farming. In *Island Nation*, Frank Broeze (1998: 191) declared,

> Pearling is still very much the business of Broome; from a moribund state with no more than ten boats and 200 people after World War II it has risen to an annual turnover of $150 million annually, with a peak employment during the season of up to 1000 people.

Writing with an eye across the Indian Ocean in its entirety, Pearson identified this transition as an example of the adaptation and change of maritime communities in the twentieth century.

> Broome is again the centre of the pearling industry, this time focussing on cultured pearls. This all began in the 1960s, and is now a multi-million dollar export earner. . . . Since the 1970s around 70 per cent of the world's cultured pearls have come from Broome.

It is because of pearling's rich history from a transoceanic perspective that he was able to write in such terms. 'Cultured pearls provide a fine example of change and commercialisation' in the context of the systemic historical changes driven by globalisation, he writes in *The Indian Ocean* (Pearson 2003: 272). 'It was in the early nineteenth century that many of the deep structural elements . . . become much less important: monsoons, currents and land barriers are all overcome by steam ships and steam trains in the service of British power and capital: the Indian Ocean world becomes embedded in a truly global economy,' the tendency towards global integration continues today, and 'Indian Ocean is now a history *in* the ocean, part of a larger, indeed global, story' (Pearson 2003: 11–12).

By shaping Broome's character as a form of littoral society, the disaster is certainly important as both event and process in the Indo-Pacific maritime world of the late nineteenth century. To place it in the history of the ocean as a whole – that is, a history of ocean-wide comparison and deep environmental structures – is more problematic. Floating stations heralded a form of industrial pearling that was marked by the technological revolution of the diving apparatus and the consequent push into deeper waters, driven by unprecedented demand for mother-of-pearl in the manufacturing centres of Great Britain, Europe and the United States (Mullins 2001: 6). But a different perspective emerges if we shift our gaze away from Haynes, Clark and other master pearlers towards the divers and crewmen they recruited to their fleets. By their presence in an industry that was transitory and ephemeral, through their labour on a permeable and fluid maritime frontier and in their fate, the disaster's nameless victims recall patterns that can be observed across a much wider geographical and temporal plane. They remind us as well that living on the shore and working on the sea involves a process of environmental adaptation, similar in at least some ways to what must also occur on the cyclone-prone coasts of the Arabian Sea and the Bay of Bengal, at the Seychelles and the Mascarene Islands and across the extended 'Indian Ocean World,' to the Philippine Archipelago and the shores of the South China Sea (Bankoff and Christensen 2016: 6–10). Exploring this as part of the common heritage of these far-flung regions and the maritime communities to be found there remains a task for historians of the ocean's dangerous seas and hazardous shores.

Note

1 Broome's output in 1900 is conflated here with the entire Australian production of mother-of-pearl.

References

Bach, John P.S. 1976. *A Maritime History of Australia*. Sydney: Thomas Nelson.
Bach, John P.S. 1955. "The Pearling Industry in Australia: An Account of Its Social and Economic Development," Report for the Department of Commerce and Agriculture, Commonwealth of Australia.
Bain, Mary Albertus. 1982. *Full Fathom Five*, Perth: Artlook Books.
Bamford, F.W. 1916. *Pearl Shelling Industry: Report and Recommendations of Royal Commission*, The Parliament of the Commonwealth of Australia, Melbourne: Government Printer.
Bankoff, Greg. 2010. "No Such Things as 'Natural Disasters': Why We Had to Invent Them," *Harvard International Review*, available at http://hir.harvard.edu/no-such-thing-as-natural-disasters (accessed 11 March 2018).
Bankoff, Greg and Joseph Christensen. 2016. "Bordering on Danger: An Introduction," in Greg Bankoff and Joseph Christensen (eds.), *Natural Hazards and People in the Indian Ocean World*, New York: Palgrave Macmillan: 1–30.
Bartlett, Norman. 1954. *The Pearl Seekers*, London: Andrew Melrose.
Battye, James Sykes. 1915. *The History of the North West of Australia*, Perth: V.K. Jones.
Bose, Sugata. 2006. *A Hundred Horizons: The Indian Ocean in the Age of Global Empire*, Cambridge, MA: Harvard University Press.
Brockman, John. 2010. *Pearling Days: The Pearling Voyage of the Sarah to the North West and Kimberley in 1880 and 1881, with an Appendix on the Death of W.H. Lowe During an Expedition N.E. of the Gascoyne in Late 1881*, Perth: Hesperian Press.
Broeze, Frank. 1998. *Island Nation: A History of Australians and the Sea*, St Leonards, NSW: Allen and Unwin.
Cairns, Lynne and Graeme Henderson. 1995. *Unfinished Voyages: Western Australian Shipwrecks 1881–1900*, Nedlands, WA: University of Western Australia Press.
Christensen, Joseph. 2016. " 'Their Inescapable Portion'? Cyclones, Disaster Relief, and the Political Economy of Australian Pearlshelling, 1865–1935", in G. Bankoff and J. Christensen (eds.), *Bordering on Danger: Natural Hazards and Peoples in the Indian Ocean World*, New York: Palgrave Macmillan: 283–311.

Christensen, Joseph. 2017. "A Patch of the Orient in Australia: Broome on the Margin of the Indo-Pacific, 1883–1939," in Kenneth R. Hall, Rila Mukherjee and Suchandra Ghosh (eds.), *Subversive Sovereigns Across the Seas: Indian Ocean Ports-of-Trade from Early Historic Times to Late Colonialism*, Kolkata: The Asiatic Society: 256–76.

Coppin, Christopher W. 1947. "A North-West Tragedy: The Big Blow of 1887," *Early Days*, 3(9): 37–40.

Drake-Brockman, Henrietta. 1946, 1963. *On the North-West Skyline*, Perth: Patersons Printing Press.

Haynes, Thomas. 1887a. Telegram to the Colonial Secretary, 28 April 1887. In Colonial Secretary's Office File 1887/3841, James Lilly – Whereabouts of John Brennan, for Information re., Cons. 527, State Records Office of Western Australia.

Haynes, Thomas. 1887b. Letter to the Colonial Secretary, 4 May 1887. In Colonial Secretary's Office File 1888/2088, Customs Duty on Stores and Royalty on Shells. Pearlers Determined to Evade Payment of Cons. 527, State Records Office of Western Australia.

Haynes, R. 1929. Biographical Notes on T.H. Haynes. In Ifor Powell Collection, PP.MS 26/1/6, File 1, P. 1010496, School of Oriental and African Studies, University of London.

Haynes, Thomas and Edward Chippindall. 1886. Letter to the Commissioner of Customs, Cossack, 1 May 1886. In Colonial Secretary's Office file 1886/1883, Pearling Industry. Import and Export Duties, Cons. 527, State Records Office of Western Australia.

Haynes, Thomas and A.J Mcrae. Petition from Pearl Shellers Cossack, 17 May 1887. In Colonial Secretary's Office File 1888/2088, Customs Duty on Stores and Royalty on Shells. Pearlers Determined to Evade Payment of, Cons. 527, State Records Office of Western Australia.

Hicks, E.W. 1887. "Account of the voyage of *Australind*," *The West Australian*, 12 May 1887: 3.

Hill, Ernestine. 1963. *The Great Australian Loneliness*, Sydney: Angus and Roberston.

Hordern, Peregrine and Nicholas Purcell. 2000. *The Corrupting Sea: A Study of Mediterranean History*, Oxford: Wiley Blackwell.

Hunt, H.A., S.S. Visser and D. Hodge (eds.). 1925. *Australian Hurricanes and Related Storms: With an Appendix on Hurricanes in the South Pacific*, Melbourne: Commonwealth Bureau of Meteorology, Bulletin No.16.

Lehane, Robert. 2014. *The Pearl King*, Brisbane: Boolarong Press.

Mayne, Blair. 1885a. Report to the Colonial Secretary, 17 October 1885. In Colonial Secretary's Office 1885/4326, Inspector of Pearl Shell Fisheries – Visit to Pearling Fleet. Report on, Cons. 527, State Records Office of Western Australia.

Mayne, Blair. 1885b. Letter to the Colonial Secretary, 23 December 1885. In Colonial Secretary's Office File 1888/2088, Customs Duty on Stores and Royalty on Shells. Pearlers Determined to Evade Payment of, Cons. 527, State Records Office of Western Australia.

McCarthy, Michael. 2006. "Naked Diving for Mother-of-Pearl," *Early Days: Journal of the Royal Western Australian Historical Society*, 13(2): 243–59.

Mukherjee, Rila. 2017. "Revisiting Michael Pearson's Indian Ocean Littoral," *Asian Review of World Histories*, 5(1): 9–30.

Mullins, Steve. 2001. "Australian Pearl-Shellers in the Mollucas: Confrontation and Comprise on a Maritime Frontier," *The Great Circle*, 23(2): 3–22.

Mullins, Steve. 2002. "James Clark and the Celebes Trading Co.: Making an Australian Maritime Venture in the Netherlands East Indies," *The Great Circle*, 24(2): 22–52.

Payne, C. 1887a. Report to the Commissioner of Police, Western Australia, 15 July 1887. In Colonial Secretary's Office file 1887/3841, James Lilly – Whereabouts of John Brennan, for information re., Cons. 527, State Records Office of Western Australia.

Payne, C. 1887b. Telegram to the Commissioner of Police, 9 May 1887. In Colonial Secretary's Office file 1887/0567, Electric Telegraph from Cossack Regarding Hurricane Off Roebuck Bay'. Cons. 527, State Records Office of Western Australia.

Pearson, Michael. 2003. *The Indian Ocean*, New York: Routledge.

Pearson, Michael. 2006. "Littoral Society: The Concept and the Problem," *Journal of World History*, 17(4): 353–73.

Powell, Alan. 2010. *Northern Voyagers: Australia's Monsoon Coast in Maritime History*, North Melbourne: Australian Scholarly Publishing.

Qasim, S. Zahoor. 1994. "The Indian Ocean and Cyclones," *Journal of Indian Ocean Studies*, 1(2): 30–40.

Reeves, Peter, Frank Broeze and Kenneth McPherson. 1988. "The Maritime Peoples of the Indian Ocean Region Since 1800," *The Mariner's Mirror*, 74(3): 241–53.

Roe, George. 1887. "Statement on the Pearling Fleet Disaster," *The Western Mail*, 7 May 1887: 25.

Saville-Kent, William. 1894. "Report to the Premier of Western Australia," *The West Australian*, 7 May: 7.

Schwartz, Stuart B. 2015. *Sea of Storms: A History of Hurricanes in the Greater Caribbean from Columbus to Katrina*, Princeton, NJ: Princeton University Press.

Smith, G. 1887. Particulars of Vessels & Boats Working the Diving Apparatus Engaged in Pearl Shelling on the North: West Coast, 18 May 1887. In Colonial Secretary's Office file 1888/2088, Customs Duty on Stores and Royalty on Shells. Pearlers Determined to Evade Payment of, Cons. 527, State Records Office of Western Australia.

Smith, T.W. 1888. Report of the Inspector of Pearl Shell Fisheries for the Season 1887–88, 24 December 1888. In Colonial Secretary's Office file 1889/240, Report for Season 1887–88'. Cons. 527, State Records Office of Western Australia.

Smith, T.W. 1889. Letter to the Hon. Colonial Secretary, 30 August 1889. In Colonial Secretary's Office file 1889/2610, Inspector Pearl Shell Fisheries – Report on operations of Pearling Fleet'. Cons. 527, State Records Office of Western Australia.

Smith, T.W. 1890. Letter to the Hon. Acting Colonial Secretary, 8 February 1890. In Colonial Secretary's Office file 1890/0768, Season 1888–1889. Report on, Cons. 527, State Records Office of Western Australia.

Streeter, Edwin. 1886a. *Pearls and Pearling Life*, London: G. Bell & Sons.

Streeter, Edwin. 1886b. Letter to the Colonial Secretary, 8 January 1886, in Colonial Secretary's Office file 1888/2088, Customs duty on Stores and Royalty on Shells. Pearlers determined to evade payment of, Cons. 527, State Records Office of Western Australia.

The Victorian Express (Geraldton).

Villiers, Alan. 1969. *Sons of Sindbad: An Account of Sailing with the Arabs in Their Dhows, in the Red Sea, Round the Coasts of Arabia, and to Zanzibar and Tanganyika; Pearling in the Persian Gulf; and the Life of Shipmasters and the Mariners of Kuwait*, New York: Charles Scribner's Sons.

Vink, Marcus P.M. 2007. "Indian Ocean Studies and the "New Thalassology"," *Journal of Global History*, 2: 41–62.

Warton, M.S. 1901. "Pearl Shelling Industry in North-West Australia," *Commonwealth Parliamentary Papers* (Australia), 1901–02, A43: 7–8.

Watson, Marcia. 1997. "The Pearling Fleet Disaster," *Western Ancestor*, 25–26, March.

The Western Mail (Perth).

The West Australian (Perth).

10

LANDSCAPE, RAJAH AND WAX PRINTS

Contemporary archaeologies of India in Mozambique

Pedro Pombo

Perceiving landscape and objects

In this chapter, I consider the possibilities of anthropology in connecting past history with contemporary times through a sensitive approach to everydayness. Sustained by ethnographic research in southern Mozambique and the Indian state of Gujarat, I aim to unveil the modes of economic, social and cultural connections between both geographies across time. These not only are alive in exceptional examples of heritage or in contemporary economic agreements but are also embedded in local culture and thus are part of the natural and sensory landscapes surrounding daily life. Proposing connections between diverse fields of enquiry, this article argues for an openness to the sensory dimensions of 'ethnographic things' (Stoller 1989), exploring how senses of landscape, scents and flavours or aesthetics can act as heritage markers and contemporary archaeologies of the past.

The landscape of the village of Macasselane, in the rural district of Manjacaze in Gaza province in southern Mozambique, translates the cashew tree plantation schemes developed by the colonial administration since the 1930s to counterbalance Indian monopoly of the processed cashew nut. What is considered the natural landscape of the district is indeed an effort to centrally control the local economy, bringing to the present the tense relations between the colonial regime and the Indian traders settled in the colony.

In a gastronomic field, the Portuguese word for 'curry,' *caril*, is used by Mozambicans to generically designate any gravy, while the curry power brand Rajah, produced in South Africa, can be found even in the smallest stores in the rural areas of southern Mozambique. Both the word *caril* and the curry powder are part of Mozambican gastronomy, in a profound assimilation of flavours denoting the long historical influence of India in this part of the African continent.

Although sometimes seen as belonging to the past, the Indian textile trade in Eastern Africa is a reality we observe simultaneously in Mozambique and in Ahmedabad, the main city in the Indian state of Gujarat. African wax prints are still produced in what once was one of the most important cotton mill centres in India and are mostly sold in stores owned by Indian-Mozambicans across the country. Some of these stores even have exclusive patterns designed in India. The fact that in Ahmedabad warehouses, we are able to see exactly the same patterns and colours as in Mozambique is a powerful testimony to the living connections between these countries and also a remainder of the history of Gujarat and its Indian Ocean trading networks. An ethnographic approach, therefore, turns visible all these translucent layers through which India is present in the landscape and life of a rural district in southern Mozambique. As a metaphor of crossing the Indian Ocean, an anthropological insight calls for the crossing of disciplines, unveiling how enduring historical processes have created cultural landscapes.

Landscape as archive

In previous research in the Manjacaze district, in the southern Mozambique province of Gaza, I engaged with an ethnography sensitive to what can be viewed as semi-transparent layers through which landscape can be perceived, observed and understood. Understanding landscape as archive, or as testimony,[1] means paying attention to its diverse components: natural and topographical elements, human occupation and agricultural fields, the architecture of buildings, its intangible and tactile qualities, paths and roads, shaded forests and open fields, the time it takes to traverse them, rhythms and sounds, flavours and gestures that happen in a particular place. Not only the landscape itself but also how it is experienced and which elements constitute it is part of this archival perspective. In this way, we can introduce the dimension of time and start unveiling the processes that built what we actually observe; landscape can be unfolded as a written text, layers of changes, natural causes and human intervention, in an archival research of historical processes. Landscape can, thus, be taken as a testimony of the history of the territory, its natural elements and the social processes that take place (Howard 2005: 30).

In their book on an historical anthropology of the Kenyan region of Siaya, Cohen and Odhiambo develop the concept of landscape as simultaneously including geographical features of a particular place and its historical, economic and social connections with other regions, acting as an 'interaction field' (Cohen and Odhiambo 1989: 4). This understanding of a place as being beyond its geographical boundaries and integrating social dynamics is worth exploring since it relates the local with wider contexts, not only turning the visible landscape into a 'cultural process' (Hirsch 1995) but unveiling the existing remains and memories of the past.

Cashew

When travelling across the Manjacaze district, as in all coastal provinces of Mozambique, we notice the predominance of cashew trees among the local flora. A dialogue between ethnographic fieldwork and archival research unveils how the landscape was deeply transformed in the first half of the twentieth century as a direct reaction to India's role in cashew nut production. Cashew is indeed an important crop, and the fruit has a significant cultural importance, being a relevant part of local natural, economic and social landscapes.

The abundance of cashew trees in Mozambique, as well as in West Africa, India, Vietnam and other South Asian countries reveals the history of its spread from Brazil, from where it probably originated, to different regions where the Portuguese established a presence.[2] Concerning the Western Indian Ocean, the cashew tree, its nut and the alcoholic beverage made with the juice of its *hipocardium*[3] are some of the layers that convey similar senses between Western India and Eastern Africa. Despite the history of the existence of cashew trees in Mozambique and India reflecting the long connections between Portuguese India and Eastern Africa,[4] the actual landscape of southern Mozambique also reveals more recent historical processes that translate the influence of India's economy in Mozambique before and after independence in both countries.

The territory of central and southern Mozambique was definitively conquered in 1895 by the Portuguese army with the defeat of the last African king of the Gaza empire, Ngungunhane. From that year onwards, the territory and its population would be inscribed in a new colonial order, sustaining the exploitation of natural resources and human labour. Since the very first years, while Gaza province was still a military command, botanical experiments were carried out in order to develop agriculture and to define which productions would be more adaptable to the local climate and soil. In the historical archives of Mozambique, we find a significant collection of boxes concerning the colonial military command and later the Circumscription of Muchopes (the colonial designation for the Manjacaze district). Several monthly reports dating between July and December 1900 explain in detail the agricultural experiments carried out and their results, among other information on infrastructure (Nogueira 1900). In the same first decades of the twentieth century, the plantation of cashew trees was progressively encouraged in the region as a viable production, and in 1915, a rail line was built connecting the town of Manjacaze with the more important cities of João Belo (actually, Xai-Xai, at the mouth of the Limpopo River) and Mawayela, in the district of Inhambane, a coastal town which had been a crown land for a long time, as well as an active port on the Mozambican coastline (Santos 1957: 27).[5] Maps are powerful tools to visually perceive the 'capture' of the territory (Noyes 1992: 106) and how developments in agriculture are complemented by new colonial infrastructures. By this time, the cashew nut had already been used in local gastronomy, and the slightly alcoholic juice and distilled spirit made with its *hipocardium* were part of the cultural and social landscapes,[6] but the plantation schemes developed by the colonial administration significantly increased local production and consumption of this fruit.

At the turn of the twentieth century, numerous Indian-origin merchant communities controlled the exportation of non-processed cashew nut to India. The vital role that Indian or Indian-origin traders (from both British and Portuguese India) had in the Mozambican economy was a constant matter of concern and is commented upon in periodic reports and inspections in the districts of the colony. Documents concerning the colonial Circumscription of Muchopes portray vividly how, in a small, rural district, Indian merchants were actively engaged in local commerce, establishing networks across the hinterland with the main centres in the south such as Inhambane, João Belo or Lourenço Marques. In 1900, the local administration received 30 requests for provisory occupation of land for commercial purposes and, with the exception of three requests (one from an Italian and two from British citizens), all were made by Indians or Indian-origin Mozambicans (Requerimentos 1900). In 1950, the panorama had not changed significantly: out of 52 commercial houses operating in the Circumscription of Muchopes, 25 were Indian and five were of Indian-origin Mozambicans (Pires 1950).

In the 1930s, India developed the mechanical shelling and processing of cashew nuts, and Mozambican exports of raw cashew became mostly directed to this market. This increase in exports was seen as an economic opportunity, and the colonial government decided to directly invest in cashew nut production to counterbalance the unofficial monopoly of this trade by Indian-origin merchants. New rules were approved to oblige the local populations to develop planting of cashew trees and to sell the cashew nuts in commercial establishments spread across the territory. In the 1950s, after many attempts to develop the industrial shelling of the nut, the first industrial complexes opened doors, proving that it was an economically viable activity (Ribeiro 2004: 193). This development intended to avoid the exportation of raw nut to India and turn Mozambique into a competitor in the processed cashew nut world market. In the mid-1960s, with large investments from Portuguese and South African groups, industrial expansion had an exponential growth, and the number of workers increased by 500 per cent between 1960 and 1970 (Ribeiro 2004: 196). Cashew nut was seen as vital to the economy of Mozambique; in an attempt to confront India's role in the world market and at the time of independence in 1975, the country processed 147,000 tons of cashew nut (Ribeiro 2004: 202).

Until recent years, Manjacaze town had a cashew nut processing factory, but the long years of civil war, with its devastating economic and social consequences, saw the revenue of this production steadily declining, and the industry slowly disappeared.

Going back to the landscape of the Manjacaze district, we can now understand how the massive presence of these trees represents a constructed landscape through past historical processes. What appears to be a 'traditional' landscape is in fact the result of enduring economic and political projects that not only changed the nature but also the lives of the local population. In this way, the landscape can be read as an historical archive, dialoguing with documents kept in archives and with the local memories that an ethnographic fieldwork unveils, reminding us 'how easy it is to accept elements of the present and observed social world as given and traditional' (Cohen and Odhiambo 1989: 95). This helps us to observe how India is present in the landscape of this Mozambican district, not only through the activity of Indian-origin traders but also indirectly, as the background reasons for economic investment in cashew plantations and later in the implementation of the nut processing industry by the Portuguese colonial government. Meanwhile, Mozambicans and Indians keep drinking the spirit made by distilling the fermented pulp of the *hipocardium*. *Totonto*, as it is called in Mozambique, or *feni*, as it is known in Goa, is part of cultural practices across the Indian Ocean, and the transparency of this drink allows us to see the past and present links between the two places.

A Rajah in the village – flavours and words

The long cultural connections between the Indian subcontinent and Mozambique can be perceived through diverse sensorial aspects that became part of what is now understood as Mozambican culture. The Indian Ocean world created cultural topographies ingrained in movements and connections, in the travel of commodities as well as in languages, religious beliefs and the settling of diverse communities along the coastal areas, while port cities were developed as nodes in vast networks (Pearson 2003; McPherson 1993; Moorthy and Jamal 2010; Mukherjee 2014). Notions of selfhood are reflected in built heritage and constructions of identities in dialogue with diverse cultural settings (Meier 2013; Gupta et al. 2010). Being part of Indian Ocean coastal Africa, North Mozambique acted as the southern border of what became Swahili culture, and in the nineteenth century, the whole of the country's territory became fully integrated into transcolonial networks linking Africa and Asia.

If art forms and architecture are tangible heritages that can speak to us about past cultural dialogues, so do more subtle heritages, such as language or gastronomy. Food is indeed a powerful social marker and a fundamental element of identity affirmation. And it is in the gastronomic field, among ingredients, scents and flavours, that we trace deep Indian influences embedded in Mozambican culinary culture. And that is why, in the daily life of a small village in the rural district of Manjacaze, we can literally find India on our plate.

When speaking in Mozambican Portuguese,[7] locals generally refer to the gravy that is served with rice or boiled corn flour as 'caril.' Any gravy, be it with vegetables, fish or meat, can loosely be called *caril*, every specific recipe having, nevertheless, its own denomination. Interestingly, *caril* is the Portuguese word for 'curry,' but in Mozambican Portuguese, it has lost its specific meaning of denominating the mixture of spices originating from India. Even if the word does not represent the curry itself, its generic use becomes quite relevant in drawing maps of culinary influences since curry, in its proper sense, became part of Mozambican gastronomy. While the word *caril* designated any kind of gravy, the 'proper' curry represents Mozambican gastronomy, along with *cafreal*,[8] *Zambezian* or *Peri Peri* (*piri piri* in Portuguese) chicken, *matapa* or samosas (clearly an Indian influence). Despite not knowing when curry entered Mozambican gastronomy, we find a reference in a text written by the Italian doctor Luis Vicente de Simoni, who arrived in Mozambique in 1819 as principal physician to the hospital of Mozambique Island. Staying two years in this post, he wrote a medical treatise on the climate and diseases of Mozambique,[9] where he mentions curry being 'peppery and full of drugs that irritates and spoils the vitality of the organs without fully satisfying their needs' (Rodrigues 2005: 637). Leaving aside the author's strong criticism, we understand that he is referring to the spicy Indian curry, made with a mix of ingredients.

This triangular relationship between India, Portugal and Mozambique gave origin to new recipes and new uses of words. The Goan influence in Mozambican cuisine reminds us how, apart from the settling of Indian communities in Mozambican territory, the senses are a vital medium through which these relations gain life. I would like to refer again to the possibility of landscape functioning as an archive and how smells and flavours can become sensorial aspects of a more inclusive notion of landscape. There is a sense of familiarity when we cross the Indian Ocean from the Mozambican coast to Western India. Despite differences, the fact of belonging to a wide geographic region under the influence of the monsoon and the circulation of botanical elements, such as the cashew tree, vegetables, fruits and flowers, enhances this sense of the familiar that bonds both sides of the ocean. We have seen how in both Goa and Mozambique cashew is a connecting element, as is the geometrically perfect flower releasing a sweet scent on both sides of the ocean, known as *frangipani* in Mozambique and *champa* in India.[10] This is the landscape where new words came into use and flavours became part of new gastronomic traditions.

Marta Rosales, in her studies on domesticity and narratives of home, quotidian life and materialities of the Goans in East Africa quotes several interviews dedicated to the importance of food as a cultural marker sustaining senses of belonging (Rosales 2010). This aspect is important to understand the history of the Indian communities in Mozambique and the cultural traits they generated. The economic motifs underlining maritime circulations were complemented by other important dimensions of life. Along with textiles and spices, dhows and steamboats coming from India to Eastern Africa carried on board persons with their senses of belonging who, in a distant land, would built notions of home through aesthetics, aromas and tastes; ingredients; and words that were part of their social and religious worldviews and concepts of personhood. The curry being a 'spiced meat, fish or vegetable stew served with rice, bread, cornmeal or another starch' (Sen 2009: 7), it is plausible that with time any gravy accompanied by rice or boiled wheat flour in Mozambican gastronomy became known as 'caril.' Sen, in his book on curry and its presence around the world, notes that the Portuguese incorporated the word 'caril' or 'caree' (most probably coming from the Tamil 'karil' or 'kari,' meaning spicy dish of vegetables and meat), as early as the seventeenth century to designate broths 'made with butter, the pulp of Indian nuts and all sorts of spices, particularly cardamoms and ginger besides herbs, fruits and a thousand other condiments poured in good quantity upon boiled Rice,' citing Pietro della Valle, a famous Italian traveller who visited Goa during his stay in India around the mid-seventeenth century. What is indeed revealing is that 'caril' is a Mozambican-Portuguese word coming not from Portugal but from Portuguese India, denoting direct and long links established between the two sides of the Western Indian Ocean. This directs us to what Maria Paula Meneses references as the 'diversity and complexities that the dishes and cooking histories can reveal' (Meneses 2009: 2). To acknowledge that food can also function as an archive and ethnographic medium is to recognise that recipes, ways of preparing food and access to the ingredients used are elements of histories that materialise in aromas and flavours. Economic history and narratives of circulation across the ocean can, thus, be also seen in a gastronomy that transcends the spheres of public life and the intimacy of home.

Prior to the larger migration of Indians sailing from Portuguese India in the nineteenth century, as also across the British Empire, Banyans from Diu (a Portuguese territory on the Gujarat coast) had been authorised to establish the Banyan Company of Mazanes in 1686 (Machado 2014), following continuous circulations between the Mozambican coast and Western India in previous centuries. At the same time, the north of the territory was administered through a particular institution titled *Prazos da Coroa* or land grants for three generations (Newitt 1995). These *prazos* became locations of 'syncretic social and cultural forms' in contact between Africa, Europe and Asia (Newitt 2002: 217). With time, large extensions of land came to be administered by Afro-European and Afro-Asian families, their kinship relations along trade routes linking the hinterland, the littoral and the local plantations. Many were Indian Catholics from Goa related to military services or administration (Newitt 2002: 227) as Mozambique belonged to the *Estado da India* (Portuguese India) until 1752 and until that time was an integral part of the vast area under Goa's administration.

The circulation of people who constructed these changing social and commercial worlds was accompanied by the travel of cultural markers as part of identities and senses of belonging. With the introduction of the curry itself to Mozambican cuisine, the Portuguese word would also have been introduced, acquiring, however, a much larger meaning. While the word *caril* became specifically Mozambican in its broad sense, the inclusion of curry in local gastronomy locates Mozambique in an incredibly large panorama of relations and also illuminates the complex and multiple histories of the Indian presence in southern Africa beyond what are today Mozambican borders. The South African provinces of Kwazulu-Natal and Cape were destinations for an important number of indentured labourers brought from India to work within various networks of the British Empire. During the nineteenth century, Indian populations settled around the Indian Ocean territories from the Eastern African coast – in the islands of Madagascar, Reunion and Mauritius, leaving a more enduring cultural impact than in previous centuries, when Indian inhabitants were mostly itinerant merchants in smaller numbers. The abolition of slavery opened a new era, when European colonial connections were sustained by the massive migration of a working force to develop agricultural works and build infrastructure in colonial possessions.

The second half of the century was also the period for effective territorial appropriation of African land and the expansion of economic and administrative structures in the continent. The development of extractive industries in the region of Johannesburg was behind enduring migration routes from Mozambique to Gauteng Province in South Africa, with deep cultural implications in Mozambique (Harries 1994) as migrants brought with them new habits, words and commodities. In this way, not only did transoceanic colonial networks link different continents, they also fomented movements across neighbouring colonies. The entwining of diverse cultural influences, religious sensibilities, languages and circulation of commodities across great distances created new visual and material cultures along the Indian Ocean with strong repercussions in the African continent.

The materiality of objects dialogued with architectural features, spatial aesthetics and modes of dressing and codifying bodies became part of the urban landscape of many of the port cities on the littoral. Objects and visual cultures can be seen as representation of identities and aesthetic choices; they also appear as consumption possibilities that reveal economic and production networks (Meier 2013; Gupta 2016). The analysis of imagery, from photographs and paintings or furniture and decorative arts that populate interior spaces, can be complemented by the study of consumerist patterns in clothes, adornments and food. In this way, even humble or discreet things can translate century-long histories and explain the past processes that structure contemporary times. This is a field of enquiry sustained by an art history approach, putting in dialogue aesthetics with architecture, urbanism, history and anthropology. Decorative arts from the past filling many museums around the word decode circulations of forms, adaptations of meanings and symbolisms and the creation of new visual languages of power and the production of culture. They cannot be studied only as geographically situated but also as revealing networks and routes that connect different places and cultures. Chinese ceramics with European motifs or Arabic inscriptions, Indo-Portuguese furniture and retabular art, Anglo-Indian architecture, ivory objects and religious statues, ceramics, carpets, embroidered silks, new forms of dressing and reinvention of recipes are some of the materialities that formed the material and affective world of oceanic routes. In contemporary times, this circulation of objects and forms can still be studied, and for that, we should direct our gaze towards what is seen as popular culture in order to discover the visual cultures that are part of current global networks. The recognition of the importance of 'things' (Appadurai 1986) takes us back to our Mozambican curry and how Indian influence in the country is made visible through an unexpectedly discrete element that embodies larger historical boundaries.

In the smallest stores, locally known as *cantinas*, or in the humble reed kitchens we can see in every Mozambican village, we can notice a small yellow packet that has become part of the visual and sensorial setting of domestic life. Along the word 'Rajah,' we can observe a drawing of a figure of a man, turban on his head, dressed in what can be seen as Indian attire. Rajah curry powder is produced in South Africa by the firm Robertsons, founded in Durban in 1924 and dedicated to the trade of herbs and spices. Durban has one of the largest Indian diaspora communities across the world, and Indian influence in South Africa can be seen through its gastronomy. Being made in South Africa, the fact that this curry is sold in Mozambique is a sign of the country's economic dependence on South Africa, since most of the products sold in the country and the most important commercial surfaces, such as Shoprite or Spar, are also South African brands and ventures. An Indian curry produced in South Africa and consumed in Mozambique is as revealing of historical and contemporary economic connections and cross-cultural landscapes as the objects found in nineteenth-century colonial photographs or in museum collections.

Going back to our little yellow box of curry powder, it is extraordinary that the everydayness of Mozambican villages is punctuated by an Indian man drawn in a curry packet, incorporating histories of circulations between India and Africa, the influence of India in Mozambique through Portuguese colonial routes and the relevance of South Africa in the country's economic and social setting since the mid-nineteenth century. The relevance of such 'things' as a simple packaged spice mixture reveals that a sensitive ethnography of what constitutes daily life can engage in meaningful dialogues with other disciplines and methodologies in order to understand the past and the present and to imagine what might be the future implications of worldwide webs of movement. What can appear to be devoid of interest becomes a meaningful object that can be seen as a remainder of an archaeology of the historical roots of elements that constitute everydayness in a southern Mozambique village. An ethnographic field sensitive to the landscape understood in its natural, human and sensorial aspects can thus reveal the intensity of meanings of what is humble and possibly taken for granted. In this case, the word *caril*, the Mozambican curry recipes and the Raja curry packet reveal different and complementary dimensions of history. The sound of the words, the smell and taste of the food and the commercial routes of a curry packet are different dimensions that express – despite or because of its dailyness – discreet reminiscences of long-term intersections across the ocean.

Wrapping colours and patterns

An essential element of the Mozambican life and visually powerful by its patterns and colours, the *capulana*, the local word for the piece of printed cotton that became a crucial dressing element, is seen everywhere. The variety of patterns, motifs and colour schemes seem infinite and are commonly worn folded around women's waistbands or as a long skirt or are tailored into fashionable dresses following recent trends in Eastern and West Africa. It was also used by men wrapped around the waist, but nowadays, it is almost confined to shirts.

This cloth became not only a sign of the dressing culture of Mozambique but also a medium of celebration and remembrance. Special prints are made to celebrate national events or important figures – Independence Day or the first president, Samora Machel, and his wife, Josina Machel – or to serve as a souvenir of celebrations of the Catholic and other Christian churches present in the country. Among the many geometric and floral patterns that fill the cloth markets in any Mozambican city or town, images of churches, politicians, Jesus Christ or the Sacred Family and dates and slogans can also be seen in market stalls. These become collectable items, acting as visual and wearable archives of memory. This is an extraordinary feature, deciphering the relevance this particular genre of cloth has in the Mozambican cultural landscape and directly connecting us with much wider locations and histories of cotton textiles in Eastern Africa. At the same time, the *capulana* also illuminates the presence of India in the shaping of textile cultures on the Eastern African coast.

Textiles have been acknowledged as one of the fundamental commodities crossing the Indian Ocean (Riello and Roy 2009; Barnes 2005) with a lasting and fundamental role in shaping and translating social and cultural backgrounds in the Swahili coast and Southeast Africa and complementing local centres of production in the African continent. Among the larger trading networks that connected the Indian subcontinent with Africa, Banyan traders from Western India were among the most powerful communities in the Western Indian Ocean, specializing in the commercialisation of textiles and enjoying privileged links between Portuguese possessions in India and those in Eastern Africa (Machado 2014). Being part of multiple trading networks connecting Eastern Africa, the Gulf, the Indian subcontinent and Southeast Asia, Portuguese colonial routes privileged, as expected, Portuguese possessions across the oceans. Mozambique sustained privileged connections with Portuguese India until the end of the nineteenth century, when trade with other countries and industrial mills in Europe and India almost completely erased the textile trade undertaken through the Portuguese ports of Diu, Daman and Goa.

Interrogating the connections between geographies of production and consumption highlights the agency of African consumers in dictating patterns and colour schemes and in giving new social meanings to the transoceanic textile trade (Machado 2009: 55). One way of understanding the relevance of textiles in the African continent is the fact that cotton fabrics produced in Western India were exchanged for ivory or slaves in 'areas that effectively constituted cloth currency zones of contact' (Machado 2009: 57), a market dominated, by the eighteenth century, by the Banyans from Diu. The diversity of cloths, patterns and colours mentioned in administrative reports, customs documents and travellers' accounts demonstrates the different uses and social categories that imported textiles acquired in East Africa, complementing a local production that had marked cultural landscapes across the continent (Machado 2014).

The nineteenth century saw important changes in this textile trade, as diverse communities from coastal areas of the Saurashtra Peninsula in western India and Bengal on the eastern Indian coast started to be engaged in this commerce (Machado 2009: 79). That century saw the development of industrialisation, machine-operated mills changing the panorama of cotton production across the globe. Indian cities that had been traditionally connected with maritime trade became new hubs of industrialisation, with Ahmedabad, Surat or Bombay gaining importance and taking advantage of the railway system of British India that connected them with steamship oceanic circuits. At the turn of the twentieth century, the Eastern African coast imported textiles from Britain, Japan, Holland and Germany, as mentioned in the chapter dedicated to the cotton trade of Zanzibar, in the report of the British Trade Mission to the Near East and Africa (1928).

Returning to Mozambique, the last years of the nineteenth century were crucial for the development of a colonial structure. The colony suddenly had vast lands to administer and new commercial networks were put in place.

The Delagoa Bay, in the south, and Beira, in the centre, became directly connected with the British territories of today's South Africa and Zimbabwe by railways, developing both cities' portuary activities.

In Mozambique, as in many other African coastal colonies in the Indian Ocean, Indian-origin trading communities played a vital role in commercial networks, adapting to new international contexts that, Markovits mentions, were linked to 'longstanding patterns of circulation' (Markovits 2006: 131).

Besides this historical contextualisation, the *capulana* is also part of a larger history of the aesthetics of clothing in the Indian Ocean world that reveals an extraordinary dissemination of forms from Africa to Southeast Asia, highlighting contemporary systems of drawing and producing the famous 'African prints' designed for the global African market and African diasporas in the world. One common characteristic is the shape of these pieces of cotton cloth, a rectangular form and between 150 cm × 110 cm for the *kangas* used in Eastern and Western Africa to the size of 180 cm × 120 cm of the most common Mozambican *capulana*. This fact translates their common origin in the handkerchiefs imported from India, which, instead of being cut individually, started to be cut in larger pieces in order to be wrapped around the body. The use of wrapping clothes has historically co-existed with more elaborate attires popularised in the Islamic regions of the continent, as seen in the Western and North African *kaftans*. The *kangas*, manufactured in Germany, North America and Britain following local taste, became fashionable in Zanzibar and along the Swahili coast at the end of the nineteenth century(Meier 2013: 104). Embodying social meanings, this cloth was a powerful visual frame of local societies and the world and of bodily aesthetics produced by the convergence of diverse cultural backgrounds, as well as a means of communicating statements(Parkin 2005).

Another cloth that became an integral part of South African material culture is the *shweshwe*, a piece of cloth dyed in indigo but nowadays using brown or red dyes as well. It is mostly drawn with repetitions of dots and small-scale geometric patterns and used across the country. Its history is related to its use by European missionaries in the mid-nineteenth century and its gradual assimilation into local dressing modes that sustained, and still sustain, its production in South Africa.

However, what has become the most famous textile in the African continent is the fabric known as the African wax print. Seen as representative of contemporary Africa's visual culture, the theme of exhibitions in reputed museums[11] and inspiration for artwork,[12] these pieces of cotton are indissociable from the present-day location of Africa in the world and the production of ideas about the continent. The chromatic richness, the extraordinary diversity of patterns ranging from those considered traditional to those incorporating objects of daily life, such as mobile phones, computers or shoes, the African print is embedded in the continent's culture and is a vehicle of the transmission of new ideas, a sense of inventiveness and new imaginations. Most of the Mozambican *capulanas* are also wax-printed cotton pieces, the exception being the chequered-patterned ones that can also be used as bedspreads offered to newly married couples. The history of the *capulana* is, thus, not only directly connected with Portuguese colonialism and India but with the history of how the African print became 'African' through a crossroad of influences and mobilities that includes not only India but also Indonesia, Holland, France, Britain and, in this new century, China.

It is accepted that the origins of the actual African print lay in the *batik* textiles produced in Indonesia from 1800 to 1945 under the rule of the Dutch East Indies. Indonesian *batiks* circulated across the Indian Ocean along with Indian textiles and gained social recognition, as some colours and motifs were for exclusive use in sacred ceremonies and for royalty. The industriali-sation of textile manufacture allowed the traditional labour-intensive mode of production to be substituted by cheaper printing techniques, making this cloth profitable for trading in Africa as well as in Europe. The most emblem-atic company producing wax prints is Vlisco, whose name is so inseparable from this textile's history that African wax prints can also be called 'Dutch wax.' Starting production at the end of the nineteenth century, Vlisco slowly adapted patterns and colours to the West African market, and in the twen-tieth century, these prints become undoubtedly 'African,' despite most of its major centres of production being located outside the continent. Mozam-bique is part of this large context, with the particularity of having a strong presence of patterns with Indian aesthetics, in floral arrangements and in intricate borders. And this fact takes us towards the cities of Ahmedabad, Surat and Bombay and the actual state of the centuries-long cotton textile manufacture.

The growing Indian trading communities in Mozambique during the nineteenth and twentieth centuries were able to sustain privileged networks between local markets and Western Indian mills. Established in major Mozambican port cities, Indian merchants were instrumental in forming a network of smaller stores across the hinterland, thereby reaching a large number of consumers. Integrating a new landscape of industrialisation in the Indian subcontinent, Ahmedabad became a hub of textile production with mills that started operations in the end of the nineteenth century. Surat, an important port city for several centuries, also developed its industry while Bombay would become the most important port on the western coast. In recent times, Indian textile production has expanded to West African markets, not only from Western Indian centres of manufacture but also by companies from Chennai in the eastern state of Tamil Nadu, which directly exports to West Africa through Nigerian traders (Lutz 2000).

In the industrial areas of eastern Ahmedabad, where the first mills were built, or in the new southwestern commercial hubs of the city, African prints are manufactured exclusively for exportation. Preliminary research has illuminated the importance of this production in the actual panorama of the city's textile trade, as we observe several catalogues with diverse African wax prints or *Dashiki* fabrics (a tunic worn by men in Western Africa with patterns designed by Vlisco and inspired by traditional Ethiopian tunics). The history of the Western Indian textiles and their transoceanic circulation can be seen in these contemporary colourful cottons, whose production is of a centuries-long story. These cottons, sold in many Mozambican stores and worn as a symbol of Mozambicanness, reveal that despite globalisation and the growing role of China in producing African prints for West and East Africa, India continues to be a centre of a fabric production that crosses the Indian Ocean. On fieldwork in Maxixe, a town in the south of the country with a strong presence of Indian-origin communities because of its proximity to the port town of Inhambane, I repeatedly heard that some of the local stores sold *capulanas* with exclusive patterns drawn in Gujarat, a story deserving further investigation. *Capulanas* with printed cornucopias that vaguely resemble Mughal aesthetics or the floral patterns inspired by traditional Gujarati block print motifs will surely be among those exclusive models created in India to satisfy Mozambican customers who buy them in stores owned by Indian-Mozambican families: a cycle of material culture 'on the move.'

One more piece of evidence deserves further fieldwork. In the heart of Bombay, we find a company specialised in the export of African wax prints with a particularity: its catalogue has a whole section on 'Mozambique fabrics' produced exclusively for that market. It is not only interesting to note the name by which they are titled but to observe their differences with the rest of the African prints: geometric patterns drawn in less contrasting forms and colours, the presence of stylised flowers or organic elements and a certain chromatic gentleness that differs from the bold and affirmative drawings of the products designed for the Western Africa markets. Interrogating these aesthetic options will illuminate the diversity of tastes and preferences that exist under the unifying notion of the African wax print, turning the singular into plural 'Africas,' denoting differences between regions and cultural backgrounds. Coming back to the *capulana*, the present-day history of textiles and the visual cultures they embody deserve to be investigated. Seen everywhere in Mozambique, *capulanas* are another remainder of complex histories, translating the Mozambique of today in the modes it has been appropriated as a medium for celebratory messages or powerful visual markers. The contemporary *capulana* remind us of the nuanced and multiple transitions from colonial to postcolonial chronologies and link the Indian presence in Mozambique with the large and diverse communities from India settled in East Africa (Oonk 2015) and the contemporary economic ties between Asia and Africa.

Conclusion

Everydayness, material culture, smells and flavours are sites where memories are constructed, re-built or contested. They are testimonies of cultural contacts across time and space. The elements that constitute daily life can be taken as simultaneously humble and powerful, as their omnipresence is where their importance lies. Besides built or intangible heritage examples that can be considered exceptional or historical events that became part of narrated history, daily gestures, landscapes and aesthetics are the ways in which the past is part of the present in what can be considered living, and lived, alternative archives. Understanding these different layers as fields of enquiry triggers an approach to the complexities of cultural processes. This also directs us towards multi-sited ethnographies, not in geographical and relational terms but by forwarding George Marcus's methodological proposal (1995) of understanding 'things' as geographies of research and meanings – in this particular case, ethnographies not only sited in different places but in different 'things' as well.

In this chapter, I have tried to argue that diverse sensorial aspects, such as the ones I have explored here, constitute an embodied history that should dialogue with other sources of historical and ethnographic knowledge, in order to change history, in the singular, into histories, in the plural, as a recognition of the constellations of narratives and encounters. Interdisciplinary research is necessary in order to focus not on a particular object or topic but on the networks they are part of. Under this perspective, a pattern in a cotton fabric is directly related with recipes, words and landscapes, opening possibilities of meaningful dialogues, allowing us to understand historical processes as unfolding in plural dimensions with affective consequences. The presence of India in Mozambique is seen not only through historical documents or statistics of the Indian-origin population in the country but also in how it became part of the everyday at so many levels.

Notes

1 The notion of landscape as testimony is inspired by the work of the Brazilian architect Paulo Tavares in taking Amazonia forest as testimony of the systematic disappearance of local communities, contesting arguments that large extensions of forest were uninhabited. This has led to an extraordinarily engaging work related to the so-called "forensic" fields of research. www.forensic-architecture.org/, accessed 20 August 2017.
2 Although this is the most accepted perspective, there are also some authors who propose the opposite travel of the tree, from India to the rest of the world: see (Ribeiro 2004: 181). Other vegetable species that become part of Mozambican gastronomic culture are also originally from South America, such as corn, cassava and groundnut (*ibidem*).
3 The cashew fruit consists of the *hipocardium*, which has the shape of a pear and an astringent pulp, and the fruit itself, which is commonly called cashew nut.

4 This connection was also at an administrative level, since Portuguese East Africa was part of the Portuguese Estado da India until 1752, when it gained its own administrative system.

5 This railway appears as a project in the map *Carta de Moçambique (esboço)* of 1914, as well as newly built roads connecting Manjacaze town with the towns of Chibuto to the west, Joao Belo to the southeast, and Zavala to the east (S.a. 1914). The opening of circulation routes was crucial for the appropriation of the territory and control of the local population.

6 It was mentioned by Junod, a missionary from the Swiss Mission, who wrote one of the most important accounts of southern Mozambique (Junod 1917).

7 Mozambican Portuguese has many words that do not exist in Portugal or are used in different contexts. Besides *caril*, among the most common in everyday life, we find the words *machamba* (an agricultural field) and appellative terms such as *mamã'* (mother), *papá* (father) or *mano* (brother), which in these forms are seen as language proper for children from Portugal.

8 The *Cafreal* chicken denotes the inverse circulation: *cafre* being a derogatory Portuguese term for black African person, having its English equivalent in the work *kaffir*. This recipe is believed to have been taken from Mozambique to Portuguese India.

9 *Tratado Medico sobre Clima e Enfermidades de Moçambique*, dated from 1821 and kept in the National Library in Rio de Janeiro, Brazil.

10 Scientific name: *Plumeria*, from the family of *Apocynaceae*.

11 'African-Print Fashion Now!', Fowler Museum at UCLA, 2017. www.fowler.ucla.edu/exhibitions/african-print-fashion-now/, accessed 20 August 2017; "Vlisco: African Fashion on a Global Stage," Philadelphia Museum of Art, 2016/7, www.philamuseum.org/exhibitions/838.html, accessed 20 August 2017.

12 Yinka Shonibare, www.yinkashonibarembe.com, accessed 20 August 2017; Omar Victor Diop, www.omarviktor.com/, accessed 20 August 2017.

References

AHM: Arquivo Histórico de Moçambique (Historical Archives of Mozambique)

SGL: Sociedade de Geografia de Lisboa (Geographical Society of Lisbon).

Appadurai, Arjun, ed. 1986. *The Social Life of Things*. Cambridge: Cambridge University Press.

Barnes, Ruth (ed.). 2005. *Textiles in Indian Ocean Societies*, London and New York: Routledge Curzon.

Cohen, D.W. and E.S. Atieno Odhiambo. 1989. *Siaya: The Historical Anthropology of an African Landscape (Eastern African Studies)*, Oxford: James Currey.

Gupta, Pamila. 2016. "Visuality and Diasporic Dynamism: Goans in Mozambique and Zanzibar," *African Studies*, 75(2): 257–77, Routledge.

Gupta, Pamila, Isabel Hofmeyr and Michael Pearson (eds.). 2010. *Eyes Across the Water – Navigating the Indian Ocean*, Cape Town: Unisa Press and Penguin India.

Harries, Patrick. 1994. *Work, Culture and Identity. Migrant Labourers in Mozambique and South-Africa, C. 1860–1910*, Portsmouth, Joanesburgo e Londres: Heineman, WItwatersrand University e James Currey Ltd.

Hirsch, Eric. 1995. "Landscape: Between Place and Space," in Eric Hirsch and Michael O'Hanlon (eds.), *The Anthropology of Landscape*, Oxford: Clarendon Press: 1–30.

Howard, Allen M. 2005. "Nodes, Networks, Landscapes, and Regions: Reading the Social History of Tropical Africa, 1700s – 1920," in Allen M. Howard and

Richard M. Shain (eds.), *The Spatial Factor in African History: The Relationship of the Social, Material, and Perceptual*, Leiden and Boston: Brill: 21–140.

Junod, Henri A. 1917. *A Vida de Uma Tribu Sul-Africana. Volume I – A Vida Social*, Lisboa: Sociedade de Geografia de Lisboa: vol. I.

Lutz, Hazel A. 2000. "India-West Africa Trade Textiles (IWATT): 'An Escape in the Life' of Gujarati Mirror-Work Embroidery," Textile Society of America Symposium Proceedings: 123–31.

Machado, Pedro. 2009. "Cloths of a New Fashion: Indian Ocean Networks of Exchange and Cloth Zones of Contact in Africa and India in the Eighteenth and Nineteenth Centuries," in Giorgio Riello and Tirthankar Roy (eds.), *How India Clothed the World: The World of South Asian Textiles, 1500–1850*, Leiden: Brill: 53–84.

Machado, Pedro. 2014. *Ocean of Trade: South Asian Merchants, Africa and the Indian Ocean, C. 1750–1850*, Cambridge: Cambridge University Press.

Marcus, George E. 1995. "Ethnography in/of the World System: The Emergence of Multi-Sited Ethnography," *Annual Review of Anthropology*, 24(1): 95–117.

Markovits, Claude. 2006. "Merchant Circulation in South Asia (Eighteenth to Twentieth Centuries): The Rise of Pan-Indian Merchant Networks," in Claude Markovits, Jacques Pouchepadass and Sanjay Subrahmanyam (eds.), *Society and Circulation: Mobile People and Itinerant Cultures in South Asia 1750–1950*, New Delhi: Anthem Press: 131–62.

McPherson, Kenneth. 1993. *The Indian Ocean: A History of People and the Sea*, Oxford: Oxford University Press.

Meier, Prita. 2013. "At Home in the World: Portrait Photography and Swahili Mercantile Aesthetics," in Gitti Salami and Monica Blackmun Visonà (eds.), *A Companion to Modern African Art*, New Jersey: John Wiley & Sons: 96–112.

Meneses, Maria Paula. 2009. "Food, Recipes and Commodities of Empires: Mozambique in the Indian Ocean Network," *Oficina Do CES*, (335).

Moorthy, Shanti and Ashraf Jamal (eds.). 2010. *Indian Ocean Studies Cultural, Social, and Political Perspectives*, New York: Routledge.

Mukherjee, Rila. 2014. "Escape from Terracentrism: Writing a Water History," *Indian Historical Review*, 41(1): 87–101.

Newitt, Malyn. 1995. *A History of Mozambique*, Bloomington and Indianapolis: Indiana University Press.

Newitt, Malyn. 2002. "Mozambique," in Patrick Chabal et al., *A History of Postocolonial Africa*, Londres: Indiana University Press: 185–235.

Nogueira, António Ribeiro. 1900. "Informações Mensais: Com.do Militar Dos M'chopes'.

Noyes, J.K. 1992. *Colonial Space: Spatiality in the Discourse of German South West Africa 1884–1915*, Chur: Harnwood Academic Publishers.

Oonk, Gijsbert. 2015. "Gujarati Asians in East Africa, 1880–2000: Colonization, De-Colonization and Complex Citizenship Issues," *Diaspora Studies*, 8(1).

Parkin, David. 2005. "Textile as Commodity, Dress as text. Swahili Kanga and Women's Statements," in Ruth Barnes (ed.), *Textiles in Indian Ocean*, London and New York: Routledge Curzon: 44–61.

Pearson, Michael. 2003. *Indian Ocean*, London: Routledge.

Pires, J.A. Mègre. 1950. "Administração Da Circunscrição Dos Muchopes. Relação Dos Comerciantes Estabelecidos Na Área Desta Circunscrição, Com Indicação

Do Número de Casas Que Cada Um Possue Nas Diversas Povoações Comerciais E Com a Distância Quilométrica a Esta Localidade. Anexo," Fundo da Administração do Concelho dos Muchopes. Caixa 314. AHM.

"Requerimentos de Ocupação Provisória de Terrenos. Dirigidos Ao Comandante Militar Dos Muchopes", 1900. Caixa 8.2, M.1. A.H.M.

Ribeiro, Fernando Bessa. 2004. "Sistema Mundial, Manjacaze E Fábricas de Caju: Uma Etnografia Das Dinâmicas Do Capitalismo Em Moçambique," Universidade de Trás-os-Montes e Alto Douro.

Riello, Giorgio and Tirthankar Roy (eds.). 2009. *How India Clothed the World: The World of South Asian Textiles, 1500–1850*, London: Brill.

Rodrigues, Eugénia. 2005. "Alimentação, Saúde e Império. O Físico-Mor Luís Vicente de Simoni E a Nutrição Dos Moçambicanos," *Arquipélago. História*, (IX): 617–56.

Rosales, Marta Vilar. 2010. "O Verdadeiro Caril Moçambicano. Transnacionalismo, Quotidianos E Materialidades Goesas Na África Colonial," in Susana Trovão and Marta Vilar Rosales (eds.), *Das Índias. Gentes, Movimentos E Pertenças Transnacionais*, Lisboa: Edições Colibri: 59–80.

S.a. 1914. "Carta de Moçambique (Esboço). 1: 3 000 000," Commissão de Cartographia. SGL – 2-G-4.

Santos, António Policarpo Sousa. 1957. "Inspecção Dos Serviços Administrativos E Dos Negócios Indígenas Da Província de Moçambique. Relatório Da Inspecção Ordinária À Extinta Circunscrição Dos Muchopes-Sede E Posto Administrativo de Chidenguele. Do Período de Janeiro de 1941 a Dezembro de 1957," *Fundo da Inspecção dos Serviços Administrativos e dos Negócios Indígenas – 1901–1968*. Caixa 28. AHM.

Sen, Collen Taylor. 2009. *Curry. A Global History*, London: Reaktion Books.

Stoller, Paul. 1989. *The Taste of Ethnographic Things: The Senses in Anthropology, Contemporary Ethnography Series*, Philadelphia: University of Pennsylvania Press.

11

LITTORAL SHELL TRACKS

Tracing Burma's transregional pearl histories

Pedro Machado

The Bay of Bengal has emerged in recent years as an important sub-region of the plural Indian Ocean, its crisscrossing circuits of migration tracing the human movements that linked southern India to Ceylon, Burma and Malaya and shaped their ecologies in particular ways in the nineteenth and early decades of the twentieth century. These circuits involved a wide array of actors whose experiences of navigating the bay's waterways mapped maritime trajectories that stitched Nagapattinam and Nagore on India's Coromandel Coast together with Penang, Melaka and Singapore (and beyond) within a context of highly commercialised exchanges of goods and the movement of significant numbers of people – most especially South Asian labourers – to work in the plantations, mines and agricultural economies of the burgeoning regional global economy – around its shores, hinterlands and interiors(Amrith 2013).

If the Bay of Bengal's oceanic histories were shaped by the migrations and labour movements of South Asians across its waters and involved also the well-studied exchanges in tea, opium and textiles, they were influenced also in significant ways by the existence of robust marine goods economies that were underpinned by a host of commercial actors, from Chinese, Indian and Malay traders to British, Australian and American merchants active across different parts of the eastern Indian Ocean from the late eighteenth into the twentieth centuries. The pearling economies of coastal Burma, including importantly those of the Mergui Archipelago that were located in its southern reaches, were primary sites of marine extraction and trade that represented vital nodes in the many flows of commodities linking the Bay of Bengal and parts of South India to Southeast Asia and the South China Sea and ultimately also to pearling's globalizing markets of the nineteenth and early twentieth centuries. Marine product extraction, involving a sustained search for pearls but more significantly in terms of quantities fished and their consumption, shell, were a critical dimension in shaping the complex waterways around which the varied littorals of the Indian Ocean took shape.[1] The pearl shell exchange and commerce of the Mergui islands, involving the shipment of significant quantities of shell in the second half of the nineteenth century to and through Penang, Singapore, the northern Australian coast and particularly southeast China, illuminate the vitality of the role of vernacular networks in sustaining intra-Asian trade. While the latter operated from the late eighteenth and especially in the nineteenth century through ports such as Singapore that had been established by an expanding British imperium in Southeast Asia and along the coast of China, these networks were structured around self-sustaining circuits traversing the waterways of the Straits of Malacca and the southern reaches of the Malay Peninsula. If the place of Chinese merchant networks cannot be overemphasised, of course, there has been a tendency as noted recently to focus on their interactions in insular Southeast Asia with regard to the marine goods trade or, when considering their place in the eastern Bay of Bengal, to privilege Upper Burma and cities such as Rangoon and Moulmein and their involvement in areas like the rice and tin trades. Chinese activities along coastal Burma, by contrast, have been given little attention, especially in the nineteenth century(Charney 2009a).

Equally, European and Australian involvement in Mergui pearling has been privileged, while the participation of Chinese and South Asian capital and labour have been marginalised or largely occluded in the scholarship. That much of the shell extracted from the Mergui Archipelago was shipped to Chinese markets is undeniable, but it is important to recognise the multiple circuits through which shipments reached the latter and also the wider importance of South Asian consumer markets for Burmese shell in the nineteenth and early twentieth centuries.

This chapter sheds light on the Mergui Archipelago and Burma's pearling histories, locating them at the interstices of translocal and transregional dynamics that connected them to commercial interests operating within the Bay of Bengal and across insular Southeast Asia and coastal China. These included, especially from the early decades of the nineteenth century, the Straits Settlements and northern Australian pearling areas like the Torres Strait as they became embedded within the expanding circuits of pearling's globalizing currents.

Early pearl trading and marine product extraction

The Mergui Archipelago comprises a vast area of over 800 islands of varying size scattered over an extensive maritime area of roughly 11,000 square miles (see Figure 11.1). An early twentieth-century visitor captured the diversity of their topography in vivid detail: 'a cluster of islands and islets, with bays and coves, headlands and highlands, capes and promontories, high bluffs and low shores, rocks and sands, fountains, streams, and cascades, mountain, plain and precipice unsurpassed for their wild and picturesque

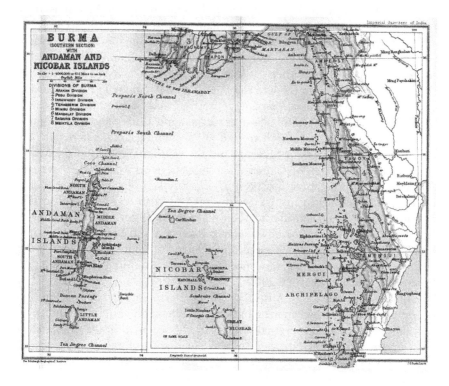

Figure 11.1 Map of Burma

Source: Map image courtesy of the Digital South Asia Library, http://dsal.uchicago.edu/, University of Chicago

beauty' (*Wingham Chronicle and Manning River Observer* 1904). Many of the islands, some as small as just a few square kilometres, had rich fishing waters but few coral reefs, the result likely of the 'enormous quantity' of mud carried to the coast and sea by the Tenasserim and Lenya Rivers; these deposits, not unlike those that flow down the Brahmaputra River to the coast of Bangladesh and are discharged regularly into the Bay of Bengal, created sizeable deltas that stretched out into nearby islands, filling the channels between them and the mainland. Islands closest to the coast thus gradually became 'absorbed into the mouths of the rivers and [were] only separated from one another by narrow creeks and mud-flats' (Rudmose Brown 1907–1909: 464). The coral reefs that were to be found existed in the southern reaches of the archipelago and were especially rich in pearl oyster banks, despite their being 'thickly populated with rich alcyonaria and black corals (*Antipathes arborea* and *A. spiralis*)' that made the pearl oysters 'none too easy to find' (Rudmose Brown 1907–1909: 467). Still, shell was found throughout these reefs at depths that did not exceed 10 to 14 metres, enabling their extraction with relative ease. Many of the archipelago's outer islands, while not necessarily possessing coral reefs, contained abundant pearl banks at depths that allowed for their collection without the aid of any kind of diving apparatus.

Shell extraction had been the work historically of the Moken, fisherfolk and sea people whose lives were intimately bound to the waterways of the archipelago's maze of small and medium-sized islands. They made their living from year-round fishing along the shores and around the reefs of the islands' disparate maritime geography. These fisherfolk lived in small communities of several dozen boats that were integral to social life and labour structured around tightly knit family units and kin. During the Indian Ocean's southwest monsoon from May to September, when the heavy rains and rough waters made sailing in the archipelago challenging if not highly dangerous, Moken erected temporary dwellings on platforms along the beach (see Figure 11.2) and waited out the return of the north-east monsoon (September to May) during which time the weather made it possible for them to resume their maritime activity.

Figure 11.2 House on stilts

Source: R.N. Rudmose-Brown, 'The Mergui Archipelago: Its People and Products', *Scottish Geographical Magazine*, 23: 463–83, 1907; and 'The Mergui Archipelago', *The Travel Magazine*, 1905, http://mergui-archipelago.net/the-travel-magazine-1905/.

Moken had historically utilised most of their energies in food collection for their own subsistence needs, gathering fish, crustaceans and oysters from the sea. According to Jacques Ivanoff and Thierry Lejard, anthropologists and ethnographers who conducted extensive fieldwork in the Mergui Archipelago over several decades, 'several thousand' Moken had been living among its islands 'for at least two centuries,' or roughly from no later than the eighteenth century. They may have been at the forefront of a coastal migration from the shores of the Malay Peninsula, 'colonizing the Tenasserim region from the south' (Ivanoff and Lejard 2002: 3). Moken sailed in *kabang*, small vessels designed to navigate and manoeuvre through the tight channels and tidal flows of the islands but robust enough to withstand some of the vagaries of the monsoon rains and tidal changes throughout the archipelago. The construction of the kabang allowed it, in the words of Jacques Ivanoff, 'to go everywhere; it can squeeze into river estuaries or hide in mangrove swamps or graze "coral flowers" right at the surface during food gathering; it can avoid shoals and sandbars and shoot across waves or face storms' (Ivanoff 2003: 91). They seem generally not to have been sailed out on open water, though, because of their specifically adapted design for 'coasting' among the islands. While individually owned, vessels were also leased occasionally among the Moken, often for payments made in the form of a percentage of the day's haul or catch.

If not a mainstay of their maritime existence, the collection of pearl shell was certainly a feature of a broader economy of extraction for the Moken that combined subsistence (oysters in particular, a key dietary element) and trade in marine products. Gathering was done in shallow waters, but experienced and skilled divers could go down to depths of up to 14 metres or so in search of shell. It is unclear how much of what was collected remained in the archipelago, but, even from the earliest days of pearl shell collection, it is likely that significant quantities were not leaving the islands. Overall, then, for the Moken, the gathering of shell and crustaceans was integrated into a routinised search for what they could gather in food collection from the sea for their livelihood.

This began to change dramatically, however, from the early decades of the nineteenth century as the Mergui Archipelago became integrated as a node in the larger Chinese marine goods economy that dominated insular Southeast Asia, with demand for shell from the islands also attracting Australian pearlers later in the century, supplying primarily European and American demand for shell. What appears to have drawn Chinese commercial interests most keenly to coastal southern Burma in the first decade or so of the nineteenth century, though, was not initially shell extraction per se but an intensified search for esculent birds' nests or *yen-wo* (Chiang 2011: 409; Blussé 1991). A translucent edible delicacy made from the glutinous secretion of swallows and swifts, birds' nests were highly sought after in China and also among overseas Chinese communities and settlements throughout

Southeast Asia for their perceived restorative and therapeutic qualities (Chiang 2011: 410–11).

Growing demand drove the trade beyond the Gulf of Thailand and Straits of Melaka and into the eastern Bay of Bengal too, where these nests were found in coastal rocky crags and were abundant among the hilly islands of the Mergui Archipelago and Tavoy Islands along the southern Burmese coast. Seeking to exploit this abundance, the governor of Cochinchina sought permission from the Burmese court in 1820 specifically to purchase nests on the Tenasserim coast in order to sell them in China and thereby increase his personal wealth. That the embassy encountered several traders involved in the esculent bird's nest trade when it stopped en route in Penang, by this time an important redistribution centre for marine products in the region, points to how entrenched it had become in commercial exchange by the early nineteenth century(Charney 2009a).[2]

Chinese merchants were thus able to monopolise the trade in such important commodities as esculent birds' nests in the Mergui Archipelago and elsewhere in the region in part by establishing cooperation with royal courts and securing supplies through payments to them for the farms of gathering and trading in these avian products, whose extraction was labour intensive due to the significant challenges of where the nests were located (for instance, NAM 1/7/37, 1894, for the considerable time and trouble it took to identify caves with viable nests, including asking local villages for information and having to confront the presence of large bat populations). It is likely that it was the expanding trade in birds' nests conducted on several of the Mergui islands and elsewhere that brought the potential of their pearling waters to the attention of Chinese merchants in the eighteenth and early nineteenth centuries. Moreover, farms included all products from the Mergui Archipelago, and pearl shell would, of course, have been among these. Its extraction was done by Moken divers working from their own vessels and harvesting shell for specific Chinese traders who appear mostly to have paid for these hauls in kind (*Selected Correspondence* 1928). These relationships endured well into the twentieth century, where they encompassed a robust exchange of shell (and other marine products) in Ranong, a Siamese border town that later in the century would operate as a collection point for marine exports from Thailand (Tagliocozzo 2011: 441). I discuss this later in the chapter.

Although Moken may also have been involved in the esculent bird's nest trade, possibly contributing the labour required to climb up the rocky crevices where the nests were to be found, evidence suggests that they focused their emerging trans-local exchange economy primarily on pearl and pearl-shell extraction. We find, therefore, a *peranakan* or locally-born Chinese merchant in Mergui, 'U Shwe I,' establishing commercial relationships with Moken for the collection of shell 'and other valuable products to be found in the sea or upon the islands.' He appears to have generally worked within these relationships to exploit the pearl banks of several islands relying on the experience and diving skills of the Moken, who could undertake several dives a day (White 1922). In addition to pearl shell, the Moken also collected trochus shell and *trepang* – edible holothurians, also known as *bêche-de-mer* in French, sea cucumbers in English and *haisen* in Chinese – for foreign traders in a marine goods economy that was expanding dramatically from the 1820s. The dynamics of this economy encompassed esculent birds' nests and a host of other products from the sea, drawing on both natural resources and the human resources of the Moken.[3]

This expansion, I should note, both reflected broader (and earlier) regional trends and was part of a larger intensification in the search for marine products from the world's oceans that unfolded over the course of the nineteenth century. Trepang and other sea products, such as tortoiseshell, had been valued imports into China from a variety of areas of insular Southeast Asia since at least the time of the Song Dynasty, stimulating the dispersal of Chinese commercial networks in the region for centuries. In the eighteenth century, for instance, in places such as Makassar – an important trading centre on the southwest peninsula of Sulawesi (Celebes) connected to local, regional and imperial Dutch networks and Maluku (the Moluccas or 'Spice Islands') – growth in the trepang trade drove Chinese commerce there amidst rising levels of consumption in China for this particular marine species (Sutherland 2011: 179). It was considered a culinary delicacy and a potent medicine with extraordinary healing properties, and Chinese doctors used its dried body wall to treat such conditions as kidney disorders, impotence and high blood pressure. Such was the scale of Chinese demand for trepang that its zones of extraction extended across the Pacific, incorporating islands such as Fiji into its reach.[4] China's markets and consuming patterns were thus a core feature of the vast networks of marine exchange that braided widely dispersed supply areas in the Indian and Pacific Oceans.

Imperial manoeuvrings

But China was not the only source of interest in Mergui shell and pearls. Growing British imperial state and private capital interest in its marine products in the nineteenth century responded to the Chinese logic of deman. These were shaped in significant ways by the compulsions of increasing – and increasingly complex – imperial territorial and maritime commitments in the Bay of Bengal and throughout many parts of insular and mainland Southeast Asia.

In Burma, tensions had been rising from the late eighteenth century between the Konbaung under Alaungpaya, who in defeating Pegu had reunited Upper and Lower Burma, and the East India Company. Involving also the region of Arakan that the Burmese had conquered in 1784 and that bordered company-administrated Chittagong, several cross-border incidents reflected the heightened state of agitation that had come to define the relationship between these two adversaries by the early nineteenth century. Indeed, the rising antagonism between them resulted in the company declaring war in March of 1824, a costly and destructive affair for both sides that lasted almost two years. The conclusion of this First Anglo-Burmese War with the Treaty of Yandabo in 1826 gave the company not only the relatively recently acquired Burmese provinces of Assam and Manipur and Arakan in the southwest but also Tenasserim in the far south of the empire. Together with control over the districts of Mergui and Tavoy, which had been occupied by the British a year before the signing of the treaty, the colonial presence thus experienced a significant expansion in Lower Burma and brought the Mergui Archipelago under nascent British imperial jurisdiction (Wright 2014: 22).

British imperial reach into coastal southern Burma reflected and in some ways helped reinforce the reality and idea of imperial acquisition then taking place in the region. It was concurrent with the commercial commitments of British merchant capital that had been developing markedly since the final decades of the eighteenth century. This was perhaps nowhere more clearly visible, as argued by Eric Tagliocozzo, than in the volume of East India Company trade, which rose rapidly in the 1770s and 1780s, especially once the Commutation Act in 1784 was passed, lowering import duties on tea – by this time widely consumed in ever greater quantities in Britain – from 119 per cent to a very favourable 12.5 per cent. As a result, British trade with China exploded (Tagliocozzo 2004a: 26).

However, the challenge of how to pay for Chinese exports was a pressing concern (the opium boom was still some years in the future), and one – albeit provisional – answer was marine products. A key part of this strategy was the acquisition of the offshore island of Penang from the Sultan of Kedah in 1786 with the explicit aim of operating as a marine products-mart along the sea route to Canton. Within a few years, Penang was attracting an increasingly greater share of regional and trans-regional shipping, with even Malay and Bugis *prahus* from South Sulawesi that had once gone to Junkceylon for ocean produce (trepang; tortoise shell, among many others) sailing rather to Penang for their cargoes(Tagliocozzo 2004a: 28).

Likewise, the value of the Mergui Archipelago for the emergent British colonial state lay precisely in its potential to contribute to the costs of administration and commercial expansion in southern Burma as a site of expanding interests in the Bay of Bengal and Southeast Asia (Charney 2009a; Win and Leng 2009: 68). British officials thus encouraged the marine products trade and sought the continued involvement of Chinese merchants already active along coastal Burma, as well as those trading from Penang, which would remain a key node for the Mergui marine products trade. The Chinese continued to control the farming of birds' nests at Tavoy in the early years of the British takeover of Tenasserim, with an unnamed merchant owning it for the five years between 1835 and 1840.

The Mergui farm for birds' nests was separated from the Tavoy farm, however, and as a demonstration of the cosmopolitan nature of the interest that the marine goods trade was attracting in these years, was contracted out to an Armenian merchant called 'Sarkies' (an abbreviated form of Sarkesian), who may have held it for a year or so before the full assertion of British control over the islands. Notably, the farm also awarded him the right to trade in all marine products from the Mergui Archipelago, and this would have included pearls and pearl shell. It is worth noting that Armenian merchants, with long histories of involvement in Indian Ocean commerce, had also been active in its pearl trading. For instance, only a few decades before Sarkies was awarded the farm, in 1800, another Armenian merchant named Gregory Baboom, with connections in Bengal, Madras and Canton, invested in the pearl fishery at Tuticorin, long a site of pearling in the Gulf of Mannar, which divided the southeastern coast of India from northwestern Sri Lanka(Ostroff 2016; Smith and Van Dyke 2003). And, reflecting the length of their pearling involvement, in the 1690s, during a six-year stay in Lhasa as a result of the extension of trade networks in Bengal and areas to its north, the Julfan merchant Hovhannes traded in pearls – along with textiles and amber – from India (Aslanian 2011: 53). Sarkies was but the most recent embodiment of the extensive involvement of Armenian commercial networks in the Indian Ocean's many and diverse trades.

Before it could develop, though, and for reasons that remain unclear, Sarkies's right to the Mergui farm was ended by the first British commissioner of Tenasserim, A. D. Maingy. Given that Maingy expected the farm to be purchased by 'the Chinese' after he departed for Tavoy, this suggests strongly that he may have sought to maintain Chinese involvement in this commerce because of its well-established structures and its prominence at Penang as well as throughout the Straits (Charney 2009a). This decision was prompted by the understanding that Chinese merchant networks were beneficial to the growing British imperial presence through the duties that were generated from their regional commerce. Moreover, it behooved British officials to promote Chinese commerce in order to avoid an adverse response from the Chi'ing state – and therefore threaten their interests in Canton – if they were regarded as actively opposing the prospects of Chinese mercantile investments by favouring other competing groups.

Yet, it appeared that Chinese merchants were not necessarily guaranteed the farm. Indeed, there was some concern from certain officials that there were 'few practical means of protecting the farm if it were to be rented out' in the Mergui Archipelago during the early years of British rule because the latter was considered something of a 'no man's land'; in other words, in these early years, it was seen as a space over which British jurisdictional control had not been formalised or secured (Charney 2009a: 212; *List of Correspondence* 1929). As if to emphasise and expose the limitations of this rule, Malay 'poachers' and 'pirates' from Penang sailed to the islands to collect birds' nests and other marine products, resulting in repeated entreaties from Maingy in the 1830s for British naval intervention that, despite the heightened concern, was never forthcoming. Instead, vessels from Penang continued to arrive in Mergui. Perhaps recognizing that these attempts to establish firmer control over the islands in the early years of British rule were likely to fail, the farm was granted eventually to Malay traders by the end of the decade (*List of Correspondence* 1929; Charney 2009a). The growing scope of Chinese involvement in the economy of Burma – for instance, in tin mining in the northwest and in the rice trade that brought Chinese junk fleets to Burma in the 1840s – meant ultimately however that Chinese commerce in esculent birds' nests and pearl shell in the Mergui islands was never displaced.

What did change in these decades, nonetheless, was that many of those Chinese active along the Burmese coasts were more often than not either based in Penang or settled in southeast Burma and that the junks plying these waters were made up of Malay (and not Chinese) crews (Tagliocozzo 2004a). Some of the traders were *peranakan* Chinese, as was the case of 'U Shwe I,' whose father had come to Mergui as a pilot on one of the ships that brought British troops across to Burma in the Second Burmese War of 1852–53. At the end of the war, his father settled in Mergui and 'lived by trading.' U Shwe I also became involved in commercial exchange in the islands, forging close relationships with several Moken for the purchase of pearls and pearl shell (White 1922: 67–8).

Quite what the quantities of pearl shell being traded in the Mergui Archipelago in the first half of the nineteenth century were is unclear. According to Kunz and Stevenson's classic work published in 1908, *The Book of the Pearl*, shell was collected by Moken divers at depths of between 11 and 15 metres, an estimate that is consistent with the accounts of travellers and observers of the pearl fisheries in the nineteenth century (Kunz and Stevenson 1908). The increasing activity of Chinese and other vessels in and around the islands of the archipelago – notwithstanding their focus on esculent birds' nests – suggests that the collection of shell was occurring regularly as Mergui became more deeply integrated into the regional marine products commercial economy. And from the second half of the century, increasingly, its waters became subject to intensified extraction that essentially industrialised the process in the 1890s but did not entirely undermine traditional harvesting methods of the Moken.

These changes are attributed often in the (limited) literature on pearling in the Mergui Archipelago to the 'discovery' of deep-water beds by British imperial interests, as well as the involvement of Australian pearlers in the final decade or so of the nineteenth century, as they expanded their search for pearl shell that was targeted primarily at European markets. While it would be hard to deny the impact that these developments had on the islands and in other pearling areas of the Burmese coast, we should be careful not to overstate them. The importance of the establishment of the Straits Settlements in 1826 is clear, as an imperial arrangement that subsumed Penang, Singapore and Malacca into a single administrative unit, resulting for instance in the marine goods trade passing increasingly through Penang and, from the 1820s, Singapore as it emerged as a prominent trans-shipment port for pearl shell along with a variety of other marine products. However, local associational networks of commercial exchange that included Chinese merchants and South Asian entrepreneurial capitalists remained vital to the financing and movement of these goods across the waterways of the eastern reaches of the Indian Ocean.[5] Indeed, while East India Company vessels and particularly English country traders from the late eighteenth and the first decades of the nineteenth century carried significant quantities of marine products from Asia to China, many of these country traders actually included Armenians and Indians, among whom Parsis appear to have been dominant. They owned several large vessels and, in sending them to Canton, were responsible for revitalizing the trade of merchants in Indian-owned and operated vessels that had been dormant for many decades (Tagliocozzo 2004a).

It is worth remembering that the junk trade was also of considerable significance. By 1835, half the value of Singapore's trade with China was carried by these vessels which, in redirecting their commerce increasingly away from ports in the Nanyang to which they had traded extensively beforehand (such as Batavia and the inter-island shipping of the Philippines), added decisively to the vitality of the British port. Indeed, overall, as noted by Eric Tagliocozzo, the 'real energy' for the transportation of marine products from Southeast Asia to China – a trade involving several source areas dispersed over a large maritime space – was provided by a range of Asian shippers, bankers and financiers. It was they, with detailed knowledge, access to financial capital, and commercial structures and mechanisms, who were largely responsible for organizing the purchase, transportation and selling of marine products in the Chinese market (Tagliocozzo 2004a: 43). In the Mergui Archipelago, therefore, it is not surprising that Chinese and Malay merchants continued to play a prominent role in the procurement of shell in the 1840s and 1850s and over the next few decades, working with Moken diving families as they had in the earlier years of the century.

At the end of each diving season, pearl shell was exported to Penang and in some cases to Singapore before being shipped on to coastal China. Perhaps because of its proximity to the Mergui Archipelago, Penang remained an important trans-shipment and financial center for the movement south of pearl shell from the coast of Burma, notwithstanding the clear dominance of Singapore as a port of call for junks and *prahus* (and of course European shipping) by the 1830s. Although at times overshadowed in the literature by Singapore, Penang maintained significant regional connections through its commercial networks to ports and towns of the northern Burmese littoral and along the Coromandel Coast in southeastern India (Leng 2009; Hussin 2006). I discuss this in greater detail I discuss this in greater detail later in the essay.

There was one other important trans-shipment node through which pearl shell – and a host of other marine products, such as green snails – reached markets in China: Ranong. Although its beginnings are unclear, Moken vessels sailed there sometime in the latter half of the nineteenth century to deliver cargoes of shell to specific Chinese merchants with whom they maintained regular and long-lasting relationships. These were then either transported directly to China or, as seems to have occurred in the majority of cases, shipped first through Penang before being transported further east. Ranong would remain a significant node through which the marine products of the Mergui Archipelago would reach Chinese markets into and throughout the twentieth century (NAM 1/7/1219, 1926).

It was this level of activity in the Mergui pearling waters – along with their aforementioned revenue-generating potential – that drew and sustained British interest, and a likely source of the first information received by imperial officials about the archipelago was Chinese merchants. Indeed, almost as soon as the British formalised their presence in Mergui in the 1820s, they began to take practical measures to exploit the pearl banks. For instance, in July 1827, A. D. Maingy – the first British commissioner of Tenasserim mentioned earlier – wrote to the assistant commissioner to inform him that pearl divers 'from Madras' had been imported into Mergui, presumably recruited from among the diving labour working in the Tuticorin or other pearl fisheries of South India (*List of Correspondence* 1929). Clearly, without adequate appreciation of Moken divers or their skills, the British drew on a labour pool with which they were familiar from decades of managing the various pearl fisheries under the governments of Company Madras and Crown Ceylon and whose labour they had sought to discipline since assuming control over these fisheries from the late eighteenth century. The aim behind the shipment of the unspecified number of divers from Madras to the Mergui Archipelago was to search specifically for pearls rather than pearl shell, a strategy that once again was informed by prior imperial experience. Pearl harvesting in South India and Sri Lanka had historically produced significant yields of this valuable marine product, and their fisheries remained vibrant in the early decades of the nineteenth century. British administrators sought to emulate what they believed to have been great Dutch success in the collection of pearls in the Gulf of Mannar in the eighteenth century once the VOC (Dutch East India Company) had withdrawn from the region after their defeat by British forces.

However, it was established by the British administration early on in Mergui that, as only 'seed-pearls were secured' there, the banks would yield but 'an insignificant revenue,' and thus the interest in developing the fisheries through further imperial endeavour or finance was initially abandoned (Kunz and Stevenson 1908: 134). This is surprising, if we assume that British officials were thinking about the possibilities of pearl exports to European markets. Seed pearls – small pearls less than two millimetres in diameter and often unevenly shaped – had been utilised in European jewellery from at least the seventeenth century and by the late eighteenth were becoming quite popular as seen, for instance, in contemporary portraiture and in the adornment practices of royal households.[6] This intensified, especially in the nineteenth century, as Victorians came to favour the delicate look of pieces made with seed pearls and often associated them with purity. Perhaps Maingy and his colleagues were unaware of this growing taste for seed pearls in Europe or considered the particularities of the Mergui varieties to be of low quality and therefore ill-suited to English markets. Whichever might have been the case, they did not pursue or encourage the exploitation of the Mergui pearl banks at first and appear to have been relatively satisfied with their continued extraction by Chinese capital, Malay and South Asian merchants amidst the robust vibrancy of Asian markets for pearls, shell and seed pearls.

'Managing' extraction

These Asian capitalists operated through a system structured around the farming of rights to collect shell, a model and practice that the British had inherited from the Burmese court in its dealings with traders operating along coastal southeast Burma. Given the seemingly modest nature of the trade in pearl shell and other marine products, it appears that the imperial authorities were content with maintaining the status quo. Farming generated enough revenue to subsidise the cost for the British of superintending the Mergui Archipelago as part of a territory – Burma – that was becoming increasingly part of broader imperial ambitions in the Indian Ocean and particularly insular and mainland Southeast Asia.

This changed from the 1870s, though, with the revival of interest among British officials in the potential of the Mergui Archipelago's pearl banks, as an integral area in the administration of Lower Burma, and other areas of the burgeoning colony, such as the Bassein coast and rivers, and the Arakan coast, as European and American consumption of pearls and pearl shell in the late nineteenth century continued to expand.[7] Herbert Warrington Smyth, a British naval officer and mining engineer who visited the Mergui Archipelago for an extended period during his five-year stay in Siam between 1891 and 1896, dated the 'investigation' of the pearl fisheries by British officials to 1874, after which interest in establishing another productive fishery possibly to match or surpass that of the Gulf of Mannar grew quickly (Smyth 1898). Some success in collecting pearls in the latter in the 1850s seems also to have revived the belief in the potential of the Mergui Archipelago to be at least equally productive. Nonetheless, it was difficult to escape the reality that, as had been the case in the 1820s, even when pearls were found (about 1 in every 15 shells, according to Smyth 1898), they were relatively small and that therefore it was unlikely that Mergui would be as greatly a profitable source of these as the other pearling zones in the Indian Ocean with which the British were becoming increasingly involved in the nineteenth century.

In pearling areas beyond Mergui, the reality for British officials and private interests seeking to profit from Burmese pearl banks was equally disappointing if nonetheless important to local imperial revenue and an element of imperial governance (OIOC P&S Department Records; *Report on the Administration of Lower Burma*, 1888). Seed pearls, mentioned previously, were mostly what was available from the large numbers of pearl-bearing oysters in Bassein district, north of the Mergui Archipelago, but along with shell, green snails, trepang and other ocean products, they formed the backbone of Burma's marine trade. Seed pearls, officials noted, "always [found] a ready sale," and as such, the revenue that their export generated was an integral component of British fiscal concerns that local authorities could do little but accept (NAM 1/15(e)/13922, 1895).[8] Additionally, pearl banks represented another site for the projection of imperial authority amidst growing British terraqueous ambitions in the Bay of Bengal and beyond and were thus of importance to the project of colony-making (Bashford 2017).

If Warrington Smyth's dating of heightened British interest is correct, it was not until the 1890s, after Burma had been incorporated administratively as a province of British India, that efforts to rationalise extraction actually took shape (Charney 2009b; Myint-U 2001). European and Australian pearlers had begun to appear on the Lower Burmese coast in search of pearls and pearl-shell by this time, concentrating their operations around the imperially named Malcolm and Page Islands while, in a reflection of the continued importance of Chinese pearlers to the Mergui marine economy, the latter concentrated their collection further north 'with Ross island as headquarters, and the neighbourhood of Ross, Elphinstone, and Grant islands as their fishing-grounds' (Sutherland 1898: 451).

The rights to fish in these waters were now sold by public auction at the court of the deputy commissioner at Mergui and, in the decade of the 1890s, if not earlier, included trepang and green snails (Sutherland 1898: 451). Auctions, similar to farming but with an openly competitive element where bidders would go up against one another to win the bid, represented also speculative opportunities for these individuals to pay a sum of money on what they predicted future hauls would yield in the following pearling season. This created at the same time a variable – but at least regular – source of income for the imperial authorities that also had the advantage for the colonial state of deflecting the risk associated with the extraction of marine products away from itself and onto the purchaser of the winning bid.[9] The auction-lease system was a variant of the farming of esculent birds' nests from previous decades and echoed the renting of the right to the pearl beds of South India and Ceylon that became the predominant form of regulation for waters the British authorities had been managing since the late eighteenth century. The inclusion of green snails and *bêche-de-mer* in the public auction, the latter having likely formed part of the farm for birds' nests as one of the marine goods merchants were given the right to collect in the 1820s as previously noted, indicated further the extent to which the British considered the waters of the Mergui Archipelago a source of marine goods and not exclusively a site of pearl or shell extraction. This was true, also, of Burma's other marine areas where the harvesting of pearls and shell was bound up with the larger marine products economy of which coastal and island Burma had always formed an integral part (Machado forthcoming).

Being guided by an administrative praxis of 'managing' Burma's pearl banks as a particular 'environment' and resource over which government sought to exert authority, and mediate use and access reflecting notions of liberal improvement resulted, though, in further intervention in how extraction of pearls and shell would be organised. Thus, in the case of the Mergui Archipelago, the Burma provincial government set about dividing the pearl banks that they believed to be scattered across their vastly dispersed islands into five 'blocks' or 'districts' that were sold, either singly or in groups, at public auction (Brown and Simpson 1907: 3; NAM 1/7/67, 1908). A winning bid guaranteed unrestricted access to that particular block's banks – some extending over extraordinarily vast areas – for an extended period of time. For instance, 'block 3' comprised 1,800 square miles scattered along the southern Burmese coast (OIOC P/4769, Pro. No. 1–5, 1894; NAM 1/7/67, 1908]. Each block was understood as 'an area of sea within which the exclusive right of pearl fishing is leased' (NAM 1/15(e)/14231: 1). These were defined along demarcated maritime lines of division that brought particular islands together into one or another discrete grouping that nonetheless was to be managed as part of a larger ecological whole. The 'block system' thus retained leases as the mechanism through which rents were collected from the pearl banks, with the deputy commissioner able to 'grant a lease of a pearl fishery for one year, or with the previous sanction of the Financial Commissioner, for any number of years not exceeding five.' At least one month before the auction, information of the terms of the lease would be advertised in English and Burmese in Mergui and throughout the 'principal ports' of Burma and the Straits Settlements. Once a successful bid had been secured – and an earnest-money payment of 10 per cent of the rent deposited into the treasury – the 'auction purchaser or successful tenderer' would be given a marked chart indicating 'the limits of every block [and therefore] the limits within which pearl-fishing is permitted by the lease' (NAM 1/15(e)/14231, 1896: 1–2).

Coinciding with the establishment of the block system, and a likely contributing factor, was the intensification of colonial Australian interest in Burma's shell. Pearlers working especially in the Torres Strait were drawn overwhelmingly – if not exclusively – to the islands of the Mergui Archipelago as 'comparatively new pearling ground' (*Northern Times and Gazette* 1895) because of their potential as a source particularly of mother-of-pearl from which pearling merchants had been making considerable profits since the 1870s through shell exports from Australia to London and other European markets as consumption began to rise sharply. Britain alone at this time imported around 1,500 tons of shell that was ultimately re-exported to the button industries of France and Austria (Martinez and Vickers 2015: 30). Prominent Australian pearlers thus began to arrive in Mergui especially in the 1890s, most notably Frank Jardine, a magistrate and cattle station owner who had become a leading figure in the Torres Strait pearling industry (Martinez and Vickers 2015: 30).[10] Reflecting the intensification of Australian interest in the archipelago's pearl banks, Jardine had come to Burma at the invitation of the British Indian government who had commissioned a report from him on the fisheries in order to gauge their commercial viability in pearl shell. Others, 'who had experience of the pearl banks of Queensland,' also arrived in Burma to gain access to Mergui's banks – in 1892, for instance, a 'Mr. Chill' had purchased the lease for 'Centre Block' for a three-year period and would attempt also to collect shell in islands off coastal Upper Burma.[11] The imperial logic informing the block system in the Mergui Archipelago was applied, equally, to other pearling areas of the Burmese coast that were dominated by South Asian, Chinese and other local merchants and traders (Machado forthcoming).

With the block system, British authorities had devised an extractive structure that could meet the revenue needs and governance aims of the incipient colonial state. Rights to each of the blocks in Mergui and Bassein could be leased either separately or together and, especially when there were several interested parties, could generate competitive bidding that would thus drive up the price of the rent on the banks. When, as occasionally though rarely happened, no bidders presented themselves at an auction, monopoly rights for each of the blocks could be awarded to any bidder whose price the district commissioner deemed appropriate for that particular block.

Moreover, rights to each or all blocks could be transferred to third parties in what became, essentially, a sub-leasing arrangement. Thus, in 1892, when Mr. Chill had purchased the rights to 'Centre Block,' as previously noted, he transferred them to the Mergui Pearling Company, whose directors and 'most of the shareholders' were based in Singapore (NAI Shimla Records No. 66C-2F-13, 1906). Other companies entered Mergui pearling in this manner in the late nineteenth century. One of their challenges, of course, was to estimate the volume of a particular block's oyster yield so as not to overpay and thereby risk losing money should the banks prove to have far less shell than had been anticipated – or, as happened to the Mergui Pearling Company in 1894, to lose money because the price of pearl shell on the London market where it was focused had fallen from £110 to £55 per ton.

As a newspaper reported dryly, '[T]he price for the company's concession is now discovered to have been too high,' the company suffering a loss of almost £10,000 (*The Queenslander* 1894). Despite the risks, another company (the Pearling and Trading Company) sent part of its fleet to the islands and its 'example has been followed by several individual owners of schooners' (*The Daily News* 1894). In this manner, the companies and schooners were allowed largely unrestricted access to their particular block or blocks. To help spread their financial risk, companies effectively 'instituted a system of sub-leasing, or rather granting a permit to would-be constituents to fish for pearl-shells on their leaseholds' (OIOC, P/4769, Pro. No. 1–5, 1894).

The block system served a further, critical purpose in the dynamics of colonial governance – the consolidation of claims to maritime space. Indeed, the territorialisation of ocean space had become an increasingly dominant feature of British and other European imperial claims from around the middle of the eighteenth century, particularly throughout the many islands and coastal areas of insular Southeast Asia. The idea and notion of extending imperial jurisdiction over maritime space was, of course, an idea with a very long history in the expansionist trajectory of European empire (Steinberg 2001; Benton 2005). In the nineteenth century, the territorialisation of oceanic space resulted in the incorporation of islands and coastal areas into an imperial legal framework that would also expose unresolved tensions and lay bare the limits of imperial jurisdiction. A case in 1893 illustrated the contours of these limits. It involved a legal challenge to the government of Burma from an Australian pearler active in the Mergui Archipelago after it had granted 'a concession of the exclusive right of fishing on these banks.' This unnamed Australian claimed through his legal representatives that he had had a right to operate in these waters because he considered 'them to be in the high seas outside the territorial waters [controlled by the government of Burma]' and that it was therefore acting unlawfully in granting monopoly rights. In response, the government contended that 'its jurisdiction extend[ed] to a distance of three miles beyond the outer edge of the archipelago,' arguing further that this jurisdiction 'include[ed] all waters lying between that line and the mainland.' The three-mile distance was a measure accepted by international law, which British authorities in Ceylon had invoked equally to extend the maritime boundaries of their island territory in 1811. This approach and thinking informed colonial governance in Burma 'to support their concession of an exclusive right of fishing' (NAI Home Department, Public B 1894; *Collection of Legislative Acts* 1811).

But in seeking to establish definitively where its 'territorial waters' lay and thus what it could claim as its maritime jurisdiction in relation to control over the Mergui Archipelago's pearling banks, the government of Burma sought the intervention of the crown's law officers in establishing the legitimacy of its position vis-à-vis claims to the contrary. The matter, as far as they were concerned, turned on '[W]hether the jurisdiction of the government of Burma and its power to grant exclusive fishing rights extends over all waters lying between the mainland of Burma and a distance of three miles beyond the outer edge of the Mergui Archipelago, or whether it is limited in the manner stated by the legal advisers of the Government of India, or otherwise.' It will come as no surprise, perhaps, that the law officers agreed that the government had correctly stated its 'territorial jurisdiction' and thus it followed 'that the government [had] no power to grant exclusive fishery rights except in waters *within* the extent of the jurisdiction so described' (NAI Home Department, Public B 1894. Emphasis mine). In making this determination, and in a statement replete with imperial hubris, they also essentially denied the possibility of the existence of any rights or claims to the banks by Moken fishermen by stating presumptively that 'we assume that in the case of the pearl fisheries in the Mergui Archipelago, there has not been as in the case of the Ceylon fisheries, an immemorial claim to the pearl oyster fishery' (NAI Home Department, Public B 1894). The reference to Ceylon was an invocation of the customary rights to pearl fishing that groups such as Tamil Paravas had negotiated and protected historically as perquisites from local and foreign rulers in the Gulf of Mannar. In the eyes of the colonial state, Moken claims were non-existent.

The case had additional significance, though. In raising questions of territoriality and maritime jurisdiction, it exposed further anxieties of an incipient colonial state struggling to solidify the 'porous' maritime boundaries of the region. Coastlines represented amorphous spaces, however, where, as Jan Heesterman reminds us, 'the littoral forms a frontier zone that is not there to separate or enclose but which rather finds its meaning in its permeability.' In other words, the pearl oyster beds of the Mergui Archipelago constituted a 'fluid frontier' that found their meaning in the permeability of their surrounding waters and coastlines (Heesterman 1980; Gillis and Torma 2015).

It was precisely this permeability, however, that was the source of considerable British imperial anxiety. These found voice specifically in the concern expressed by the secretary to the government of India in correspondence with the chief commissioner of Burma over the existence of 'no clear proof . . . of the Mergui islands having been at any time officially declared to be part of Tenasserim [Lower Burma] and under the administration of the Chief Commissioner of Burma.' Calcutta thus urged that a 'draft notification' be submitted 'bringing them formally into the province of Tenasserim and under the Chief Commissioners' administration' (NAI Political Department 1894). The urgency for such a notification related also to the larger imperial project of boundary-making that had been inaugurated in the late 1860s around the demarcation of space between Tenasserim, as the southernmost region of Burma, and Siam. As the demarcation 'partly related to some of the islands in the southern part of the Mergui Archipelago,' there was concern over their inclusion 'with the British government' (NAI Political Department 1894).

In the face of competing French imperial interests in Siam, border-making was an integral strategy in consolidating a notion of imperial boundedness and incorporation that was seen both to reflect and engender the power of the state and render this power visible through its enforcement.[12] This echoed – albeit with somewhat different valences – British vexations earlier in the century over establishing boundaries with the court of Siam after they had conquered southern Burma and turned it into the Tenasserim Province (Winichakul 1994; see also Tagliocozzo 2004b). The permeability of the southern border would, however, remain a fact of life for British authorities, with Moken regularly sailing to Ranong to deliver pre-arranged cargoes of pearl shell to Chinese merchants into the 1920s and 1930s. And 'Siamese' poachers would sail to certain blocks regularly to fish for pearls and shell, both undermining the rights of the lessees and jeopardizing the future revenue of colonial income because 'a lower price would be paid for this monopoly in future and Government therefore will also lose' (NAM 1/7/1190, 1924). With limited policing of the blocks, there was little chance of preventing this coastal activity that had been ongoing since at least the early nineteenth century, well before the establishment of British interest in the Mergui Archipelago.

If the block system signaled deepening European and Australian participation in the Mergui Archipelago and helped solidify British attempts at establishing maritime borders in Burma, it also encouraged the involvement of local and regional merchants and pearl entrepreneurs. Ethnic Burmese, for instance, continued to be active in the extraction of shell by purchasing licences from the government or sub-leasers.[13] Malay traders, in an extension of their long participation in pearling as noted earlier, were also active in Mergui, particularly through the maintenance of relationships that were established over years with Moken divers and collectors of shell (NAM 1/7/1094, 1902). But among the most prominent merchants in the islands were Penang-based Chinese merchants, many of whom were by the end of the nineteenth century locally born or Peranakan Chinese. They transported shell from Mergui regularly to Penang, where its value was often double what it was in Burma, before their cargoes were trans-shipped onto China. Some Burma-born Chinese also participated in this commerce, but they appear to have been outnumbered by Chinese merchants operating from Penang in the late nineteenth century (Smyth 1898: 296; Leng 2009: 29). At least as important were South Asian merchants who sub-leased rights to harvest pearls and shell in the blocks. Many of these merchants were India-born but included a small if growing number of locally born Indians from the early years of the twentieth century. Nakarattar Chettiar capitalists were also important traders, and for some, the Mergui fisheries represented an extension of earlier family involvement in the Ceylon Strait and Gulf of

Mannar (OIOC, P&S, Burma 1898; Rudner 1994: 58). More significant, however, was the involvement of Tamil Marakkayar Muslim merchants with ancestral ties to South India but who were by the late nineteenth century in Mergui hailing from Penang as Jawi Peranakan, hybrid Malay-South Indian communities whose members would play prominent roles in the political life of Penang and lead the Malay-Muslim reform movement there in the 1920s (Fujimoto 1989; Lewis 2016). In other areas of Burmese pearl and shell harvesting, such as Bassein and Arakan, locally born Chinese and Tamil-speaking South Indian traders played prominent roles.[14] There were also Bombay merchants and 'Surati traders,' who may have been residing in Rangoon and were not necessarily based in Surat, purchasing leases for the fisheries. As with the Bombay merchants, they were likely Gujarati Khojas with connections to the small coastal state of Kutch (NAM 1/15(e)/14231, 1896; NAM 1/15(e)/14448, 1897; Markovits 2013). All of these groups participated actively in the extraction of shell and pearls and were largely responsible for sustaining its translocal and transregional ties in the nineteenth and twentieth centuries (Machado forthcoming for further detail).

Arresting extraction

While the block system became the dominant, structural apparatus through which the colonial state sought to manage – and profit from – the extraction of pearls and shell from Burma's banks by all interested parties, it did not go unchallenged. Within a few years of its implementation, misgivings began to be expressed in Mergui about certain aspects of its extractive effects, specifically related to questions about the regeneration of oyster stocks and the impact this could have on yields. Thus, while 'all the fishing rights' to the archipelago were sold again for a three-year period in 1895, when this ended in 1898, they were sold for only two years, as government officials worried about over-fishing (NAI Shimla Records, No 66C-2F-13, 1906).

As concerns began to grow, there were some who nonetheless remained unconvinced of this threat. Frank Jardine, for instance, whom the British Indian government had commissioned to produce a report on the fisheries and who was therefore in a position to exert considerable influence on officials, was firm in the belief that 'although several of the first-worked beds have been temporarily abandoned they are not in anything approaching a worked out condition.' He was convinced, for instance, that the 'whole of the north-eastern corner of the concession lying between Sir John Macolm, Ravenshaw, Paway [sic] Islands, and the southern boundary of No. 2 Block, is one immense bed of pearl shell' (*Northern Territory Times and Gazette*, 1895). Jardine's optimistic view no doubt inspired an idea more broadly that the archipelago's waters held great and untapped potential for large-scale exploitation by pearlers. This appeared to be confirmed by the dramatic rise in the volume of shell collected as a result of the creation of the block system: whereas only 26 tons had been extracted in the 1891–92 season, this grew to 294 tons in 1893–94 and by the 1894–95 season had increased markedly to 315 tons (NAM 1/7/1063, 1900). But at least according to official figures, there was a steady decline in yields after this period, dropping down to 111 tons in 1899–1900 and 66 tons in 1900–01 (NAM 1/7/1063, 1900; Brown and Simpson 1907: 4; Butcher 2004: 127). This prompted R. N. Rudmose Brown and Jas J. Simpson, authors in 1907 of an official report on the archipelago, to claim that the block system 'was undoubtedly detrimental to the pearl banks, inasmuch as individuals of companies leasing these blocks recklessly exploit them' (Brown and Simpson 1907: 3).

Other, arguably more vocal concerns, were voiced among government officers beyond the Mergui Archipelago concerning the deleterious effects of granting monopoly rights over pearl banks. District officers were concerned over how the extraction of shell along the Bassein and Arakanese coasts was depriving local populations of a valuable food source through intense searching for seed pearls that resulted in oyster shells – including the flesh of the oyster – being discarded in great number, in some years totaling tens of millions of oysters (NAM 1/15(e)/14238, 1896). As a result, several merchants were denied access to the banks and periods of closure instituted in attempts to replenish stocks. There remained an underlying commitment, nonetheless, to finding all possible means of making the collection of shell as profitable as possible in Bassein and Arakan, including encouraging the use of diving apparatus to locate yet-to-be-discovered banks at greater depths (further details in Machado forthcoming).

So, despite the ambivalence of colonial administrators towards the block system as an institutional structure for managing Burma's pearl fisheries as a marine resource, it remained in place into the first decades of the twentieth century. There was, though, one significant change of fundamental importance, implemented to ameliorate concerns of over-fishing and guarantee continued revenue from the fisheries in the Mergui Archipelago: the auction system, whereby blocks were put up to public auction, was abolished in the late 1890s and replaced by one of fees or licences on each of the pumps being used by pearlers on diving vessels (NAM 1/7/1094, 1902). Pumps, as the next section will elaborate, were an integral apparatus of the new technology that had been introduced into the Mergui Archipelago towards the end of the nineteenth century, the so-called 'diving dress' or 'suit' that required the use of pumps to provide air to divers who were going down to far-greater depths than was possible through 'naked' diving, where none of this technology was utilised to extract shell. Indeed, the introduction of a licencing system on individual pumps was also a move to accommodate the elaborated use of the diving suit in Mergui pearling, while the rights to collect shells, green snails and trochus shell 'without apparatus' continued to be sold by auction (OIOC P/4769, Pro. No. 1–5, 1894; Kunz and Stevenson 1908: 136).

Not embraced by all in the colonial administration – some thought that there would be great difficulty in fixing the fee and that it 'would be liable to attract the scum and dregs of the two hemispheres' – licences were generally agreed upon to be the most expedient way forward for government, especially in light of the decline of European and Australian involvement in the archipelago by the end of the nineteenth century (NAM 1/7/1063, 1900).[15] Moreover, with the auction system, the rights to collect pearl shell, green snails, trochus and other marine products had been sold together as part of a block, but now they were being sold separately. The new system, it was thus noted,

> brought an increase of revenue which [is attributed] chiefly to the fact that pearling with machinery and diving for g.s. [green snails] are carried on by entirely different classes of people and need a different kind of knowledge, so that to sell them together was manifestly wasteful.
>
> (NAM 1/7/1094, 1902)

But the change was not only positively endorsed by the Revenue Department – local pearlers welcomed it too, claiming in a letter to the lieutenant governor of Burma in 1900 that it would 'induce more people taking up [sic] the concern' (NAM 1/7/1063, 1900). With the fee set at Rs400 per pump, the result of careful calculations that were based on how much the blocks had been leased for in previous years, the licence system was understood to broaden the involvement of local pearlers and establish continued revenue for local government offices (NAM 1/7/1063, 1900). At the same time, though, it raised serious questions about diving as a physical and labour practice – fundamental to the overall functioning of the entire industry – in which the colonial state sought to intervene increasingly from the late nineteenth century.

Penetrating depths

Diving for and collecting pearls and shell, as noted earlier, had for years before the consolidation of British rule in Burma in the nineteenth century been mostly carried out by Moken divers in a coastal economy that combined subsistence with the exchange of marine products. Divers could reach impressive depths of well over 10 metres in their search for shell, with some claiming that the Moken had actually 'cleared' the banks of the Mergui Archipelago 'nearly all down to a depth of six fathoms' (Smyth 1898: 295). Moken divers maintained relationships with Chinese merchants, as these called at the islands with greater frequency from the late eighteenth and especially first decades of the nineteenth centuries in search of shell and other marine products. As British interests in Burma grew from the 1820s, the prospect of exploiting pearling waters through the use of the same rationalised labour force that had been employed in the banks over which the East India Company and crown had exerted control in the Gulf of Mannar resulted in Tamil divers being shipped to the archipelago. The details of this endeavour are not available, but it would appear that it did not develop as a government scheme. Rather, in the first half of the nineteenth century, the extraction of shell was undertaken predominantly by Moken diving labour that continued to be engaged by Chinese and also Malay traders on a seasonal and sustained basis, as they were also by Penang-based merchants. This did not change substantially in the following decades, as Moken divers continued to labour among the islands' oyster beds for specific traders.

The Burmese colonial state's introduction of the block system in the early 1890s, with its overt attempt at rationalizing pearl fishing in the archipelago and elsewhere in the colony, did not necessarily alter these arrangements in its initial years. Blocks were sold in their entirety or together at auction, and the rights thereby granted the lessee to exploit their banks did not encompass the labour that was actually required to collect shell. The assumption, on the part of colonial officers, seems to have been that the use of Moken divers, going down to collect shell without utilizing any of the equipment of so-called dress diving, would persist with lessees. And, indeed, this appears to have been the case.

However, the introduction of the diving suit into the Mergui Archipelago by European and Australian pearling capital around 1894 as an element of 'modern' maritime technology created, as it would elsewhere in the pearling world, the separate and distinct category of 'naked' diving.[16] In Burma, as more generally throughout Southeast Asia, divers were capable of attaining depths of around 12 to 14 metres prior to the introduction of the dresses, spending a limited amount of time searching for and collecting oysters before having to return to the surface. Divers were thus restricted to work in relatively shallow water 'even though they knew that pearl oysters were often abundant in deeper waters' (Butcher 2004: 124). Having been developed through different stages over the course of the nineteenth century, the diving dress – consisting of a helmet, corselet, a suit made of waterproof canvas and weighted boots – allowed divers to go down to far greater depths than was otherwise possible. The associated use of a hand pump and hose through which air was carried to the helmet and a rope attached to the diver to enable, by tugging at it, the conveying of different signals to the crew completed the diving ensemble. Despite its cumbersome and somewhat restrictive nature, the dress meant that divers were able to reach depths over twice that of diving without the apparatus and that their time underwater was also greatly extended. Any technological advantage that would allow divers to reach these greater depths was, of course, an extremely attractive if costlier proposition for pearlers who, unsurprisingly, embraced the adoption of the diving dress. And for the colonial state, it introduced a vertical dimension to the territorialisation of oceanic space by making it possible to claim and exploit beds at unprecedented depths.

Never fully supplanted as a labour mode, though, naked diving continued to exist often as a complementary form for the extraction of pearl shell as well as an array of marine products. In the Mergui Archipelago (the dress was not used elsewhere in Burma), naked diving remained a vibrant endeavour practiced exclusively by Moken divers, who were engaged by merchants, including in blocks where pumps and dress diving were being utilised simultaneously, to collect shells, green snails and trochus shell found in shallower waters. But after considered debate about its merits and demerits, the agreement on the part of colonial offices to introduce the licencing system comprised of 'fees on pumps being used' brought to the fore the question of 'diving without apparatus' (NAM 1/7/1094, 1902). Specifically, the question centred on how the *right* of collecting the aforementioned marine products should be apportioned – in other words, should the right to collect shell without the use of diving equipment be sold separately 'along with the other rights,' or should naked diving be somehow incorporated into a fee structure that was associated with what was levied on pumps. Revenue department officials, in particular, were concerned that the latter had actually rendered naked pearling 'free' and therefore sought a resolution to an activity for which there continued to be considerable interest among pearl shell and marine product traders in the Mergui Archipelago (NAM 1/7/1094, 1902).

Although urged by these traders even before the auction-lease system had been abolished that it would indeed be desirable to sell the 'right of collecting m.o.p. [mother-of-pearl] shells without diving apparatus . . . along with the other rights,' government officers were hesitant – at least initially – to grant this change. For some, fully cognisant that naked diving was in the hands of Moken seafarers, believed that these divers 'might benefit by the fact of such pearling being free' (NAM 1/7/1094, 1902). But this was dismissed as untrue according to the Mergui revenue officer, for the Moken 'hardly get fair play at the hands of the licensees, to whom they look for food and what clothing they need.' The notion that Moken divers were being exploited by 'individual Chinese and Malays' reflected colonial stereotyping of groups with whom Moken divers and families had cultivated relationships over many decades of pearl fishing in the archipelago's waters. This notion was a guiding principle, nonetheless, and resulted in revenue officials and the financial commissioner jointly endorsing that the 'exclusive right of working without diving apparatus in the various blocks of the pearling area . . . be leased separately' (NAM 1/7/83, 1908). Its inclusion in the 1905 Burma Fisheries Act enshrined what had already become commonly accepted by Burma's local colonial officers (NAM 1/7/67, 1908).

This did not entirely resolve matters from the government's standpoint, however, for 'free' diving remained widely practiced among the archipelago's islands. Several Chinese merchants operating in Mergui in the first two decades of the twentieth century 'employ[ed]' Moken divers 'without licence [sic] for pearling' (NAM 1/7/1094, n.d.). Clearly driven by an imperative to derive as much taxation from the collection of any and all marine products in the region's waters as possible, this concern reflected also ongoing efforts to define maritime borders that were, as noted earlier, indeterminate and traversed constantly by the movement of goods, boats and people. Moken divers thus continued to either dive for traders who sailed to the archipelago or, as seems to have been more common, to sail the relatively short distance to Ranong, where they delivered their cargoes of assorted marine products to specific Chinese – and in some cases Malay – traders with whom they had pre-arranged agreements. Understanding little of the dynamics of these relationships, colonial officers sought the criminalisation of this behaviour, with imprisonment a possibility or large fines being issued to traders who, upon inspection, could not produce a licence that had to be kept onboard the vessel (NAM 1/7/1063, 1901). It is difficult to get a sense of how successful this approach was, but the almost total absence of colonial naval patrol vessels meant that local officials were forced to rely on the logic, applied as much to the idea of Moken naked diving as to the extraction through dress diving, that the 'holders of licences would . . . inform against any unlicenced pumps who would be competing unfairly with them' (NAM 1/7/1063, 1900). Quite to what degree this may have been true is hard to discern. But even with the complaints of some prominent merchants – like those made by Ebrahim Ahmed in the 1920s – about Moken trading to Ranong in marine products fished from areas to which these merchants had been granted de facto exclusive rights, this economy continued to thrive as an irrepressible feature of the exchange of marine products in Burma's coastal waters.

Pearl and shell harvesting in the Mergui Archipelago, then, was characterised at the turn of the century by co-existence of naked and dress diving. The numbers of pumps being used in the islands had grown from around 60 in the mid-1890s to possibly as many as 80 by the early years of the twentieth century but do not appear to have grown much beyond this number. Indian and Chinese merchant investments, noted earlier, contributed to this number of pumps through significant investments in boats and dresses. Schooners employed mostly Filipino, Malay and Japanese divers in the small boats that actually carried the pumps and that sailed to the pearl banks before returning to the larger vessel operating as a 'floating station,' where their hauls were discharged. While Australian involvement in Mergui had been prominent, until around the turn of the century, many of the dress divers had been brought to the islands from the pearling grounds of the Torres Strait and Aru Islands. Thereafter, while the number of Australian- or European-owned pumps dropped significantly, dress diving remained a feature of pearling in the archipelago, with growing numbers of Japanese divers – as would be the case beyond Burma of course – labouring to collect shell at great depths.

In areas 'outside the open pearling grounds' – the blocks into which the islands of the archipelago continued to be divided – diving was organised through leases and not the pump system, with divers working in waters where 'exclusive rights of pearling and taking of green snails etc [were granted] within a definite area' (NAM 1/7/83, 1908). This was, a government official wrote in Moulmein in 1908, so as to avoid the 'interfere[nce] with persons diving for pearls under licences in the public pearling area' (NAM 1/7/67, 1908). This appears to have been part of efforts to allow the exploration of waters that could contain pearl banks, specifically around the Moskos Islands that lay to the north of the Mergui Archipelago.[17]

The complementarity of dress and naked diving, coupled with the investments in equipment and boats by Asian traders and merchants and the ongoing relationships of Moken divers and mariners with Chinese traders, created a thriving pearling economy in the transregional Burmese waters. The bustling cosmopolitan town of Mergui, which served as the capital of the pearling industry for the archipelago – it was where pearlers in many instances brought their haul of pearl shell and other marine products for sale and where prices were negotiated – reflected its dynamism, as a visiting journalist described in 1913:

> Nestling between river and jungle . . . half hidden until one comes abreast of it . . . Mergui is not the sleepy place that it looks from the sea; there is plenty of life and stir in its streets and market places. Its bazaar is alive with a glowing panorama of half the races of the East – Chinaman and Burman jostle one another; Madras coolies, Malays and Siamese are all to be seen . . . while among them move Japanese and Filipinos . . . Mergui is a thriving town, which is growing year by year.
>
> (*Oamaru Mail*, 1913)

Pearling remained a mainstay of local and transregional economies into the 1920s and 1930s, where, even for those with broader investments in, for instance, tin mining, it remained a significant part of their portfolio. Also, part of the appeal of pearling in the coastal and island waters of Burma may well have been that, as pointed out by John Butcher, 'a much higher proportion of the pearl oysters in the Mergui Archipelago contained pearls [when they did] than in some other pearling areas such as the Aru Island and the Torres Strait' (Butcher 2004: 128). There was thus always the possibility that pearlers might strike it lucky, despite the odds that they would not.

Conclusion

If the prospect of discovering an oyster among the many shells that divers were bringing to the surface was enough to induce investment in Burma's pearl banks, it appears that the industry – like others in the Indian Ocean – suffered from the competition from cultured pearls by the 1930s and the effects of that decade's economic depression.[18]

Yet, in another sign of its resiliency, investors turned increasingly to pearl cultivation in the 1950s when the Burma Pearl Fishing and Culture Syndicate (BPFCS), a private Japanese-Myanmar joint-venture farm, began cultivating pearls at Domel Island (Tun 1998: 3). This had already been attempted in the early years of the century when an unnamed syndicate that had been in operation for a decade cultivated pearls that had 'reached a commercial basis' (*Observer* 1910). It would appear that the development of the cultured pearl industry occurred primarily in the postwar years under the influence of the BPFCS. After moving to Sir J. Malcolm Island in 1956, the country's Revolutionary Government (brought to power by the military coup in 1962) nationalised the joint-venture farm in 1963, and after some reshuffling over the years, it was eventually transformed into a separate enterprise in 1989 under the Ministry of Mines and renamed the Myanmar Pearl Enterprise (MPE). Since the introduction of economic reforms from this time, three joint-venture companies – 'both local and foreign' – began white South Sea Pearl production in addition to the government-owned MPE (Tun 1998: 3). Investments from Japanese, Australian, Tahitian and Thai companies, in partnership with MPE, stimulated an expansion of the industry that was grounded in seeding techniques developed locally after Japanese knowledge had been successfully transferred in the 1950s. Yields of mother-of-pearl fluctuated over the thirty years between 1967/68 and 1995/96 from 20–30 metric tonnes to 90 metric tonnes, while production of cultured South Sea Pearls was equally uneven over the same period. Sales revenue, relatively modest, could reach significant levels as it did in 1990 when a little over $5 million worth of pearls were sold.

These efforts reflect a continuity of interest in the potential of the Mergui Archipelago as a maritime zone of extraction. More broadly, in the last two decades of the twentieth and first few years of the twenty-first centuries, there has been a resurgence in the shipment of ocean products between Southeast Asia and China. Spurred by record economic growth since the 1980s, ocean commerce in traditional conduits of trade between the two regions has revitalised an exchange that had never really disappeared but that had existed in the shadow of other, more important lines of commerce for much of the twentieth century. Encompassing different sets of actors and networks of business organisation, the marine goods economy (including a variety of fish, too, of course) has flourished along the coasts of the Southeast Asian mainland and throughout its islands as varying sub-ethnic groups have shipped cargoes of shellfish from the Indian Ocean coast of southern Thailand (astride the Andaman Sea), dried fish from Cambodia's Tonle Sap (the country's great lake), edible sea cucumbers collected throughout the region from Taipei and Taiwan and shark fins from Manila in the

Philippines to discerning Chinese markets. From Burma, too, traditionally sought marine goods 'are shuttling en masse to China' and include very expensive species of holothurians among other items (Tagliocozzo 2011: 441). Harvesting the ocean, as much now as in the past, represents an enduring arena of business for a range of interested parties and will likely continue to do so in the future.

Notes

1 While my conceptual understanding of "littoral" has been influenced by Michael Pearson's important essay, "Littoral Society: The Concept and the Problems," *Journal of World History* 17.4 (December 2006): 353–73, I use the term differently as encompassing multiple coastal areas and reflecting the plurality of coastal and inter-coastal histories with connections also to urban areas. For further discussion of new approaches to littorals, see Jennifer L. Gaynor, *Intertidal History in Island Southeast Asia: Submerged Genealogy & the Legacy of Coastal Capture* (Ithaca: Cornell University Press, 2016).

2 The holder of the Burmese royal birds' nest farm for southeast Burma, 'Thiwa-Kyawthu-Nawratta,' paid 20,000 ticals (or perhaps their value in kind) for the right of collection and exchange for Tavoy Islands and the Mergui Archipelago, a right he appears to have held for several years.

3 Trepang was an important marine good connecting Southeast Asia to China through the South China Sea; see Heather Sunderland, "Trepang and Wangkang: The China Trade of Eighteenth-Century Makassar, 1720s – 1840s," *Bijdragen tot de Taal-, Land- en Volkenkunde* 156 (2000): 451–72; and James Francis Warren, *The Sulu Zone, 1768–1898: The Dynamics of External Trade, Slavery and Ethnicity in the Transformation of a Southeast Asian Maritime State* (Singapore: Singapore University Press, 1981). The latter discusses the regional slaving expeditions that *Taosugdatus* (princes) organized in the nineteenth century for sea-peoples to be used in the collection of trepang.

4 Edward Melillo discusses how, amidst the expansion of whaling in the Pacific from the end of the eighteenth century, mariners from Nantucket and New England merchants from Salem Harbour forged close connections to Fiji and became involved extensively in the export of sea cucumbers, which were found in abundance throughout the island's warm coastal shoals, to China. Taking advantage of different valuation systems, North American entrepreneurs with connections to Canton (and also Manila) exchanged trepang for Chinese silks, jade, tea, porcelain and lacquered goods that were becoming increasingly popular in Euro-American markets. See "Making Sea Cucumbers Out of Whales' Teeth: Nantucket Castaways and Encounters of Value in Nineteenth-Century Fiji," *Environmental History* 20 (2015): 449–74; and also Gregory Cushman, *Guano and the Opening of the Pacific World: A Global Ecological History* (Cambridge: Cambridge University Press, 2013).

5 According to Eric Tagliocozzo, some of Singapore's advantages were that it was geographically better positioned than Penang to major collecting areas for marine goods located in insular southeast Asian waters and its status as a 'free' port. See Tagliocozzo, Eric, "A Necklace of Fins: Marine Goods Trading in Maritime Southeast Asia, 1780–1860," *International Journal of Asian Studies* 1.1 (2004): 23–48.

6 See, for instance, the collections of royal Portuguese jewellery at the Museu Nacional de Arte Antiga, in Lisbon, Portugal.

7 This was prompted not only by the accumulated wealth of Euro-American industrialists but also by development of button-production using shell and the broadening markets that a nascent middle class was creating for a variety of pearls and especially products made from mother-of-pearl.

8 For further details, see Joseph Christensen Machado, "Precious Networks: Exploring Burma's Pearling Histories," in *Pearls, People and Power: The Global Pearl Trades of the Indian Ocean World, 16th–20th Centuries*, edited by Joseph Christensen Machado and Steven Mullins (Ohio University Press, forthcoming).

9 The 'intermittent character of the fisheries' (i.e., the variable nature of the availability of oysters along pearling banks from one season to the next) was well-established and commented upon in a report by W. A. Herdman on the Gulf of Mannar fisheries: *Report to the Government of Ceylon on the Pearl Oyster Fisheries of the Gulf of Manaar* (London, 1903), 3.

10 The fourth chapter of the book further discusses Jardine's relationship with James Clarke, the major pearling figure in northern Australia.

11 This would have necessitated coming to an 'arrangement with the turtle bank lessees,' an arrangement that Chill was ultimately unable to secure. See NAM, 1/15(e)/13699, Secretary to the Financial Commissioner, Burma, to the Commissioner, Irawaddy Division, 17 April 1894; *idem*, Secretary to the Financial Commissioner, Burma to Mr. Chill, 14 May 1894; *idem*, Mr. Chill to Secretary to the Financial Commissioner, Burma, 25 May 1894; NAM, 1/15(e)/13435, Secretary to the Financial Commissioner, Burma, to the Commissioner, Irawaddy Division, Bassein, 31 August 1893.

12 Eric Tagliocozzo has explored these dynamics in relation to illegality and the establishment of borders in Southeast Asia in the context of imperial rivalries between the British and Dutch. See *Secret Trades, Porous Borders: Smuggling and States along a Southeast Asian Frontier, 1865–1915* (New Haven and London: Yale University Press, 2005).

13 See, for instance, the "Revenue Chalans [receipts]" detailing purchasers of pearling license in the 1920s in NAM, 1/7/1190.

14 This information is derived from several files in NAM, such as 1/7/1219; 1/7/1190; 1/15(e)/16175; and 1/15(e)/13922.

15 This concern that the licencing system would attract 'undesirables' was dismissed on the grounds that approximately Rs 5,000 in capital was required by anyone seeking 'to start pearling operations.'

16 This terminology had been used at least a decade or two earlier, for instance in descriptions of the pearling industry in northwestern Australia.

17 See, for instance, the proposal put forward in 1912 by a London 'partnership' to extend the size of a lease that had already been granted earlier in the Moskos Islands for the purposes, among others, of extending 'the pearl and shell industry by opening up new areas' and of 'restocking denuded banks.' NAM, 1/7/83, F. C. Colomb to Deputy Commissioner, Tavoy, 5 November 1912.

18 The development of cultured pearls by Kokichi Mikimoto, a Japanese noodle-shop owner who perfected the ancient Chinese practice of inserting a spherical piece of mother-of-pearl into oyster shells to induce the oyster to produce a pearl, is well known. See, for instance, Robert Eunson, *The Pearl King: The Story of the Fabulous Mikimoto* (Tokyo: Charles E. Tuttle, 1963).

References

Amrith, Sunil. 2013. *Crossing the Bay of Bengal: The Furies of Nature and the Fortunes of Migrants*, Cambridge: Harvard University Press.

Anon. 1894. "West Kimberley Notes," *The Daily News*, 1 September.

Anon. 1894. "Notices to Correspondents," *The Queenslander*, 24 November.

Anon. 1895. "The Mergui Pearl Fisheries," *Northern Territory Times and Gazette*, 31 May.

Anon. 1904. "Traveller – The Salones," *The Wingham Chronicle and Manning River Observer*, 18 June.

Anon. 1910. "Nutshell Interviews," *Observer*, 26 February.

Anon. 1913. "The Mergui Archipelago," *Oamaru Mail*, 22 April.

Aslanian, Sebouh. 2011. *From the Indian Ocean to the Mediterranean: The Global Trade Networks of Armenian Merchants from New Julfa*, Berkeley, New York and London: University of California Press.

Bashford, Alison. 2017. "Terraqueous Histories," *The Historical Journal*, 60: 253–72.

Benton, Lauren. 2005. "Legal Spaces of Empire," *Comparative Studies in Society and History*, 47(4): 700–24, October.

Blussé, Leonard. 1991. "In Praise of Commodities: An Essay on the Cross-Cultural Trade in Edible Birds' Nests," in Roderich Ptak and Dietmar Rothermund (eds.), *Emporia, Commodities and Entrepreneurs in Asian Maritime Trade, c. 1400–1750*, Stuttgart: Franz Steiner Verlag.

Butcher, John G. 2004. *The Closing of the Frontier: A History of the Marine Fisheries of Southeast Asia c. 1850–2000*, Singapore: Institute of Southeast Asian Studies.

Charney, Michael. 2009a. "Esculent Bird's Nest, Tin and Fish: The Overseas Chinese and Their Trade in the Eastern Bay of Bengal (Coastal Burma) During the First Half of the Nineteenth Century," in Geoff Wade (ed.), *China and Southeast Asia, Volume IV: Interactions from the End of the Nineteenth Century to 1911*, London: Routledge.

Charney, Michael. 2009b. *A History of Modern Burma*, Cambridge: Cambridge University Press.

Chiang, Bien. 2011. "Market Prices, Labor Input, and Relation of Production in Sarawak's Edible Birds' Nest Trade," in Eric Tagliocozzo and Wen-Chin Chang (eds.), *Chinese Circulations: Capital, Commodities, and Networks in Southeast Asia*, Durham and London: Duke University Press.

A Collection of Legislative Acts, Ceylon Government, Regulation No. 3 of 1811.

Cushman, Gregory. 2013. *Guano and the Opening of the Pacific World: A Global Ecological History*, Cambridge: Cambridge University Press.

Eunson, Robert. 1963. *The Pearl King: The Story of the Fabulous Mikimoto*, Tokyo: Charles E. Tuttle.

Fujimoto, Helen. 1989. *The South Indian-Muslim Community and the Evolution of the Jawi Peranakan in Penang Up to 1948*, Tokyo: Gaikokugo Daigaku.

Gaynor, Jennifer L. 2016. *Intertidal History in Island Southeast Asia: Submerged Genealogy & the Legacy of Coastal Capture*, Ithaca: Cornell University Press.

Gillis, John and Franziska Torma (eds.). 2015. *Fluid Frontiers: New Currents in Marine Environmental History*, Cambridge: The White Horse Press.

Heesterman, J.C. 1980. "Littoral et intérieur de l'Inde," in Leonard Blussé, H.L. Wesseling and George D. Winius (eds.), *History and Underdevelopment: Essays on Underdevelopment and European Expansion in Asia and Africa*, Leiden: Leiden University Press.

Herdman, W.A. 1903. *Report to the Government of Ceylon on the Pearl Oyster Fisheries of the Gulf of Manaar*, London.

Hussin, Nordin. 2006. *Trade and Society in the Straits of Melaka: Dutch Melaka and English Penang, 1780–1830*, Singapore: National University of Singapore Press.

Ivanoff, Jacques. 2003. "Moken Boats," *Nest*, 22: 86–109.

Ivanoff, Jacques and Thierry Lejard (in collaboration with Luca and Gabriella Gansser). 2002. *A Journey Through the Mergui Archipelago*, Bangkok: White Lotus Press.

Kunz, George Frederick and Charles Hugh Stevenson. 1908. *The Book of the Pearl: The History, Art, Science and Industry of the Queen of Gems*, New York: The Century Co.

Lewis, Su Lin. 2016. *Cities in Motion: Urban Life and Cosmopolitanism in Southeast Asia, 1920–1940*, Cambridge: Cambridge University Press.

Machado. forthcoming. "Precious Networks: Exploring Burma's Pearling Histories," in Machado, Joseph Christensen and Steven Mullins (eds.), *Pearls, People and Power: The Global Pearl Trades of the Indian Ocean World, 16th–20th Centuries*, Ohio University Press.

Markovits, Claude. 2013. "South Asian Business in the Empire and Beyond, c. 1800–1950," in Joya Chatterji and David Washbrook (eds.), *Routledge Handbook of the South Asian Diaspora*, Abingdon and New York: Routledge.

Martinez, Julia and Adrian Vickers. 2015. *The Pearl Frontier: Indonesian Labor and Indigenous Encounters in Australia's Northern Trading Network*, Honolulu: University of Hawai'i Press.

Melillo, Edward. 2015. "Making Sea Cucumbers Out of Whales' Teeth: Nantucket Castaways and Encounters of Value in Nineteenth-Century Fiji," *Environmental History*, 20: 449–74.

Myint-U, Thant. 2001. *The Making of Modern Burma*, Cambridge: Cambridge University Press.

Ostroff, Samuel. 2016. "Between Promise and Peril: Credit and Debt at the Pearl Fisheries of South India and Sri Lanka, c. 1800," in Chia Yin Hsu, Thomas M. Luckett and Erika Vause (eds.), *The Cultural History of Money and Credit: A Global Perspective*, Lanham, MA: Lexington Books.

Pearson, Michael. 2006. "Littoral Society: The Concept and the Problems," *Journal of World History*, 17(4): 353–73, December.

Rudmose Brown, R.N. 1907–1909. "The Mergui Archipelago: Its People and Products," *Scottish Geographical Magazine*, 23(9): 464.

Rudmose Brown, R.N. and Jas J. Simpson. 1907. *Report to the Government of Burma on the Pearl Oyster Fisheries of the Mergui Archipelago and Moskos Islands*, Rangoon: Office of the Superintendent, Government Printing.

Rudner, David West. 1994. *Caste and Capitalism in Colonial India: The Nattukotai Chettiars*, Berkeley, CA: University of California Press.

Smith, Carl T. and Paul A. Van Dyke. 2003. "Four Armenian Families," *Review in Culture*, International Edition, (8): 40–50, October.

Steinberg, Philip E. 2001. *The Social Construction of the Ocean*, Cambridge: Cambridge University Press.

Sutherland, Heather. 1898. "South Tenasserim and the Mergui Archipelago," *Scottish Geographical Magazine*, 14(9): 449–64.

Sunderland, Heather. 2000. "Trepang and Wangkang: The China Trade of Eighteenth-Century Makassar, 1720s – 1840s," *Bijdragen tot de Taal-, Land- en Volkenkunde*, 156: 451–72.

Sutherland, Heather. 2011. "A Sino-Indonesian Commodity Chain: The Trade in Tortoiseshell in the Late Seventeenth and Eighteenth Centuries," in Eric Tagliocozzo and Wen-Chin Chang (eds.), *Chinese Circulations: Capital, Commodities, and Networks in Southeast Asia*, Durham and London: Duke University Press.

Tagliocozzo, Eric. 2004a. "A Necklace of Fins: Marine Goods Trading in Maritime Southeast Asia, 1780–1860," *International Journal of Asian Studies*, 1(1): 23–48.

Tagliocozzo, Eric. 2004b. "Ambiguous Commodities, Unstable Frontiers: The Case of Burma, Siam, and Imperial Britain, 1800–1900," *Comparative Studies in Society and History*, 46(2): 354–77, April.

Tagliocozzo, Eric. 2005. *Secret Trades, Porous Borders: Smuggling and States Along a Southeast Asian Frontier, 1865–1915*, New Haven and London: Yale University Press.

Tagliocozzo, Eric. 2011. "A Sino-Southeast Asian Circuit: Ethnohistories of the Marine Goods Trade," in Eric Tagliocozzo and Wen-Chin Chang (eds.), *Chinese Circulations*. Durham: Duke University Press.

Tun, Tint. 1998. "Myanmar Pearling: Past, Present and Future," *SPC Pearl Oyster Information Bulletin #12*: 3–7, December.

Warren, James Francis. 1981. *The Sulu Zone, 1768–1898: The Dynamics of External Trade, Slavery and Ethnicity in the Transformation of a Southeast Asian Maritime State*, Singapore: Singapore University Press.

Warrington Smyth, H. 1898. *Five Years in Siam from 1891 to 1896*, London: John Murray.

Wei Leng, Loh. 2009. "Penang as Commercial Centre: Trade and Shipping Networks," *JMBRAS*, 82(Part 2): 25–37.

White, Walter Grainge. 1922. *The Sea Gypsies of Malaya*, Philadelphia: J.B. Lippincott Company.

Win, Daw and Loh Wei Leng. 2009. "Regional Links: Yangon, Penang and Singapore," *JMBRAS*, 82(Part 2): 67–79.

Winichakul, Thongchai. 1994. *Siam Mapped: A History of the Geo-Body of a Nation*, Honolulu: University of Hawai'i Press.

Wright, Ashley. 2014. *Opium and Empire in Southeast Asia: Regulating Consumption in British Burma*, Basingstoke: Palgrave Macmillan.

Archival Collections

−Office of Indian and Oriental Collections, British Library, London (OIOC)
P&S Department Records, 1874.
National Archives of India, Delhi (NAI).
P/4769, Pro. No. 1–5, "Report," 16 February 1894.
P/4769, Pro. No. 1–5, "Report," 16 February 1894.
P&S Department Records, Burma, 1898.

−National Archives of India, Delhi (NAI)
Shimla Records, No. 66C-2F-13, Revenue Secretary to Government of Burma to Secretary to Government of India, 26 May 1906.
Home Department, Public B, June 1894, Nov. 1/3, "Enclosure – Mergui Pearl Fisheries," 19 December 1893.
Home Department, Public B, June 1894, Nov. 1/3, "Opinion of the Law Officers," 19 December 1893.

Political Department, Sir E.C. Buck KT, CSI, Secretary to the Government of India to Chief Commissioner of Burma, 23 May 1894.

Secretary of State for India, 2 May 1894.

–National Archives of Myanmar, Yangon (NAM)

1/7/37, "Diary of Maung Ba Hein," 12 February 1894.

1/7/1219, E. Ahmed to Deputy Commissioner, 10 September 1926; same to same, 16 October 1926.

1/7/67, H.L. Tilly to Deputy Commissioner, Tavoy, 4 July 1908.

1/7/67, G.E.T. Green to Commissioner, Tavoy, 13 July 1908.

1/7/67, Offg. Commissioner of the Tenasserim Division, Moulmein, to the Deputy Commissioner, Tavoy, 4 July 1908.

1/7/83, Secretary to the Financial Commissioner, Burma, to Colonel K.M. Foss, Rangoon, 23 September 1908.

1/7/83, F. C. Colomb to Deputy Commissioner, Tavoy, 5 November 1912.

1/7/1063, "Statement Showing Quantity and Value of M.O.P. shell exported from Mergui during 5 years," 3 January 1900.

1/7/1063, Secretary to the Financial Commissioner to the Commissioner, Tenasserim Division, 6 March 1900.

1/7/1063, Ebrahim Ahmed, Mohamed Salim et al to Lieutenant Governor of Burma, Mergui, 22 February 1900.

1/7/1063, "Draft Pearling Licencing Form," 31 January 1901.

1/7/1094, Revenue Department, Mergui, to Commissioner, Moulmein, 24 June 1902.

1/7/1094, "Salon diving", n.d.

1/7/1190, Deputy Commissioner, Mergui, to District Superintendent of Police, 8 March 1924.

1/7/1190, "Revenue Chalans"

1/15(e)/13922, Secretary to Financial Commissioner, Burma, to Commissioner, Irawaddy Division, Bassein, 2 March 1895.

1/15(e)/13699, Secretary to the Financial Commissioner, Burma, to the Commissioner, Irawaddy Division, 17 April 1894.

1/15(e)/13699, Secretary to the Financial Commissioner, Burma to Mr. Chill, 14 May 1894.

1/15(e)/13699, Mr. Chill to Secretary to the Financial Commissioner, Burma, 25 May 1894.

1/15(e)/13435, Secretary to the Financial Commissioner, Burma, to the Commissioner, Irawaddy Division, Bassein, 31 August 1893.

1/15(e)/14231, "Rules for Regulating the Pearl Fisheries of Lower Burma, 1896.

1/15(e)/14231, Deputy Commissioner, Bassein, to Commissioner, Irrawaddy Division, Bassein, 29 June 1896.

1/15(e)/14238, Deputy Commissioner, Bassein, to Commissioner, Irawaddy Division, Bassein, 31 August 1896.

1/15(e)/14448, Deputy Commissioner, Bassein, to Commissioner, Irrawaddy Division, Bassein, 5 May 1897.

Part IV

REMINISCENCES

Figure 12.1 Michael Pearson advancing on the Bay of Bengal in a dinghy from Masulipatnam, India, 2011

Source: All photographs in this chapter are from the author's personal collection.

12

MICHAEL NAYLOR PEARSON

The discipline of history, the sea and the man

Rila Mukherjee

I had of course encountered Michael Pearson through his *Merchants and Rulers in Gujarat* as a university student, but I first met him at an Indian Ocean conference at Leiden organised by his UTS Sydney colleagues Stephen Muecke and Devleena Ghosh in 2006. 'Littoral Society: The Concept and the Problems' had just been published in the *Journal of World History* that year, and I like to think that Michael knew this article heralded a new phase in his writing life. Although he had published an earlier version as 'Littoral Society: The Case for the Coast' in *The Great Circle* in 1985, this particular article was more consciously geographical and anthropological and placed the littoral firmly on the maritime map.

If Alan Villiers and Auguste Toussaint heralded the first wave of Indian Ocean studies of the 1950s and 1960s, Michael Pearson, K. N. Chaudhuri and Kenneth McPherson represented the second wave that rose in the 1980s (Armitage et al. 2018: 37). This second generation fuelled the intensely oceanic approach of the first wave. As the Australian Association for Maritime History states on its website (https://aamh.asn.au/), 'maritime history is the study of people and their activities in, on, around and under the waters of the world. This includes oceans, estuaries, rivers, and creeks.' Like his predecessor Frank Broeze, Michael believed that maritime history was the study of the relationship between humans and the sea. Broeze had identified six broad overlapping categories: using the resources of the sea and its subsoil, transportation, political power projection, scientific exploration, leisure, and culture and ideology (Broeze 1989: 6).

Like Broeze, Michael defined maritime history as widely as possible. He knowingly disregarded disciplinary boundaries sometimes, although he had started out, very self-consciously, as a historian. At that time, in the words of Broeze (Broeze 1995: x–xiii), the field of maritime history was just emerging, its practitioners were few and far between and the 'field' and scope of maritime history was yet to be defined. Moreover, maritime history was still to be dis-entangled from national histories. Michael's conception of the sea and human interactions within it is now reinforced by a new generation of scholars. Although Sanjay Subrahmanyam has recently observed that Michael was not always rigorous in his use of archival material (Subrahmanyam 2017: 222), Michael himself always claimed that he was like a magpie, taking bits and pieces from across disciplines to formulate his arguments. This was his greatest strength, reading widely to understand the sea, the exercise culminating in his magnum opus *The Indian Ocean*, which was published in 2003. Peter Ridgway, sometime president of the Australian Association of Maritime History, conceived of an Indian Ocean maritime history atlas inspired by Michael's work (Ridgway 2005).

*

Although he wrote about an Indian Ocean world, Michael remained acutely conscious of the dangers of imagining the spatial boundaries of this world. He often quoted Braudel's work wherein inland Cracow was also sometimes part of the Mediterranean world through networks that varied in time and scope. But Michael also felt that perceived commonalities across the Indian Ocean sometimes stretched its physical boundaries, and he repeatedly asked these questions: How far inland? How far could an oceanic world extend? What common patterns or themes could we find? The questions he asked are important, since Central Africa, the Ottoman East, the India-Burma borderlands or camels and Bedouins are now seen as constituting an Indian Ocean world. The Indian Ocean world seems in danger of losing its ocean!

Partly, the present ambiguity regarding the spatial limits of an Indian Ocean world results from Michael's writings. His Indian Ocean world is dominated by flows and circulations – his work was marked by a political ontology that took as its starting point flows, circulations and the destabilising immanence of liquid (Steinberg and Peters 2015). Historian Pedro Machado too has emphasised flows and connections in his 'world on the move' in eighteenth-century Gujarat. Local and inter-regional circuits of production, commercialisation, exchange and consumer demand shaped the eighteenth-century global economy's contours and parameters, and Machado argued that larger histories of global exchange need to be attentive to the multiple strands that underlie its structure (Machado 2014: 14). Despite arguments against concentrating only on flows and connections, a conceptualisation of the world as fundamentally consisting of water-borne social processes is also visible in Michael's edited volume *Trade, Circulation and Flow in the Indian Ocean World* of 2015:

> We see the Indian Ocean in its broadest sense, but does this mean we have an Indian Ocean World? The latter term implies some unity, some connections, which make this body of water something that can be studied and analyzed, just like say a state or a city or a famous person . . . this matter is still open. Yet several of

the chapters in this book show ties and connections, elements of commonality, stretching all over the Indian Ocean, so that we can indeed write of an Indian Ocean World.

(Pearson 2015a)

But there were also differences. Michael's position on the land-sea binary was not always clear; at times, he would argue that the influence of the sea stretched far inland; at other times, he wrote of far-reaching terrestrial influences on oceans. He wrote that much that purported to be oceanic history was methodologically flawed – most products came from land, ships were built on land, sailors returned home to their families – we could not just set sail and ignore the land from which we came. So, for Michael, although the aquatic part of our globe needed more focus, we could not ignore the land altogether (Pearson 2014a; Mukherjee 2018). But 'how far inland' oceanic influences stretched remained for him an unresolved problem (Pearson 2011: 82).

Michael's most recent publication to date is 'Places in the Indian Ocean World,' where he firmly places port cities on the Indian Ocean map:

We all enact change over time, but are not nearly as concerned with where we are writing about. One recent trend in general historiography may help our maritime studies. This is the matter of *place*. To illustrate this, let me say a little about three particular spaces, that is, ships, then coasts, and finally port cities.

(Pearson 2017: 4–5, my italics)

Although he subscribed to the notion of an Indian Ocean world and, like Auguste Toussaint (Toussaint 1974), he also endorsed the notion of multiple Indian Oceans, Michael remained profoundly sceptical of oceans as units of world historical analysis. The diversity and randomness across as well as *within* waterscapes left him unconvinced on matters of unities and connectivities. The oceanic world was just too hybrid, with many spatial and temporal inconsistencies, as Canizares-Esguerra and Breen have pointed out in the context of the Atlantic:

works of Atlantic history have repeatedly emphasized themes of interconnection, circulation, encounter, and exchange. . . . One major disadvantage of this 'national Atlantic' framework is that it maps modernity's more celebrated features – religious toleration, free market capitalism, democracy, and experimental science – almost exclusively onto the British and Dutch Atlantic. By contrast, the Iberian empires have been depicted as decadent, conservative, or mired in a particularly exploitative attitude toward their indigenous and enslaved subjects.

(Canizares-Esguerra and Breen 2013: 597)

Michael cautioned that all oceanic history was not always world history, perceiving, as Bashford has now noted, a slide from the maritime 'worlds' of Braudel's Mediterranean to the maritime 'world' of global history (Bashford 2017: 2; Pearson 2015b: 145, 148, 151). Recently, Nile Green too has critiqued the presumption of connection that undergirds much of the Indian Ocean world work. His work on Bombay and Barcelona puts pressure on maritime worlds as explanatory frameworks, as ecumenes with historically contingent rather than self-evident effects (Green 2013; Burton et al. 2013: 499–500).

*

Michael always emphasised the ozone of the sea and the brackishness of estuarine waters. I like to think that his deliberate use of models from other disciplines not only sharpened his thinking and enhanced his written output but also imparted the tang of salt air to his writings. 'Littoral societies' (Pearson 2006) had heralded a new wave of oceanic history writing that Michael titled 'amphibian' histories, what Steinberg and Peters have termed 'thinking *with* the sea' and 'wet ontology' and what Alison Bashford has now titled as 'terraqueous' histories – where the original meaning of 'terraqueous' was expansive in terms of the description and comprehension of matter and processes. In its original usage in Anglophone texts, terraqueous matter could and did include 'atmosphere, mass of air, vapours, and clouds' (Steinberg and Peters 2015; Bashford 2017: 8).

Michael called this new kind of history 'oceanic' history, where he deliberated the influence of the land on the sea and vice versa (Pearson 2014b). He insisted on the historian's need to 'get wet' while writing of the sea and, as Steinberg writes, to unpack

> the fundamental binary between land and water (or dry space and wet space) that underpins the modern notion of state territoriality. Swamps, estuaries, islands (especially barrier islands), and even spaces that may be quite far from coasts, such as wetlands, ships, and ice floes all complicate the land-sea divide and thereby lead us to question assumed understandings wherein landmasses are the spaces of society and oceans are simply zones of exchange.
>
> (Steinberg 2013: 163)

Michael saw estuaries marking the divide between land and sea, making an oceanic world:

> I have elaborated at perhaps too much length the difficulties of writing a history of the Indian Ocean . . . rather than try to be purely maritime, the best we can hope for is to be amphibious, to move easily between land and sea. . . . Perhaps estuaries could provide us

a clue: 'Estuaries are of a dual nature: they let the river flow into the sea, and they let the sea make its way inland.'

(Pearson 2007: 28–9)

Steinberg and Peters have furthered this geographic vision of the Indian Ocean. Steinberg has argued the sea is not a metaphor, that there is a fundamental flaw in the bulk of ocean-themed literature, maritime history, analytical work on cultural attitudes towards the ocean and a raft of scholarship in cultural studies in which the fluvial nature of the ocean is used to signal a world of mobilities, between-ness, instabilities and becomings. While all of these perspectives on the sea serve a purpose in that they suggest ways for theorising an alternative ontology of connection, Steinberg cautions that they fail to incorporate the sea as a real, experienced social arena. Even as ocean-region-based studies gain popularity, they all too often fail to engage the *aqueous centre* (my emphasis) that lies at the heart of every maritime community. Studies that seek to highlight political-economic connections across ocean basins tend to ignore the sea altogether, while those that highlight it as a site for challenging modernist notions of identity and subjectivity tend to treat the ocean solely as a metaphor. Steinberg argues that in order for ocean-region-based studies to reach their potential, the ocean must be engaged as a material space characterised by movement and continual reformation across all of its dimensions. By turning to the fluidity of the ocean that lies in the middle of the ocean region, we can gain new perspectives not just on the space that unites the region but on space itself and how it is produced (and reproduces itself) within the dynamics of spatial assemblages. Looking at the world from an ocean-region-based perspective thus becomes a means not just for highlighting a new series of global processes and connections but for transforming the way we view the world as a whole (Steinberg 2013: 156).

'Littoral societies' therefore changed my whole way of thinking, leading me to perceive the Indian Ocean world not just as lands fringing an ocean but as a composite blend of oceans, seas, marshes, lagoons, lakes, rivers and estuaries, each with distinctive features. How best could I describe this world?

*

Prior to the Leiden meeting in 2006, I had dared to send Michael a draft of my first book, *Strange Riches: Bengal in the Mercantile Map of South Asia*, for comments. *Strange Riches* had very little of maritime influences; it was a solidly terrestrial book, situating Bengal within the South Asian mercantile world. I had sent across soft copies to Peter Marshall and Christopher Bayly as well; Bayly never bothered to get back (and indeed why should he have?), but Peter Marshall commented incisively on the draft and asked me to revise certain arguments.

But most surprising was Michael's help. He had never met me, did not even know of me, and yet he took the trouble not only to comment extensively in that first message but kept up a running correspondence with me by email from that time until we met in Leiden. I remember a particularly stupid argument I had with him on email – I claimed that the port of Lahori Bandar was probably more important to the Mughal economy than Surat, even in the early eighteenth century. Michael disagreed, but when I stuck to my position, somewhat untenably in retrospect, he diplomatically kept silent. This is Michael, a gentleman to the last; he never undertakes arguments even when he knows he is right. Live and let live is his motto, although he once confided to me that he felt he never got the recognition he felt was his due in Australia. There must have been considerable disappointment and also some sadness in him, but this was countered by the recognition and affection he got from so many scholars around the world. Michael is truly blessed in that sense, and I think he knows it. He once said it was the late Ashin Das Gupta who brought him 'into' the Indian Ocean. In his turn, he was the first to introduce me to the works of Philip Steinberg, Isaac Land and Kimberley Peters to sharpen the geographic focus in my writing that he had observed earlier on.

*

Fast-forward to 2011. I had quit Jadavpur University in Kolkata in 2007 and joined as professor of history at the University of Hyderabad, over 1,400 kilometres away. I organised a conference on ports as gateways and managed to fund Michael's airfare from his base on the Gold Coast. He came with his wife, Denni, and the first thing he said was he was happy to be at Hyderabad but felt he should point out to me that he was now retired and could not return the invite. This was a surprisingly humble admission to make; I replied he was invited as a scholar and not as a potential invitation-wielding machine! The co-editor of this volume, Prof. Radhika Seshan of the University of Pune, and two of the contributors of this volume – Prof. Kenneth R. Hall of Ball State University, USA, and Dr. Amélia Polónia of the University of Porto, Portugal – were also present at that meeting.

The ports meeting of 2011 was significant for it opened the way to future collaborations. In 2015, Amélia invited Radhika, Michael (and Denni) and myself (along with my husband) to the Connected Oceans meeting in Porto and arranged several field trips to Portugal's maritime regions. The proceedings of that meeting came out as a forum edited by Amélia in the *International Journal of Maritime History* in February 2017. And in January 2017, Radhika guest-edited a special issue of the *Asian Review of World Histories* on Michael's work in which all of us featured. Ken Hall has been lead editor in some of our collective outputs, the most recent of which are *Subversive Sovereigns Across the Seas: Indian Ocean Port-Cities from Early Historic*

Times to late Colonialism (2017) and the soon-to-be-out *Cross-Cultural Networking in the Eastern Indian Ocean Realm c. 100–1800*.

The ports meeting not only yielded new definitions of port towns when it was published as *Vanguards of Globalisation: Port-Cities from the Classical to the Modern* in 2014 but also saw a field trip to Masulipatnam, Motupalli (I like to think this inspired Radhika's study of Motupalli's southern Bay of Bengal linkages in this volume!), Undavalli and Amaravati in undivided Andhra Pradesh via the Bhongir, Kondapalli and Devarakonda forts and a road trip to northern Karnataka: to Bidar, to the Bahmani capital-necropolis complex at Gulbarga-Firuzabad-Holkunda and lastly to Bijapur (see Figure 12.2). Michael profoundly disapproved of the time Denni and I spent in local markets looking at (and sometimes buying) locally produced 'bling'; he would heave a patient sigh as we dashed into yet another fashion jewellery shop. Some photographs from that memorable trip are included in this chapter.

I particularly remember Michael's excitement on two occasions on that particular trip: once when we burst through the aquamarine lagoons of Masulipatnam (see Figure 12.3) and saw the sea, and Michael cried out, 'Rila, the Bay of Bengal,' and another time when we approached the Ibrahim Rauza in Bijapur. Michael had been keen on the visit to Bijapur from

Figure 12.2 Michael Pearson at Bijapur, 2011

Figure 12.3 Michael Pearson at the pier in Masulipatnam, 2011

the start; he wanted to revisit the places of his youth, and I think he wanted to share with Denni a place he had known when writing his first book – *Merchants and Rulers in Gujarat*. In Bijapur, Michael walked along the city walls, although the rest of us were exhausted. That evening, we went to a very seedy rooftop restaurant for drinks. The location was magical; night had fallen, and from our table, we could see the lights of Bijapur twinkling below.

This first meeting morphed into an enduring friendship. In October 2011, I left Hyderabad to join as director of the Institut de Chandernagor near Kolkata. My remit was to put the institute on the global map, and to that end, I organised many international meetings during the four years I was there. I managed to invite Michael (and Denni) again, in December 2012, for a meeting on waterscapes (the proceedings came out in 2016 as *Living With Water*) and, in November 2013, to a meeting on world history which we held on a boat in the Sundarbans because for some reason it was impossible to hire a conference hall and arrange accommodation either in Kolkata or Chandernagore that winter season. Denni and her sister Barbara accompanied us. Amélia and Radhika were there as well. We stayed on an estuarine island; every night, the hosts arranged a concert or a play performed by local artists. They lit bonfires, which helped ward off the winter chill. Cocktails were served around the fire. Michael enjoyed the estuarine landscape of the Sundarbans and kept on photographing the mangroves growing out of the water. Perhaps the grey, muddy soil of the Sundarbans reinforced his interest in water histories, for he was consciously moving away from the sea into the coastal fringe by then; this was evident in the last keynote he would deliver later at Chandernagore in January 2015. It was titled 'Territoriality and the Decline of the Ecotone,' which remains sadly unpublished to date, as Michael could send across only an unfinished draft. The Sundarbans was a marine world composed of half water and half land, a landscape particularly suited to his littoral fancy. The papers presented at that memorable meeting came out as a special issue in the *Asian Review of World Histories* in January 2015.

In January 2015, I invited Michael once again for a meeting titled Territoriality in Coastal Societies but could only fund partial airfare. Michael kindly agreed to this. From Chandernagore, all of us flew to Kochi, where the Institut de Chandernagor – in collaboration with the Indian Museum, Kolkata – had organised a panel on maritime history at the Kochi-Muziris Biennale. Ken Hall was with us for the conference and for the Kochi trip as well. I and Denni, who had accompanied Michael, left the next day to fly to Kathmandu for another conference, but Michael and Ken stayed back to visit Pattanam, identified with the ancient port of Muziris, before going on to a conference organised by Radhika in Pune. Michael then went on to IIT Gandhinagar, and Ken flew back from Mumbai. Michael's essay on territoriality, sadly unfinished, formed the focal point of my 'Maritime – Aquatic; Territorial – Territoriality: Tracing Michael N. Pearson's Work on the Sea' (2018).

Michael always liked coming into Kolkata, and that time, he even flew in by Air Asia, only a few days after the fateful Air Asia crash of December 2015. Because he was turfed out of Calcutta Club in 2013 for appearing

Figure 12.4 Michael Pearson at a temple at Saptagrama [Satgaon], 2015

Figure 12.5 Michael Pearson in a toy shop, Kondapalli, Andhra Pradesh, 2011

in jeans and a shawl, this time, he carried a suit for a potential visit to the club! He always visited our dentist friend Sid for his dental repair work while in Kolkata because, as Michael noted, Kolkata rates were so much less expensive than the Australian, where his social security did not cover dental work. He loved biryani; he said coming from a farming family, he loved his meat and potatoes. We always made sure that we sourced him good biryani wherever we found ourselves; we had a particularly fine one in Masulipatnam in 2011. (See Figure 12.6.)

*

Michael and I also met at two Indian Ocean conferences at Fremantle and Abu Dhabi in 2012 and 2015 and at the connected oceans conference in Porto as mentioned, also in 2015. I have always felt that Michael was instrumental in arranging the invitations to the first two, although he never said anything of the sort (and I never asked him). The 2012 Fremantle conference resulted in his edited volume *Trade, Circulation, and Flow in the Indian Ocean World*. That was probably Michael's last edited work. Abu Dhabi in the spring of 2015 was the second-to-last time I saw Michael; he came with an oil-free frying pan that Denni had thoughtfully sent across

Figure 12.6 Michael Pearson at the old Masulipatnam shipyard, 2011

for me. We had more biryani there. We met again at Amélia's conference at Porto that summer; Radhika was also there. That was the last time we met. We spent some lovely summer days together at the English tennis club in Porto. Sadly, Michael was not functioning too well by then. He had lost weight, his speech was somewhat slurred and he forgot things. I teased him about the Trojans cap he wore; he said 'very funny.' He had suffered several small strokes earlier that year. He had his massive stroke in December that same year. I have not seen him since.

*

Knowing Michael opened up many collaborative ventures for me. I met some of the Fremantle organisers of 2012 (Jim Warren and Joe Christensen from Murdoch, Australia) again at a panel Radhika and I organised at the Water History conference in Montpellier in 2013. Sadly, Radhika had a foot injury just prior and so dropped out of that meeting, but Joe Christensen, who joined us at the Montpellier meeting is represented in this volume, and the Murdoch group and I have met thenceforth at Perth, Singapore and Manila in 2014, 2016 and 2018.

The Chandernagore meetings of 2012, 2013 and 2015 had organised extensive field trips within Bengal. In 2012, we visited the terra cotta temples of Bishnupur to study the boat panels on the Jor Bangla temple walls. It was a long road trip, but Michael said it was worth it. In 2013, we went to the inland capitals of Sultani Bengal at Gaur, Tanda and Pandua after our visit to the Sundarbans. Since Michael was a historian who had specialised in the west coast of India and African and Arabian Sea networks – and we must also remember Michael was the first maritime historian to bring the East African coast into the Indian Ocean maritime world – I always liked to expose him to the east coast political regimes and their Bay of Bengal links. We also visited the Buddhist site of Jagjivanpur near Malda on that trip, but I remember Michael was not particularly turned on by that site.

In 2015, after the Chandernagore conference, many of us, including Ken Hall and the Pearsons, visited Saptagrama (Satgaon); Michael was particularly interested in the boat panels at the Ananta Basudev temple at Bansberia. Ken, I and my husband, and the Pearsons spent a quiet few days at the estuarine site of Tajpur on the Bay of Bengal thereafter; Michael had a head massage on the beach and generally relaxed. He beach combed, collecting pottery sherds; these most likely link to ninth- to tenth-century Sumatran and Javanese ceramics but have not been dated as yet. Sadly, that was the last time I would invite Michael. His stroke occurred in December of that year.

*

What I remember most about Michael is his infectious enthusiasm. Usually a quiet man, he is always open to new ideas and things; he keenly observes everything around him and absorbs what he considers useful and relevant. He had tremendous physical and mental energy – and a wry sense of humour. The resort we stayed at in the Sundarbans in 2013 had construction still going on in some of the cottages. Denni's sister who accompanied us had checked into a cottage whose window panes had yet to be put up. When she got up the next morning, she was surprised to see shutters in place; the evening before there had just been an opening. On her exclaiming on this, Michael remarked, 'Barbie, this is the mysterious East; things come up in the night by magic!' Michael always mocked orientalism of all kinds! He remained up to date on the latest slang words. At a party organised by the Indian Museum, Kolkata, on the Floatel ship (on the occasion of the Water History conference) in 2012, he called our son a 'chick magnet'! It was only much later that I became familiar with the term.

I hope this chapter will not be taken as just a catalogue of trips we undertook with Michael and the conferences we attended together; on the contrary, I have particularly mentioned these to emphasise the collective nature of our work after meeting and collaborating with Michael. I feel that I got to know Michael as a scholar and man more through our road trips than at the conferences where he usually spoke very little. Nor was he always vocal at social occasions; I have the impression he disliked big parties and preferred informal get-togethers. One journalist who spent a whole day with him at Bishnupur on the occasion of the water conference in 2012 could not get a single 'quotable' quote out of him. According to this journalist, he just kept saying 'Mmm hmm. Maritime history. It's very important. You know, this is serious stuff.' And yet, every day we spent together was a journey of discovery; every evening was party time when he was around! And, of course, our parties were never complete without mutton biryanis.

References

Armitage, David, Alison Bashford and Sujit Sivasundaram (eds.). 2018. *Oceanic Histories*, Cambridge: Cambridge University Press.

Bashford, Alison. 2017. "Terraqueous Histories," *The Historical Journal*: 1–20.

Broeze, Frank. 1989. "From the Periphery to the Mainstream: The Challenge of Australia's Maritime History," *The Great Circle*, 11(1): 1–13.

Broeze, Frank. 1995. "Introduction: Maritime History at the Crossroads: A Critical Review of Recent Historiography," in Frank Broeze (ed.), *Maritime History at the Crossroads: A Critical Review of Recent Historiography*, St. John's, Newfoundland: IMEHA: ix–xxi.

Burton, Antoinette, Madhavi Kale, Isabel Hofmeyr, Clare Anderson, Christopher J. Lee and Nile Green. 2013. "Sea Tracks and Trails: Indian Ocean Worlds as Method," *History Compass* 11(7): 497–502.

Cañizares-Esguerra, Jorge and Benjamin Breen. 2013. "Hybrid Atlantics: Future Directions for the History of the Atlantic World," *History Compass*, 11(8): 597–609.

Green, Nile. 2013. "Maritime Worlds and Global History: Comparing the Mediterranean and Indian Ocean Through Barcelona and Bombay," *History Compass*, 11(7): 513–23.

Machado, Pedro. 2014. *Ocean of Trade: South Asian Merchants, Africa and the Indian Ocean, c. 1750–1850*, Cambridge: Cambridge University Press.

Mukherjee, Rila. 2018. "Maritime – Aquatic; Territorial – Territoriality: Tracing Michael N. Pearson's Work on the Sea," *Journal of Indian Ocean World Studies*, 2(1): 57–72.

Pearson, M.N. 2006. "Littoral Society: The Concept and the Problems," *Journal of World History*, 17(4): 353–73.

Pearson, M.N. 2007. "Studying the Indian Ocean World: Problems and Opportunities," in H.P. Ray and E.A. Alpers (eds.), *Cross Currents and Community Networks: The History of the Indian Ocean World*, New Delhi: Oxford University Press: 15–33.

Pearson, M.N. 2011. "History of the Indian Ocean: A Review Essay," *Wasafiri*, 26(2): 78–85.

Pearson, M.N. 2014a. "Oceanic History," in Prasenjit Duara, Viren Murthy and Andrew Sartori (eds.), *A Companion to Global Historical Thought*, Chichester: John Wiley and Sons.

Pearson, M.N. 2014b. "Indian Ocean Port-Cities: Themes and Problems," in Rila Mukherjee (ed.), *Vanguards of Globalization: Port-Cities from the Classical to the Modern*, New Delhi: Primus Books: 63–77.

Pearson, M.N. 2015a. "Introduction: Maritime History and the Indian Ocean World," in Michael Pearson (ed.), *Trade, Circulation, and Flow in the Indian Ocean World*, Basingstoke: Palgrave Macmillan.

Pearson, M.N. 2015b. "Notes on World History and Maritime History," *Asian Review of World Histories*, special issue *Problematizing World History*, 3(1): 137–51.

Pearson, M.N. 2017. "Places in the Indian Ocean World," *The Journal of Indian Ocean World Studies*, 1(1): 4–23.

Ridgway, Peter. 2005. "Indian Ocean Maritime History Atlas," *The Great Circle*, 27(1): 34–51.

Steinberg, Philip E. 2013. "Of Other Seas: Metaphors and Materialities in Maritime Regions," *Atlantic Studies*, 10(2): 156–69.

Steinberg, Philip E. and K. Peters. 2015. "Wet Ontologies, Fluid Spaces: Giving Depth to Volume Through Oceanic Thinking," *Environment and Planning D: Society and Space*, 33(2): 247–64.

Subrahmanyam, Sanjay. 2017. "Review of Fernando Rosa, *The Portuguese in the Creole Indian Ocean*," *International Journal of Maritime History*, 29(1): 221–23.

Toussaint, Auguste. 1974. *L'Ocean Indien au XVIIIe siecle*, Paris: Flammarion.

13

AFTERWORD

Radhika Seshan

We began by talking of the ways in which Michael Pearson has influenced the writing of Indian Ocean histories, and we are also ending with the influences that he has on writing such histories. In another essay (Seshan 2017: 2), I had said that Michael's work had focused broadly on three areas – the link between water history and world histories, littoral societies and port cities. But beyond these, what has been of particular importance to us has been his ability to move from land to water and back again, in what he called 'amphibian' approaches, and his encouragement to all of us to attempt the same. However, here, I will go into other aspects not touched upon in that brief essay.

In the introduction to this collective, much has been said on Michael's work. I will therefore not repeat any of that here. Rather, I will concentrate on some aspects that have not been taken up in this volume. One is the concern with port cities; the other is the coast of India, particularly the west coast, where Michael began his work. Here, my focus is that of a maritime historian, working with and through a conventional archive.

In his initial works, Michael depended extensively on the imperial Portuguese archives. Amélia Polónia and Fabiano Bracht in this volume have taken up some of the themes that marked that early phase, but what I want to underline here is the many ways in which he used this archive and the different ways of looking that he underlined through his use. Take, for example, his work on *Coastal Western India* (Pearson 1981). While the book was about the range of Portuguese records available in India (in Goa, specifically) for the scholar of imperial encounters, the preface itself made clear his dissatisfaction with the then existing state of affairs. He pointed to the existence of 'colonial history per se, a study of Europeans in Asia which concentrates exclusively on Europeans,' which, he said, was 'intellectually unsatisfactory because it is illogical to deny any influence at all from the Asian environment on the Europeans living there' (Pearson 1981: xvi). In that work itself, therefore, he began to outline some of the themes that have occupied him over the years since then – brokers, port cities, banyas and brahmins and their role as agents and interlocutors and much more. One

AFTERWORD

part of this, I think, is what he later formulated much more clearly in his work on littoral societies, even if he himself later said that he was rather unsure of his concept (Pearson 2014: 68).

An abiding area of his interest has been overlapping circuits of engagement across the ocean. Here, he has been coming back to the port cities at fairly regular intervals. He has pointed to the importance of the location of cities, of the social milieu within the ports and the connections both across the water and along the coasts that these cities shared. It is in this area that I would like to make a few points that came out of some informal discussions with Michael – I'm sure he'll recognise them.

On a trip to the east coast, to the old port of Motupalli (the theme of my paper in this collective), Michael quizzed me extensively on the connections that Motupalli had with the Bay of Bengal networks. When I told him that my starting point was Marco Polo, he said that it would then be necessary to locate Motupalli 'across both the Bay and the Ocean' and told me that I needed to study it as a river port that stretched inwards to the land to get its resources and across the Bay to Pegu and Burma, as well as southwards towards Sri Lanka and both east and west from there. When I asked him whether it was possible to see any of the western India ports in the same way, he told me to study Chaul and Rajapur – two ports that, he said, were possibly engaged in the same way across territorial and aquatic spaces but in a different chronological period. However, he himself did not take up any case studies of ports, after his initial foray into the port city of Goa.

That said, it is clear that his concerns with ports – as amphibious spaces and as geographical locations – has been an ongoing but primarily a theoretical and conceptual one. The port with its umland, foreland and hinterland was a space that needed to be studied, but the distinctiveness of each port had to be underlined.[1] Models are, he implies, to be tested and then modified as and when necessary. Thus, there may be some ports which do not have an umland (the immediate space surrounding a port, from where food most often comes) but only forelands and hinterlands. This perhaps needs to be extended a little, to argue that the foreland (the overseas world connected by water) may not be overseas but along the coast. We have instances of coastal trade, where ships from Malabar were to be seen in Gujarat and vice versa, carrying the products of each region to the other. So, can we then argue that both foreland and hinterland need to be studied in the context of broader engagements with both land and sea?

Michael has never been very sure of the land-sea binary, for he has argued both that the influence of the sea stretched far inland and that the influence of the land stretched far out to sea. But what of the coastal spaces he called the *marge*? These were the spaces of fisherfolk, of pirates, of petty traders, who also doubled, when necessary, as soldiers for the rulers of the coastal regions. In the late seventeenth century, for instance, the Maratha admiral Kanhoji Angre was reported by the English factors at Surat to have as his 'soldiers' on board his ships, the *galbats* that patrolled the coast between Kalyan and Rajapur, both sailors and fishermen. This overlap of occupation is something that Michael has hinted at but never engaged with directly. The question of pirates is of course a thorny one, for we need to remember that 'piracy' was also a label, to be used against anyone – or any group – that challenged the 'sovereignty' of the Europeans on the coast (Pearson 1981: 25).

A third area that Michael has been dealing with is the notion of cosmopolitanism in port cities. While agreeing that port cities were likely to bring together a diverse population, he asked how this population communicated with each other. Languages were not static; as he said, in his understanding,

> versions of Arabic dominated up to the sixteenth century. . . . Later creole Portuguese spread widely. . . . Other Europeans found Portuguese to be most useful.
>
> (Pearson 2014: 73)

In his collection of essays published in 2005, this aspect of language is particularly underlined, for he has pointed to the linguistic ability of the brokers. Sanjay Subrahmanyam has spoken of a world where Persian was the standard language of communication, but can this be accepted? Persian words have of course found their way into many Indian dialects and languages and are to be found in Swahili as well, but would Persian not have been the language of the higher classes, rather than that of the common folk? On the east coast, in Fort St. George, the English had a Persian translator for the letters that came from the Golconda and Bijapur governments and their administrators and Tamil and Telugu translators for other correspondence. And here, they appointed Portuguese settlers for the purpose. The issue of language, of translation and cross-cultural influences, is something that we need to take up much more seriously. Along with this, particularly for the India part, we also need to look at issues of caste and language and of (possibly) the ways in which language was used as a tool of keeping people at a distance. Michael has said that the result of such investigations may show that the Indian Ocean ports had a greater mix of people than ports on other oceans, but then, this would also prove the point that he and Ashin Das Gupta started with, of the distinctive nature of the Indian Ocean world and the need to study it, both in itself and in comparison with other aquatic spaces.

Let me now move on to the west coast of India. Michael began with Gujarat and went on to Goa and then around and across the Arabian Sea. To repeat a question that he asked, 'Can we see the seas and shores of the Indian Ocean as being a discrete unit that can be investigated like a state, or a city, or a ruler?' (Pearson 1998: 8). The point here is that when talking of the west coast of India, we cannot stick to the geographical limits of the Indian coastline alone but have to take western India and east Africa together as a unit. Going back to his concerns with ports, societies, littorals and margins, should we not see this unit only as one of the circuits of cultural, economic, linguistic and political connections, of overlaps and conflicts, but of an underlying unity as well? A concern that he has pointed out with this question is that this may lead us back to the old idea of the transformative nature of European intervention into Asian and African waters, so that we go back to the period 1500–1800 as being a definitive one, as some of the contributors have done in this collective. Perhaps one answer to this concern is to highlight the cultural continuities (and discontinuities) from an earlier time into the period with which Michael has been most concerned, as Patrick Manning does in this volume. Again, here, I will go back to something that Michael did not take up in a big way but to which he has pointed regularly – case studies, focusing on specific ports and the connections of one port and its people with others, across land and sea.

What were the networks that dominated this world? What changed and what continued in the period 1500–1800? How were the Europeans perceived in this world? Were family and/or spatial networks of importance both on land and on sea? We have, in India, the examples of Virji Vora operating from Surat along the Konkan coast and into the interior, up to Agra and Burhanpur and on the east coast, the family of Malaya Chetti. Virji Vora operated through a large number of agents, but the records do not indicate that these agents were part of his family. His partner, Abdul Ghafur, in contrast, did bring his son into his business, and his grandson in the early eighteenth century made a case for himself for getting the governorship of Surat. Vora and Ghafur had extensive trade connections with the Red Sea/Persian Gulf areas in addition to those across India, but Indian historians have not looked at whom they dealt with in these regions. Should we not engage with African scholars of these times to flesh out our histories? Malaya Chetti, on the east coast, clearly worked with his family and with the steadily declining Vijayanagar Empire; once that empire vanished, the family too declined in power and visibility. But trade as a whole did not come to an end, and so, going back to Michael's work, should we not ask about the processes of networking, rather than networks of operation alone?

Michael has said that he has been a 'shameless magpie' in his work. It is these tendencies that inform this collective for we have, we hope, brought together scholars who represent at least some of the areas that he borrowed from.

Note

1 It is to be remembered that while by and large umland and foreland are regarded as being the same, he made a distinction in his work (Pearson 2014: 66).

References

Pearson, M.N. 1981. *Coastal Western India: Studies from the Portuguese Records*, Xavier Centre for Historical Research, No. 2, Goa: Concept Publishing House.

Pearson, M.N. 1988. *Before Colonialism: Theories on Asian-European Relations 1500–1750*, New Delhi: Oxford University Press.

Pearson, M.N. 2005. *The World of the Indian Ocean: Studies in Economic, Social and Cultural History*, Burlington: Ashgate.

Pearson, M.N. 2014. "Indian Ocean Port-Cities: Themes and Problems," in Rila Mukherjee (ed.), *Vanguards of Globalization: Port-Cities from the Classical to the Modern*, New Delhi: Primus: 63–77.

Pearson, M.N. 1998. *Port Cities and Intruders: The Swahili Coast, India, and Portugal in the Early Modern Era*, Baltimore and London: Johns Hopkins University Press.

Seshan, R. 2017. "Ports and Littoral Societies: A Tribute to Michael Naylor Pearson," *Asian Review of World Histories*, 5(1): 1–7, January.

INDEX

Note: Page numbers in *italics* indicate figures, and those in bold indicate table.

Aboriginal labour 181
Abu Dhabi conference 259–260
Afonso, Ignácio Caetano 146–147, 148, 152
Africa: as constitutive locus 42–44; intellectuals and intellectual work 43; Protestants 43; slave diaspora 42
Africa in Stereo (Jaji) 43
African Americans 43
African wax prints 207–209
Afro-Asian solidarity 43
Afro-Brazilian Umbanda spiritual traditions 44
Agnew, John 51, 52–53
Ahmedabad, textile production in 208; African wax prints 208–209
Ainurruvar (the 500) 52, 53
Alaungpaya 220
Alavi, Seema 40
Americas 24
Ananta Basudev temple 261
Andaya, Barbara Watson 54
Andhra Coast 55
Anglo-Burmese War 221
Anglo-Dutch War 134
Anim-Addo, Anyee 38, 42
Antunes, Cátia 97
apothecaries *see* physicians/surgeons/ apothecaries
Arabic periodicals 39–40
Arabic press 39
Arasaratnam, Sinappah 58
Arjunawiwaha kakawin 84
Arthasastra 69
Asian Review of World Histories 254

Atlantic and Indian oceans: sub-imperial configurations 38–39; transoceanic carceral assemblages 37–38
Australind 175, 180, 185
autonomy of Moor people 133–134
Ayurvedic medicine 139

Babad Dalem (Balinese account) 72
Babad Tanah Jawi 68, 81
Bach, John 177, 183, 186, 187, 190
Bain, Mary Albertus 183, 187
Bali: Majapahit's conquest and reconquest of 71–72
Bankoff, Greg 11
Banyan traders 206
Bashford, Alison 252
Bastos, Cristina 142–143
Basu, Helene 44
Batavia 124–134; Asian slaves 125; as a colonial city 124–126; cross-cultural relations 125; historical analysis 125; population 125, 127–131, **129–131**; *see also* Moor people, in Batavia
Battuta, Ibn 59
Bayly, Christopher 253
Bay of Bengal 12, 54; human movements 214; mercantile networks 59; oceanic histories 214; Portuguese presence and control 107
Behreh, Madho 166
Bell, Peter 162–164
Black Death 22–23; mortality 23
Book of One Thousand Questions 41

INDEX

Book of the Pearl, The (Kunz and Stevenson) 223
Bracht, Fabiano 10
Brah-Widjaja 81
Braudel, Fernand 34, 51, 250, 252
Broeze, Frank 13, 191
Broome 177, 178, 183, 185–191
Brown, R. N. Rudmose 234
Buddhist Vihara 54
Burke, Peter 137–138
Burma 11–12, 214–239; auction system 235; block system 233–234, 236; British interests in 235–236; diving and divers 235–239; map of 216; overview 214–215; perl trading/pearling economies 214, 215–220
Burma Fisheries Act 237
Burma Pearl Fishing and Culture Syndicate (BPFCS) 240
Burton, Antoinette 43

cakravartins (universal monarchs) 69
Calcutta 166–169
Calumba roots 147, 148
Camuttirapatti 53
cantinas 204
Cape of Good Hope 24
caril 201
cashew 198–200
China 62; Southeast Asia and 240–241
Chola kingdom/rule 52–55; external policy 54; inscriptions 52–53
Christensen, Joseph 11, 260
climate: disease and 23; monsoons and 20; temperatures 23
Coelho, Manoel Rodrigues 150
Collis-Buthelezi, Victoria 42–43
colonisation and decolonisation 26–29
Columbian Exchange 24
Colvelle and Gilmore & Co. 166
commerce: global nexus 23–26; Islamic expansion and 21–23
Commonwealth Royal Commission 187
Commutation Act in 1784 221
Conrad, Joseph 177
contact zone 138, 143, 151
Conti, Niccolo 57
coral reefs, Mergui Archipelago 216–217
Coromandel Coast 54
Corrupting Sea, The (Horden and Purcell) 11

Coutinho, Rodrigo da Sousa 140
cowrie shells 22
creative misunderstanding 139
Cross-Cultural Networking in the Eastern Indian Ocean Realm c. 100–1800 255
cultural diversity 21
cyclones, Western Australia 188–189

da Câmara, Francisco António da Veiga Cabral 140
da Gama, Vasco 23
"Dairy Maid, The" 182
Dalgado, Sebastião 150
Damar, Arya 72
Dampier Archipelago 182
Dark Princess (du Bois) 43
Dashiki fabrics 209; *see also* African wax prints
da Silva, Barroso 150
Daut, Aboe Bakar 134
Dauwd, Abd Allah 134
David Scott 156–157, 166–169
decolonisation *see* colonisation and decolonisation
Delagoa Bay 207
Delhi Sultanate 22
DeLoughrey, Elizabeth 42
Demak 80, 84
Desantara 65–66
Dharmasastra 69
diving for pearls/shell, in Mergui Archipelago 235–239; Moken divers 235, 236, 237–238, 239
Domel Island 240
dos Reis, João 140
Drake-Brockman, Henrietta 190
Drewal, Henry 44
Dutch East India Company 9–10, 124–134; *see also* Batavia; Moor people, in Batavia

Eastern Seas 175
Eckel, Leslie 41, 42
Eighty Mile Beach 175, 177, 180, 182, 190
El Nino Southern Oscillation 20
empire building 97; theories on 98–101
English East India Company (EIC): colonial government 159; European shipowners and 159; labour market

270

INDEX

159–160; political ascendancy 159;
  recruitment process 159
epidemic disease 23, 24
erivirapattinam 53
Estado da India 203
Esty, Jed 41
exchange system 40
*Eyes Across the Water: Navigating
  the Indian Ocean* (Gupta, Hofmeyr,
  Pearson) 5

Federal Council of Australasia 185
First Global Age (1400 to 1800) 9
Fisher, Michael 159–160
fisherfolk, Mergui Archipelago 217
food, Mozambique 200–205
Fremantle conference 259, 260
frontier 137–138

Gelgel Dynasty of Bali 71
geography of ocean spaces 5–10
Getieven 127
ghatserangs 168, 169
Giri 81–82
Glossário Luso Asiático (Dalgado) 150
Goa, India 137; diseases 141–142;
  hospitals 142–143; physicians,
  surgeons and apothecaries 143–147;
  population 143
'God's Shadow' 79
Gordillo, Gaston 41
Great Australian Loneliness, The (Hill)
  190
Great Depression 190
Green, Nile 252
guild inscriptions 59
Gulf of Mannar 236
Gupta, Ashin Das 254
Gupta, Pamila 5

Haan, F. de 126–127
Hall, Kenneth R. 8, 254–255, 261
Haynes, Thomas Henry 175, 177,
  180–181, 183–184, 186, 188,
  189, 191
hazardousness of place 11
Heesterman, J. C. 2, 3, 13
Hikayat Banjar 64, 67
Hikayat Raja-Raja Pasai 67
Hill, Ernestine 190
Hindu-Buddhism 8
Hofmeyr, Isabel 5

Horden, Peregrine 11
Hospital Militar 147
Hospital Real 140–147

Ieyasu, Tokugawa 111
Immigration Restriction Act 183, 186
Indian Museum, Kolkata 257
Indian Ocean: as a human space 1, 2
Indian Ocean, The (Pearson) 191
*Indian Ocean Studies: Cultural, Social,
  and Political Perspectives* (Moorthy
  and Jamal) 5
Indian Opinion (Gandhi) 40
Indian sailors *see* sailors (lascars)
Institut de Chandernagor 257
International Missionary Council 43
Islam: Delhi Sultanate and 22;
  Java and 8
Islamic conversions 63
Islamic expansion and commerce 21–23
Islamic states, Majapahit and 76–84
Island Nation (Broeze) 191
Ivanoff, Jacques 218

Jabavu, D. D. T. 43
Jadavpur University in Kolkata 254
Jaji, Tsitsi 43
Jamal, Ashraf 5
Japan: European guns 109; Jesuits
  in 97–98, 109–116; Portuguese in
  109–116
Jardine, Frank 233
Java 8; cultural accomplishments 63;
  Hindu-Buddhist perspective 62;
  Islamic states 76–84; knowledge
  networking contacts 62; Muslim
  sultanate 72–76; religious evolutions
  8; textual communities 84–89; *see
  also* Majapahit empire/era
Jesuits in Japan 9, 97–98; Portuguese
  and 9, 98, 109–116; Roman church
  9, 97–98
João Lopes Pinheiro root 147, 148,
  149–152

Kadaram 54
Kadiri monarch 84
Kakatiyas, Warangal 55–59
Karashima, Noboru 59
Kertanagara, King 65
Khan, Genghis 22
Khan, Hussain 167–168

271

INDEX

Khuri-Makdisi, Ilham 39–40
Khyber Pass 20
knowledge creation 138–139
knowledge networking 8
knowledge production 10, 139
Kulke, Hermann 58
Kunz, George Frederick 223
Kyburt, Kartik 166

labour contractors 160
labour market 10, 159–160
La Guma, Alex 40–41
Land, Isaac 254
landscape, Mozambique: as archive
197–198; objects and 196–197
lascars *see* sailors (lascars)
Lavery, Charne 42
Lee, Chris 40
Lejard, Thierry 218
Lewis, Martin 36–37
Lokapalas 78
Luke, John 161, 162, 164

Machado, Pedro 11–12, 250
Machel, Josina 205
Machel, Samora 205
Mada, Gajah 63, 72, 75, 81
Mahendravarman 55
Maingy, A. D. 222
Majapahit empire/era: aggressive
initiatives 69; authority 63, 65;
Babad chronicle literature on 68;
battle with Sunda Straits ruler 69–70;
conquest of Bali 71–72; demise 67;
ethical character of monarchs 69;
literary conceptions 66; Malay-
language chronicles on 67–68;
Muslim sultanate and 72–76; ports-
of-trade 63–64; as regional empire
and identity 64, 65–72; rise of
Islamic states and 76–84; sphere of
influence 65; tributaries 64
Majid, Ibn 23
Malay Peninsula 65
Mamallapuram 55
Mami Wata 44
Marcus, George 210
Maria, Queen 147
Maritime History of Australia, A (Bach)
177
Markovits, Claude 207
Marshall, Peter 253

Masulipatnam, Motupalli 57, 255, 259
Mauritius 166
Maynard, John 40
medicinal roots, in Portuguese India
147–152
Medieval Warm Period 21
Mediterranean: Braudel's notion of 34
Merchants and Rulers in Gujarat
(Pearson) 13, 249, 256
Mergui Archipelago 11–12; Chinese
marine goods economy 218–220;
coral reefs 216–217; diving and
divers 235–239; early pearl trading
and marine product extraction
215–220; geographical description
215–216; imperial manoeuvrings
220–226; pearl and shell extraction
226–235
Moken: Chinese merchants and
219–220; coastal migration from
Malay Peninsula 218; collection of
pearl shell 218; collection of trochus
shell 220; diving for perl and shells
235, 236, 237–238, 239; food
collection 218
Moken divers 235–239
Mongol conquests (1206–1280) 22
monsoons 20
Montebello Islands 188
Moore, John 161, 162
Moor people, in Batavia 9–10,
126–134; autonomy 133–134;
Gujarati sailors 132; hospital for
134; as indigenous setters 126;
occupations 131–133; population
127–131, **129–131**; sailors 131–133
Moorthy, Shanti 5
Mordexim 141–142, 150
Motupalli 55–57, 59, 255, 265
Mozambique 11, 196–210; African
wax prints 207–209; *cantinas* 204;
capulanas 205, 207, 208, 209;
cashew 198–200; cloth markets
205; colours and patterns 205–209;
food 200–205; Indian-origin
trading communities 207; landscape
196–198; Rajah (curry power) 11,
196–197, 204
Muhammad 79
Mukherjee, Rila 51
*Muslim Cosmopolitanism in the Age of
Empire* (Alavi) 40

272

INDEX

Muslim sultanate, in Java 72–76
Myanmar Pearl Enterprise (MPE) 240

Nadri, Ghulam A. 10
Nagapattinam 54
Nagarakertagama (Mpu Prapanca) 62, 63, 64, 65, 66, 67, 68–69, 71, 78, 80, 84
namban-jin 109
Naqshbandi Sufi networks 40
National Archives of the Republic of Indonesia 131
Nikitin, Athanasius 57
Nina, Patan Mochamat 134
Northwest Coast of Australia 175
Nusantara 63

occupations of Moor people 131–133
Opium Wars 169
ordered space 52

padinenvisaya 53
Panditos (Pundits) 139, 140
Paniyanatu 53
Pararaton 68–69
Parker, Geoffrey 109
Patah, Raden 80–83
pattanapagudi inscriptions 53, 59
pearl and shell extraction, in Burma 214–239; arresting 233–235; diving and divers 235–239; managing 226–233; *see also* Mergui Archipelago
Pearling and Trading Company 186
Pearling Fleet Disaster of 1987 11, 175–192; in history 190–192; as process 187–190; as turning point 183–187
Pearl Shell Fishery Regulation Act 181, 183–184, 188
Pearson, Michael 1, 5, 7, 19, 20–21, 158, 249–262; Abu Dhabi conference 259–260; aquatic vision 2–4; *Coastal Western India* 264; East African coast 24; enthusiasm 261; on environment 177, 178; Fremantle conference 259, 260; Kolkata and 257, 259; Leiden meeting 253–254; littoral society 177; as a magpie 250; maritime history and 249; maritime studies for 1; *Merchants and Rulers in Gujarat* 13, 249, 256;

'Places in the Indian Ocean World' 251; Subrahmanyam on 250; *Trade, Circulation and Flow in the Indian Ocean World* 250, 259; visit to Bijapur 255–257; works 32, 51, 137, 179; writings 250–252
Pekojan 126–127, 128, 131, 133
periodicals 39–40
Persian Gulf 20
Peters, Kimberley 252, 253, 254
Pharmacopea Tubalense 150, 152
physicians/surgeons/apothecaries, in Portuguese India 143–147
Pinheiro, João Lopes 149–150
Pinto, Fernão Mendes 109
Pires, Tomé 2
place: fundamental aspects 51, 52–53; space and 51
'Places in the Indian Ocean World' (Pearson) 251
plague 22–23
Polo, Marco 58, 265
Polónia, Amélia 9, 97, 254
Pombo, Pedro 11
Popescu, Monica 42
Portugal 24; Afro-Brazilian Umbanda spiritual traditions 44
Portuguese: informal networks 101; medicinal roots 147–152; overseas expansion/settlement 101–106; physicians, surgeons and apothecaries 143–147; role of state and individuals in 101–106; trade networks in the East 106–108
Portuguese in Japan 109–116; business settlement 109; products 109; self-organised networks 110
post-human oceanic thesis/models 41–42
Prazos da Coroa 202
Purcell, Nicholas 11

Raffles, Thomas Stamford 126
Rajah (curry power) 11, 196–197, 204
Ramon, Pedro 116
Red Sea 20
Ricci, Ronit 41
Ridgway, Peter 250
Robson, George 168
Rosales, Marta 201–202
Rossum, Van 132
Royal Mail Packet Service 38

273

INDEX

sailors (lascars): case of *David Scott*
166–169; historiographical context
157–161; lived experiences aboard
the *Union* 161–166; overview
156–157
Sangam literature 52
Second World War 190
Senapati, Panembahan 68
Seshan, Radhika 8, 254
Shari'a 77
Shimada, Ryuto 9–10
Siddis, in India 44
Silk Road 22
Silu, Merah 79
Simpson, Jas J. 234
Sir J. Malcolm Island 240
South Africa 11
South African Indians 43
South China Sea 109
Souza, George Bryan 131
space 51; ordered 52
Sree Pas-Sair 175, 181, 188
Stanley, Frederick 167
Stanley, John 169
Stapel, F. W. 127
Steinberg, Philip E. 3, 5, 252–253, 254
stereo-sound systems 43
Stevenson, Charles Hugh 223
*Strange Riches: Bengal in the
Mercantile Map of South Asia*
(Mukherjee) 253
Streeter, Edwin 184
Strum, John 163
Subbaruyulu, Y. 53
Subrahmanyam, Sanjay 249
*Subversive Sovereigns Across the Seas:
Indian Ocean Port-Cities from Early
Historic Times to late Colonialism*
254–255
Sumatra 63
Sundarbans 257, 261
surgeons *see* physicians/surgeons/
apothecaries
syphilis 24

Tagliocozzo, Eric 221
Tanegashima Island 109
Territoriality and the Decline of the
Ecotone 257
Territoriality in Coastal Societies 257
textiles/textile industry 205–209;
African wax prints 207–209;

commercialisation 206; trading
networks 206
textual communities, Java 84–89
textual honours system 40
Thomas, John 161–162
tinai 51
Todalia genus 150
Toussaint, Auguste 251
*Trade, Circulation and Flow in the
Indian Ocean World* (Pearson) 250,
259
translation 40
trans-Pacific route 23
Treaty of Yandabo 221

Union 156; Bell's testimony 162–164;
food 164–165; ill-treatment of
European crews 162–163; lascar's
lived experiences 161–166; Moore's
testimony 161, 162; Thomas's
testimony 161–162
University of Hyderabad 254
Usana Jawa (Balinese account) 71–72

Vaidya 139
*Vanguards of Globalisation:
Port-Cities from the Classical
to the Modern* 255
Velha Goa 143

wali sanga 78, 80
Warrington, Herbert 226
West Australian 175, 181, 187–188
Western Australia 175–192; customs
revenue 186; cyclones 188–189;
floating stations 183–184, 185;
government 184–185
Western Australian Pearl Shell and
Beche-de-mer Fishery (Extra-
territorial) Act 185
Western Mail 175
wet ontologies 2
White, Richard 138
Wigen, Karen 1
World Pacifist Congress 43
Wuruk, Hayam 65, 69

Xavier, Francis 110

Yawabumi 65
Yellow River Valley 22
Yersina pestis 22

274